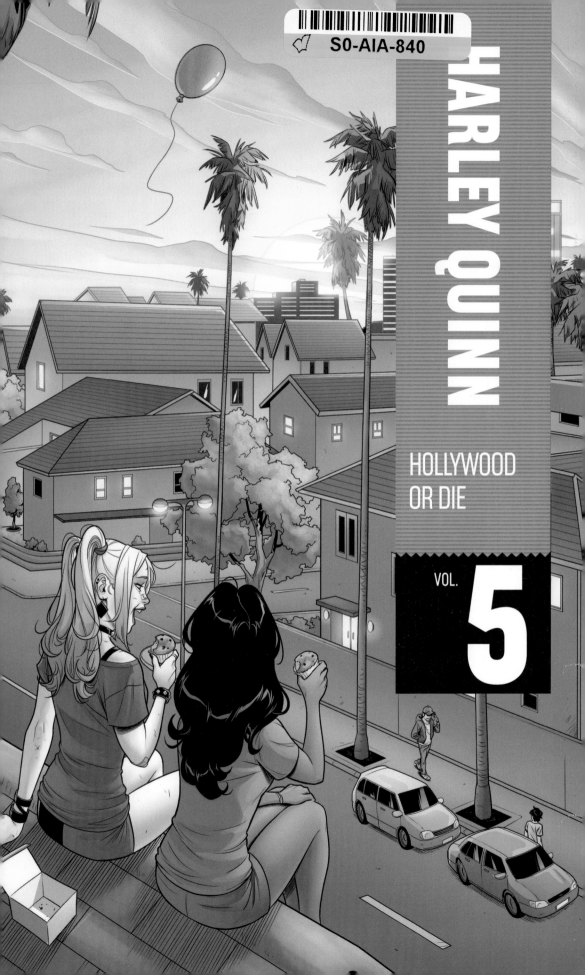

HARLEY QUINN

HOLLYWOOD OR DIE

VOL. **5**

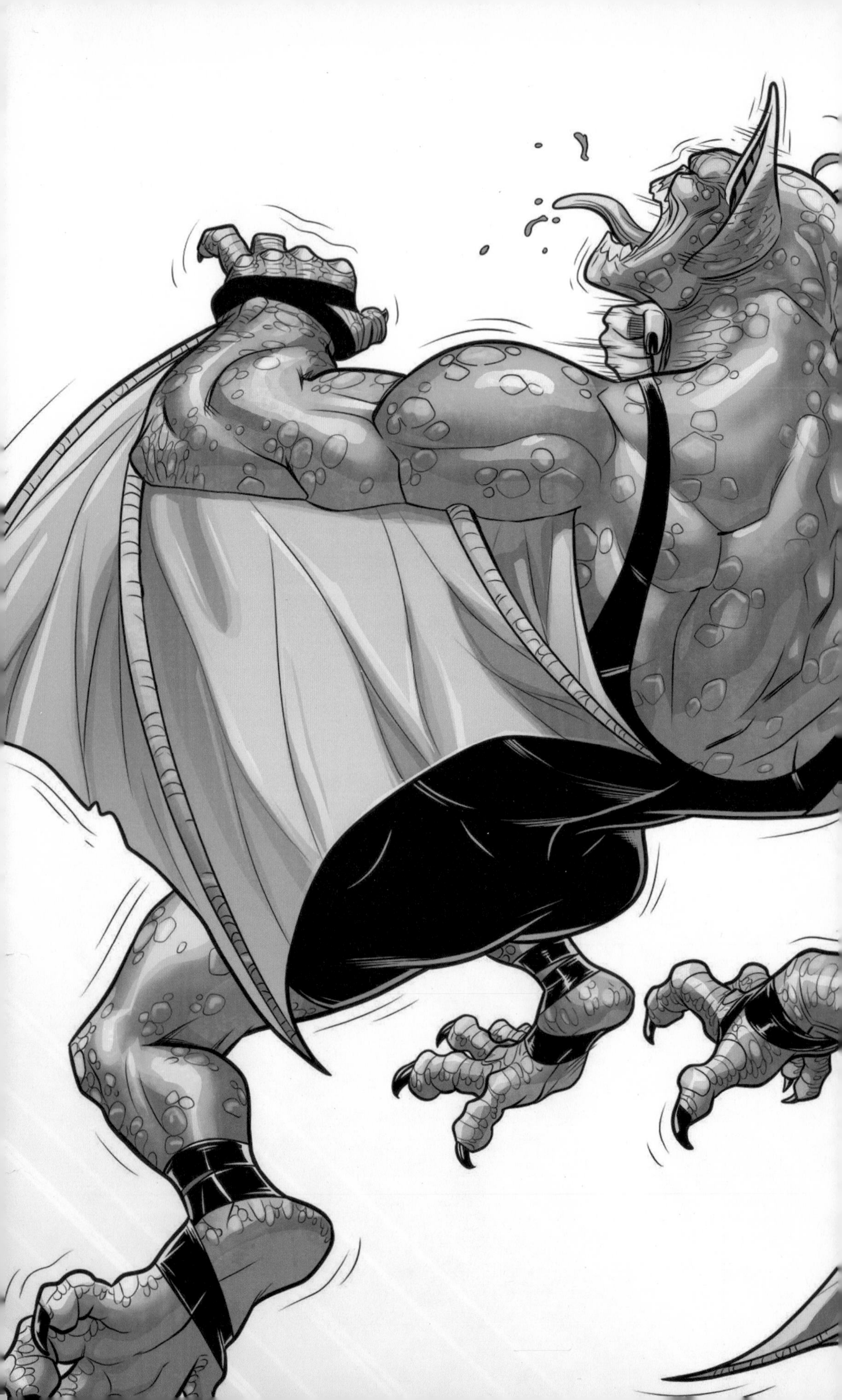

HARLEY QUINN
HOLLYWOOD OR DIE

writer

SAM HUMPHRIES

artists

SAMI BASRI
ABEL
RILEY ROSSMO
NICOLA SCOTT
NGOZI UKAZU
JOE QUINONES

colorists

HI-FI
IVAN PLASCENCIA
ANNETTE KWOK
NGOZI UKAZU
JOE QUINONES

letterer

DAVE SHARPE

collection cover artists

GUILLEM MARCH and **ARIF PRIANTO**

HARLEY QUINN created by **PAUL DINI** and **BRUCE TIMM**.
SUPERMAN created by **JERRY SIEGEL** and **JOE SHUSTER**.
By special arrangement with the Jerry Siegel family.

VOL.

5

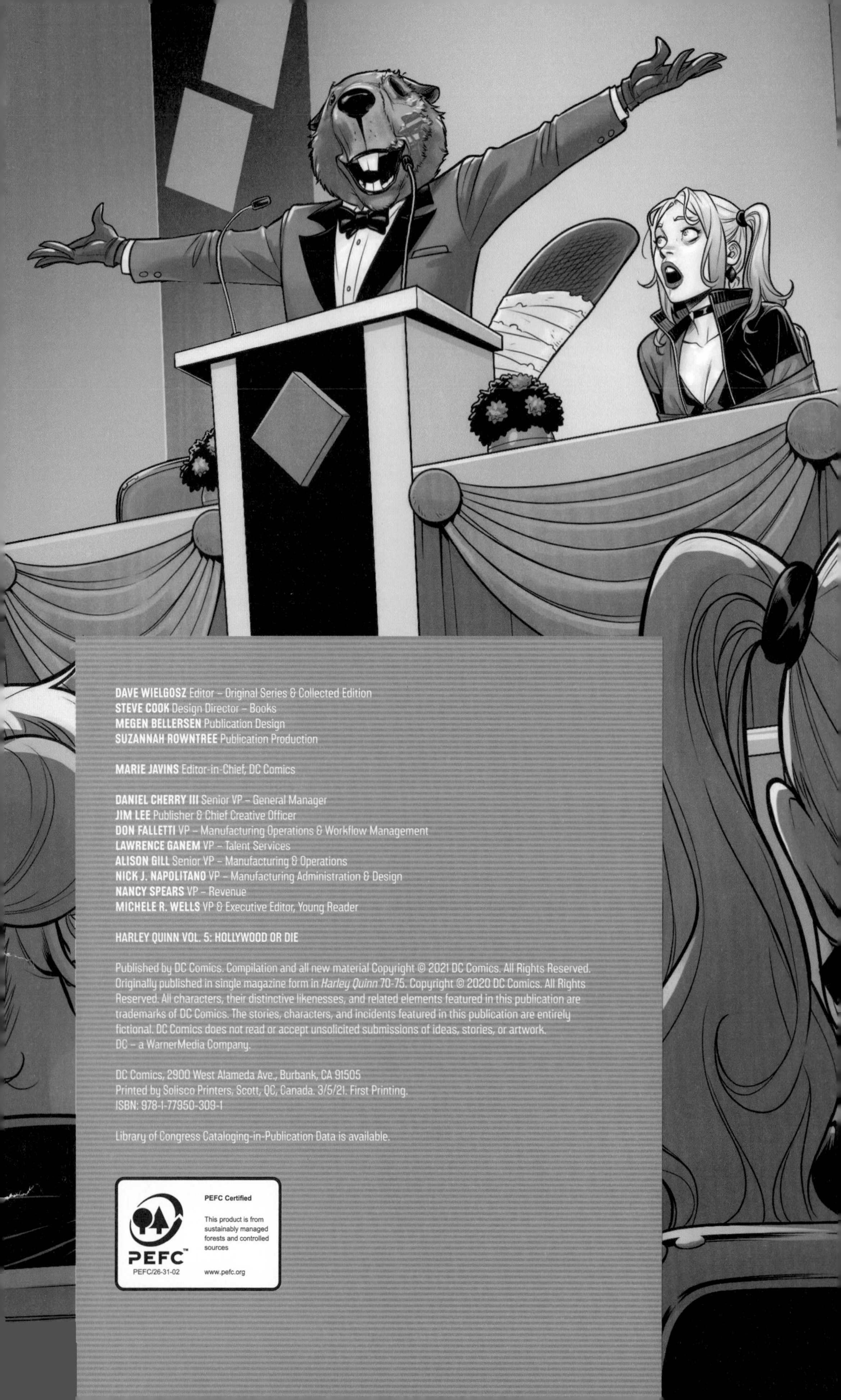

DAVE WIELGOSZ Editor – Original Series & Collected Edition
STEVE COOK Design Director – Books
MEGEN BELLERSEN Publication Design
SUZANNAH ROWNTREE Publication Production

MARIE JAVINS Editor-in-Chief, DC Comics

DANIEL CHERRY III Senior VP – General Manager
JIM LEE Publisher & Chief Creative Officer
DON FALLETTI VP – Manufacturing Operations & Workflow Management
LAWRENCE GANEM VP – Talent Services
ALISON GILL Senior VP – Manufacturing & Operations
NICK J. NAPOLITANO VP – Manufacturing Administration & Design
NANCY SPEARS VP – Revenue
MICHELE R. WELLS VP & Executive Editor, Young Reader

HARLEY QUINN VOL. 5: HOLLYWOOD OR DIE

DC Comics, 2900 West Alameda Ave., Burbank, CA 91505
Printed by Solisco Printers, Scott, QC, Canada. 3/5/21. First Printing.
ISBN: 978-1-77950-309-1

Library of Congress Cataloging-in-Publication Data is available.

PEFC Certified
This product is from sustainably managed forests and controlled sources
PEFC/26-31-02
www.pefc.org

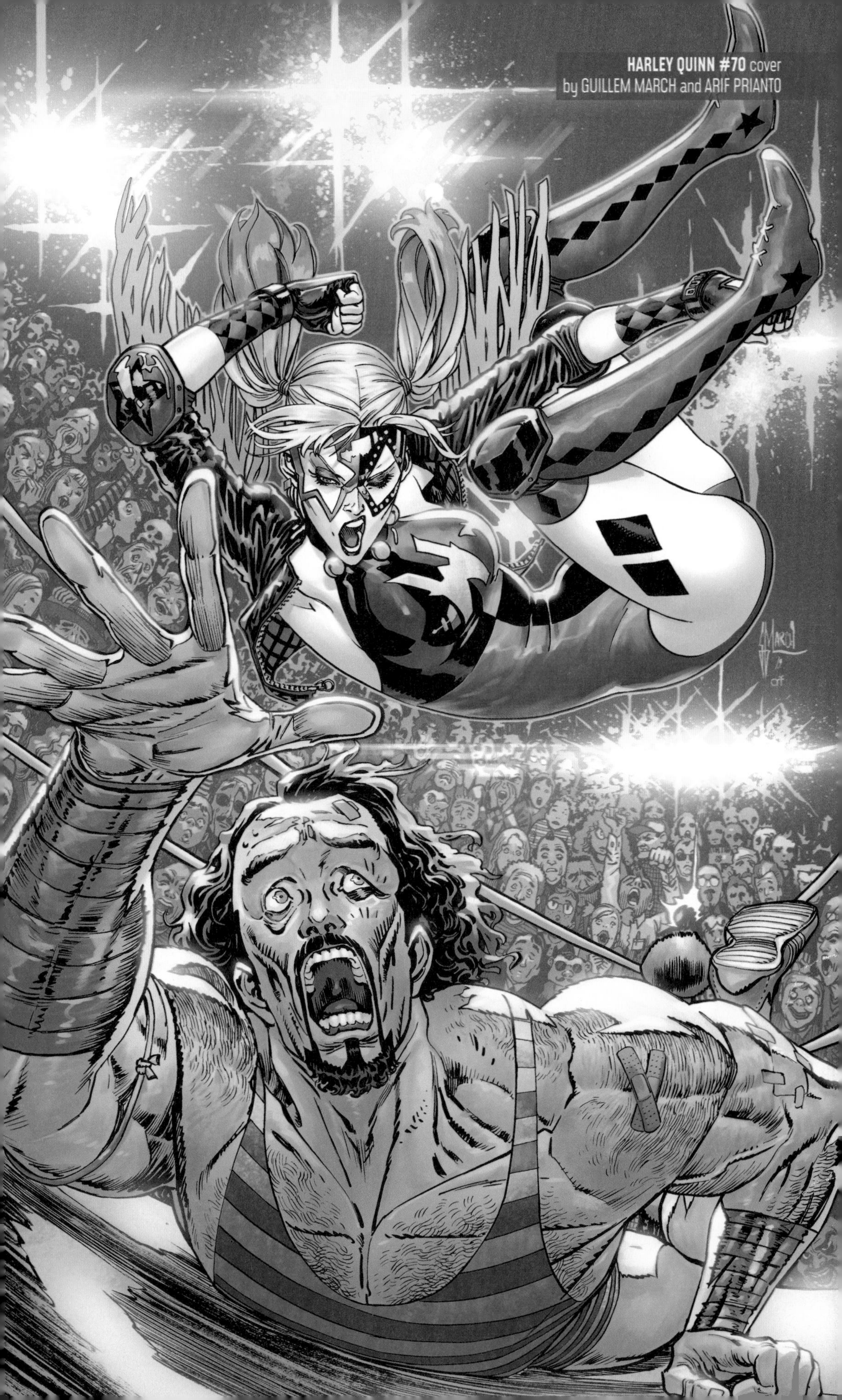

HARLEY QUINN #70 cover
by GUILLEM MARCH and ARIF PRIANTO

HARLEY QUINN #70 variant cover
by FRANK CHO and SABINE RICH

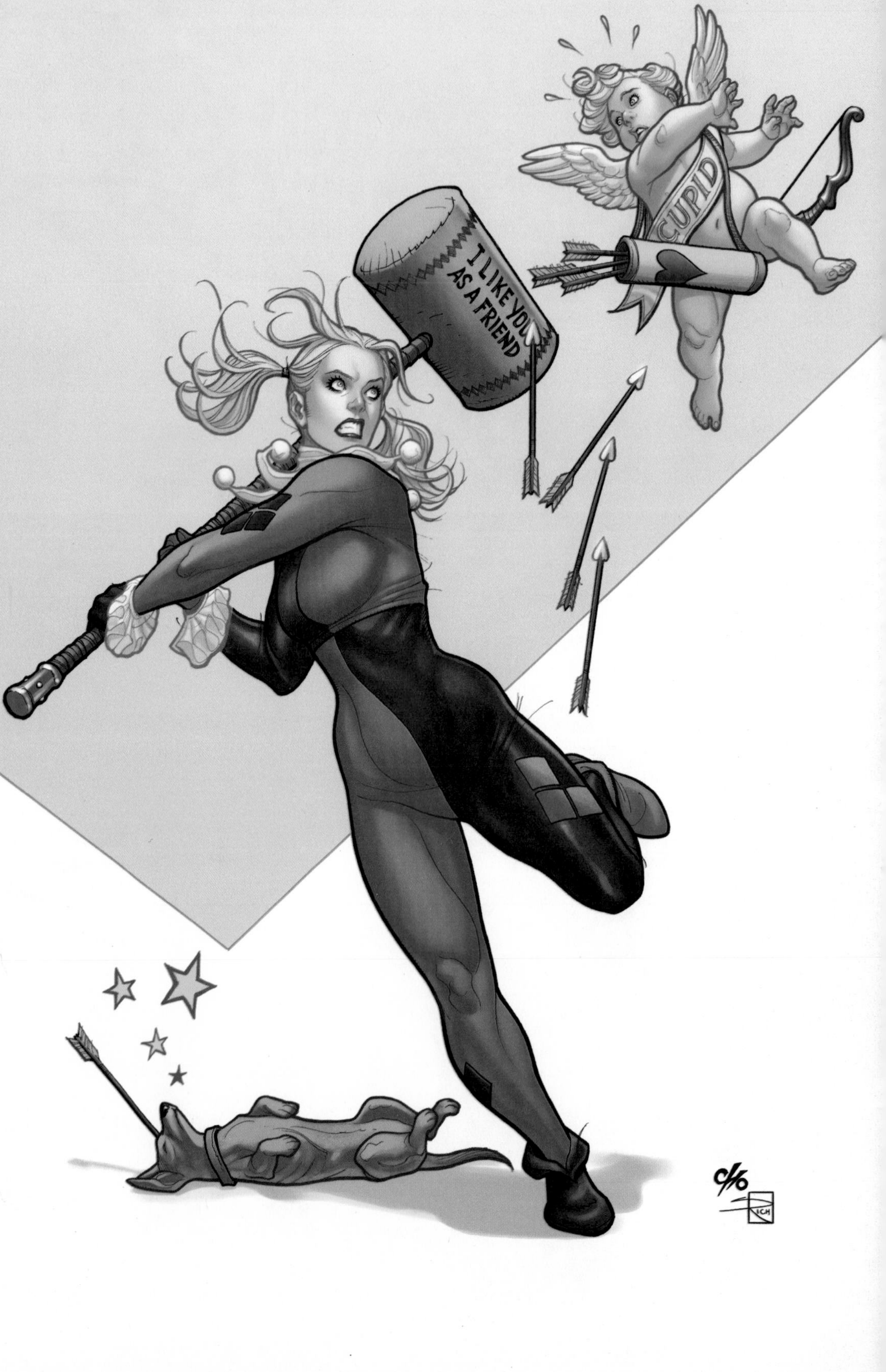

I LIKE YOU AS A FRIEND
CUPID

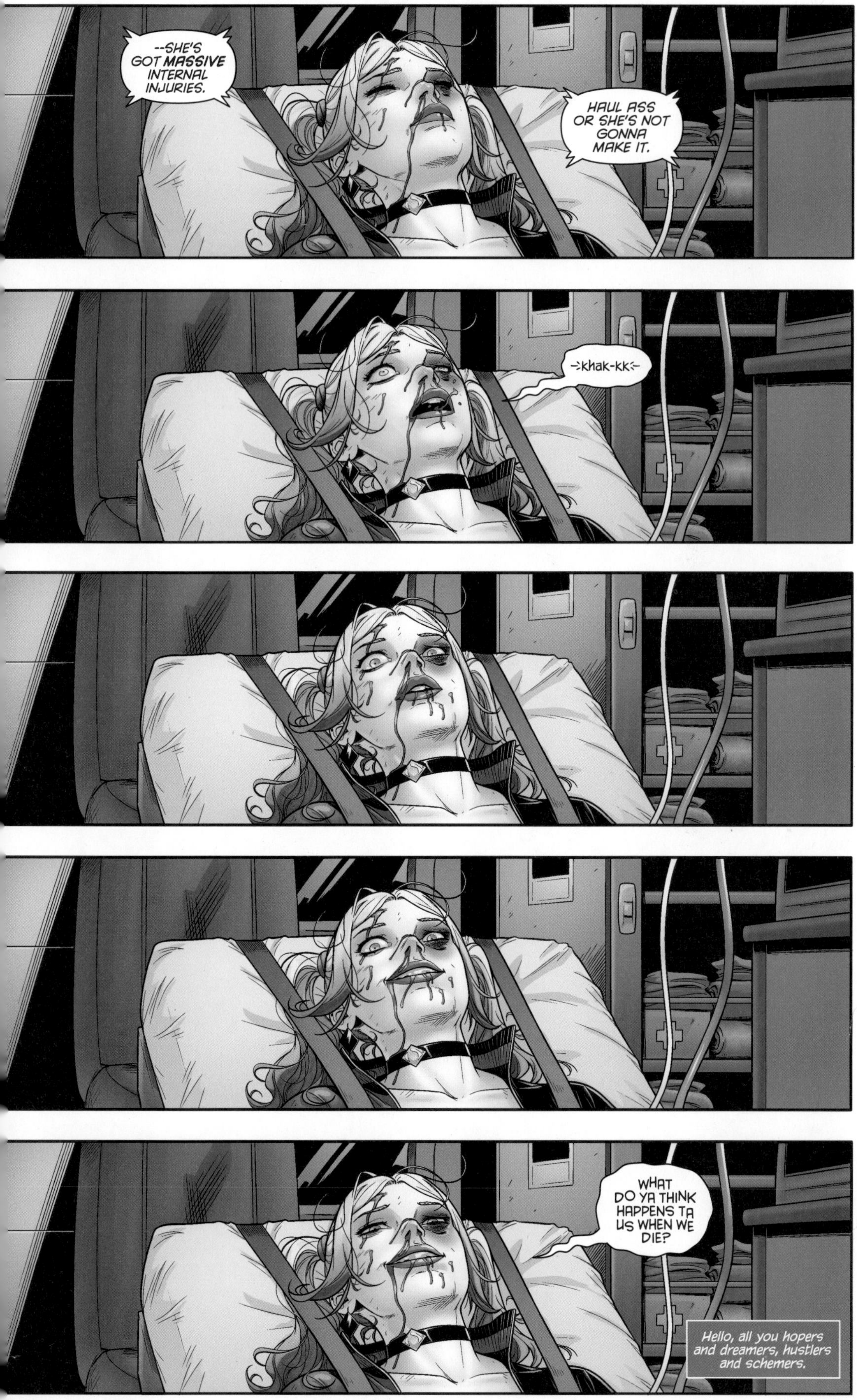
--SHE'S GOT MASSIVE INTERNAL INJURIES.
HAUL ASS OR SHE'S NOT GONNA MAKE IT.
-khak-kk-
WHAT DO YA THINK HAPPENS TA US WHEN WE DIE?
Hello, all you hopers and dreamers, hustlers and schemers.

Los Angeles was heavy with ocean air the night the Jade Feather disappeared.

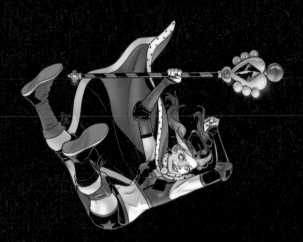

Those doldrums of March, with Thanagar in retrograde, and the houses of the Amazon and the Detective in thirty degree overlap.

Those free-flowing, unpredictable weeks of Tamaran season where humans transform into beasts, antagonists become lovers, and fortunes sour in the time it takes to turn a page.

The season of trouble, opportunity, pandemonium and death.

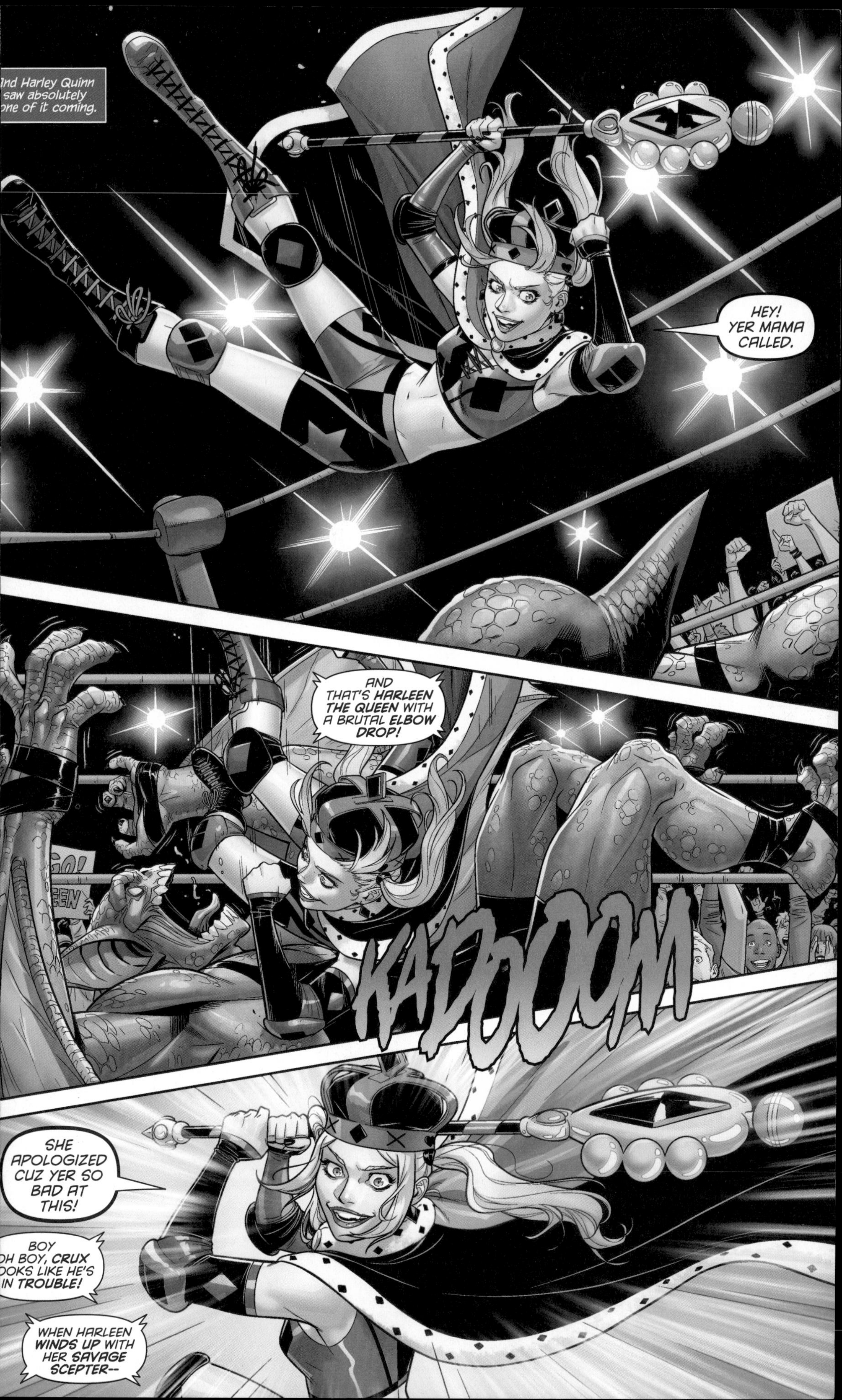
And Harley Quinn saw absolutely none of it coming.
HEY! YER MAMA CALLED.
AND THAT'S HARLEEN THE QUEEN WITH A BRUTAL ELBOW DROP!
KADOOOM
SHE APOLOGIZED CUZ YER SO BAD AT THIS!
BOY OH BOY, CRUX LOOKS LIKE HE'S IN TROUBLE!
WHEN HARLEEN WINDS UP WITH HER SAVAGE SCEPTER--

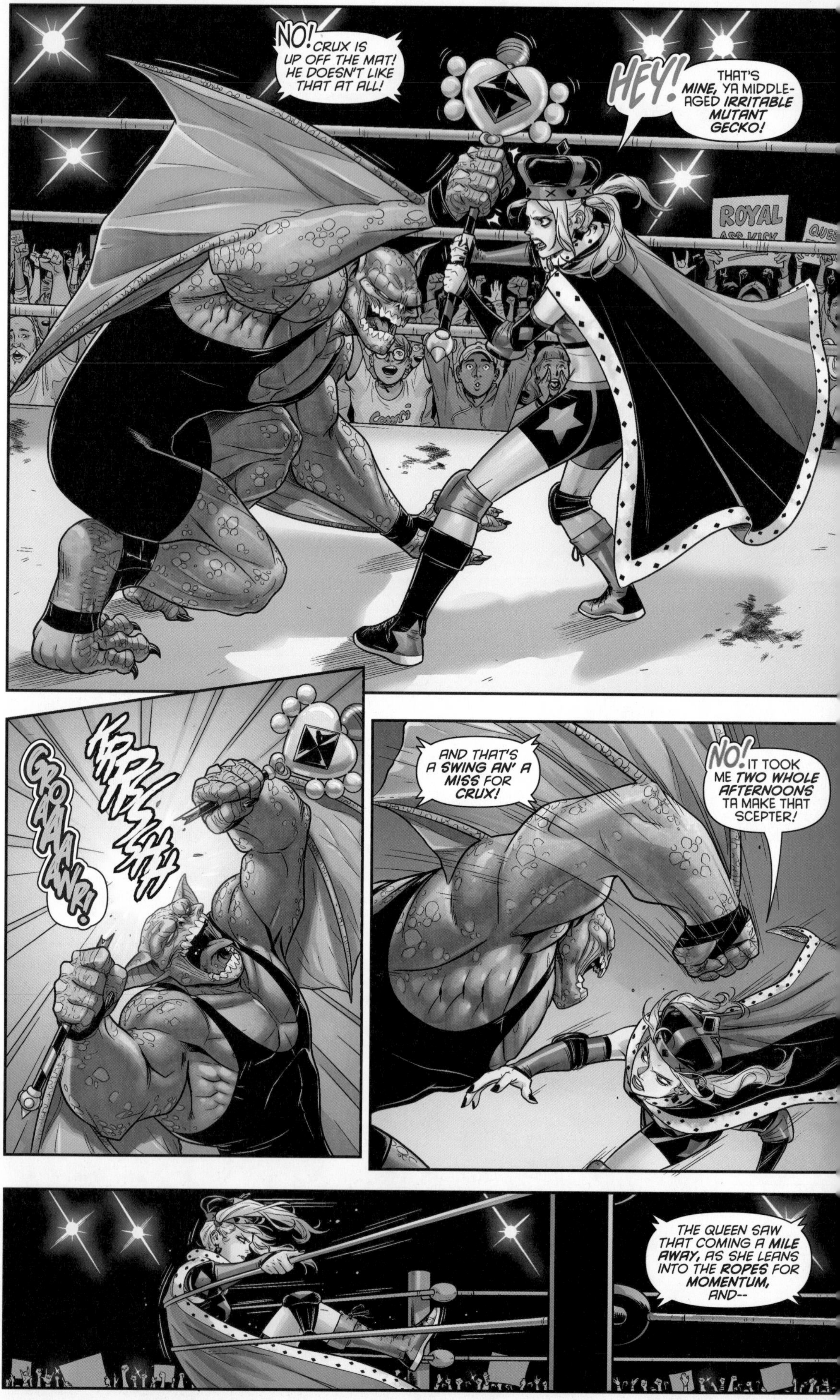
NO! CRUX IS UP OFF THE MAT! HE DOESN'T LIKE THAT AT ALL!
HEY!
THAT'S MINE, YA MIDDLE-AGED IRRITABLE MUTANT GECKO!
ROYAL
KRRUNCHH
GROAAAAAWR!
AND THAT'S A SWING AN' A MISS FOR CRUX!
NO! IT TOOK ME TWO WHOLE AFTERNOONS TA MAKE THAT SCEPTER!
THE QUEEN SAW THAT COMING A MILE AWAY, AS SHE LEANS INTO THE ROPES FOR MOMENTUM, AND--

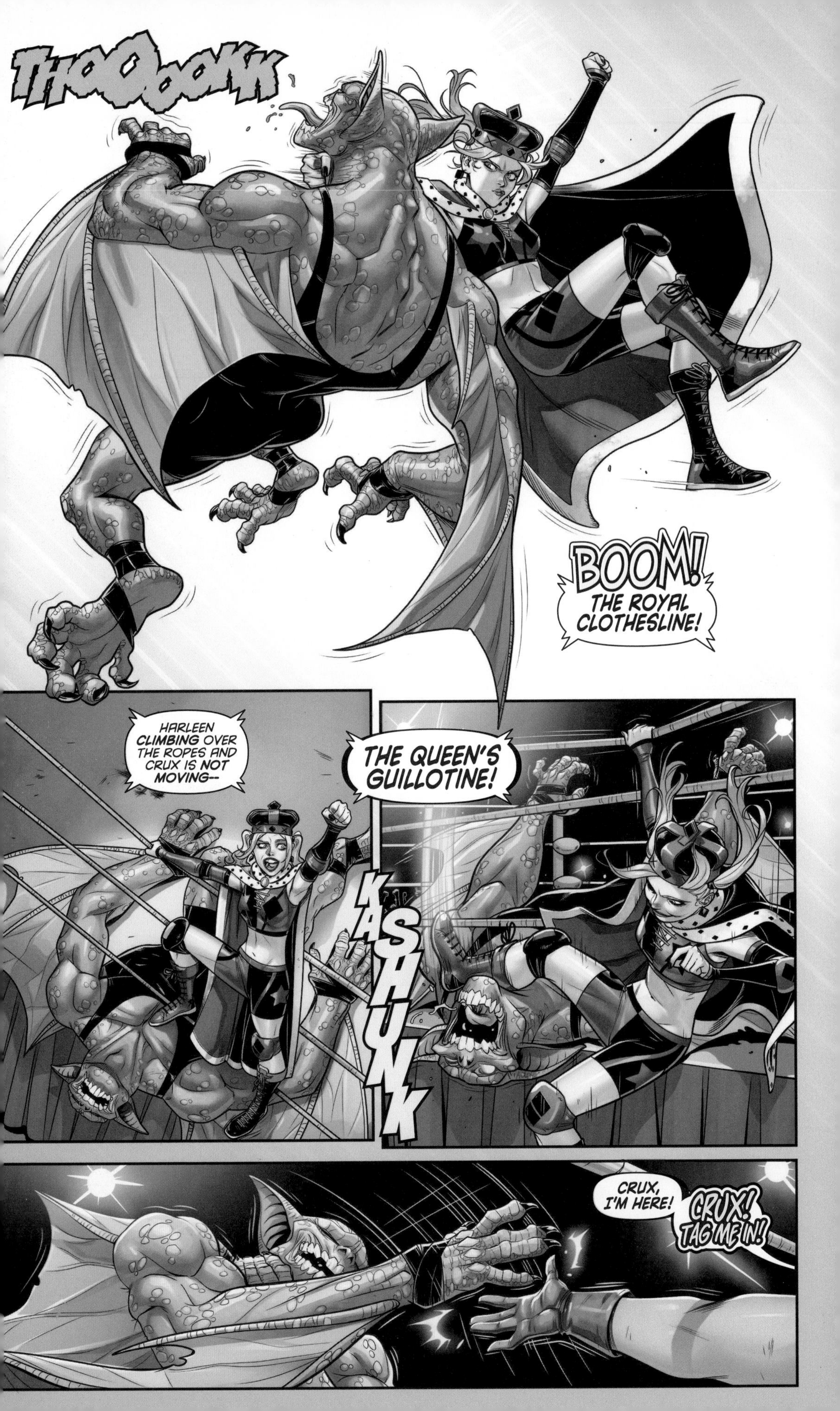

THOOOOKK
BOOM! THE ROYAL CLOTHESLINE!
HARLEEN CLIMBING OVER THE ROPES AND CRUX IS NOT MOVING--
THE QUEEN'S GUILLOTINE!
KASHUNK
CRUX, I'M HERE!
CRUX! TAG ME IN!

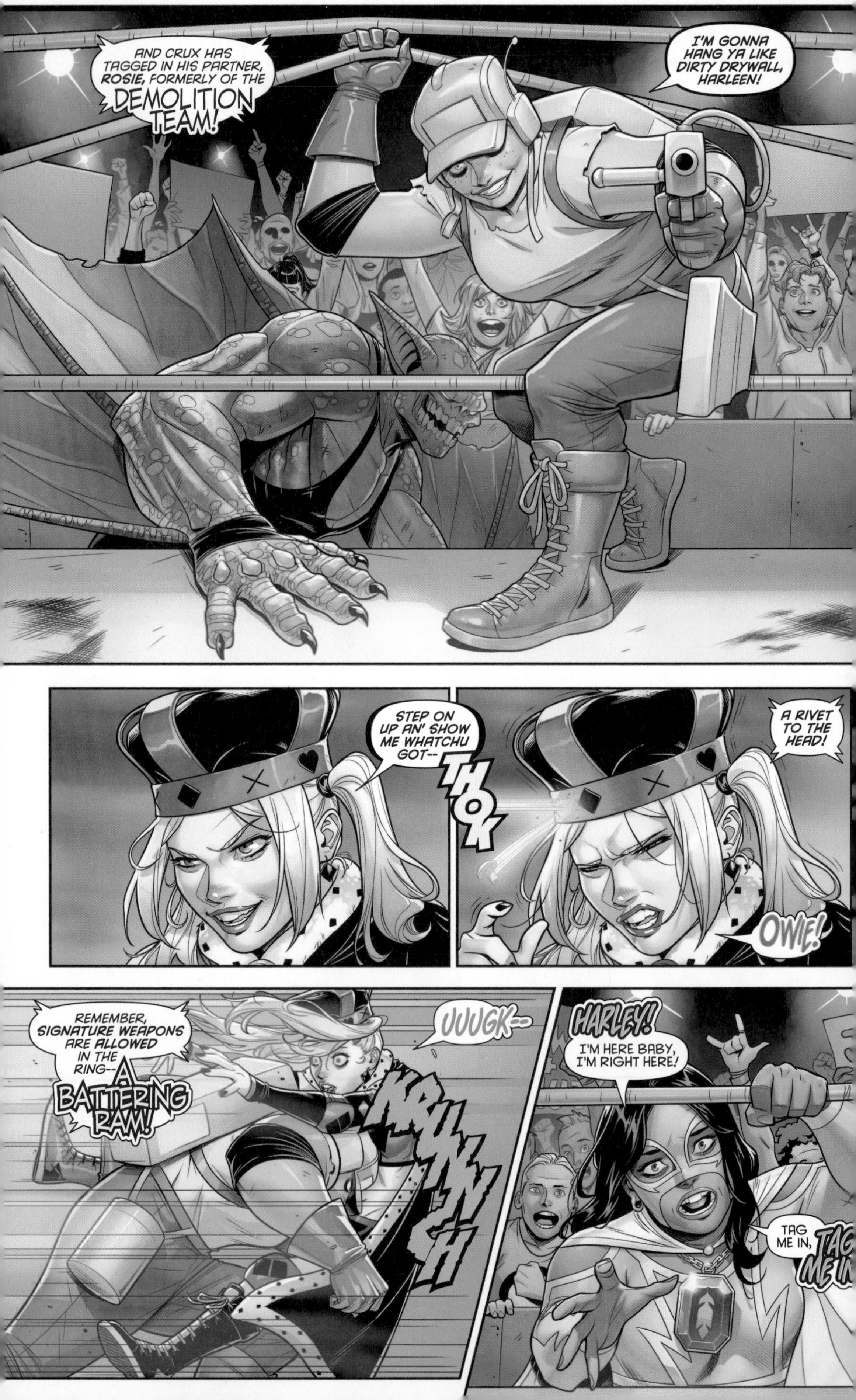
AND CRUX HAS TAGGED IN HIS PARTNER, ROSIE, FORMERLY OF THE DEMOLITION TEAM!
I'M GONNA HANG YA LIKE DIRTY DRYWALL, HARLEEN!
STEP ON UP AN' SHOW ME WHATCHU GOT--
THOK
A RIVET TO THE HEAD!
OWIE!
REMEMBER, SIGNATURE WEAPONS ARE ALLOWED IN THE RING-- A BATTERING RAM!
UUUGK--
KRUNNCH
HARLEY!
I'M HERE BABY, I'M RIGHT HERE!
TAG ME IN,

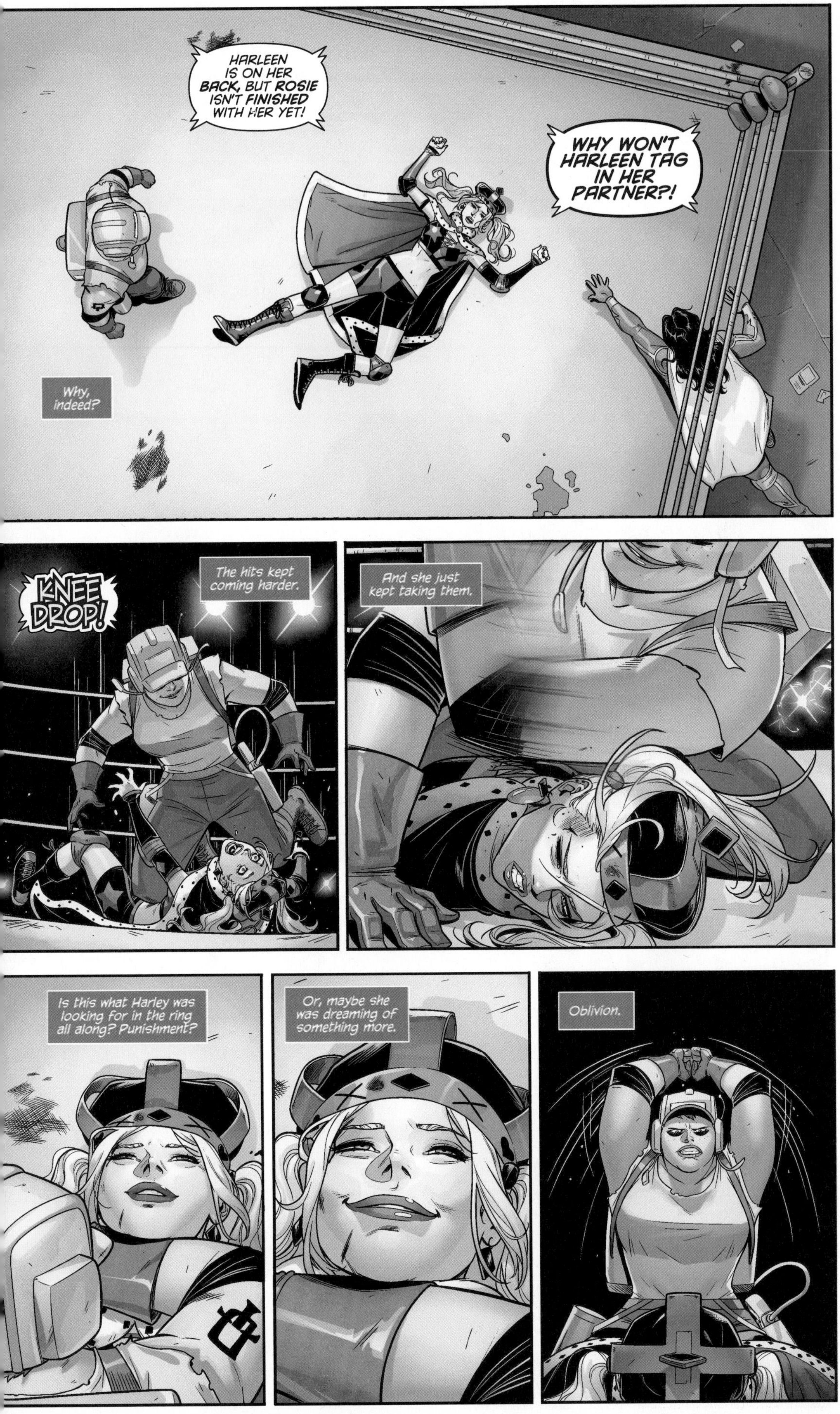
HARLEEN IS ON HER BACK, BUT ROSIE ISN'T FINISHED WITH HER YET!
WHY WON'T HARLEEN TAG IN HER PARTNER?!
Why, indeed?
KNEE DROP!
The hits kept coming harder.
And she just kept taking them.
Is this what Harley was looking for in the ring all along? Punishment?
Or, maybe she was dreaming of something more.
Oblivion.

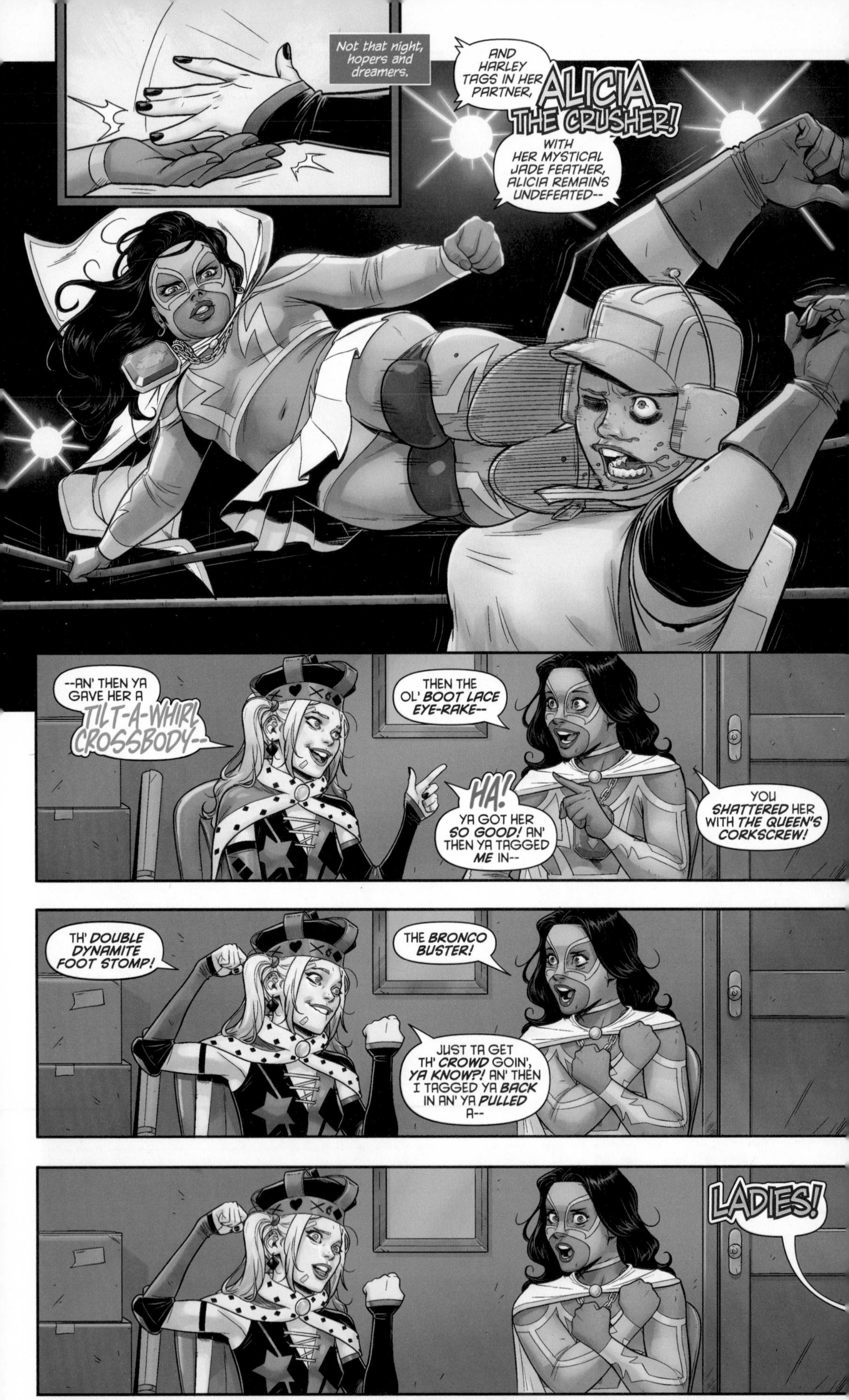
Not that night, hopers and dreamers.
AND HARLEY TAGS IN HER PARTNER, ALICIA THE CRUSHER!
WITH HER MYSTICAL JADE FEATHER, ALICIA REMAINS UNDEFEATED--
--AN' THEN YA GAVE HER A TILT-A-WHIRL CROSSBODY--
THEN THE OL' BOOT LACE EYE-RAKE--
HA!
YA GOT HER SO GOOD! AN' THEN YA TAGGED ME IN--
YOU SHATTERED HER WITH THE QUEEN'S CORKSCREW!
TH' DOUBLE DYNAMITE FOOT STOMP!
THE BRONCO BUSTER!
JUST TA GET TH' CROWD GOIN', YA KNOW?! AN' THEN I TAGGED YA BACK IN AN' YA PULLED A--
LADIES!

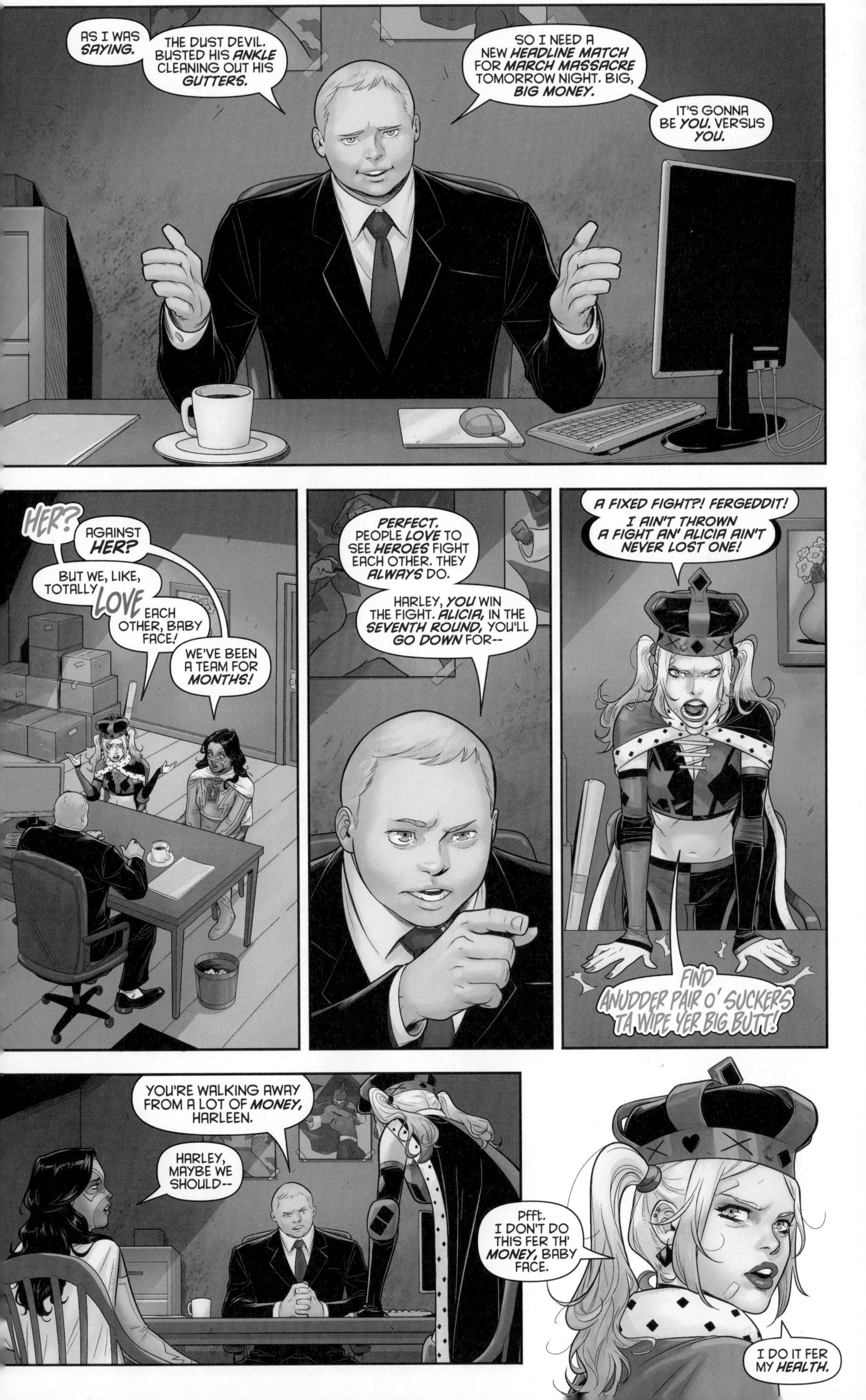
AS I WAS SAYING.
THE DUST DEVIL. BUSTED HIS ANKLE CLEANING OUT HIS GUTTERS.
SO I NEED A NEW HEADLINE MATCH FOR MARCH MASSACRE TOMORROW NIGHT. BIG, BIG MONEY.
IT'S GONNA BE YOU. VERSUS YOU.
HER?
AGAINST HER?
BUT WE, LIKE, TOTALLY LOVE EACH OTHER, BABY FACE!
WE'VE BEEN A TEAM FOR MONTHS!
PERFECT. PEOPLE LOVE TO SEE HEROES FIGHT EACH OTHER. THEY ALWAYS DO.
HARLEY, YOU WIN THE FIGHT. ALICIA, IN THE SEVENTH ROUND, YOU'LL GO DOWN FOR--
A FIXED FIGHT?! FERGEDDIT!
I AIN'T THROWN A FIGHT AN' ALICIA AIN'T NEVER LOST ONE!
FIND ANUDDER PAIR O' SUCKERS TA WIPE YER BIG BUTT!
YOU'RE WALKING AWAY FROM A LOT OF MONEY, HARLEEN.
HARLEY, MAYBE WE SHOULD--
Pfft. I DON'T DO THIS FER TH' MONEY, BABY FACE.
I DO IT FER MY HEALTH.

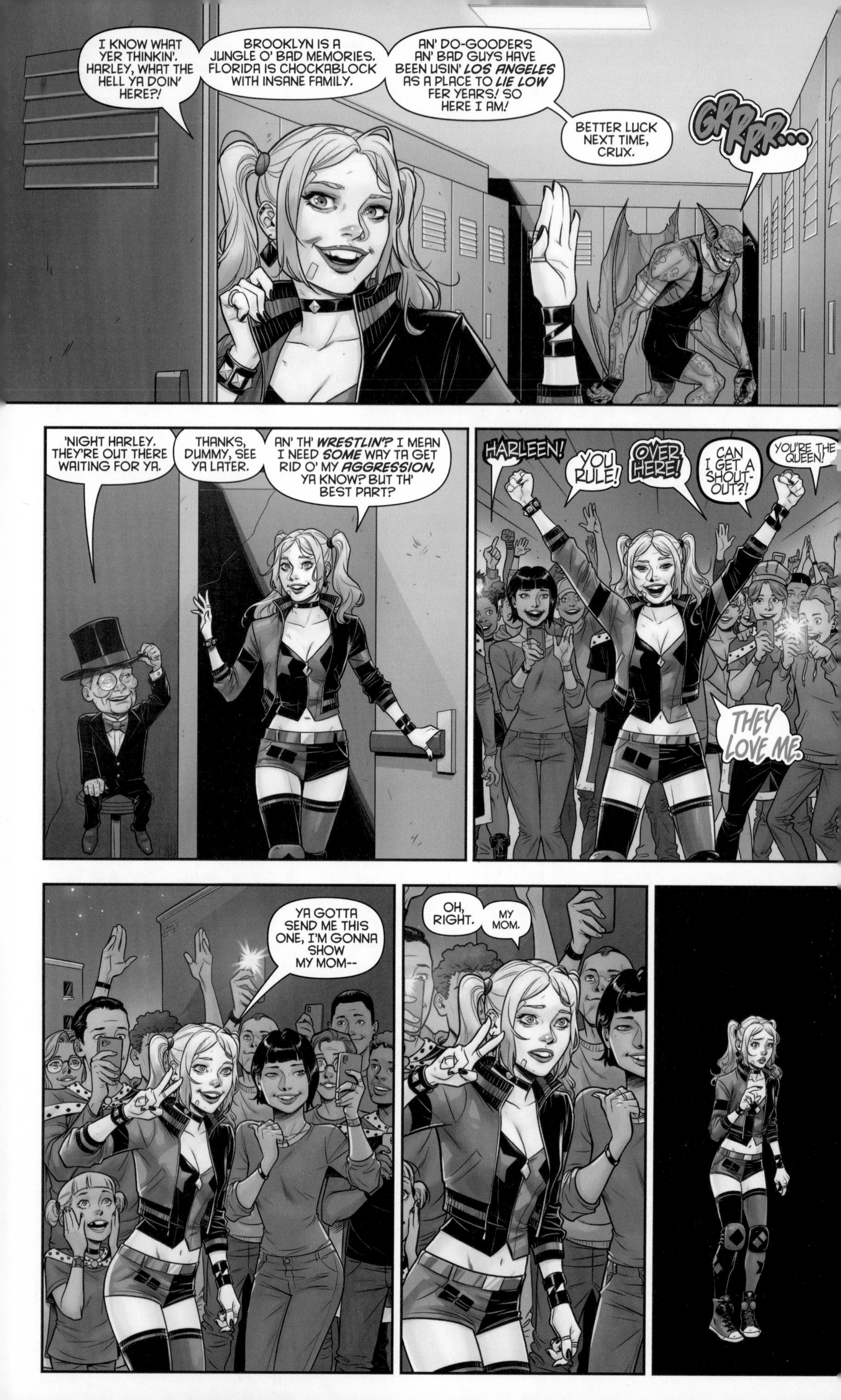
I KNOW WHAT YER THINKIN'. HARLEY, WHAT THE HELL YA DOIN' HERE?!
BROOKLYN IS A JUNGLE O' BAD MEMORIES. FLORIDA IS CHOCKABLOCK WITH INSANE FAMILY.
AN' DO-GOODERS AN' BAD GUYS HAVE BEEN USIN' LOS ANGELES AS A PLACE TO LIE LOW FER YEARS! SO HERE I AM!
BETTER LUCK NEXT TIME, CRUX.
GRRRR...
'NIGHT HARLEY. THEY'RE OUT THERE WAITING FOR YA.
THANKS, DUMMY, SEE YA LATER.
AN' TH' WRESTLIN'? I MEAN I NEED SOME WAY TA GET RID O' MY AGGRESSION, YA KNOW? BUT TH' BEST PART?
HARLEEN!
YOU RULE!
OVER HERE!
CAN I GET A SHOUT-OUT?!
YOU'RE THE QUEEN!
THEY LOVE ME.
YA GOTTA SEND ME THIS ONE, I'M GONNA SHOW MY MOM--
OH, RIGHT.
MY MOM.

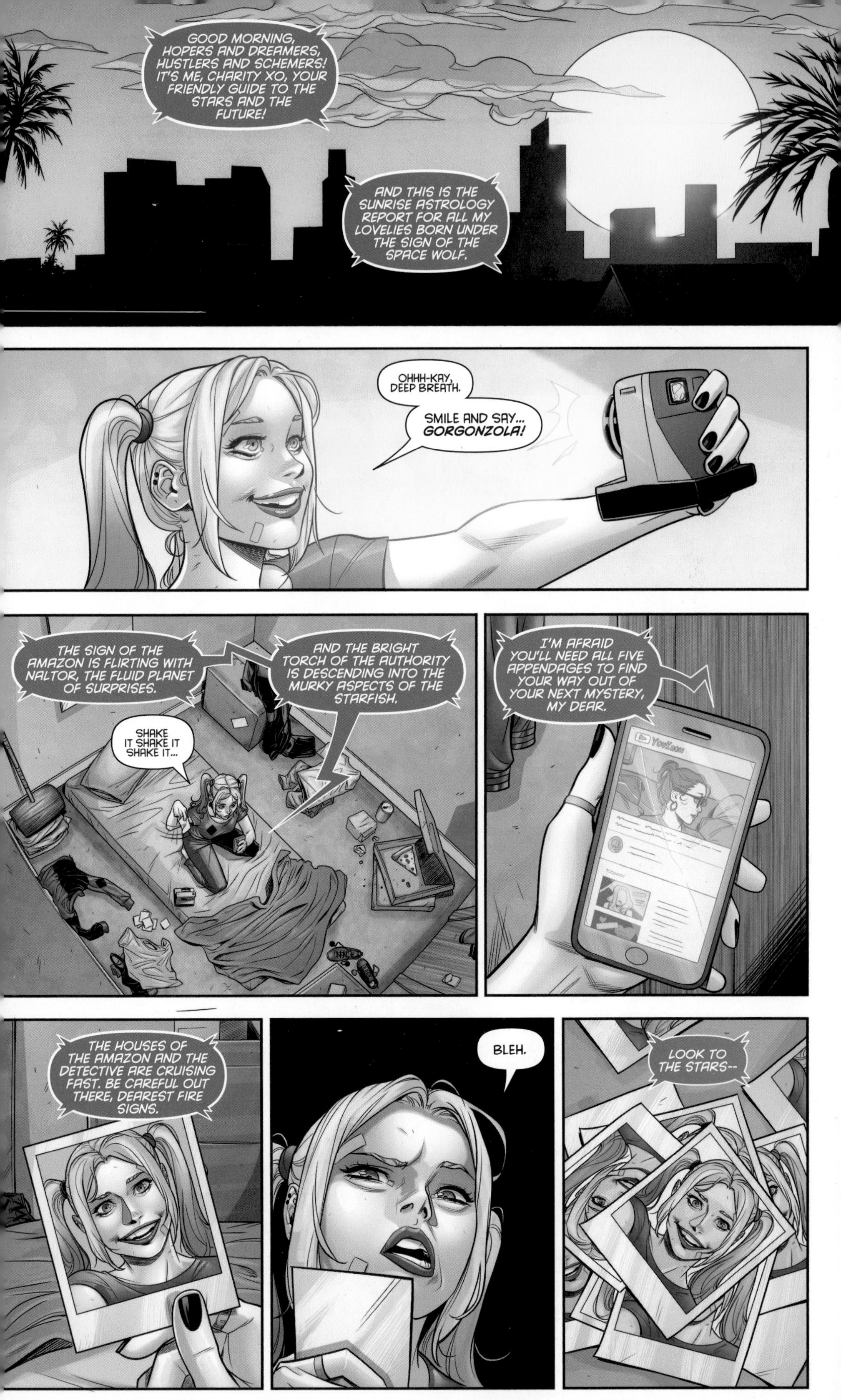
GOOD MORNING, HOPERS AND DREAMERS, HUSTLERS AND SCHEMERS! IT'S ME, CHARITY XO, YOUR FRIENDLY GUIDE TO THE STARS AND THE FUTURE!
AND THIS IS THE SUNRISE ASTROLOGY REPORT FOR ALL MY LOVELIES BORN UNDER THE SIGN OF THE SPACE WOLF.
OHHH-KAY, DEEP BREATH.
SMILE AND SAY... GORGONZOLA!
THE SIGN OF THE AMAZON IS FLIRTING WITH NALTOR, THE FLUID PLANET OF SURPRISES.
AND THE BRIGHT TORCH OF THE AUTHORITY IS DESCENDING INTO THE MURKY ASPECTS OF THE STARFISH.
SHAKE IT SHAKE IT SHAKE IT...
I'M AFRAID YOU'LL NEED ALL FIVE APPENDAGES TO FIND YOUR WAY OUT OF YOUR NEXT MYSTERY, MY DEAR.
THE HOUSES OF THE AMAZON AND THE DETECTIVE ARE CRUISING FAST. BE CAREFUL OUT THERE, DEAREST FIRE SIGNS.
BLEH.
LOOK TO THE STARS--

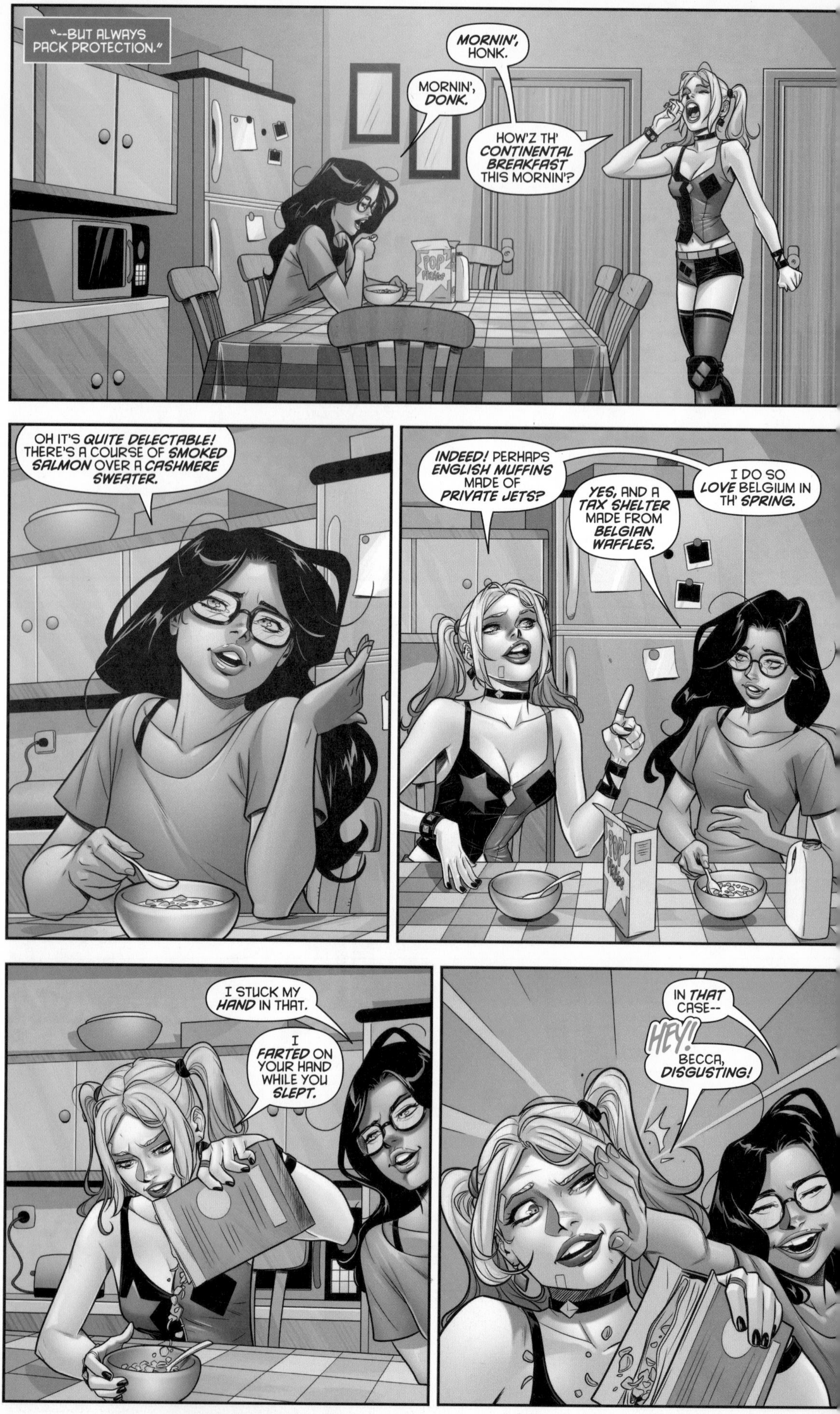
"--BUT ALWAYS PACK PROTECTION."
MORNIN', HONK.
MORNIN', DONK.
HOW'Z TH' CONTINENTAL BREAKFAST THIS MORNIN'?
OH IT'S QUITE DELECTABLE! THERE'S A COURSE OF SMOKED SALMON OVER A CASHMERE SWEATER.
INDEED! PERHAPS ENGLISH MUFFINS MADE OF PRIVATE JETS?
YES, AND A TAX SHELTER MADE FROM BELGIAN WAFFLES.
I DO SO LOVE BELGIUM IN TH' SPRING.
I STUCK MY HAND IN THAT.
I FARTED ON YOUR HAND WHILE YOU SLEPT.
IN THAT CASE--
HEY!
BECCA, DISGUSTING!

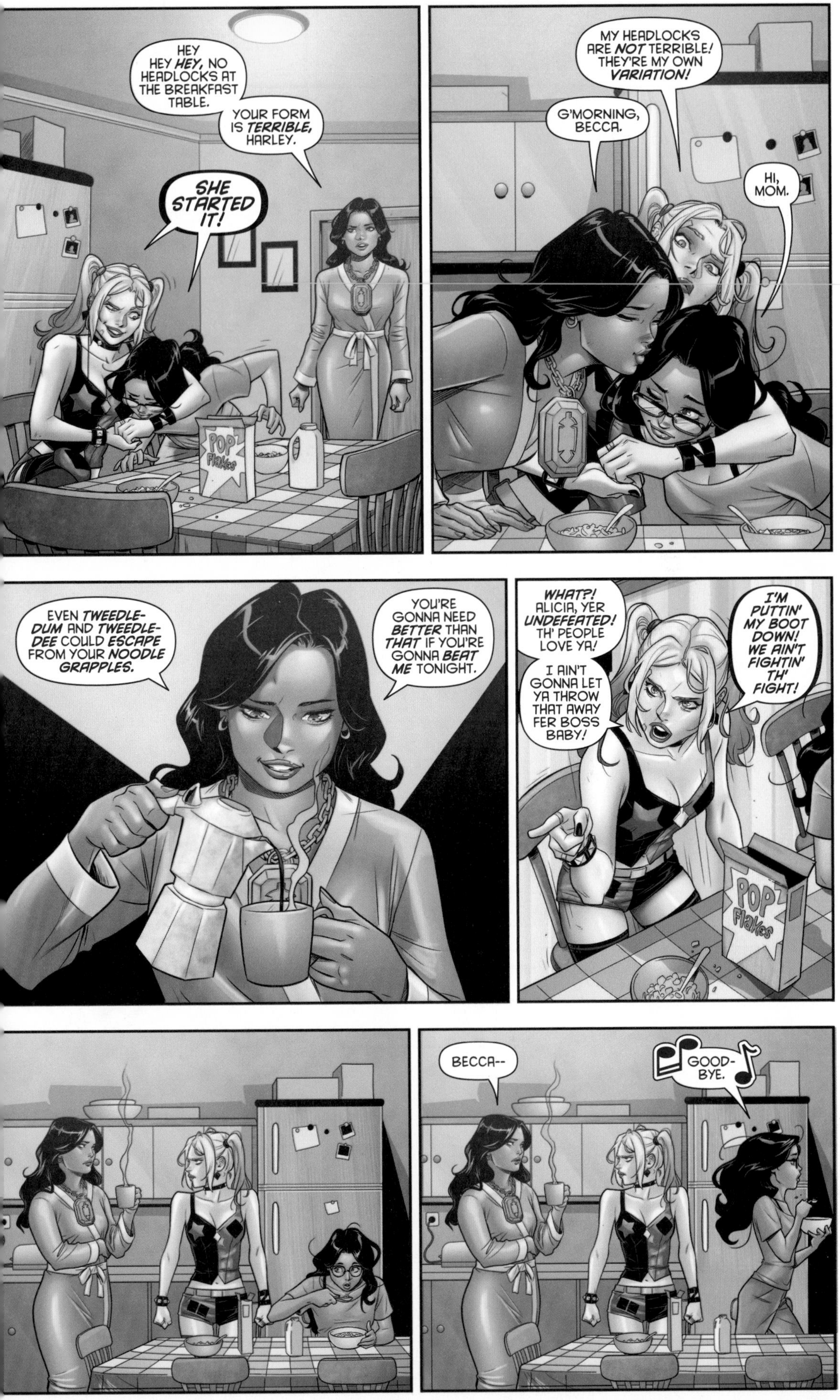
HEY HEY *HEY*, NO HEADLOCKS AT THE BREAKFAST TABLE.
YOUR FORM IS *TERRIBLE,* HARLEY.
SHE STARTED IT!
MY HEADLOCKS ARE *NOT* TERRIBLE! THEY'RE MY OWN *VARIATION!*
G'MORNING, BECCA.
HI, MOM.
EVEN *TWEEDLE-DUM* AND *TWEEDLE-DEE* COULD *ESCAPE* FROM YOUR *NOODLE GRAPPLES.*
YOU'RE GONNA NEED *BETTER* THAN *THAT* IF YOU'RE GONNA *BEAT ME* TONIGHT.
POP Flakes
WHAT?! ALICIA, YER *UNDEFEATED!* TH' PEOPLE LOVE YA!
I AIN'T GONNA LET YA THROW THAT AWAY FER BOSS BABY!
I'M PUTTIN' MY BOOT DOWN! WE AIN'T FIGHTIN' TH' FIGHT!
POP Flakes
BECCA--
GOOD-BYE.

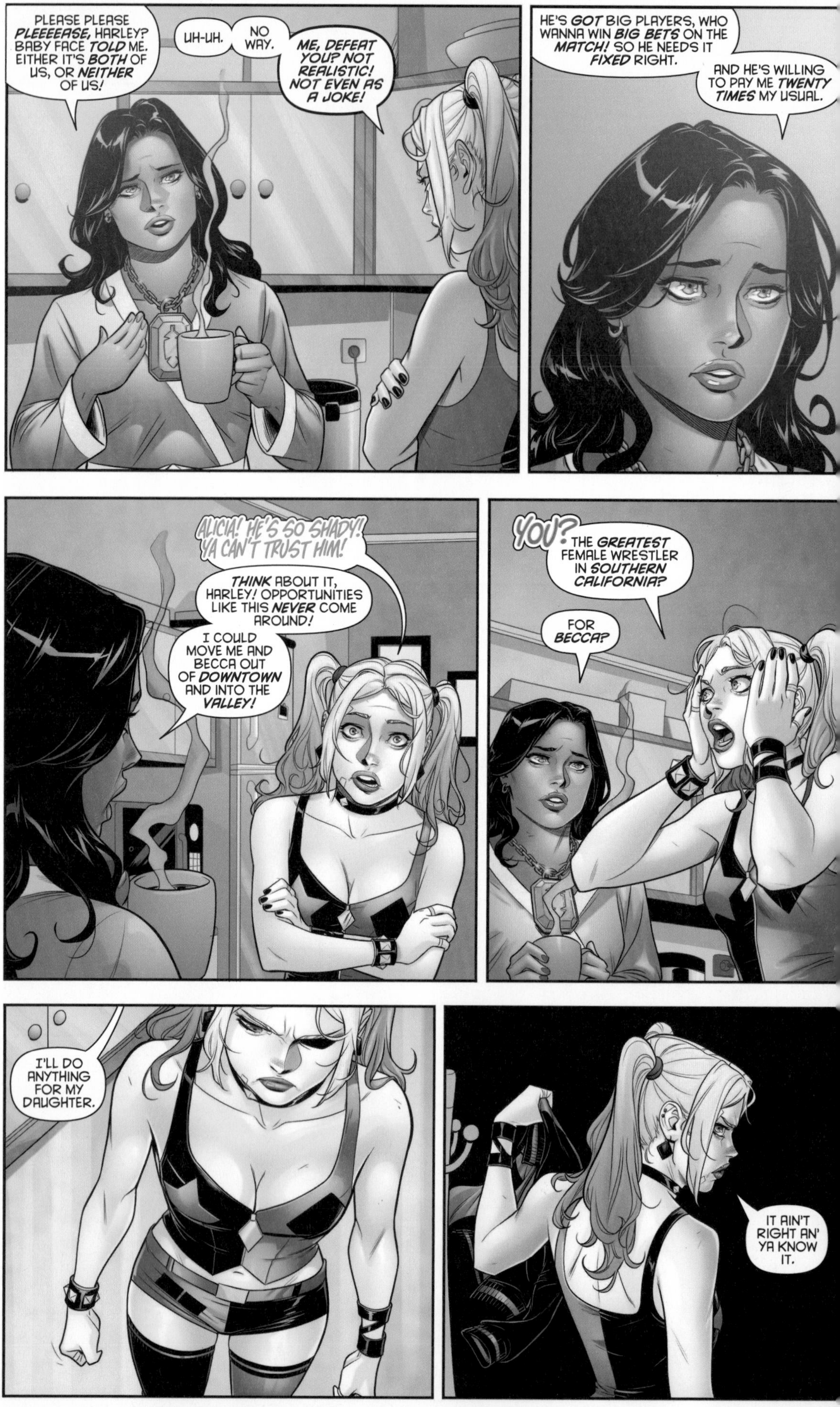

PLEASE PLEASE PLEEEEEASE, HARLEY? BABY FACE TOLD ME. EITHER IT'S BOTH OF US, OR NEITHER OF US!
UH-UH.
NO WAY.
ME, DEFEAT YOU? NOT REALISTIC! NOT EVEN AS A JOKE!
HE'S GOT BIG PLAYERS, WHO WANNA WIN BIG BETS ON THE MATCH! SO HE NEEDS IT FIXED RIGHT.
AND HE'S WILLING TO PAY ME TWENTY TIMES MY USUAL.
ALICIA! HE'S SO SHADY! YA CAN'T TRUST HIM!
THINK ABOUT IT, HARLEY! OPPORTUNITIES LIKE THIS NEVER COME AROUND!
I COULD MOVE ME AND BECCA OUT OF DOWNTOWN AND INTO THE VALLEY!
YOU? THE GREATEST FEMALE WRESTLER IN SOUTHERN CALIFORNIA?
FOR BECCA?
I'LL DO ANYTHING FOR MY DAUGHTER.
IT AIN'T RIGHT AN' YA KNOW IT.

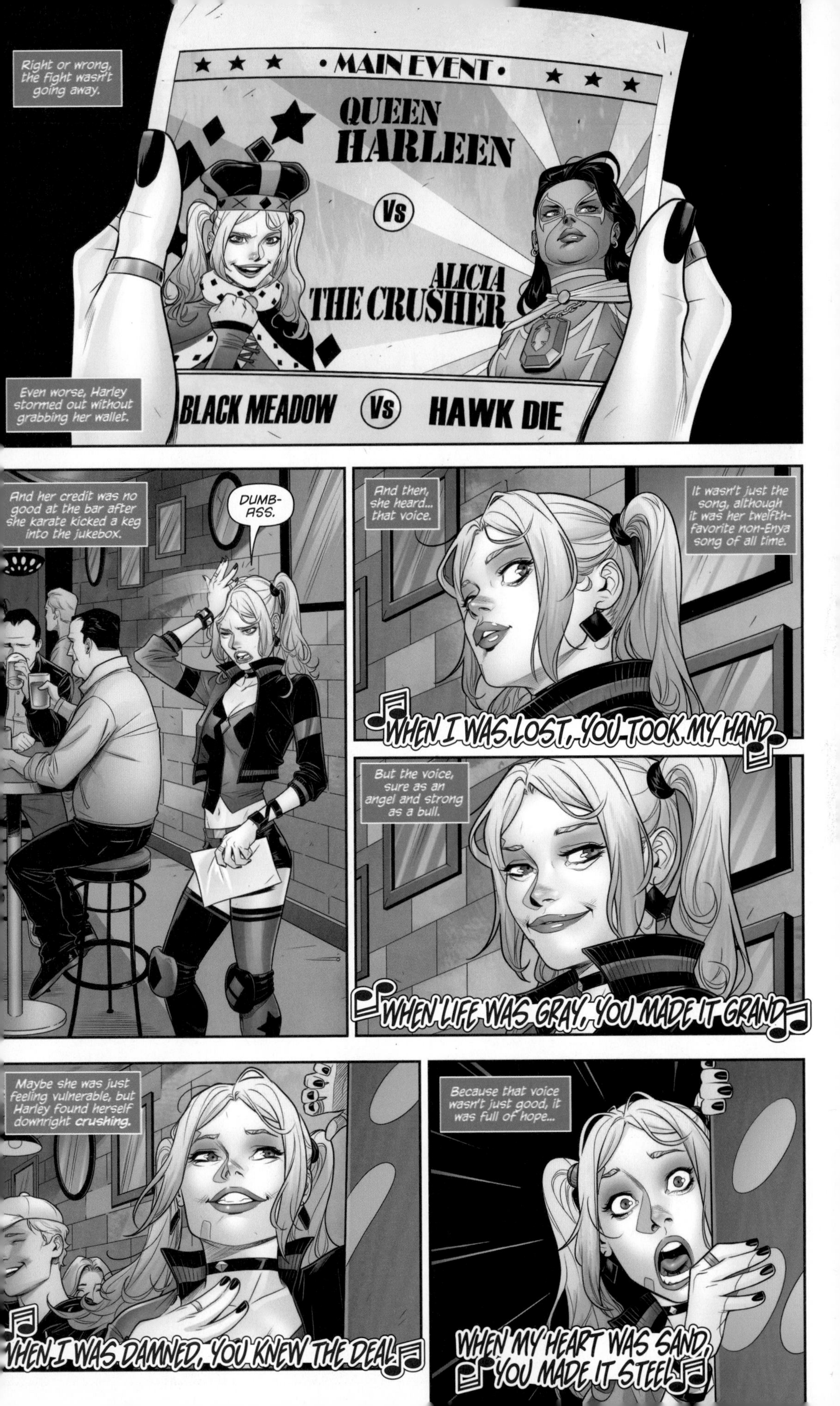

Right or wrong, the fight wasn't going away.
MAIN EVENT
QUEEN HARLEEN
Vs
ALICIA THE CRUSHER
Even worse, Harley stormed out without grabbing her wallet.
BLACK MEADOW
Vs
HAWK DIE
And her credit was no good at the bar after she karate kicked a keg into the jukebox.
DUMB-ASS.
And then, she heard... that voice.
It wasn't just the song, although it was her twelfth-favorite non-Enya song of all time.
WHEN I WAS LOST, YOU TOOK MY HAND
But the voice, sure as an angel and strong as a bull.
WHEN LIFE WAS GRAY, YOU MADE IT GRAND
Maybe she was just feeling vulnerable, but Harley found herself downright crushing.
WHEN I WAS DAMNED, YOU KNEW THE DEAL
Because that voice wasn't just good, it was full of hope...
WHEN MY HEART WAS SAND, YOU MADE IT STEEL

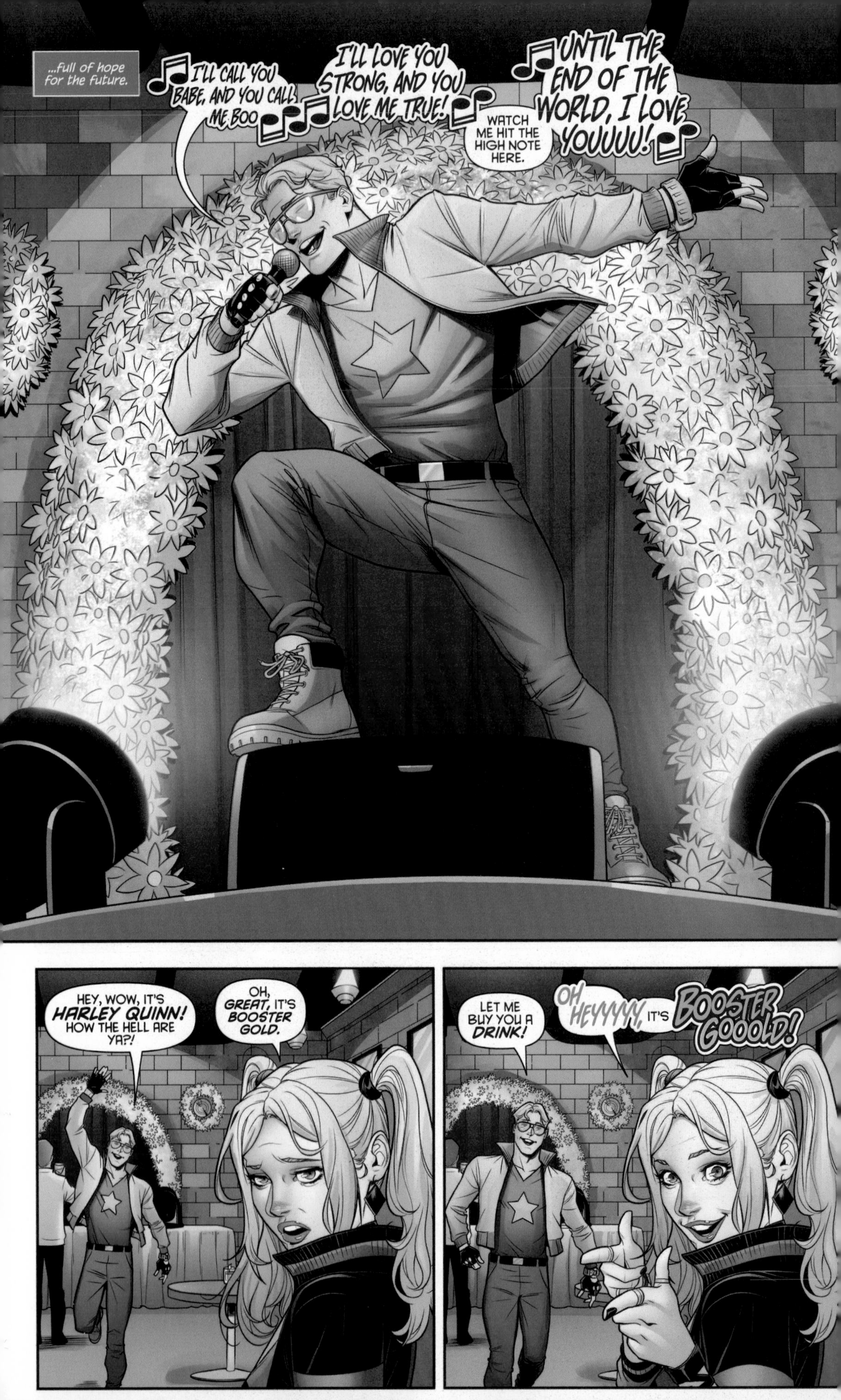
...full of hope for the future.
I'LL CALL YOU BABE, AND YOU CALL ME BOO
I'LL LOVE YOU STRONG, AND YOU LOVE ME TRUE!
WATCH ME HIT THE HIGH NOTE HERE.
UNTIL THE END OF THE WORLD, I LOVE YOUUUU!
HEY, WOW, IT'S HARLEY QUINN! HOW THE HELL ARE YA?!
OH, GREAT, IT'S BOOSTER GOLD.
LET ME BUY YOU A DRINK!
OH HEYYYY, IT'S BOOSTER GOOOLD!

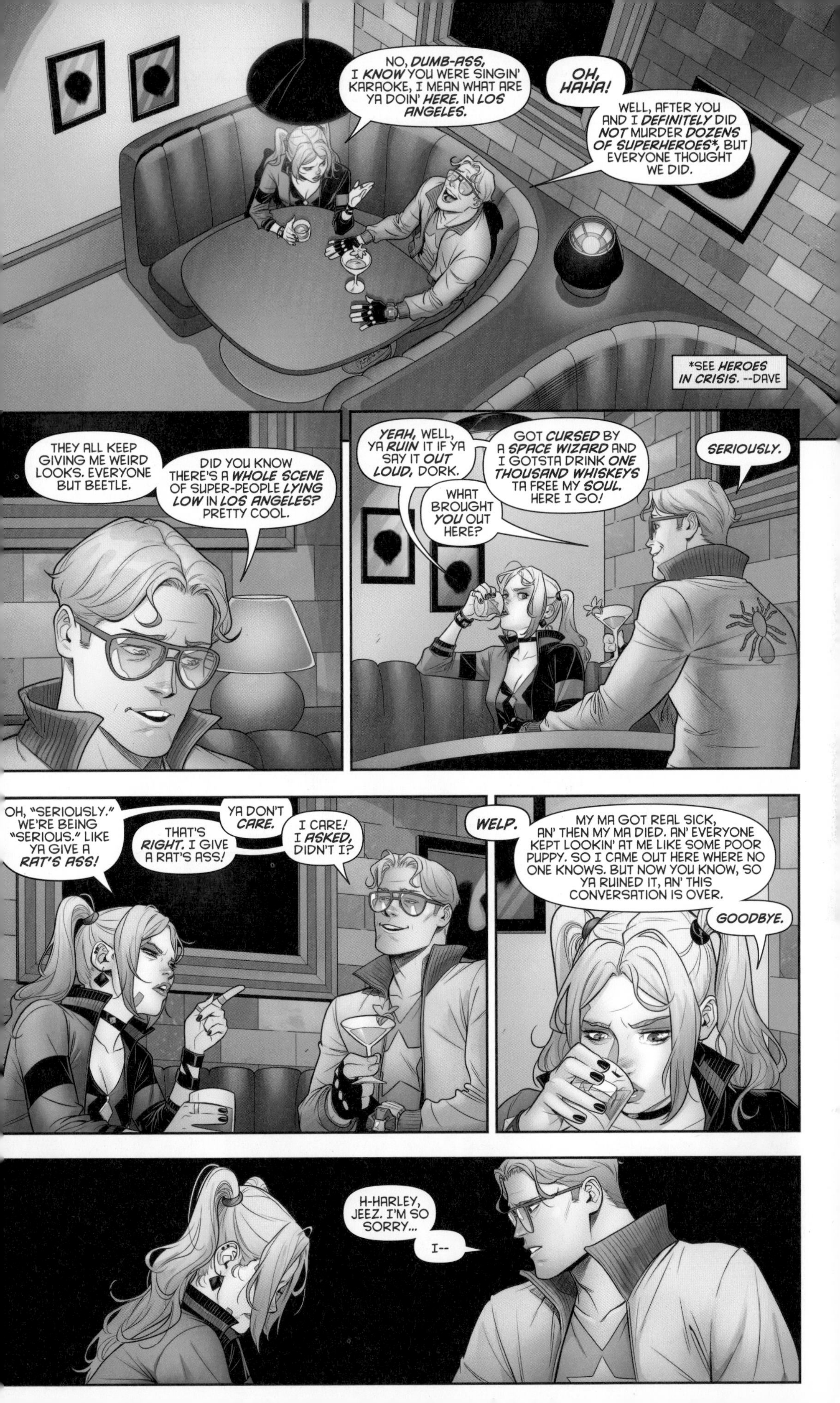
NO, DUMB-ASS, I KNOW YOU WERE SINGIN' KARAOKE, I MEAN WHAT ARE YA DOIN' HERE. IN LOS ANGELES.
OH, HAHA!
WELL, AFTER YOU AND I DEFINITELY DID NOT MURDER DOZENS OF SUPERHEROES*, BUT EVERYONE THOUGHT WE DID.
*SEE HEROES IN CRISIS. --DAVE
THEY ALL KEEP GIVING ME WEIRD LOOKS. EVERYONE BUT BEETLE.
DID YOU KNOW THERE'S A WHOLE SCENE OF SUPER-PEOPLE LYING LOW IN LOS ANGELES? PRETTY COOL.
WHAT BROUGHT YOU OUT HERE?
GOT CURSED BY A SPACE WIZARD AND I GOTSTA DRINK ONE THOUSAND WHISKEYS TA FREE MY SOUL. HERE I GO!
YEAH, WELL, YA RUIN IT IF YA SAY IT OUT LOUD, DORK.
SERIOUSLY.
OH, "SERIOUSLY." WE'RE BEING "SERIOUS." LIKE YA GIVE A RAT'S ASS!
THAT'S RIGHT. I GIVE A RAT'S ASS!
YA DON'T CARE.
I CARE! I ASKED, DIDN'T I?
WELP.
MY MA GOT REAL SICK, AN' THEN MY MA DIED. AN' EVERYONE KEPT LOOKIN' AT ME LIKE SOME POOR PUPPY. SO I CAME OUT HERE WHERE NO ONE KNOWS. BUT NOW YOU KNOW, SO YA RUINED IT, AN' THIS CONVERSATION IS OVER.
GOODBYE.
H-HARLEY, JEEZ. I'M SO SORRY...
I--

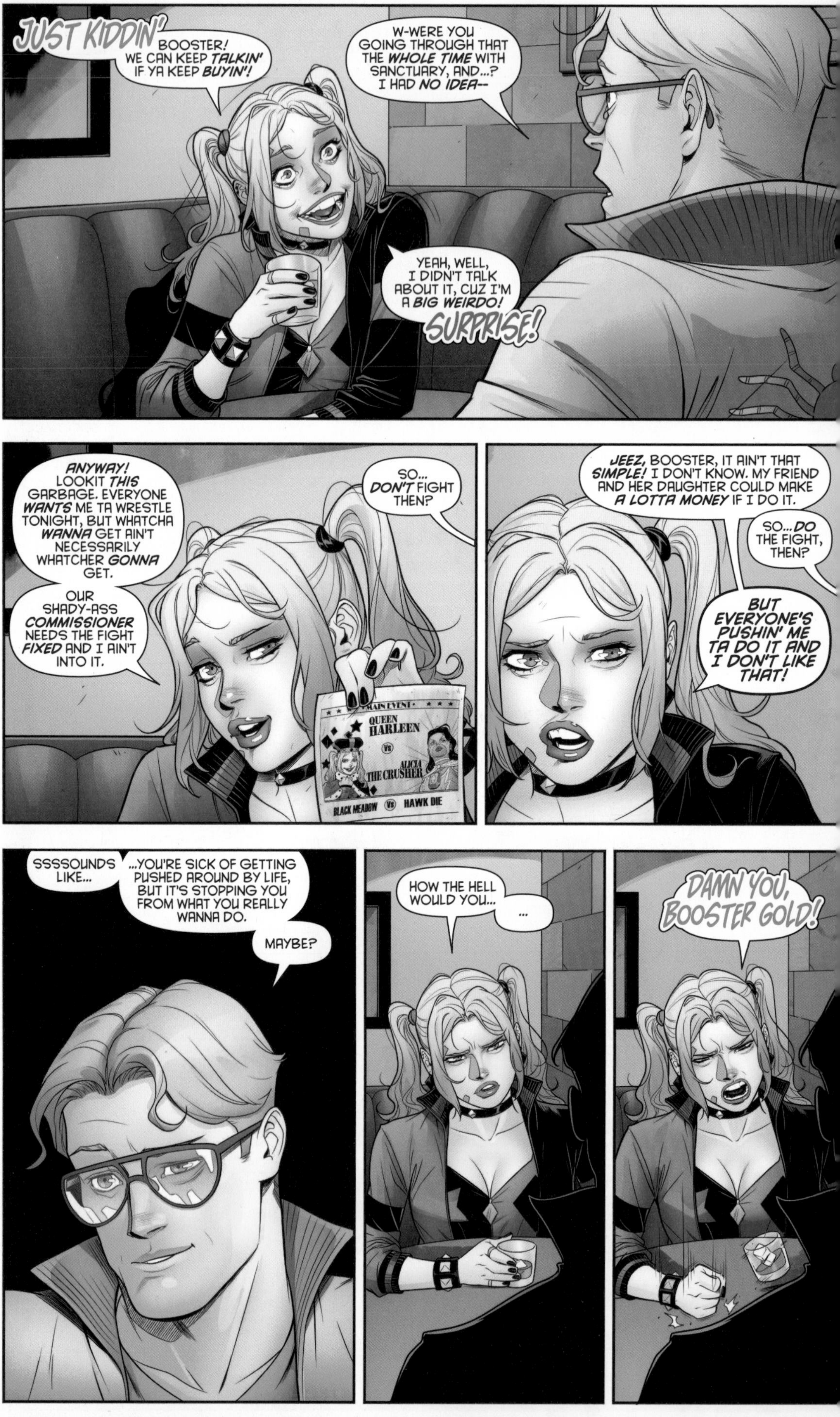

JUST KIDDIN' BOOSTER! WE CAN KEEP TALKIN' IF YA KEEP BUYIN'!
W-WERE YOU GOING THROUGH THAT THE WHOLE TIME WITH SANCTUARY, AND...? I HAD NO IDEA--
YEAH, WELL, I DIDN'T TALK ABOUT IT, CUZ I'M A BIG WEIRDO! SURPRISE!
ANYWAY! LOOKIT THIS GARBAGE. EVERYONE WANTS ME TA WRESTLE TONIGHT, BUT WHATCHA WANNA GET AIN'T NECESSARILY WHATCHER GONNA GET.
OUR SHADY-ASS COMMISSIONER NEEDS THE FIGHT FIXED AND I AIN'T INTO IT.
SO... DON'T FIGHT THEN?
MAIN EVENT
QUEEN HARLEEN
VS
ALICIA THE CRUSHER
BLACK MEADOW VS HAWK DIE
JEEZ, BOOSTER, IT AIN'T THAT SIMPLE! I DON'T KNOW. MY FRIEND AND HER DAUGHTER COULD MAKE A LOTTA MONEY IF I DO IT.
SO...DO THE FIGHT, THEN?
BUT EVERYONE'S PUSHIN' ME TA DO IT AND I DON'T LIKE THAT!
SSSSOUNDS LIKE...
...YOU'RE SICK OF GETTING PUSHED AROUND BY LIFE, BUT IT'S STOPPING YOU FROM WHAT YOU REALLY WANNA DO.
MAYBE?
HOW THE HELL WOULD YOU...
...
DAMN YOU, BOOSTER GOLD!

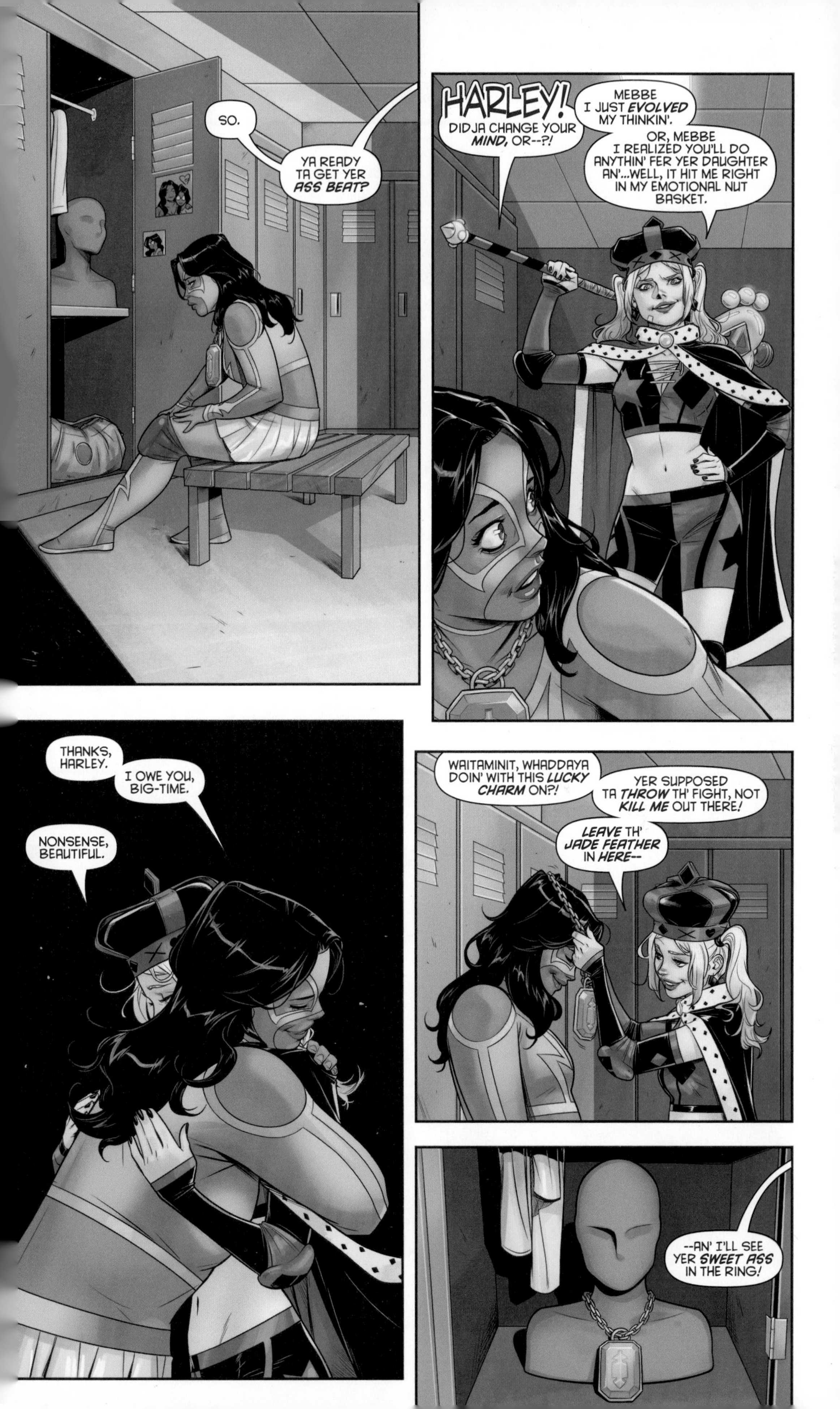

SO.
YA READY TA GET YER *ASS BEAT?*
HARLEY!
DIDJA CHANGE YOUR *MIND,* OR--?!
MEBBE I JUST *EVOLVED* MY THINKIN'.
OR, MEBBE I REALIZED YOU'LL DO ANYTHIN' FER YER DAUGHTER AN'...WELL, IT HIT ME RIGHT IN MY EMOTIONAL NUT BASKET.
THANKS, HARLEY.
I OWE YOU, BIG-TIME.
NONSENSE, BEAUTIFUL.
WAITAMINIT, WHADDAYA DOIN' WITH THIS *LUCKY CHARM* ON?!
YER SUPPOSED TA *THROW* TH' FIGHT, NOT *KILL ME* OUT THERE!
LEAVE TH' *JADE FEATHER* IN *HERE--*
--AN' I'LL SEE YER *SWEET ASS* IN THE RING!

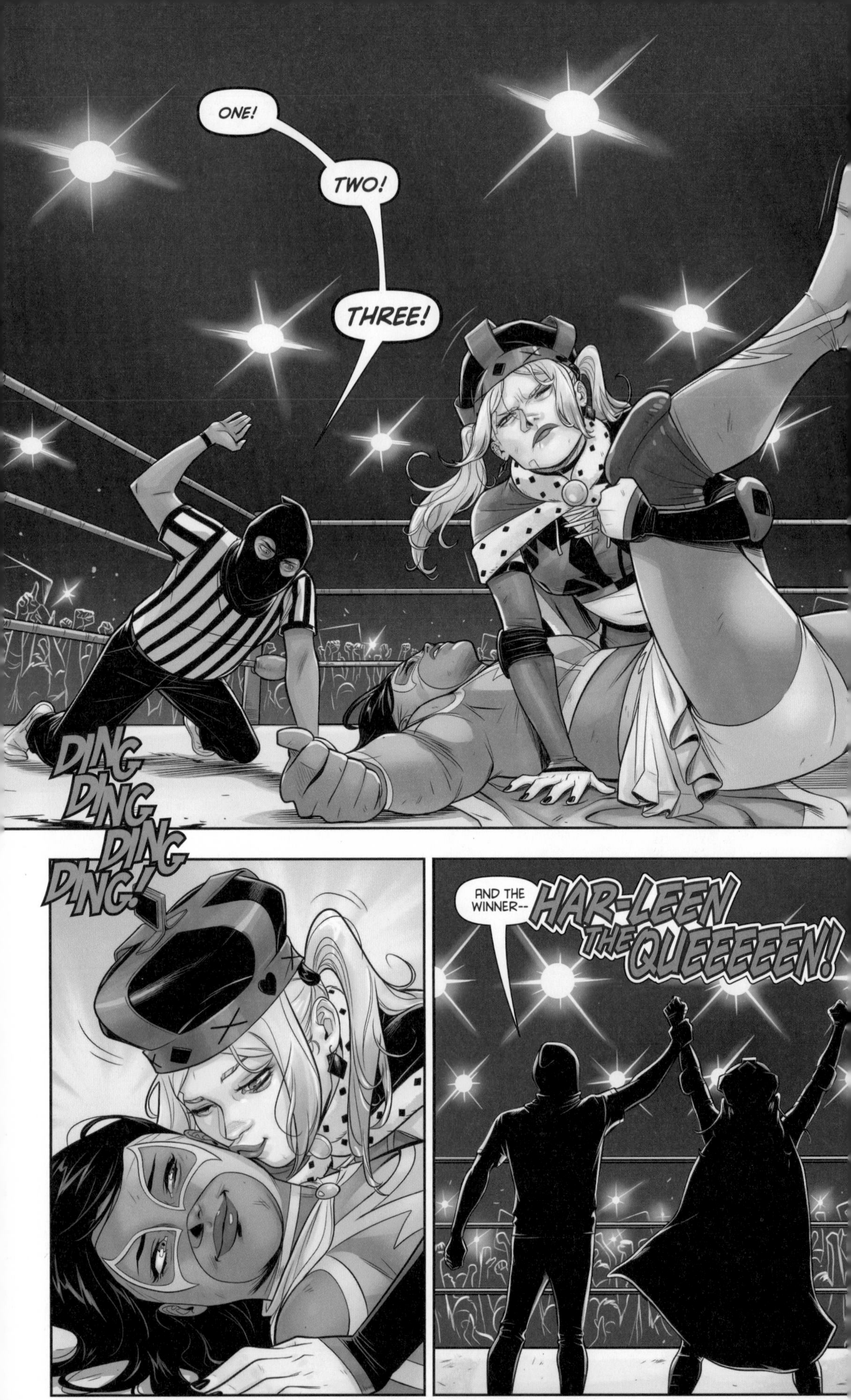
ONE!
TWO!
THREE!
DING DING DING DING!
AND THE WINNER--
HAR-LEEN THE QUEEEEEEN!

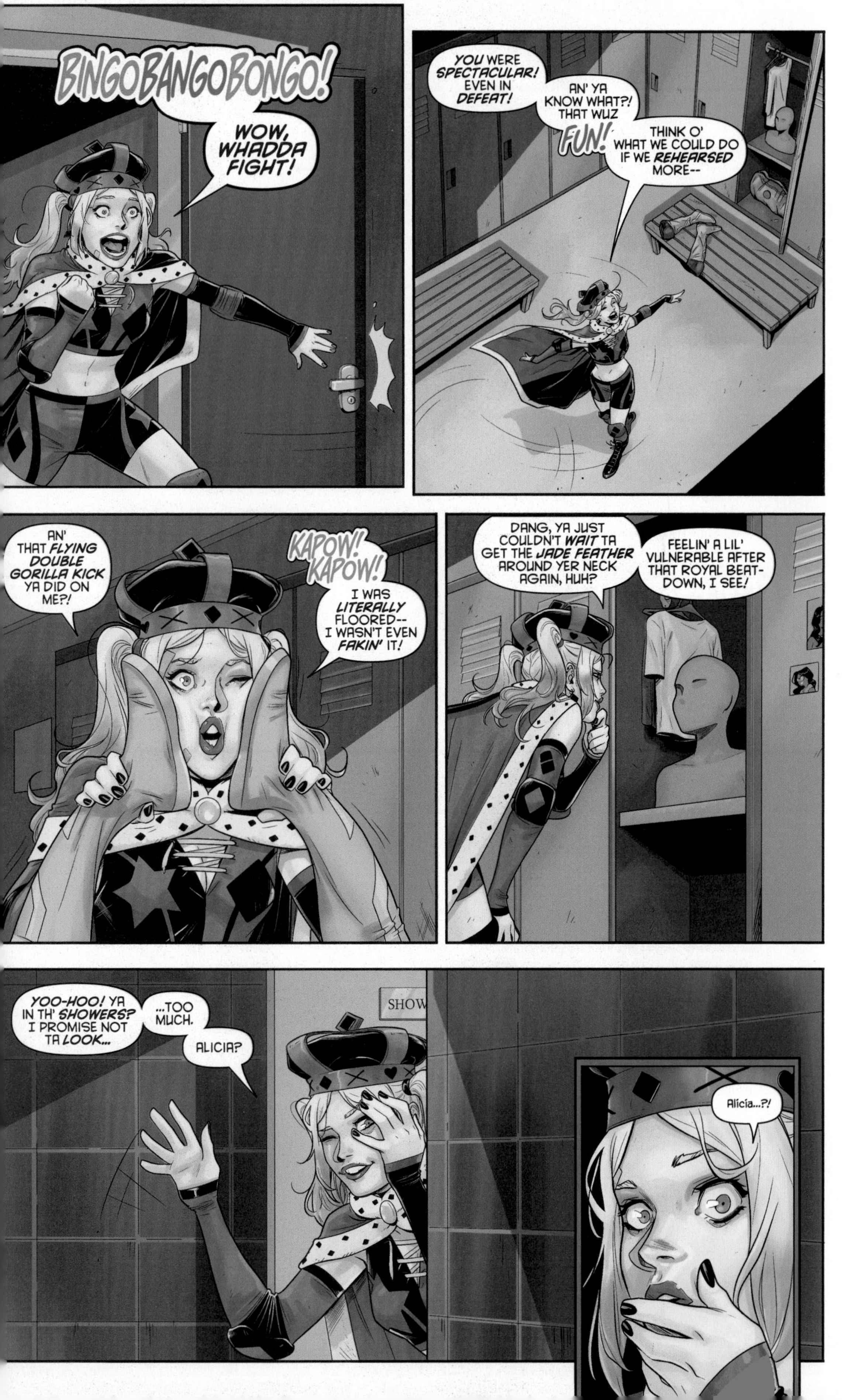
BINGOBANGOBONGO!
WOW, WHADDA FIGHT!
YOU WERE SPECTACULAR! EVEN IN DEFEAT!
AN' YA KNOW WHAT?! THAT WUZ FUN!
THINK O' WHAT WE COULD DO IF WE REHEARSED MORE--
AN' THAT FLYING DOUBLE GORILLA KICK YA DID ON ME?!
KAPOW! KAPOW!
I WAS LITERALLY FLOORED-- I WASN'T EVEN FAKIN' IT!
DANG, YA JUST COULDN'T WAIT TA GET THE JADE FEATHER AROUND YER NECK AGAIN, HUH?
FEELIN' A LIL' VULNERABLE AFTER THAT ROYAL BEAT-DOWN, I SEE!
YOO-HOO! YA IN TH' SHOWERS? I PROMISE NOT TA LOOK...
...TOO MUCH.
SHOW
ALICIA?
Alicia...?!

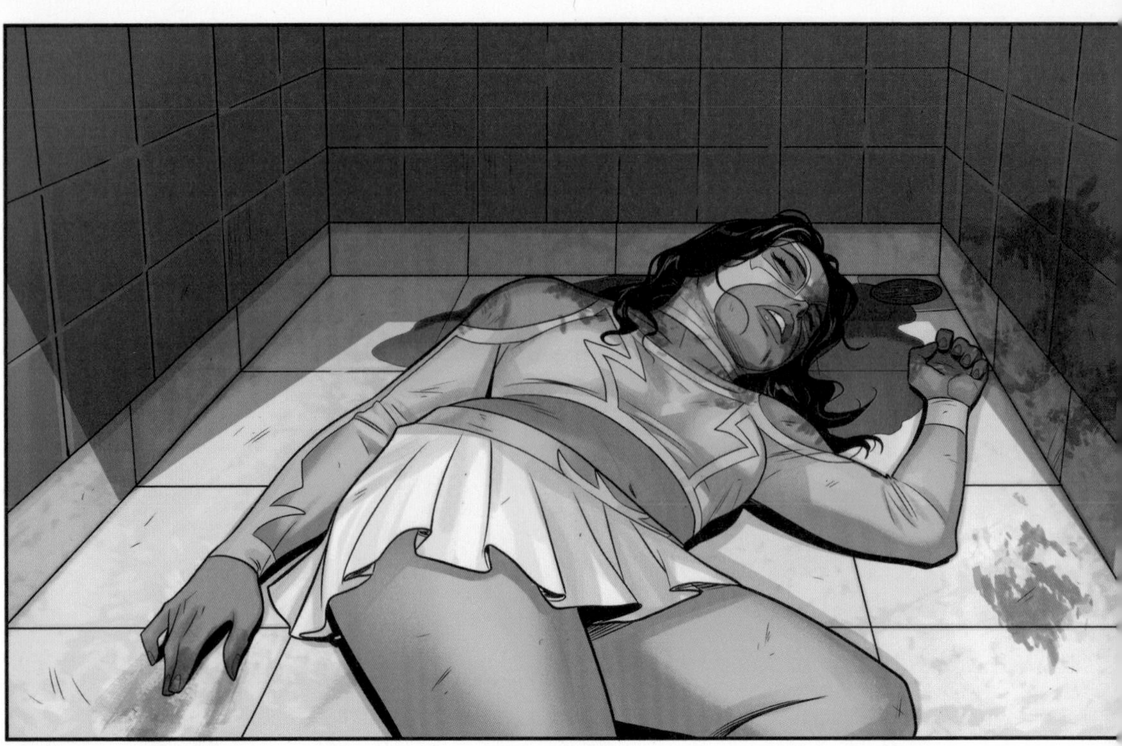

DC COMICS PROUDLY PRESENTS THE NEW HARLEY QUINN EPIC,

CALIFORNIA OR DEATH

CHAPTER 1 HARLEEN THE QUEEN

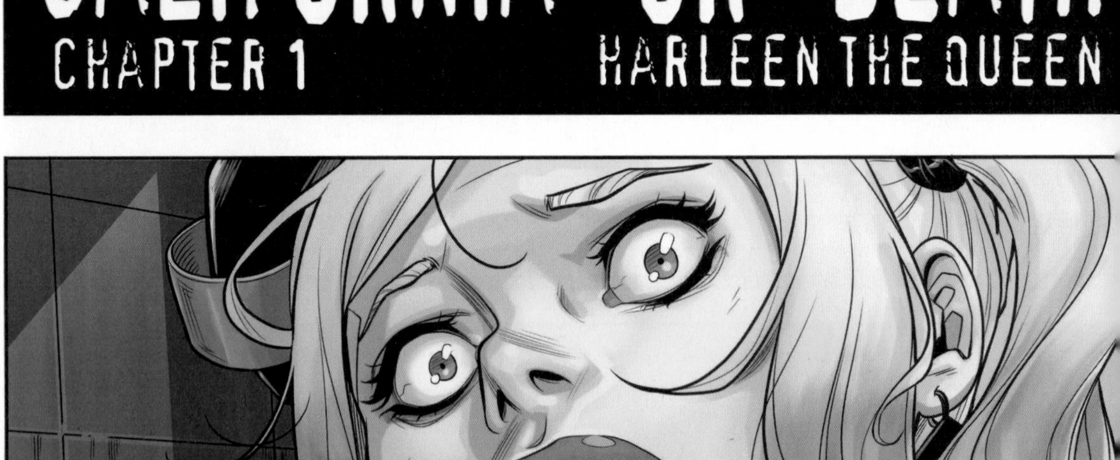

SAM HUMPHRIES WRITER SAMI BASRI ARTIST HI-FI COLORS
DAVE SHARPE LETTERS GUILLEM MARCH & ARIF PRIANTO COVER
FRANK CHO & SABINE RICH VARIANT COVER DAVE WIELGOSZ EDITOR
BEN ABERNATHY GROUP EDITOR
HARLEY QUINN CREATED BY PAUL DINI & BRUCE TIMM

NEXT ISSUE: YA CAN'T GET AWAY WITH MURDER!

HARLEY QUINN #71 cover
by RILEY ROSSMO and IVAN PLASCENCIA

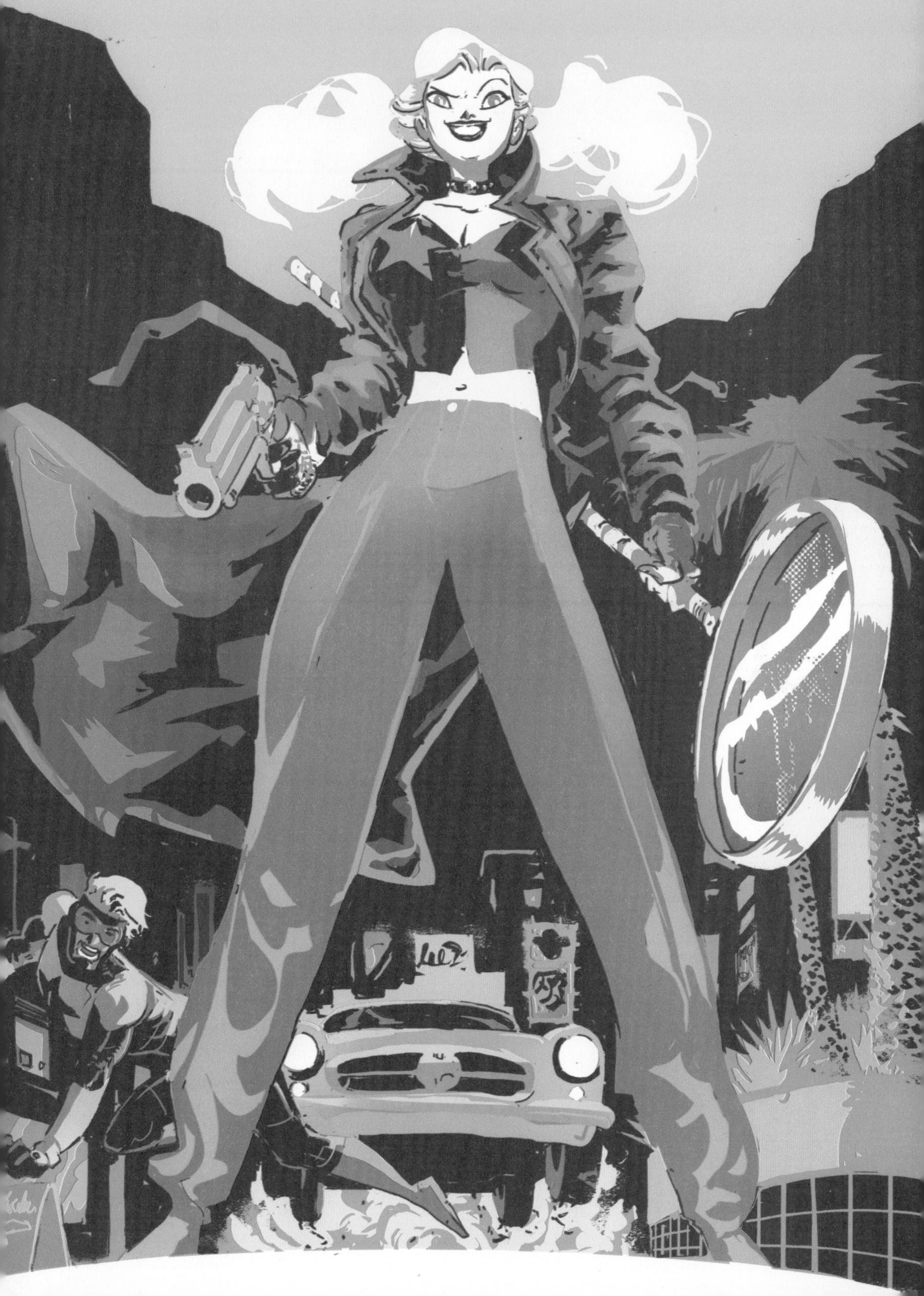

HARLEY QUINN #71 variant cover
by FRANK CHO and SABINE RICH

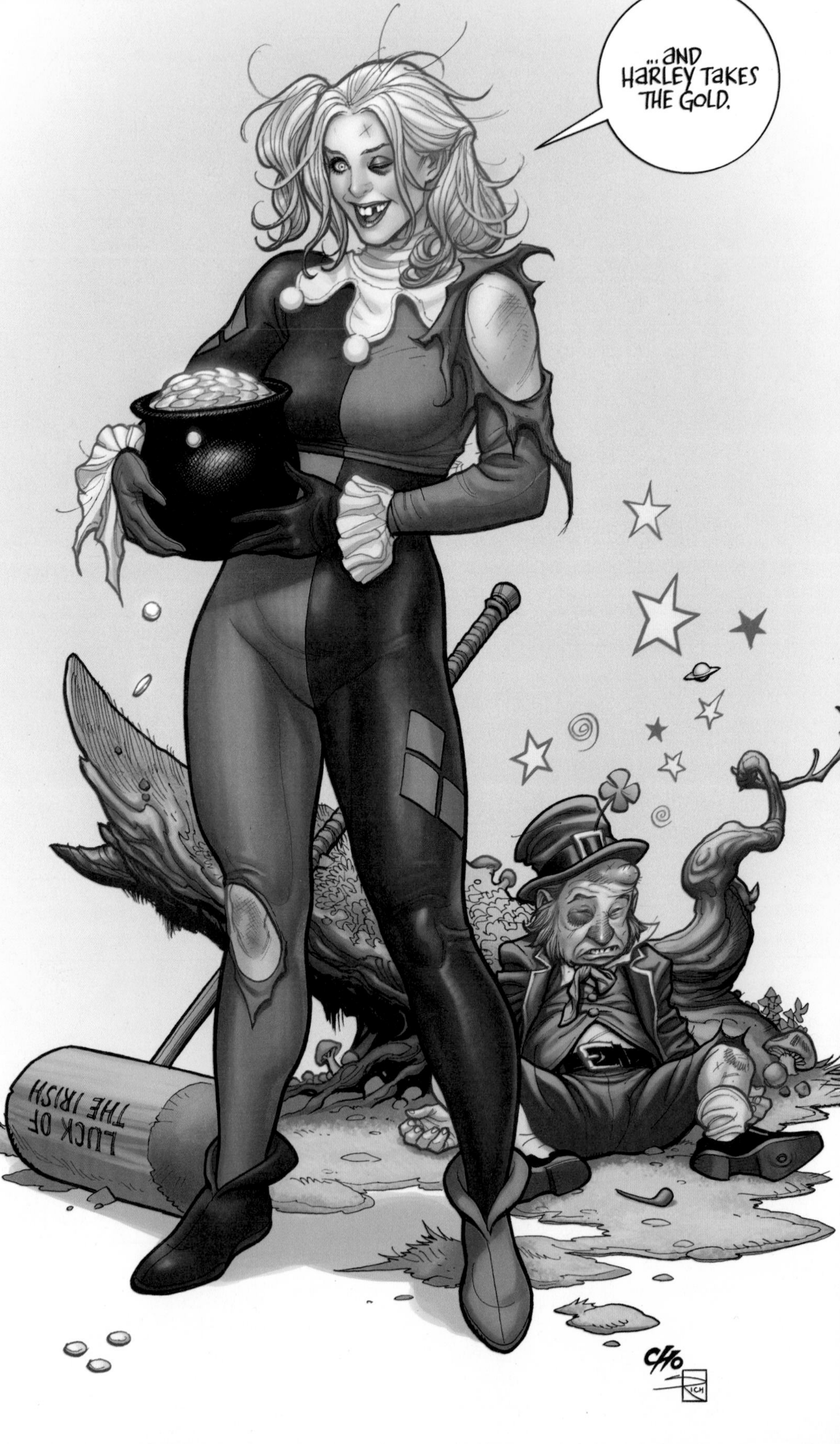
...AND HARLEY TAKES THE GOLD.
LUCK OF THE IRISH
CHO
RICH

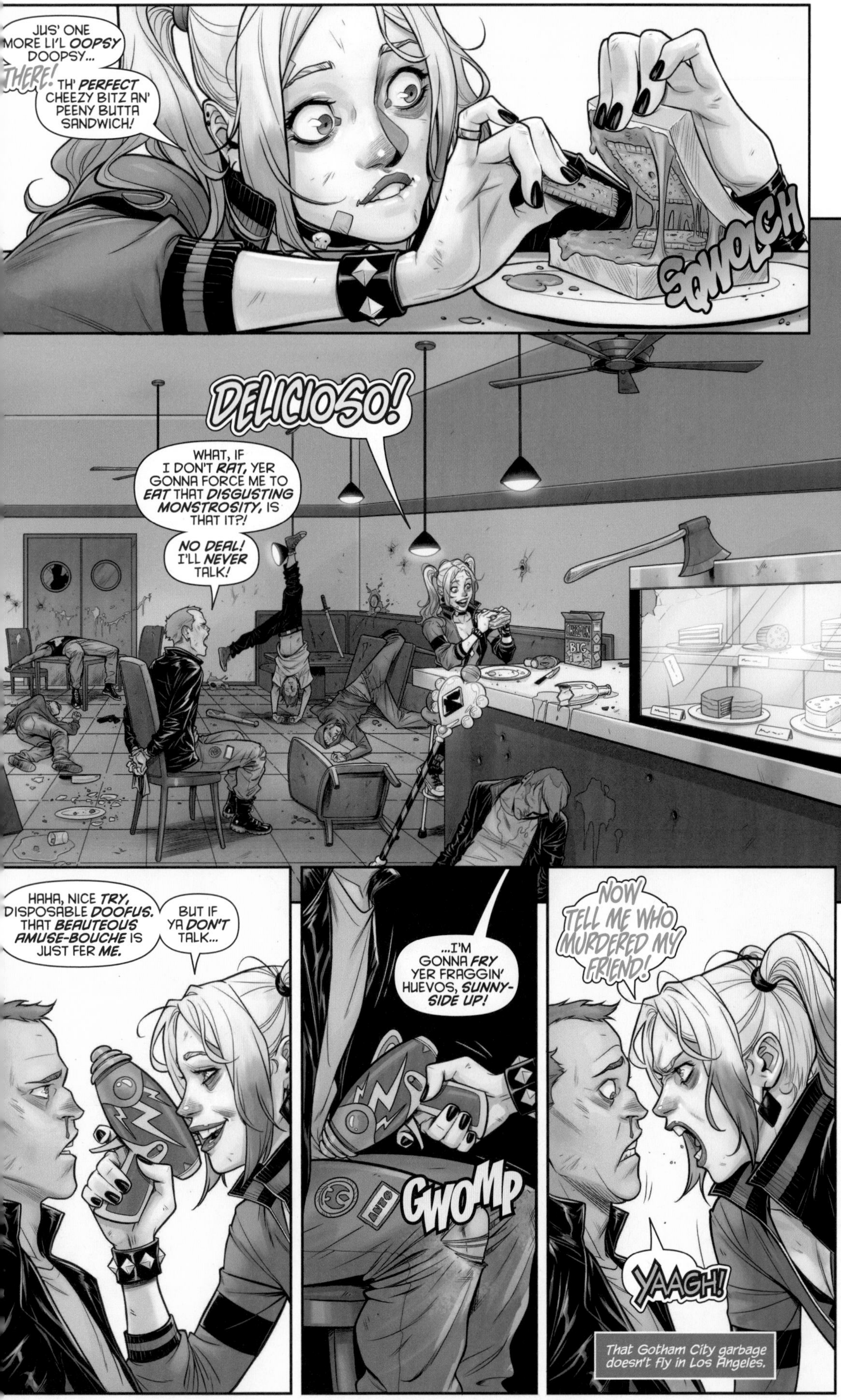
JUS' ONE MORE LI'L OOPSY DOOPSY...
THERE!
TH' PERFECT CHEEZY BITZ AN' PEENY BUTTA SANDWICH!
SQWOLCH
DELICIOSO!
WHAT, IF I DON'T RAT, YER GONNA FORCE ME TO EAT THAT DISGUSTING MONSTROSITY, IS THAT IT?!
NO DEAL! I'LL NEVER TALK!
HAHA, NICE TRY, DISPOSABLE DOOFUS. THAT BEAUTEOUS AMUSE-BOUCHE IS JUST FER ME.
BUT IF YA DON'T TALK...
...I'M GONNA FRY YER FRAGGIN' HUEVOS, SUNNY-SIDE UP!
GWOMP
NOW TELL ME WHO MURDERED MY FRIEND!
YAAGH!
That Gotham City garbage doesn't fly in Los Angeles.

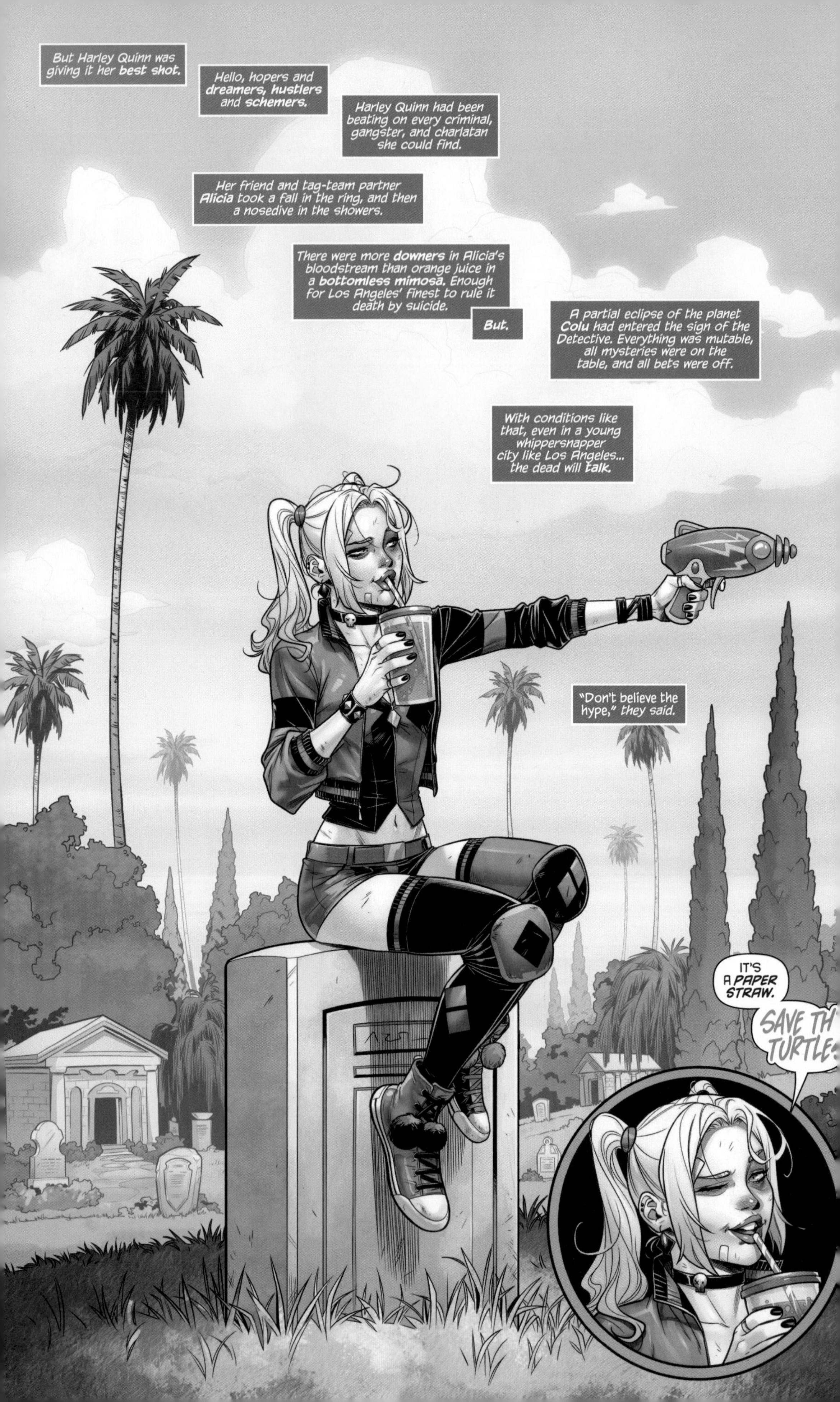

But Harley Quinn was giving it her best shot.
Hello, hopers and dreamers, hustlers and schemers.
Harley Quinn had been beating on every criminal, gangster, and charlatan she could find.
Her friend and tag-team partner Alicia took a fall in the ring, and then a nosedive in the showers.
There were more downers in Alicia's bloodstream than orange juice in a bottomless mimosa. Enough for Los Angeles' finest to rule it death by suicide.
But.
A partial eclipse of the planet Colu had entered the sign of the Detective. Everything was mutable, all mysteries were on the table, and all bets were off.
With conditions like that, even in a young whippersnapper city like Los Angeles... the dead will talk.
"Don't believe the hype," they said.
IT'S A PAPER STRAW.
SAVE TH TURTLE

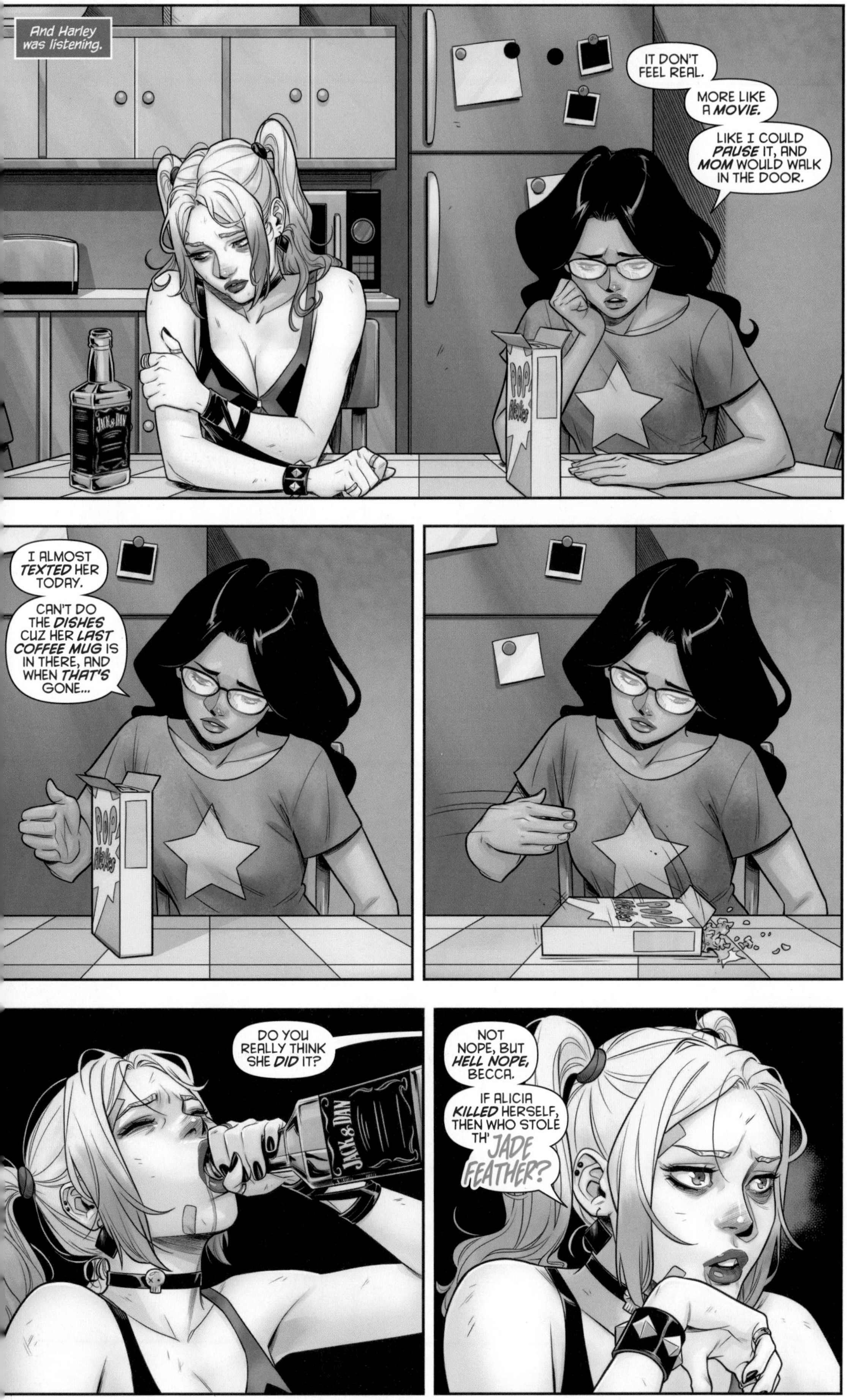
And Harley was listening.
IT DON'T FEEL REAL.
MORE LIKE A MOVIE.
LIKE I COULD PAUSE IT, AND MOM WOULD WALK IN THE DOOR.
JACK & DAN
POP Flakes
I ALMOST TEXTED HER TODAY.
CAN'T DO THE DISHES CUZ HER LAST COFFEE MUG IS IN THERE, AND WHEN THAT'S GONE...
DO YOU REALLY THINK SHE DID IT?
JACK & DAN
NOT NOPE, BUT HELL NOPE, BECCA.
IF ALICIA KILLED HERSELF, THEN WHO STOLE TH' JADE FEATHER?

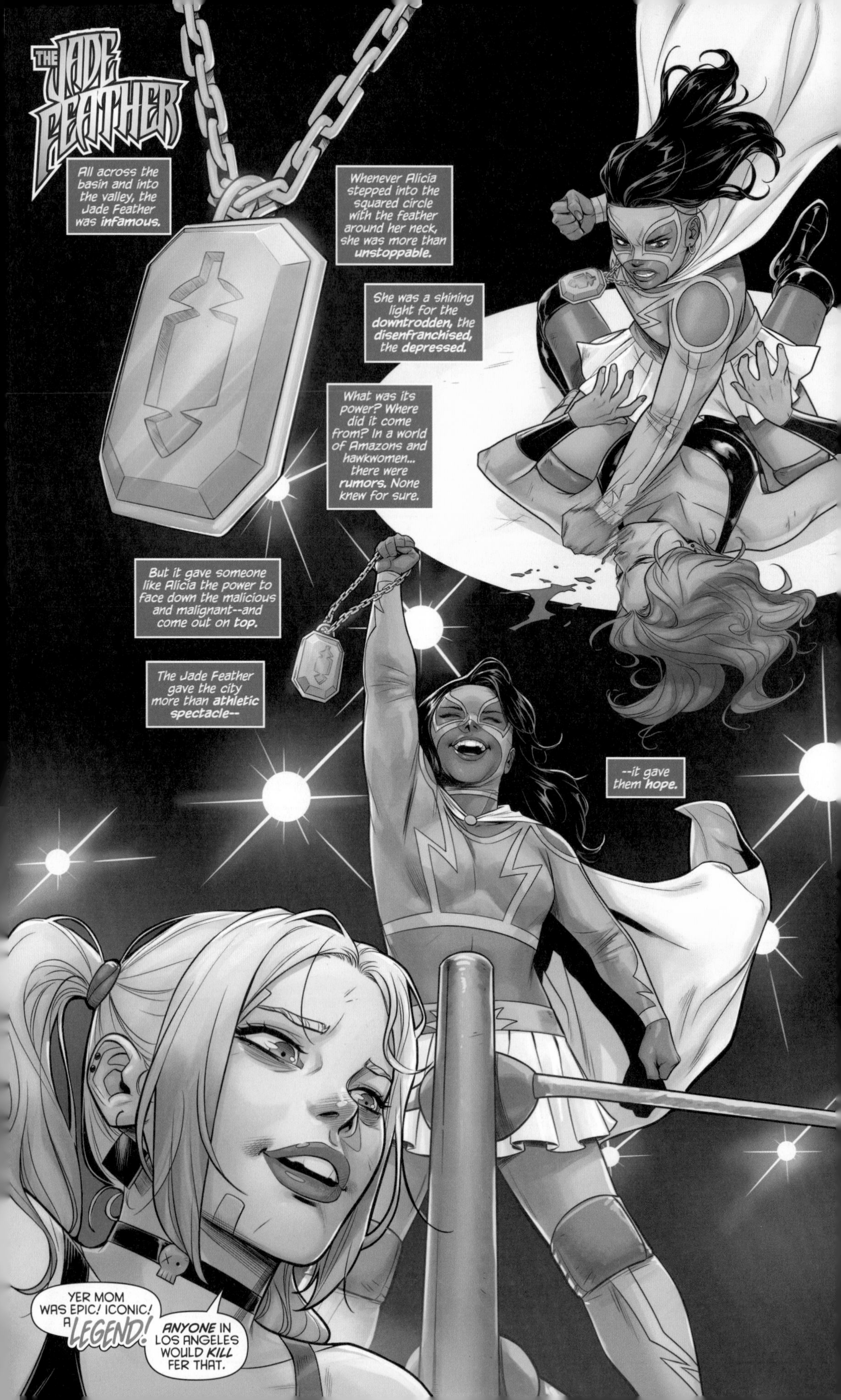

THE JADE FEATHER
All across the basin and into the valley, the Jade Feather was infamous.
Whenever Alicia stepped into the squared circle with the feather around her neck, she was more than unstoppable.
She was a shining light for the downtrodden, the disenfranchised, the depressed.
What was its power? Where did it come from? In a world of Amazons and hawkwomen... there were rumors. None knew for sure.
But it gave someone like Alicia the power to face down the malicious and malignant--and come out on top.
The Jade Feather gave the city more than athletic spectacle--
--it gave them hope.
YER MOM WAS EPIC! ICONIC! A LEGEND!
ANYONE IN LOS ANGELES WOULD KILL FER THAT.

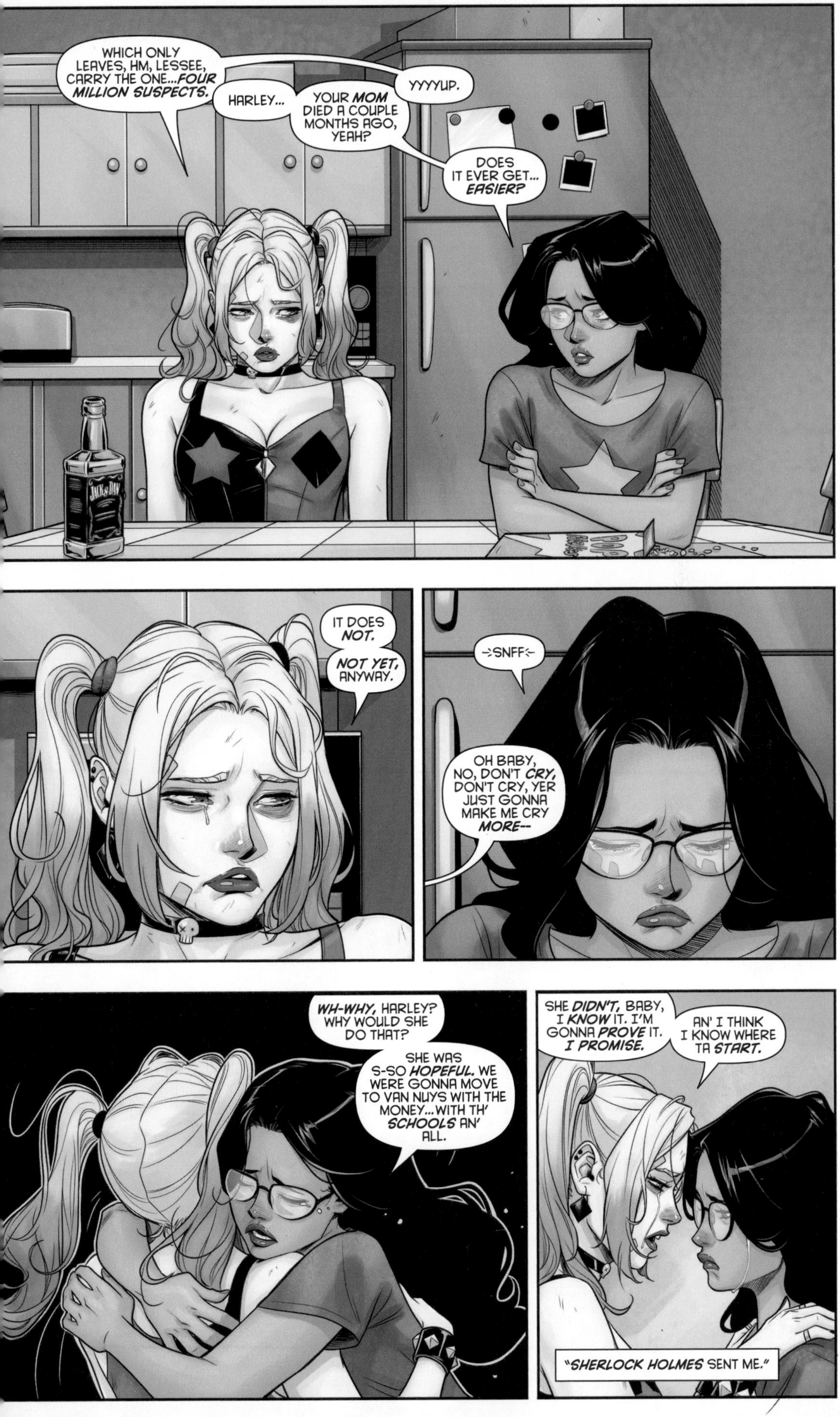
WHICH ONLY LEAVES, HM, LESSEE, CARRY THE ONE...FOUR MILLION SUSPECTS.
YYYYUP.
HARLEY...
YOUR MOM DIED A COUPLE MONTHS AGO, YEAH?
DOES IT EVER GET... EASIER?
IT DOES NOT.
NOT YET, ANYWAY.
SNFF
OH BABY, NO, DON'T CRY, DON'T CRY, YER JUST GONNA MAKE ME CRY MORE--
WH-WHY, HARLEY? WHY WOULD SHE DO THAT?
SHE WAS S-SO HOPEFUL. WE WERE GONNA MOVE TO VAN NUYS WITH THE MONEY...WITH TH' SCHOOLS AN' ALL.
SHE DIDN'T, BABY, I KNOW IT. I'M GONNA PROVE IT. I PROMISE.
AN' I THINK I KNOW WHERE TA START.
"SHERLOCK HOLMES SENT ME."

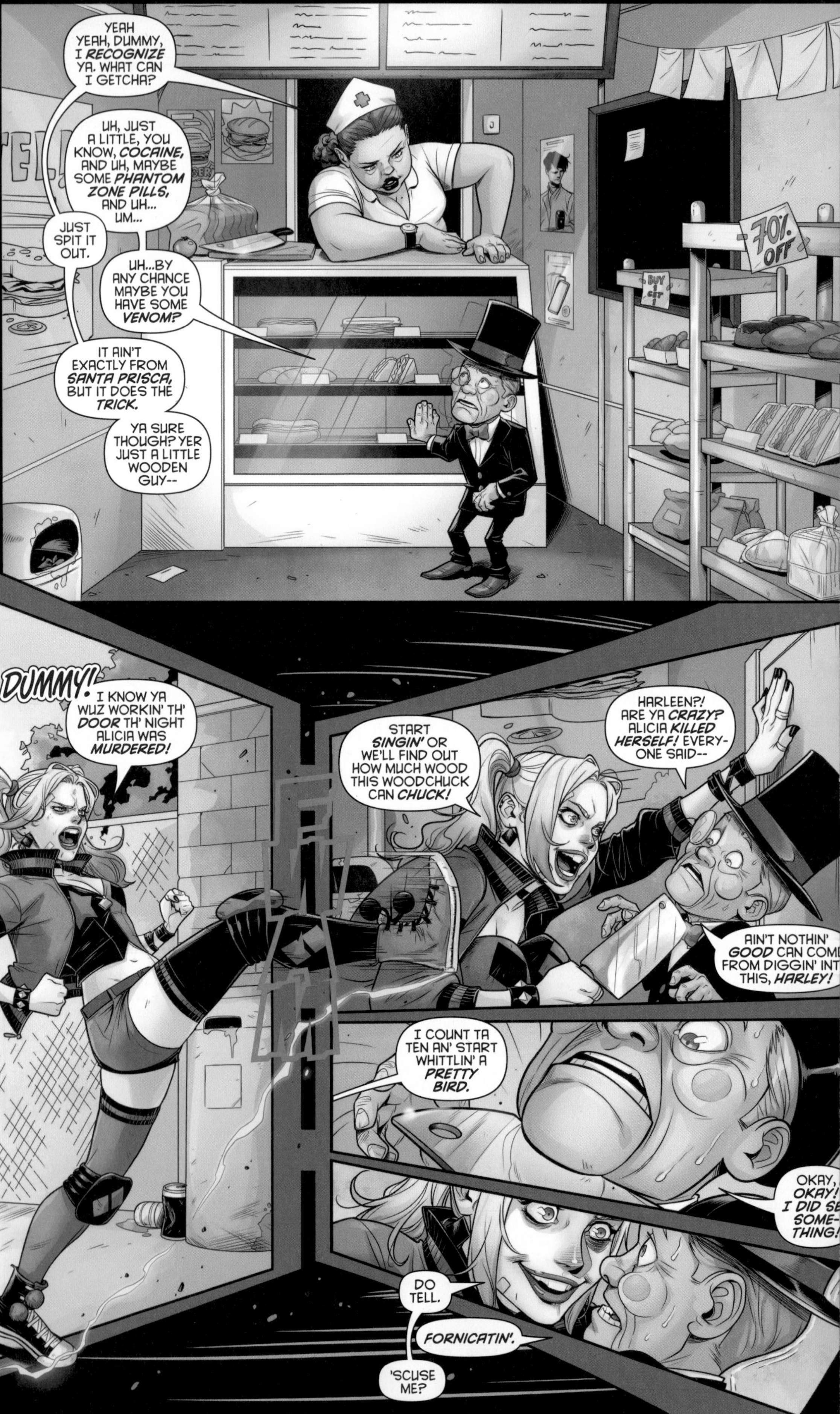

YEAH YEAH, DUMMY, I RECOGNIZE YA. WHAT CAN I GETCHA?
UH, JUST A LITTLE, YOU KNOW, COCAINE, AND UH, MAYBE SOME PHANTOM ZONE PILLS, AND UH... UM...
JUST SPIT IT OUT.
UH...BY ANY CHANCE MAYBE YOU HAVE SOME VENOM?
IT AIN'T EXACTLY FROM SANTA PRISCA, BUT IT DOES THE TRICK.
YA SURE THOUGH? YER JUST A LITTLE WOODEN GUY--
-70% OFF
DUMMY!
I KNOW YA WUZ WORKIN' TH' DOOR TH' NIGHT ALICIA WAS MURDERED!
START SINGIN' OR WE'LL FIND OUT HOW MUCH WOOD THIS WOODCHUCK CAN CHUCK!
HARLEEN?! ARE YA CRAZY? ALICIA KILLED HERSELF! EVERY-ONE SAID--
AIN'T NOTHIN' GOOD CAN COME FROM DIGGIN' INT THIS, HARLEY!
I COUNT TA TEN AN' START WHITTLIN' A PRETTY BIRD.
OKAY, OKAY! I DID SE SOME-THING!
DO TELL.
FORNICATIN'.
'SCUSE ME?

MOMMA, WHAT'S A FORNICATIN'?

I'LL TELL YA NEXT *NEVERUARY*. NOW LET ME AN' HARLEY HAVE *ADULT TALK*.

ROSIE, *LOOK*, I KNOWS YOU AN' *TAD RYERSTAD* WERE GOIN' TA *POUND TOWN* IN TH' *SHOWERS*--

--AN' I KNOW YER *MARRIED*...BUT NOT TA *EACH OTHER*.

DON'T MAKE ME *NARC* ON YA. I JUST WANNA KNOW IF YA SAW ANYTHIN' *WEIRD* THAT NIGHT.

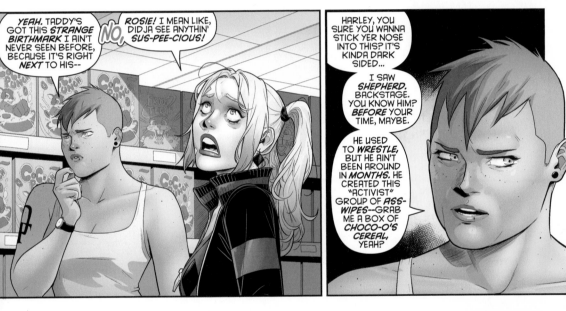

YEAH. TADDY'S GOT THIS *STRANGE BIRTHMARK* I AIN'T NEVER SEEN BEFORE, BECAUSE IT'S RIGHT *NEXT* TO HIS--

NO, ROSIE! I MEAN LIKE, DIDJA SEE ANYTHIN' *SUS-PEE-CIOUS!*

HARLEY, YOU SURE YOU WANNA STICK YER NOSE INTO THIS? IT'S KINDA DARK SIDED...

I SAW *SHEPHERD.* BACKSTAGE. YOU KNOW HIM? *BEFORE* YOUR TIME, MAYBE.

HE USED TO *WRESTLE,* BUT HE AIN'T BEEN AROUND IN *MONTHS.* HE CREATED THIS "ACTIVIST" GROUP OF *ASS-WIPES*--GRAB ME A BOX OF *CHOCO-O'S CEREAL,* YEAH?

THEY CALL THEMSELVES *ACCESS AMERICA.* GET IT? "AXIS" AMERICA.

THOSE *NAZI SCUMBAGS?!* WHERE DO THEY HANG OUT?

I DUNNO, DO I? IT'S NOT LIKE I HAUNT *WHITE SUPREMACIST MEETINGS.*

WAIT, I THINK TADDY HAD TO *DROP OFF* SHEPHERD'S *OLD SHOES* ONCE, LEMME TEXT HIM FOR THE *ADDRESS.*

OH, YOU WANNA SEE A PIC OF THE *BIRTH-MARK?*

ROSIE, NO!

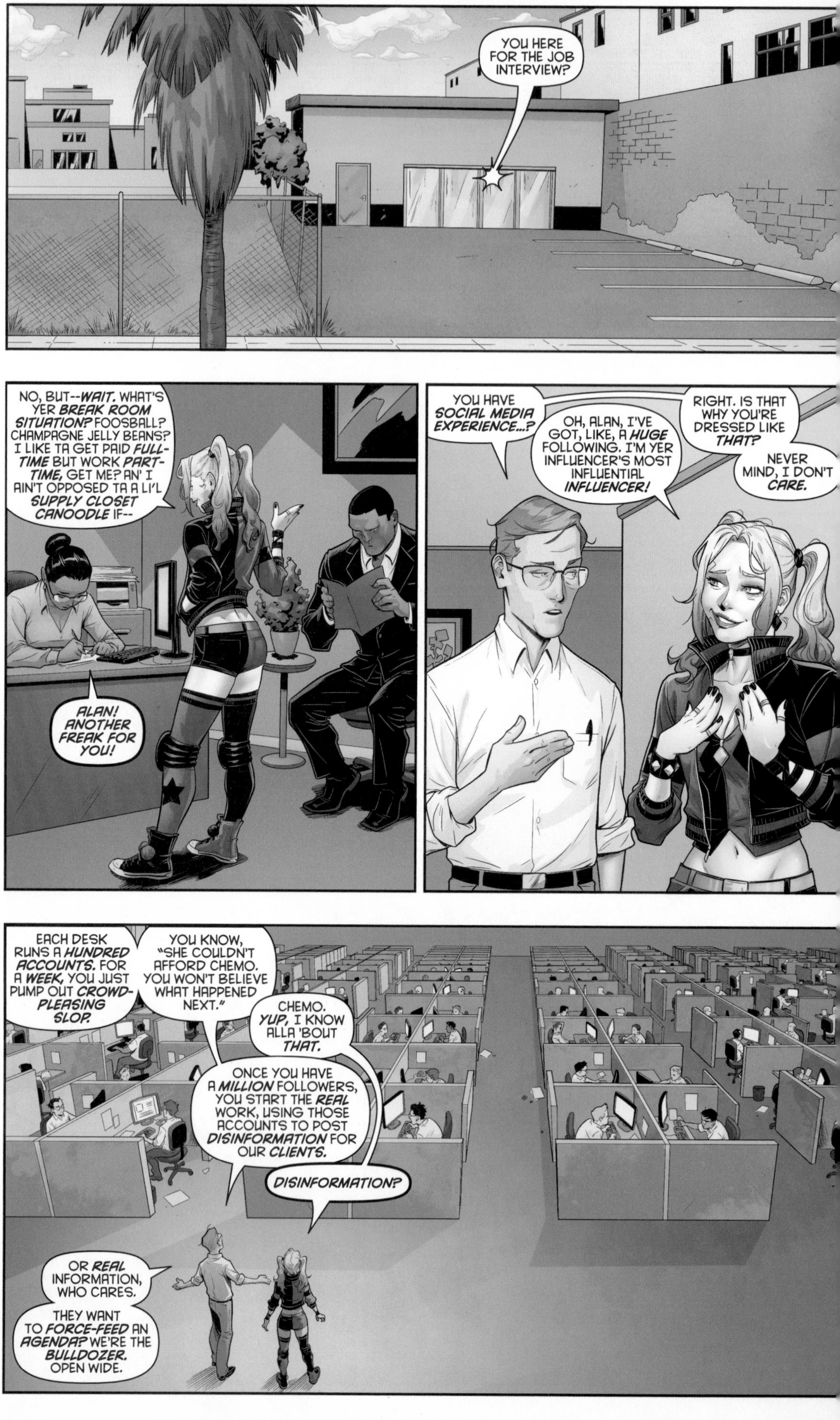

YOU HERE FOR THE JOB INTERVIEW?
NO, BUT--WAIT. WHAT'S YER BREAK ROOM SITUATION? FOOSBALL? CHAMPAGNE JELLY BEANS? I LIKE TA GET PAID FULL-TIME BUT WORK PART-TIME, GET ME? AN' I AIN'T OPPOSED TA A LI'L SUPPLY CLOSET CANOODLE IF--
ALAN! ANOTHER FREAK FOR YOU!
YOU HAVE SOCIAL MEDIA EXPERIENCE...?
OH, ALAN, I'VE GOT, LIKE, A HUGE FOLLOWING. I'M YER INFLUENCER'S MOST INFLUENTIAL INFLUENCER!
RIGHT. IS THAT WHY YOU'RE DRESSED LIKE THAT?
NEVER MIND, I DON'T CARE.
EACH DESK RUNS A HUNDRED ACCOUNTS. FOR A WEEK, YOU JUST PUMP OUT CROWD-PLEASING SLOP.
YOU KNOW, "SHE COULDN'T AFFORD CHEMO. YOU WON'T BELIEVE WHAT HAPPENED NEXT."
CHEMO. YUP, I KNOW ALLA 'BOUT THAT.
ONCE YOU HAVE A MILLION FOLLOWERS, YOU START THE REAL WORK, USING THOSE ACCOUNTS TO POST DISINFORMATION FOR OUR CLIENTS.
DISINFORMATION?
OR REAL INFORMATION, WHO CARES.
THEY WANT TO FORCE-FEED AN AGENDA? WE'RE THE BULLDOZER. OPEN WIDE.

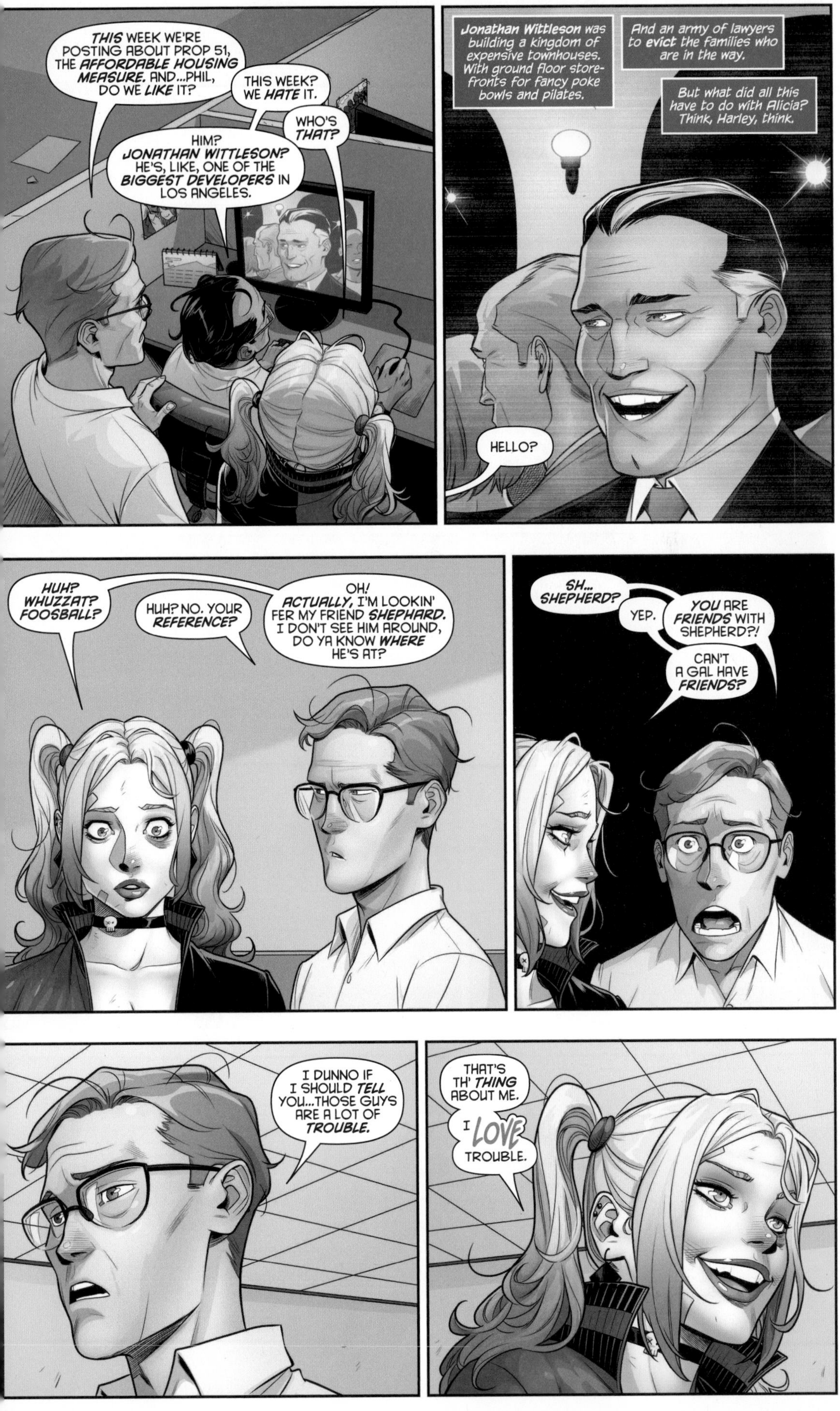
THIS WEEK WE'RE POSTING ABOUT PROP 51, THE AFFORDABLE HOUSING MEASURE. AND...PHIL, DO WE LIKE IT?
THIS WEEK? WE HATE IT.
WHO'S THAT?
HIM? JONATHAN WITTLESON? HE'S, LIKE, ONE OF THE BIGGEST DEVELOPERS IN LOS ANGELES.
Jonathan Wittleson was building a kingdom of expensive townhouses. With ground floor store-fronts for fancy poke bowls and pilates.
And an army of lawyers to evict the families who are in the way.
But what did all this have to do with Alicia? Think, Harley, think.
HELLO?
HUH? WHUZZAT? FOOSBALL?
HUH? NO. YOUR REFERENCE?
OH! ACTUALLY, I'M LOOKIN' FER MY FRIEND SHEPHARD. I DON'T SEE HIM AROUND, DO YA KNOW WHERE HE'S AT?
SH... SHEPHERD?
YEP.
YOU ARE FRIENDS WITH SHEPHERD?!
CAN'T A GAL HAVE FRIENDS?
I DUNNO IF I SHOULD TELL YOU...THOSE GUYS ARE A LOT OF TROUBLE.
THAT'S TH' THING ABOUT ME.
I LOVE TROUBLE.

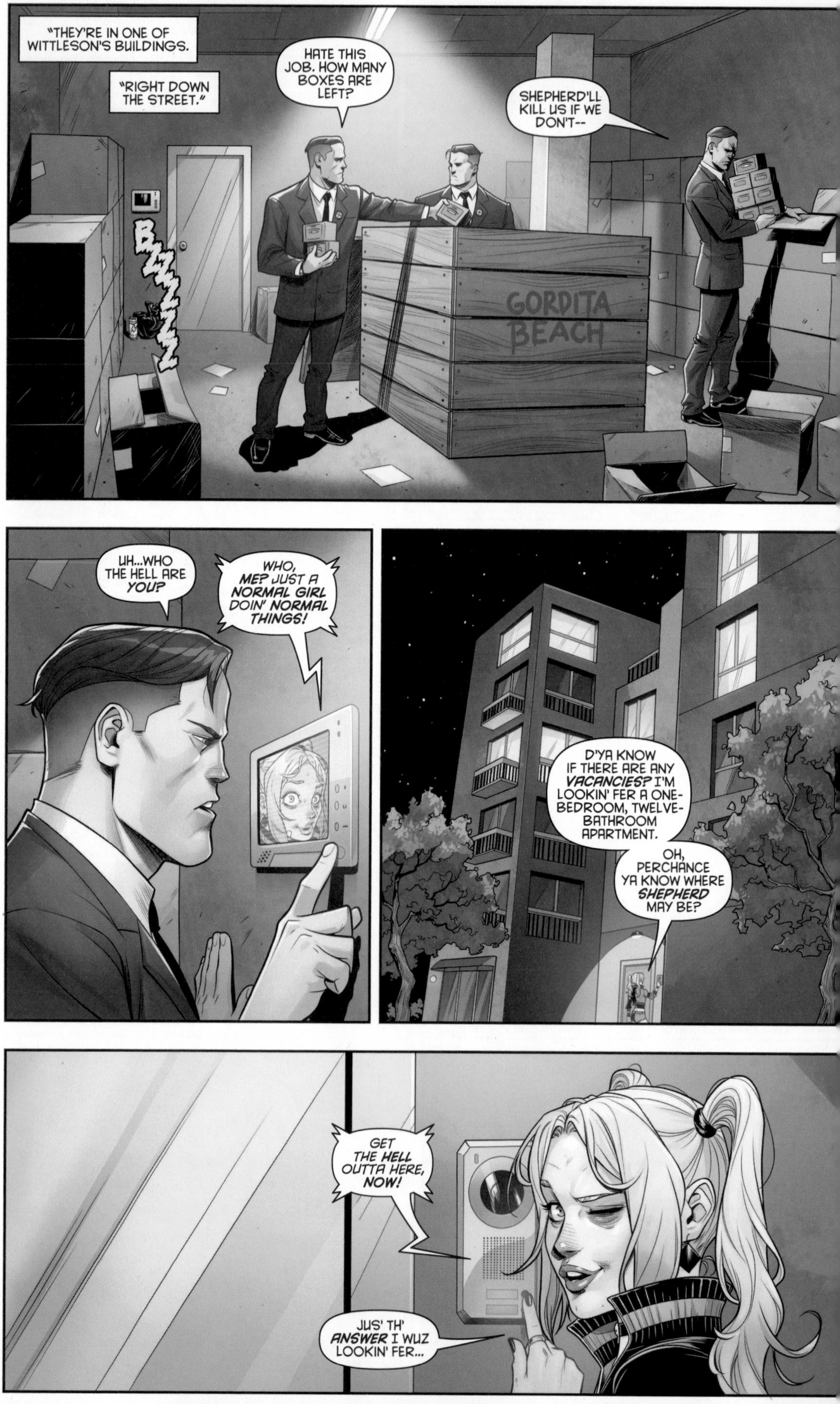
"THEY'RE IN ONE OF WITTLESON'S BUILDINGS.
"RIGHT DOWN THE STREET."
HATE THIS JOB. HOW MANY BOXES ARE LEFT?
SHEPHERD'LL KILL US IF WE DON'T--
BZZZZZZ
GORDITA BEACH
UH...WHO THE HELL ARE YOU?
WHO, ME? JUST A NORMAL GIRL DOIN' NORMAL THINGS!
D'YA KNOW IF THERE ARE ANY VACANCIES? I'M LOOKIN' FER A ONE-BEDROOM, TWELVE-BATHROOM APARTMENT.
OH, PERCHANCE YA KNOW WHERE SHEPHERD MAY BE?
GET THE HELL OUTTA HERE, NOW!
JUS' TH' ANSWER I WUZ LOOKIN' FER...

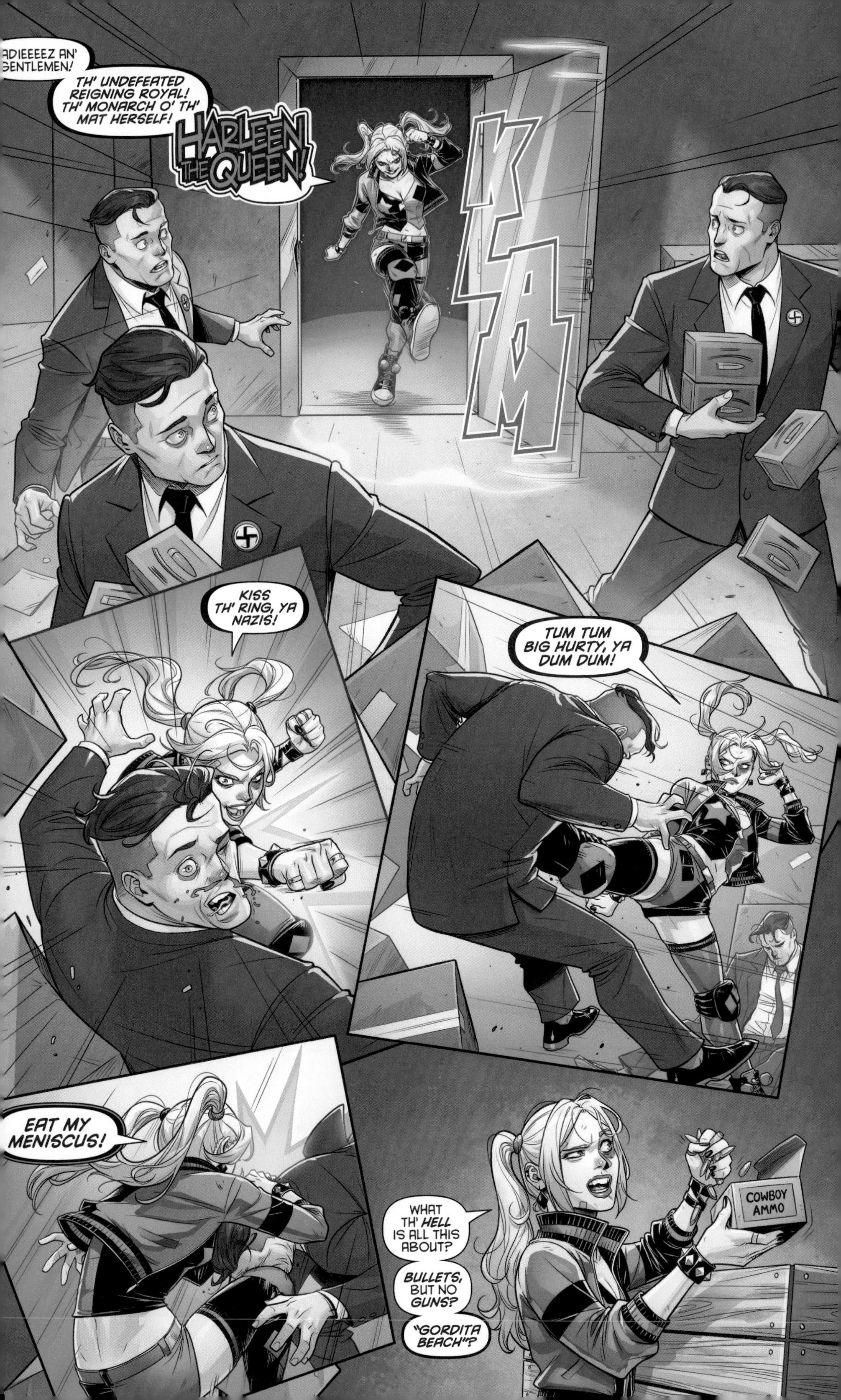

ADIEEEEZ AN' GENTLEMEN!
TH' UNDEFEATED REIGNING ROYAL! TH' MONARCH O' TH' MAT HERSELF!
HARLEEN THE QUEEN!
KLAM
KISS TH' RING, YA NAZIS!
TUM TUM BIG HURTY, YA DUM DUM!
EAT MY MENISCUS!
WHAT TH' HELL IS ALL THIS ABOUT?
BULLETS, BUT NO GUNS?
"GORDITA BEACH"?
COWBOY AMMO

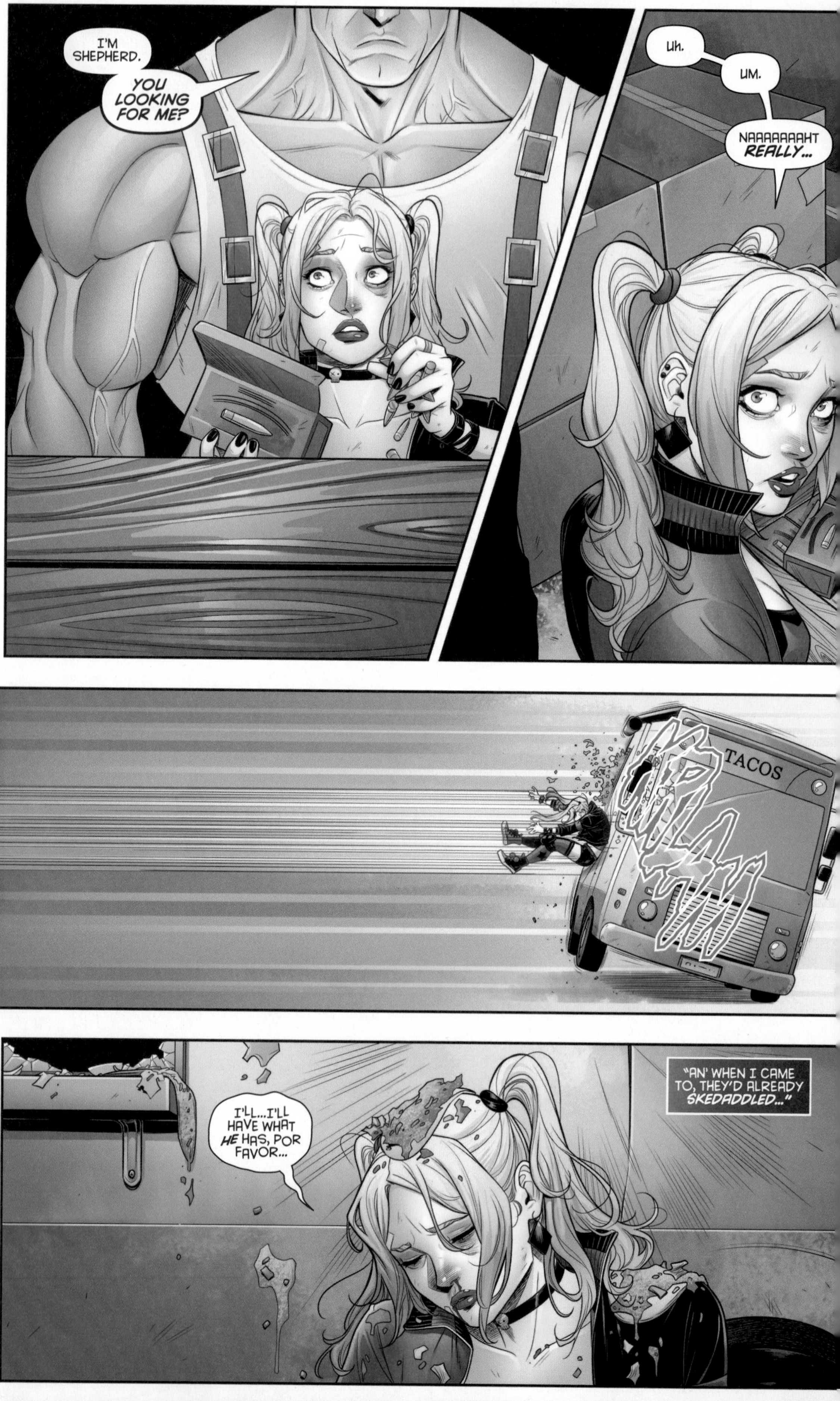

I'M SHEPHERD.
YOU LOOKING FOR ME?
UH.
UM.
NAAAAAAAHT REALLY...
TACOS
"AN' WHEN I CAME TO, THEY'D ALREADY SKEDADDLED..."
I'LL...I'LL HAVE WHAT HE HAS, POR FAVOR...

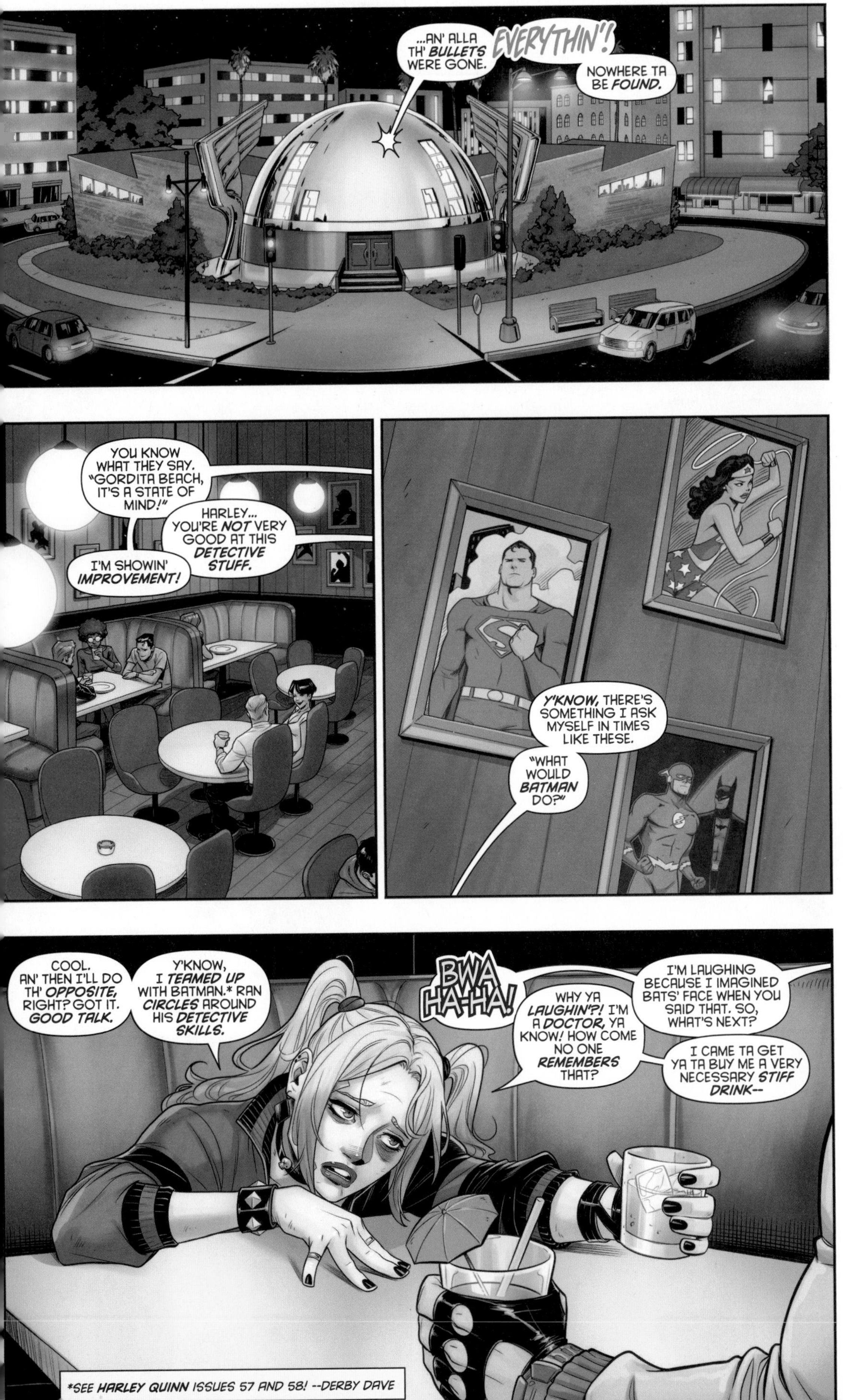
...AN' ALLA TH' BULLETS WERE GONE.
EVERYTHIN'!
NOWHERE TA BE FOUND.
YOU KNOW WHAT THEY SAY. "GORDITA BEACH, IT'S A STATE OF MIND!"
HARLEY... YOU'RE NOT VERY GOOD AT THIS DETECTIVE STUFF.
I'M SHOWIN' IMPROVEMENT!
Y'KNOW, THERE'S SOMETHING I ASK MYSELF IN TIMES LIKE THESE.
"WHAT WOULD BATMAN DO?"
COOL. AN' THEN I'LL DO TH' OPPOSITE, RIGHT? GOT IT. GOOD TALK.
Y'KNOW, I TEAMED UP WITH BATMAN.* RAN CIRCLES AROUND HIS DETECTIVE SKILLS.
BWA HA-HA!
WHY YA LAUGHIN'?! I'M A DOCTOR, YA KNOW! HOW COME NO ONE REMEMBERS THAT?
I'M LAUGHING BECAUSE I IMAGINED BATS' FACE WHEN YOU SAID THAT. SO, WHAT'S NEXT?
I CAME TA GET YA TA BUY ME A VERY NECESSARY STIFF DRINK--
*SEE HARLEY QUINN ISSUES 57 AND 58! --DERBY DAVE

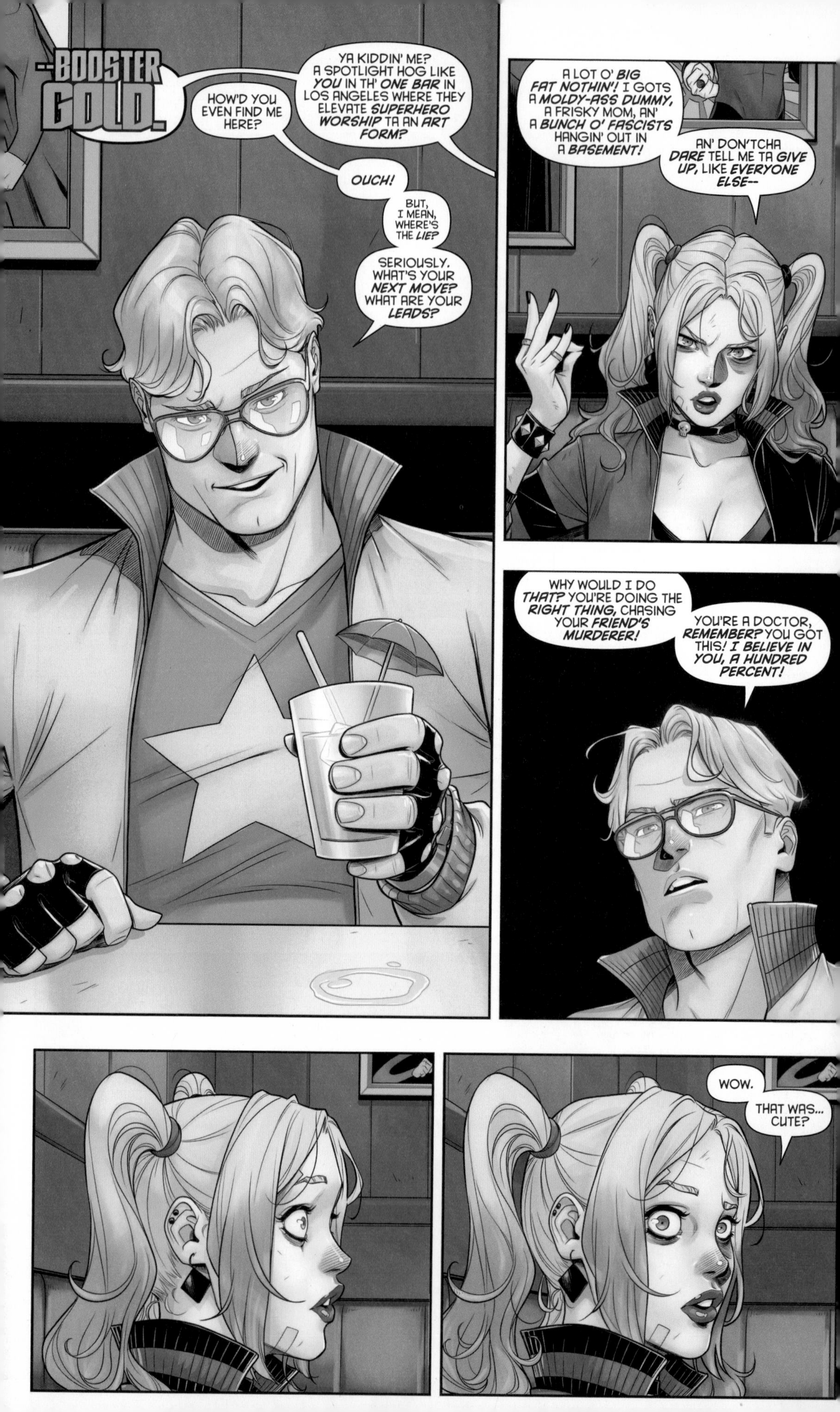

--BOOSTER GOLD.
HOW'D YOU EVEN FIND ME HERE?
YA KIDDIN' ME? A SPOTLIGHT HOG LIKE YOU IN TH' ONE BAR IN LOS ANGELES WHERE THEY ELEVATE SUPERHERO WORSHIP TA AN ART FORM?
OUCH!
BUT, I MEAN, WHERE'S THE LIE?
SERIOUSLY. WHAT'S YOUR NEXT MOVE? WHAT ARE YOUR LEADS?
A LOT O' BIG FAT NOTHIN'! I GOTS A MOLDY-ASS DUMMY, A FRISKY MOM, AN' A BUNCH O' FASCISTS HANGIN' OUT IN A BASEMENT!
AN' DON'TCHA DARE TELL ME TA GIVE UP, LIKE EVERYONE ELSE--
WHY WOULD I DO THAT? YOU'RE DOING THE RIGHT THING, CHASING YOUR FRIEND'S MURDERER!
YOU'RE A DOCTOR, REMEMBER? YOU GOT THIS! I BELIEVE IN YOU, A HUNDRED PERCENT!
WOW.
THAT WAS... CUTE?

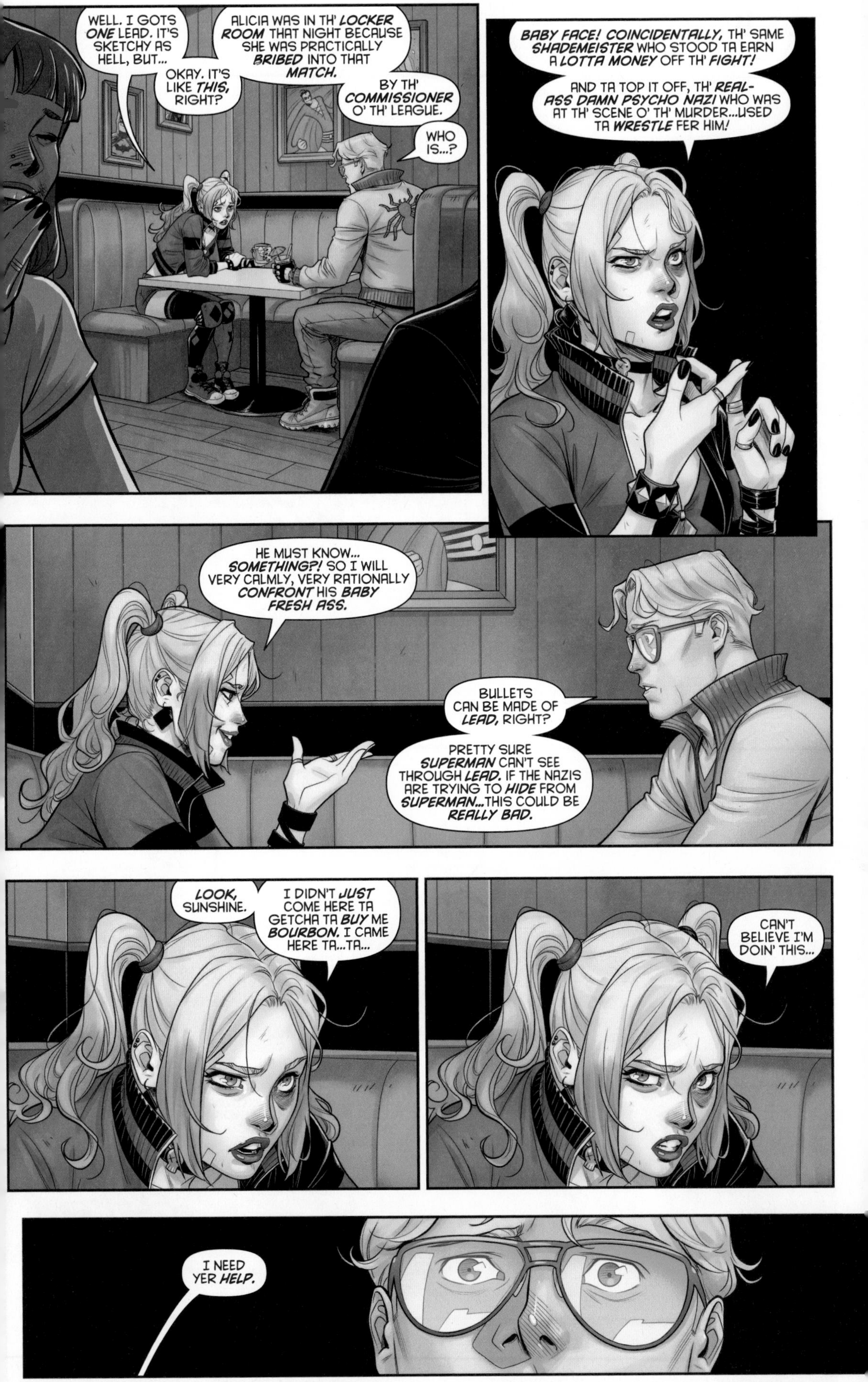
WELL. I GOTS ONE LEAD. IT'S SKETCHY AS HELL, BUT...
OKAY. IT'S LIKE THIS, RIGHT?
ALICIA WAS IN TH' LOCKER ROOM THAT NIGHT BECAUSE SHE WAS PRACTICALLY BRIBED INTO THAT MATCH.
BY TH' COMMISSIONER O' TH' LEAGUE.
WHO IS...?
BABY FACE! COINCIDENTALLY, TH' SAME SHADEMEISTER WHO STOOD TA EARN A LOTTA MONEY OFF TH' FIGHT!
AND TA TOP IT OFF, TH' REAL-ASS DAMN PSYCHO NAZI WHO WAS AT TH' SCENE O' TH' MURDER...USED TA WRESTLE FER HIM!
HE MUST KNOW... SOMETHING?! SO I WILL VERY CALMLY, VERY RATIONALLY CONFRONT HIS BABY FRESH ASS.
BULLETS CAN BE MADE OF LEAD, RIGHT?
PRETTY SURE SUPERMAN CAN'T SEE THROUGH LEAD. IF THE NAZIS ARE TRYING TO HIDE FROM SUPERMAN...THIS COULD BE REALLY BAD.
LOOK, SUNSHINE.
I DIDN'T JUST COME HERE TA GETCHA TA BUY ME BOURBON. I CAME HERE TA...TA...
CAN'T BELIEVE I'M DOIN' THIS...
I NEED YER HELP.

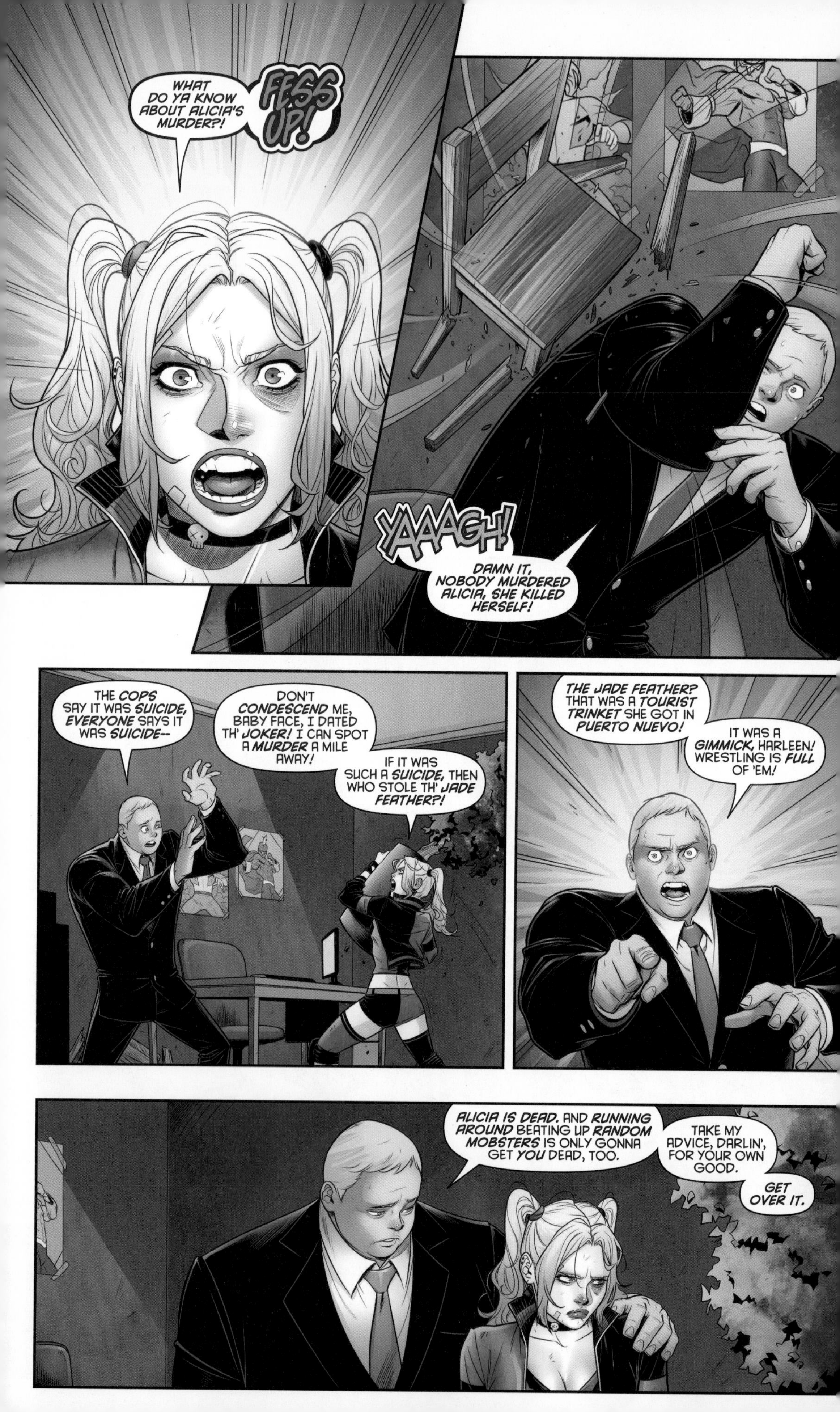

WHAT DO YA KNOW ABOUT ALICIA'S MURDER?!
FESS UP!
YAAAGH!
DAMN IT, NOBODY MURDERED ALICIA, SHE KILLED HERSELF!
THE COPS SAY IT WAS SUICIDE, EVERYONE SAYS IT WAS SUICIDE--
DON'T CONDESCEND ME, BABY FACE, I DATED TH' JOKER! I CAN SPOT A MURDER A MILE AWAY!
IF IT WAS SUCH A SUICIDE, THEN WHO STOLE TH' JADE FEATHER?!
THE JADE FEATHER? THAT WAS A TOURIST TRINKET SHE GOT IN PUERTO NUEVO!
IT WAS A GIMMICK, HARLEEN! WRESTLING IS FULL OF 'EM!
ALICIA IS DEAD. AND RUNNING AROUND BEATING UP RANDOM MOBSTERS IS ONLY GONNA GET YOU DEAD, TOO.
TAKE MY ADVICE, DARLIN', FOR YOUR OWN GOOD.
GET OVER IT.

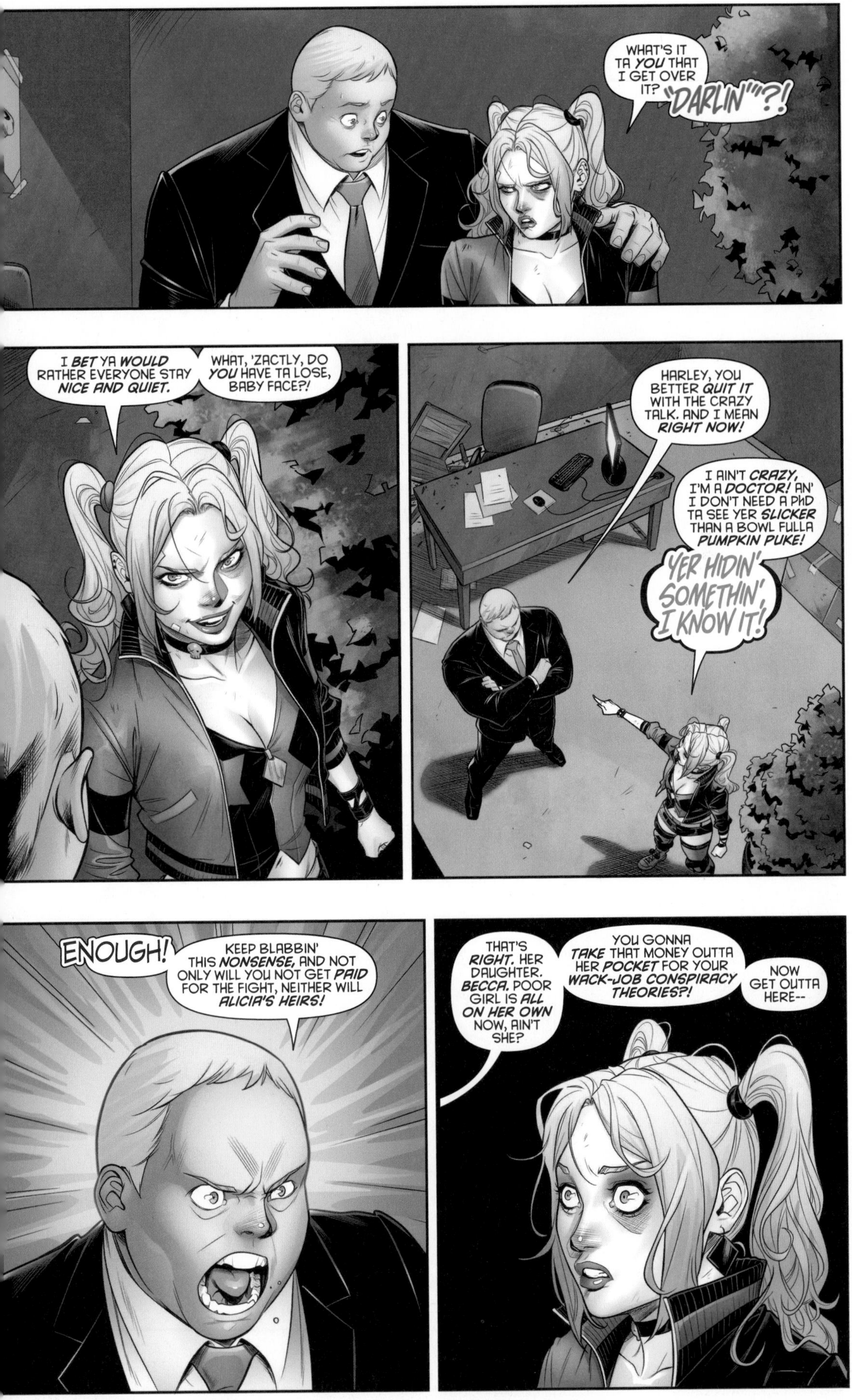

WHAT'S IT TA YOU THAT I GET OVER IT? "DARLIN'"?!
I BET YA WOULD RATHER EVERYONE STAY NICE AND QUIET.
WHAT, 'ZACTLY, DO YOU HAVE TA LOSE, BABY FACE?!
HARLEY, YOU BETTER QUIT IT WITH THE CRAZY TALK. AND I MEAN RIGHT NOW!
I AIN'T CRAZY, I'M A DOCTOR! AN' I DON'T NEED A PhD TA SEE YER SLICKER THAN A BOWL FULLA PUMPKIN PUKE!
YER HIDIN' SOMETHIN', I KNOW IT!
ENOUGH!
KEEP BLABBIN' THIS NONSENSE, AND NOT ONLY WILL YOU NOT GET PAID FOR THE FIGHT, NEITHER WILL ALICIA'S HEIRS!
THAT'S RIGHT. HER DAUGHTER. BECCA. POOR GIRL IS ALL ON HER OWN NOW, AIN'T SHE?
YOU GONNA TAKE THAT MONEY OUTTA HER POCKET FOR YOUR WACK-JOB CONSPIRACY THEORIES?!
NOW GET OUTTA HERE--

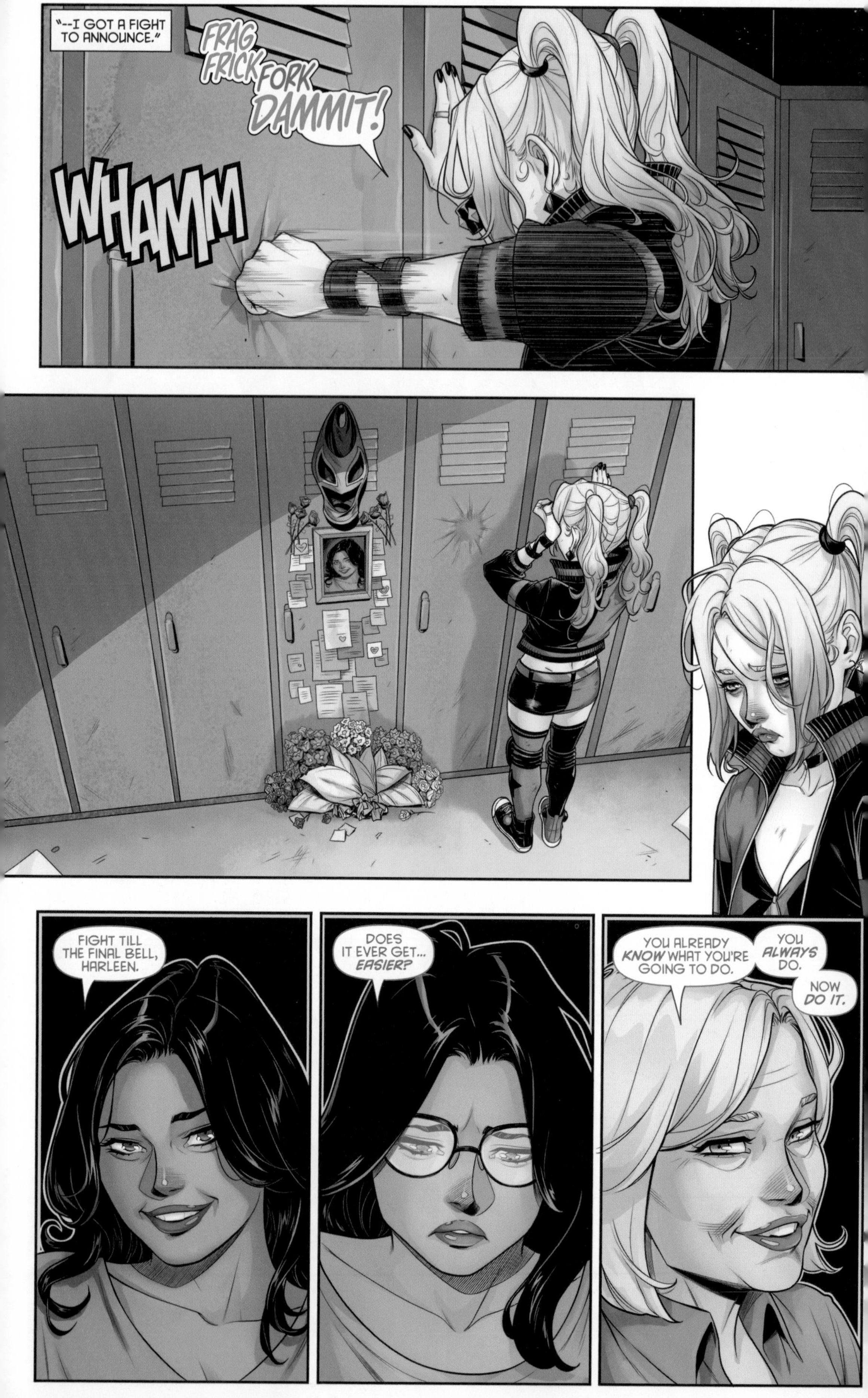

"--I GOT A FIGHT TO ANNOUNCE."
FRAG FRICK FORK DAMMIT!
WHAMM
FIGHT TILL THE FINAL BELL, HARLEEN.
DOES IT EVER GET... EASIER?
YOU ALREADY KNOW WHAT YOU'RE GOING TO DO.
YOU ALWAYS DO.
NOW DO IT.

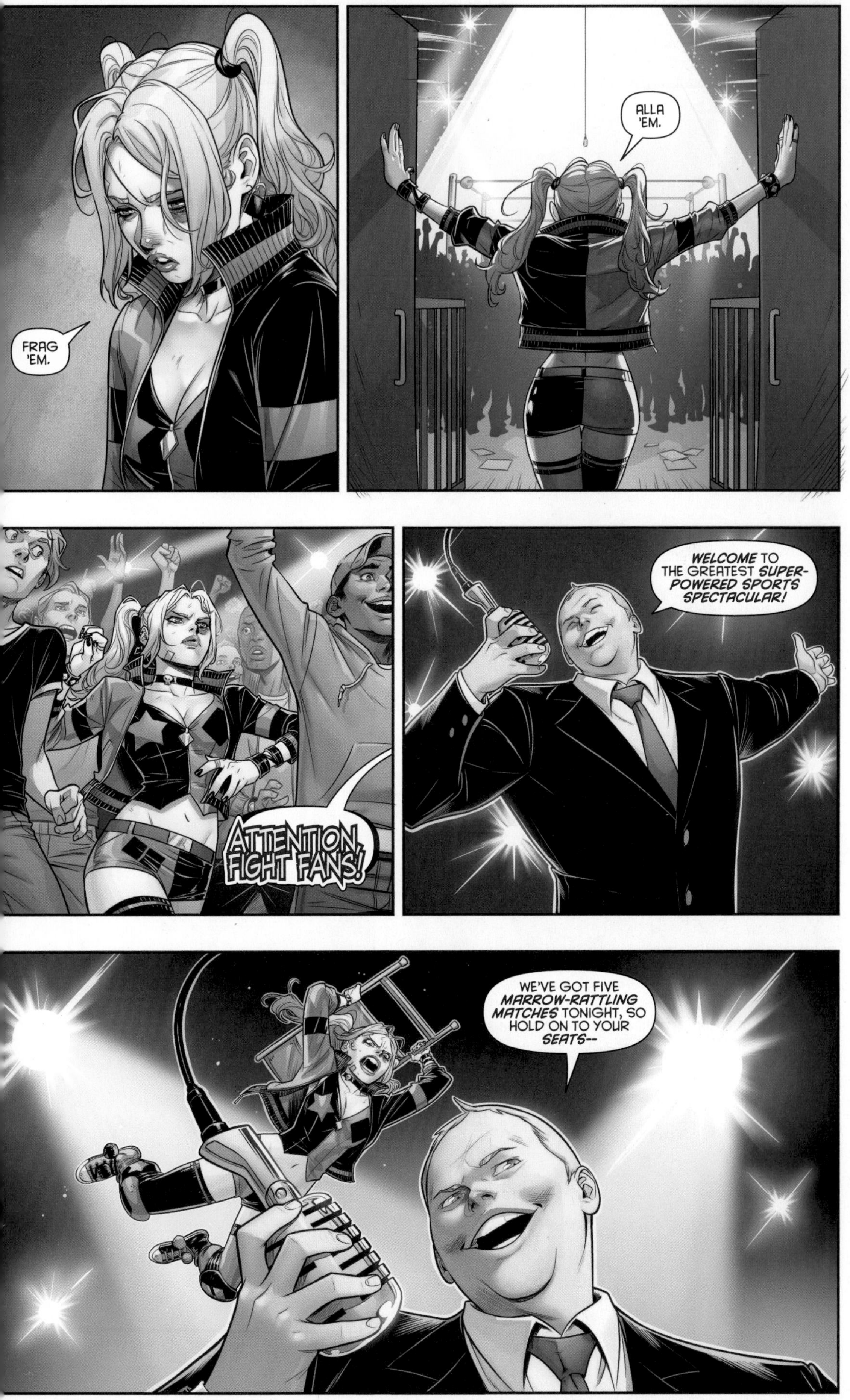
FRAG 'EM.
ALLA 'EM.
ATTENTION, FIGHT FANS!
WELCOME TO THE GREATEST SUPER-POWERED SPORTS SPECTACULAR!
WE'VE GOT FIVE MARROW-RATTLING MATCHES TONIGHT, SO HOLD ON TO YOUR SEATS--

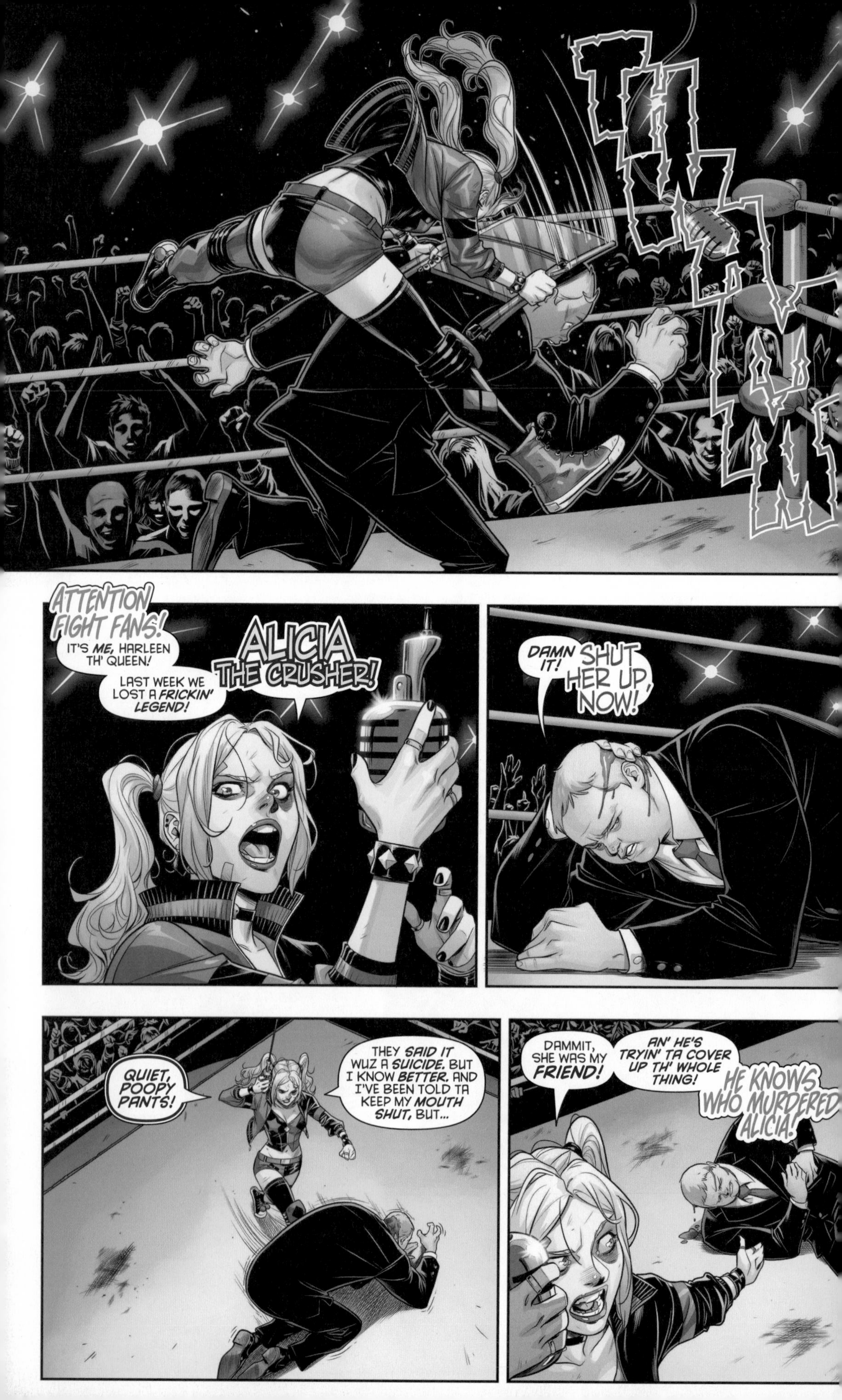
ATTENTION FIGHT FANS!
IT'S *ME,* HARLEEN TH' QUEEN!
LAST WEEK WE LOST A *FRICKIN' LEGEND!*
ALICIA THE CRUSHER!
DAMN IT!
SHUT HER UP, NOW!
QUIET, POOPY PANTS!
THEY *SAID IT* WUZ A *SUICIDE.* BUT I KNOW *BETTER.* AND I'VE BEEN TOLD TA KEEP MY *MOUTH SHUT,* BUT...
DAMMIT, SHE WAS MY *FRIEND!*
AN' HE'S TRYIN' TA COVER UP TH' WHOLE THING!
HE KNOWS WHO MURDERED ALICIA!

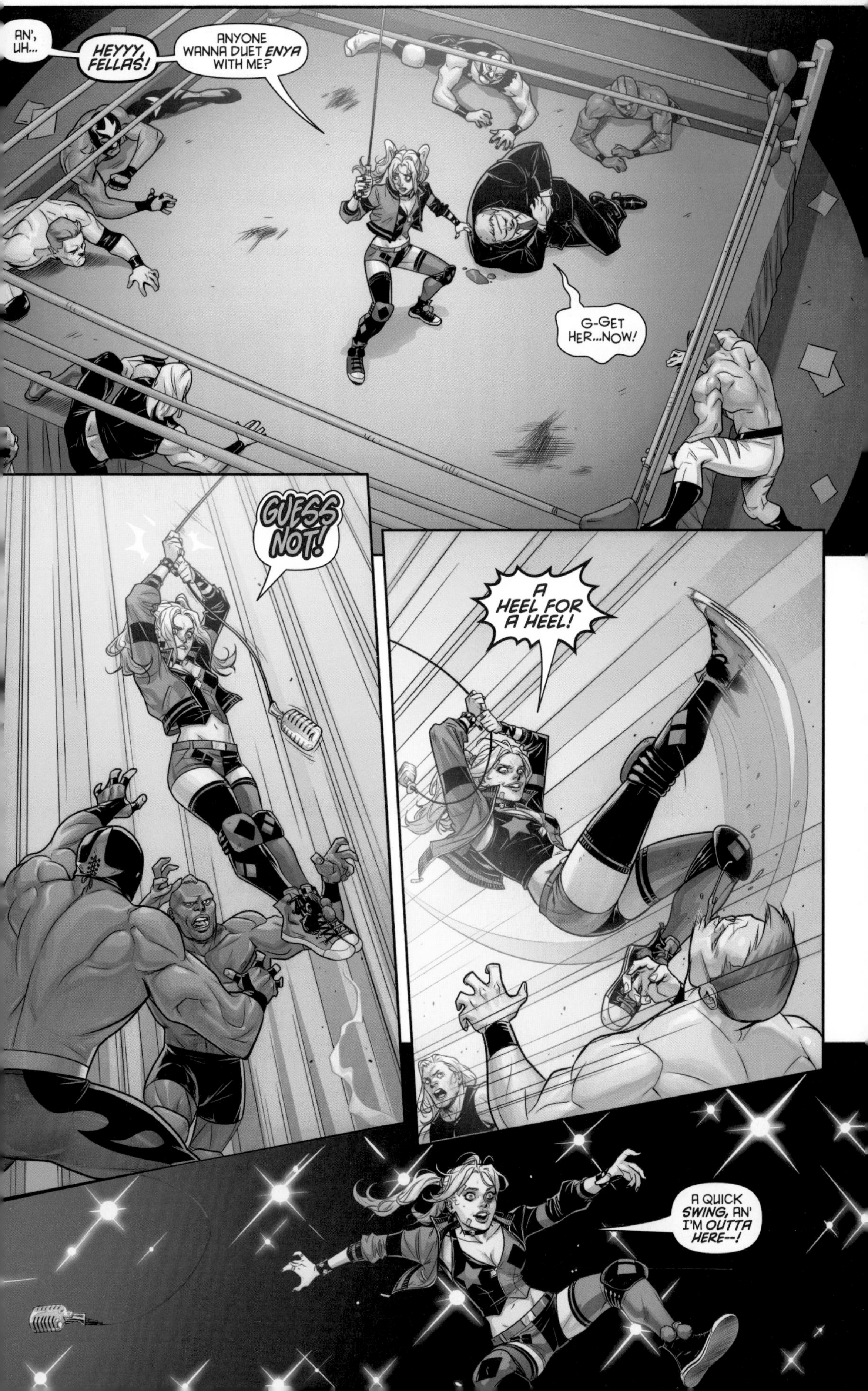
AN', UH...
HEYYY, FELLAS!
ANYONE WANNA DUET ENYA WITH ME?
G-GET HER...NOW!
GUESS NOT!
A HEEL FOR A HEEL!
A QUICK SWING, AN' I'M OUTTA HERE--!

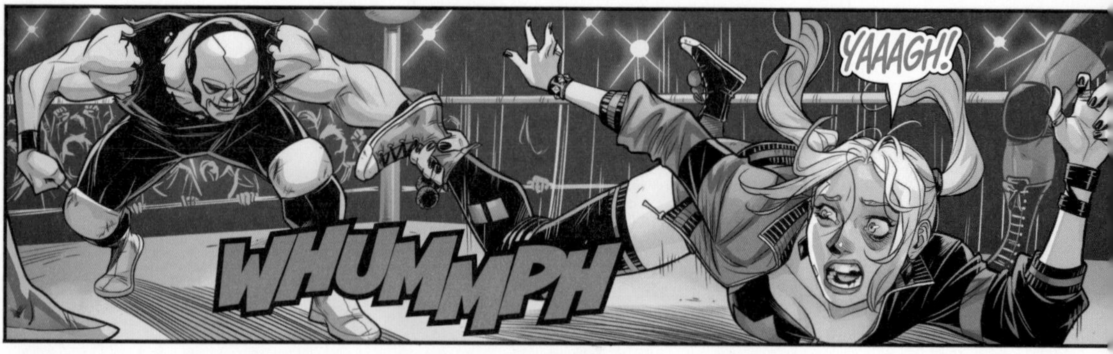
YAAAGH!
WHUMMPH

CALIFORNIA OR DEATH

CHAPTER 2 WORLD'S GREATEST DETECTIVE

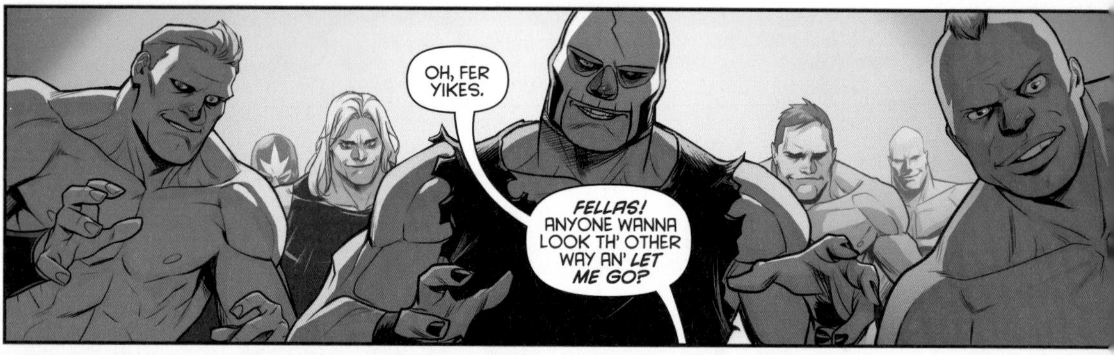
OH, FER YIKES.
FELLAS! ANYONE WANNA LOOK TH' OTHER WAY AN' *LET ME GO?*

SAM HUMPHRIES WRITER SAMI BASRI ARTIST HI-FI COLORS
DAVE SHARPE LETTERS RILEY ROSSMO & IVAN PLASCENCIA COVER
FRANK CHO & SABINE RICH VARIANT COVER
DAVE WIELGOSZ EDITOR
BEN ABERNATHY GROUP EDITOR
HARLEY QUINN CREATED BY PAUL DINI & BRUCE TIMM
BOOSTER GOLD CREATED BY DAN JURGENS

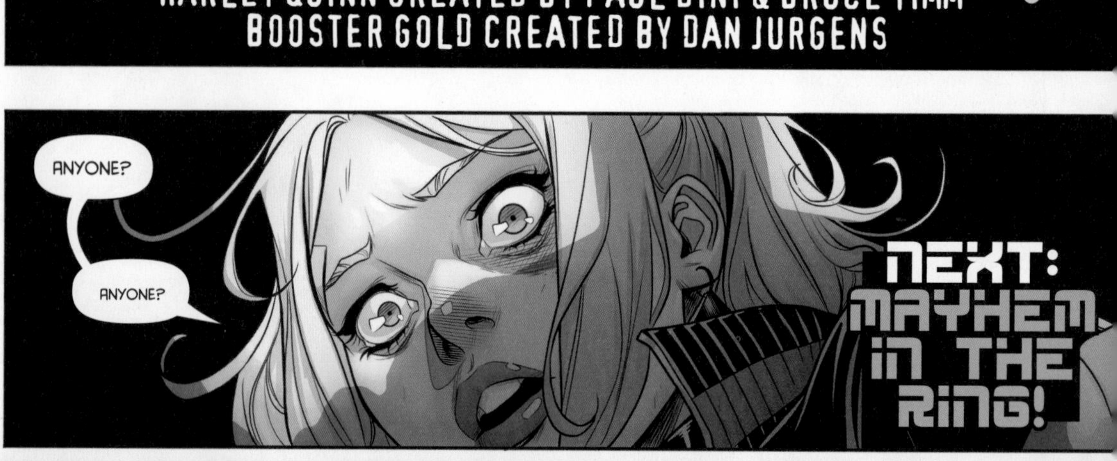
ANYONE?
ANYONE?
NEXT: MAYHEM IN THE RING!

HARLEY QUINN #72 cover
by GUILLEM MARCH and ARIF PRIANTO

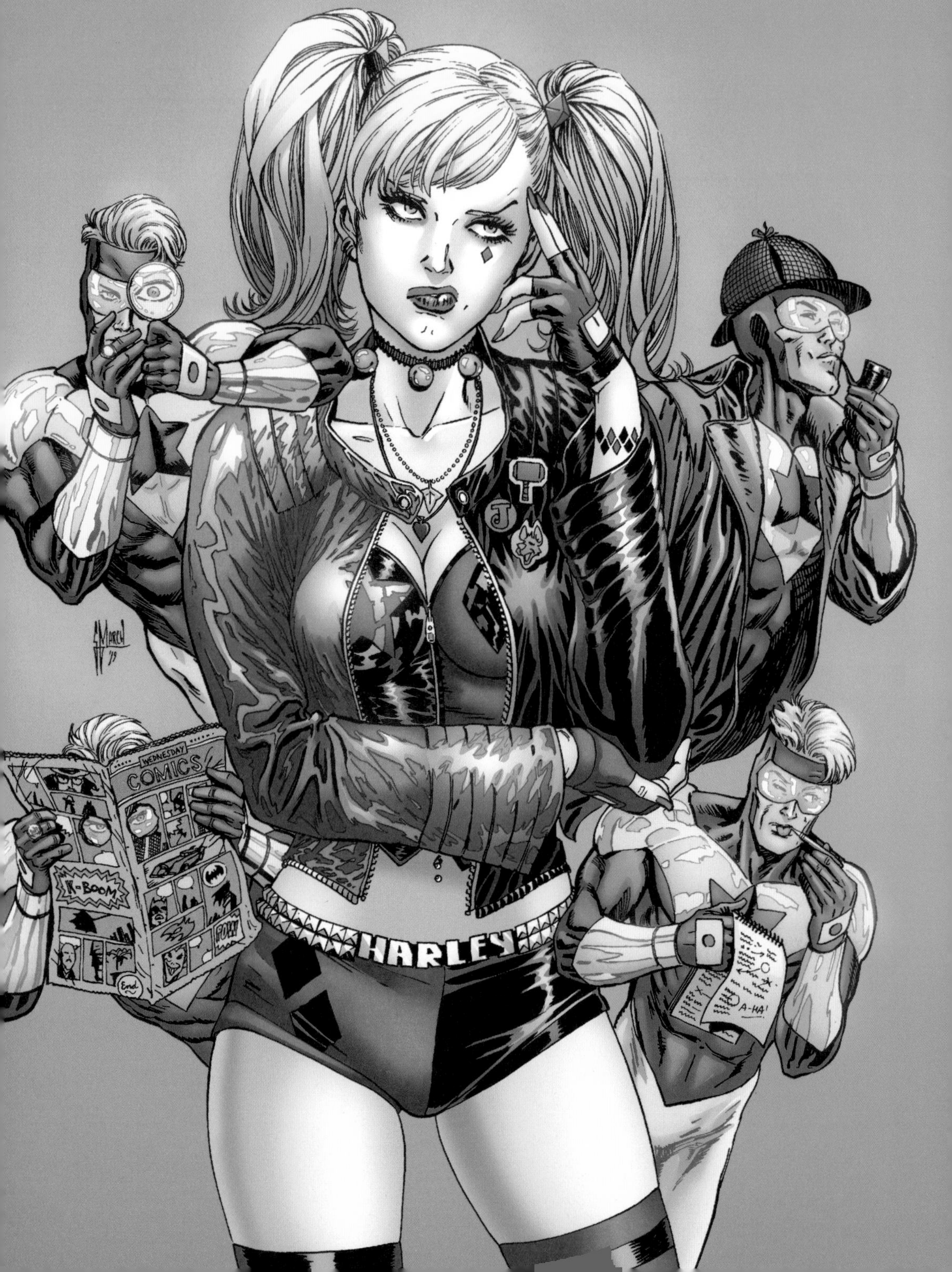
WEDNESDAY
COMICS
K-BOOM
POW
End
A-HA!
HARLEY

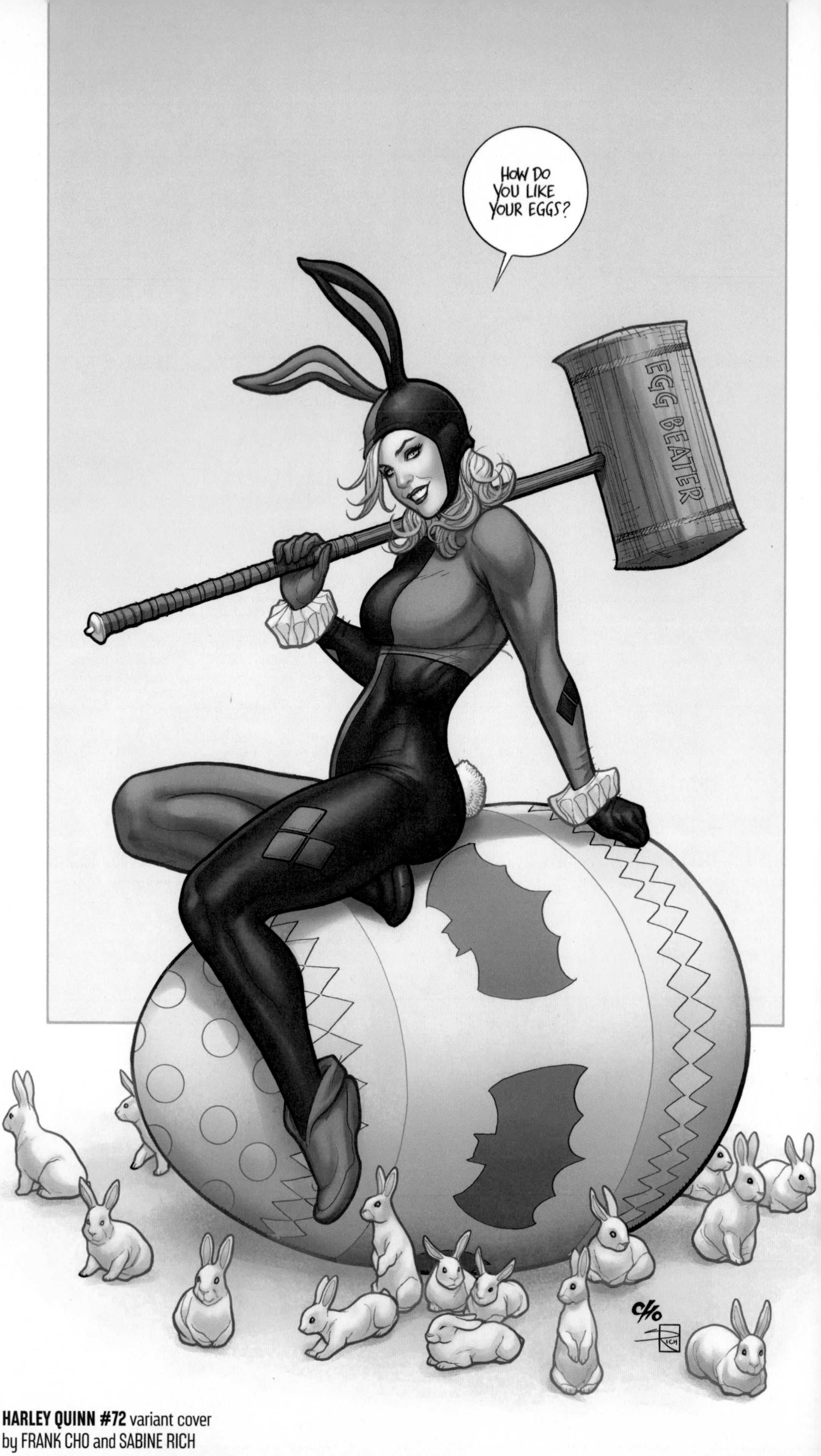
HOW DO
YOU LIKE
YOUR EGGS?
EGG BEATER
CHO
RICH

HARLEY QUINN #72 variant cover
by FRANK CHO and SABINE RICH

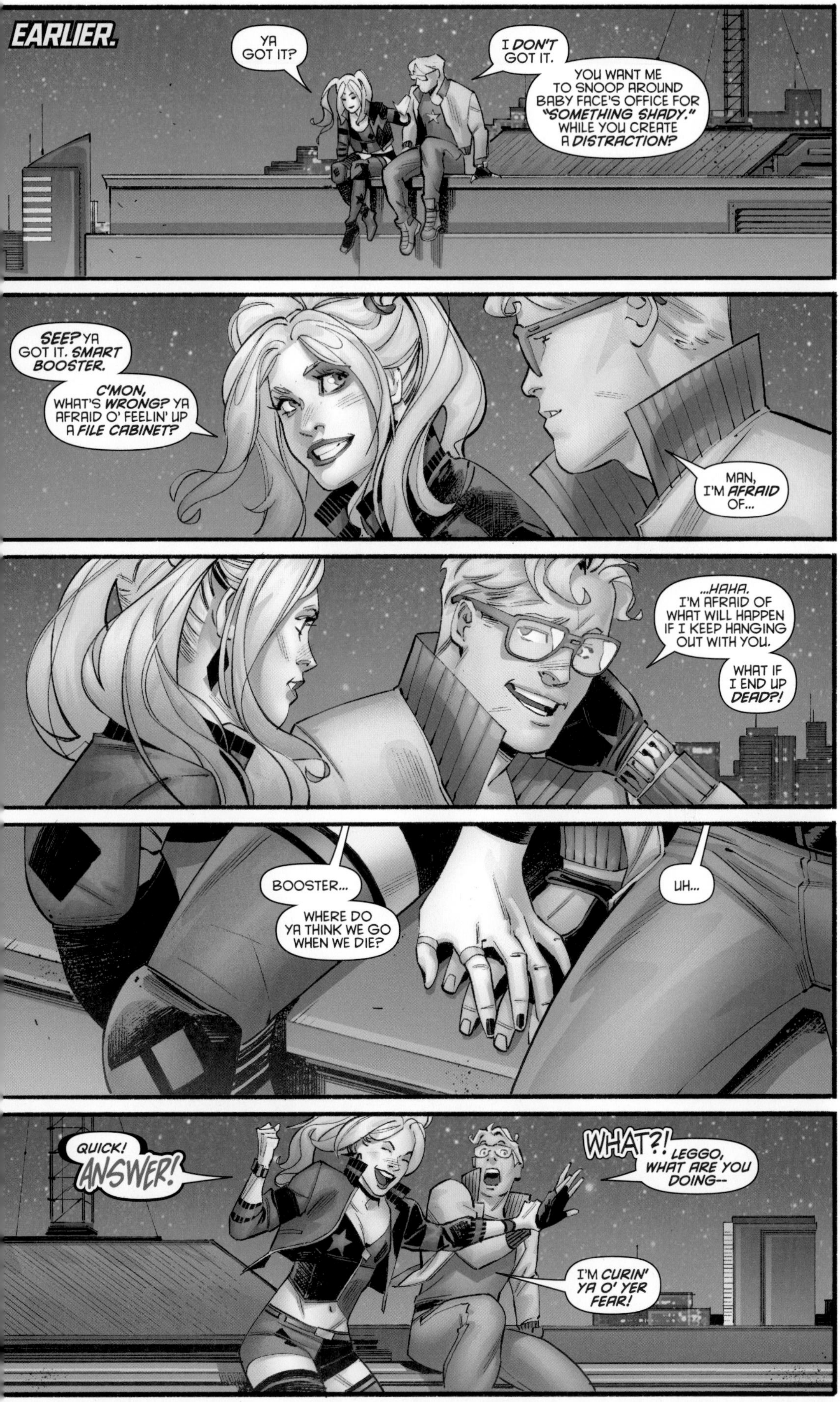
EARLIER.
YA GOT IT?
I DON'T GOT IT.
YOU WANT ME TO SNOOP AROUND BABY FACE'S OFFICE FOR "SOMETHING SHADY." WHILE YOU CREATE A DISTRACTION?
SEE? YA GOT IT. SMART BOOSTER.
C'MON, WHAT'S WRONG? YA AFRAID O' FEELIN' UP A FILE CABINET?
MAN, I'M AFRAID OF...
...HAHA. I'M AFRAID OF WHAT WILL HAPPEN IF I KEEP HANGING OUT WITH YOU.
WHAT IF I END UP DEAD?!
BOOSTER...
WHERE DO YA THINK WE GO WHEN WE DIE?
UH...
QUICK! ANSWER!
WHAT?! LEGGO, WHAT ARE YOU DOING--
I'M CURIN' YA O' YER FEAR!

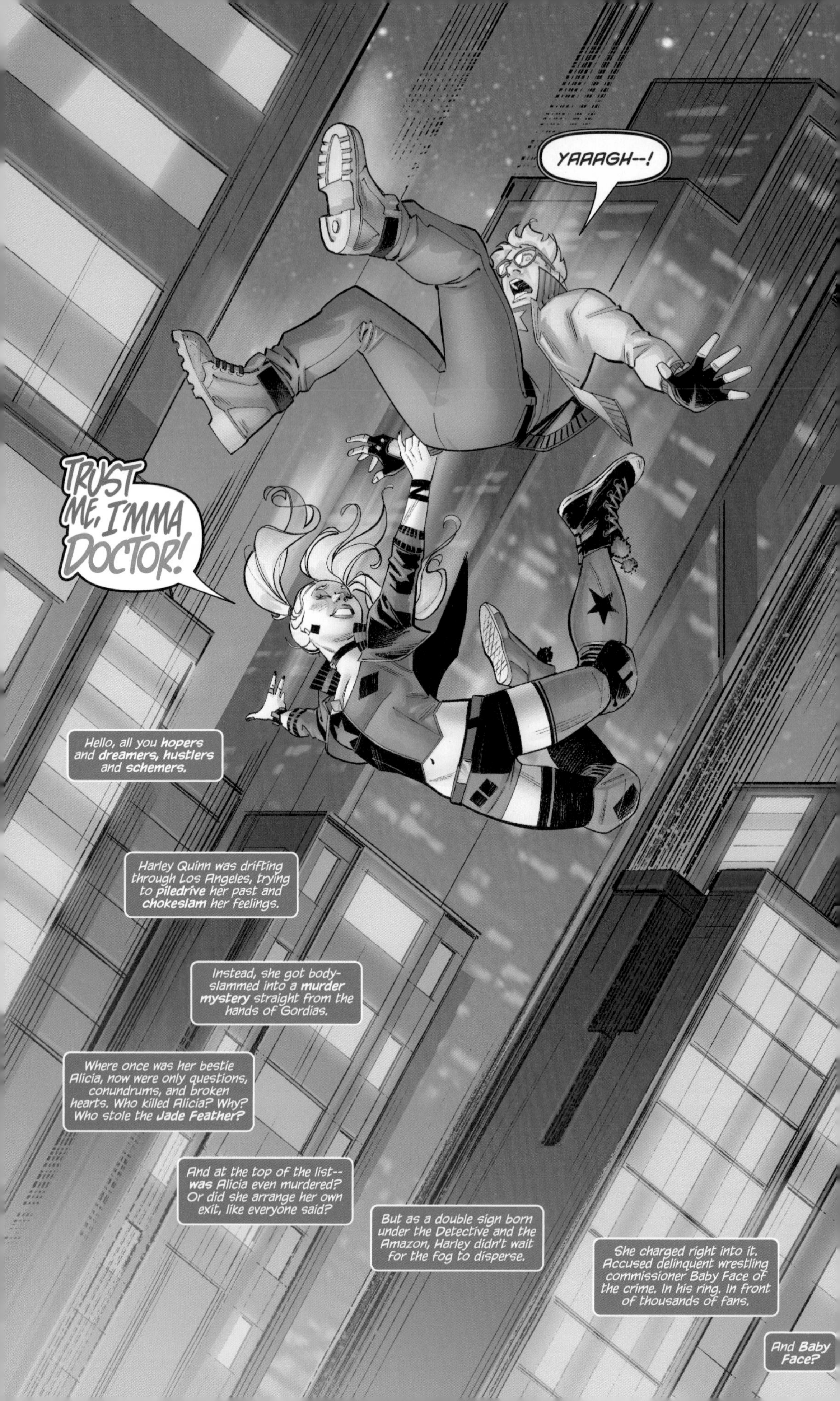

YAAAGH--!
TRUST ME, I'MMA DOCTOR!
Hello, all you **hopers** and **dreamers, hustlers** and **schemers.**
Harley Quinn was drifting through Los Angeles, trying to **piledrive** her past and **chokeslam** her feelings.
Instead, she got body-slammed into a **murder mystery** straight from the hands of Gordias.
Where once was her bestie Alicia, now were only questions, conundrums, and broken hearts. Who killed Alicia? Why? Who stole the **Jade Feather?**
And at the top of the list--**was** Alicia even murdered? Or did she arrange her own exit, like everyone said?
But as a double sign born under the Detective and the Amazon, Harley didn't wait for the fog to disperse.
She charged right into it. Accused delinquent wrestling commissioner Baby Face of the crime. In his ring. In front of thousands of fans.
And **Baby Face?**

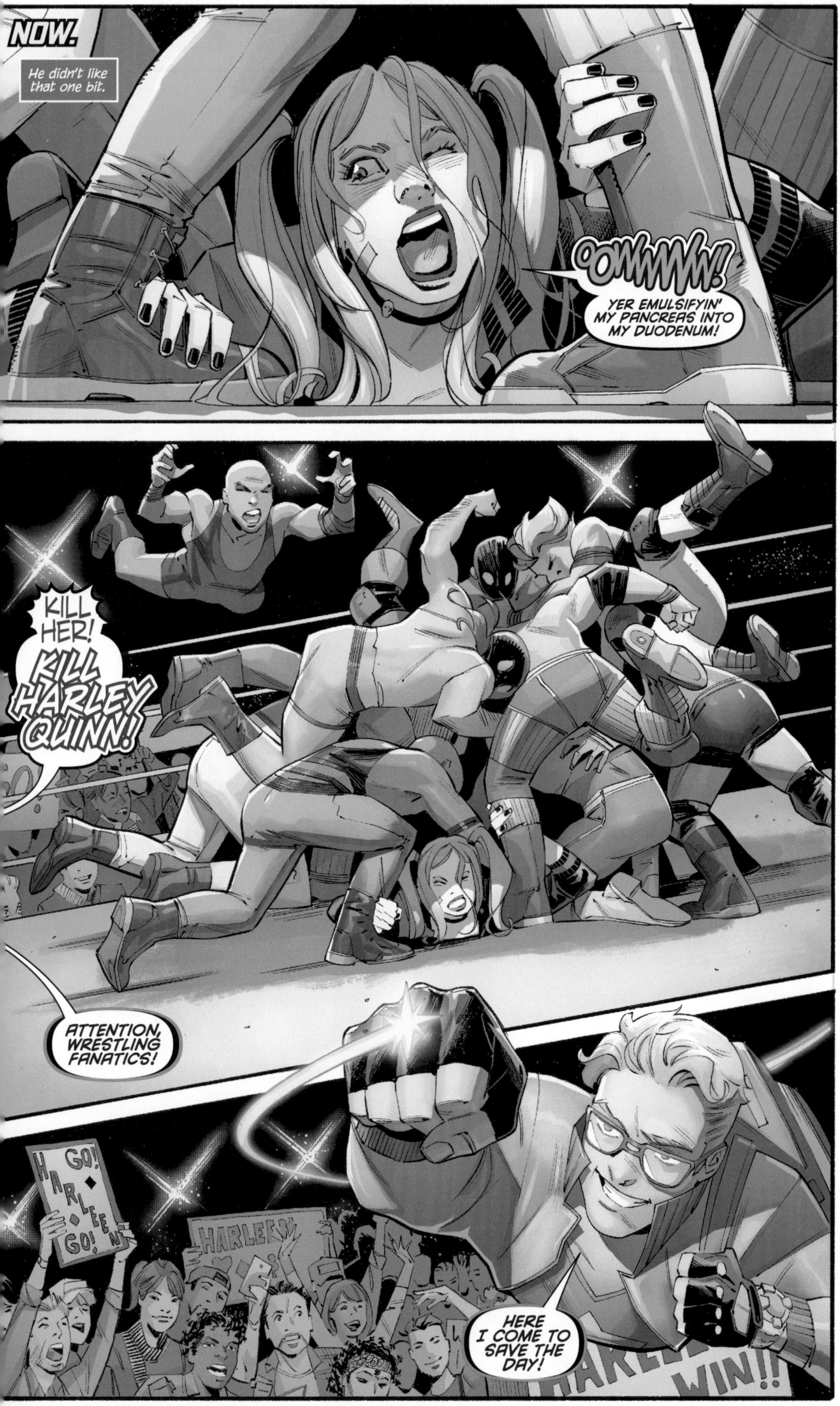
NOW.
He didn't like that one bit.
OOWWWW!
YER EMULSIFYIN' MY PANCREAS INTO MY DUODENUM!
KILL HER! KILL HARLEY QUINN!
ATTENTION, WRESTLING FANATICS!
HERE I COME TO SAVE THE DAY!
GO! HARLEEN GO!
HARLEEN
WIN!!

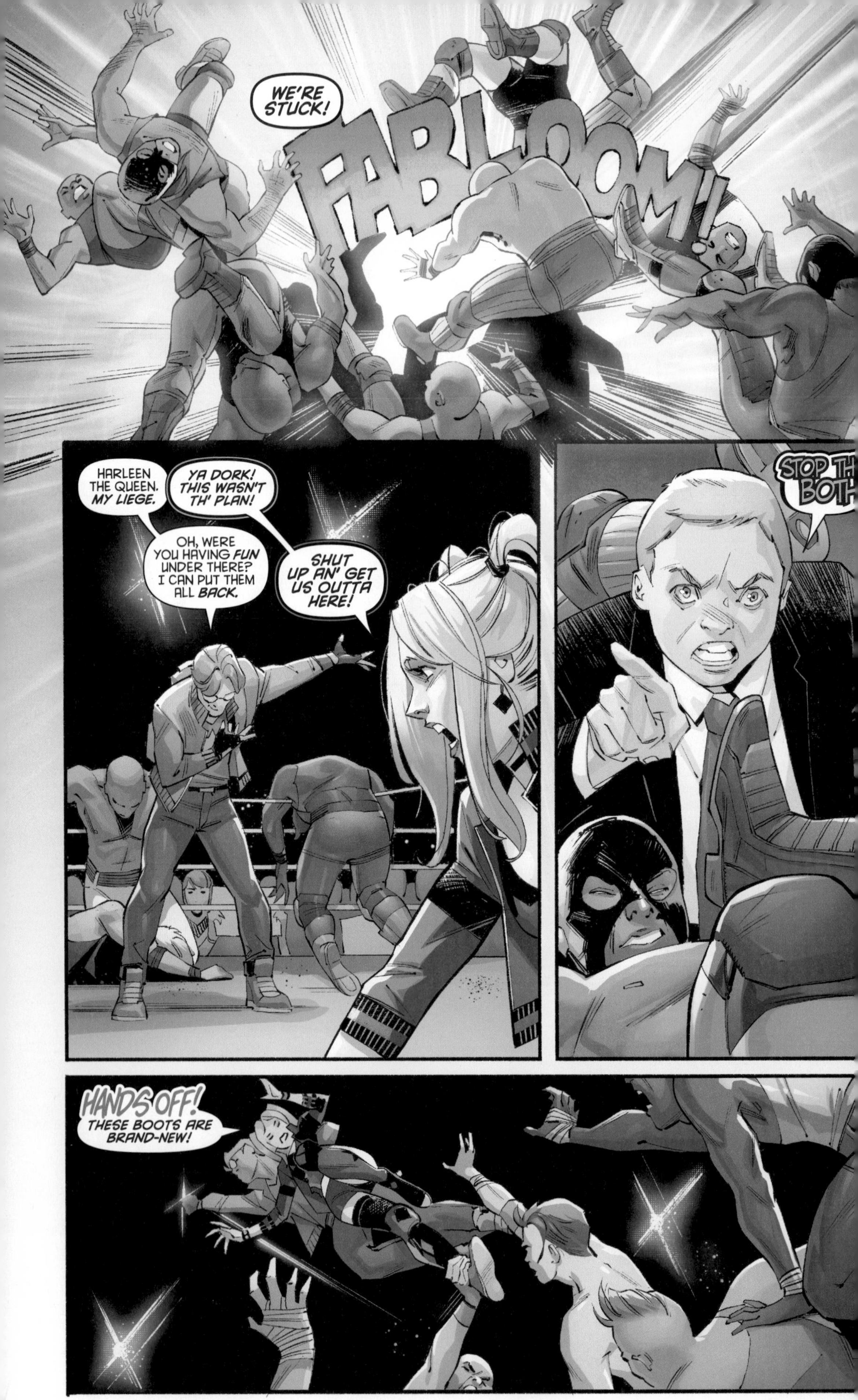

WE'RE STUCK!
FABLOOM!
HARLEEN THE QUEEN. MY LIEGE.
YA DORK! THIS WASN'T TH' PLAN!
OH, WERE YOU HAVING FUN UNDER THERE? I CAN PUT THEM ALL BACK.
SHUT UP AN' GET US OUTTA HERE!
STOP TH
BOTH
HANDS OFF! THESE BOOTS ARE BRAND-NEW!

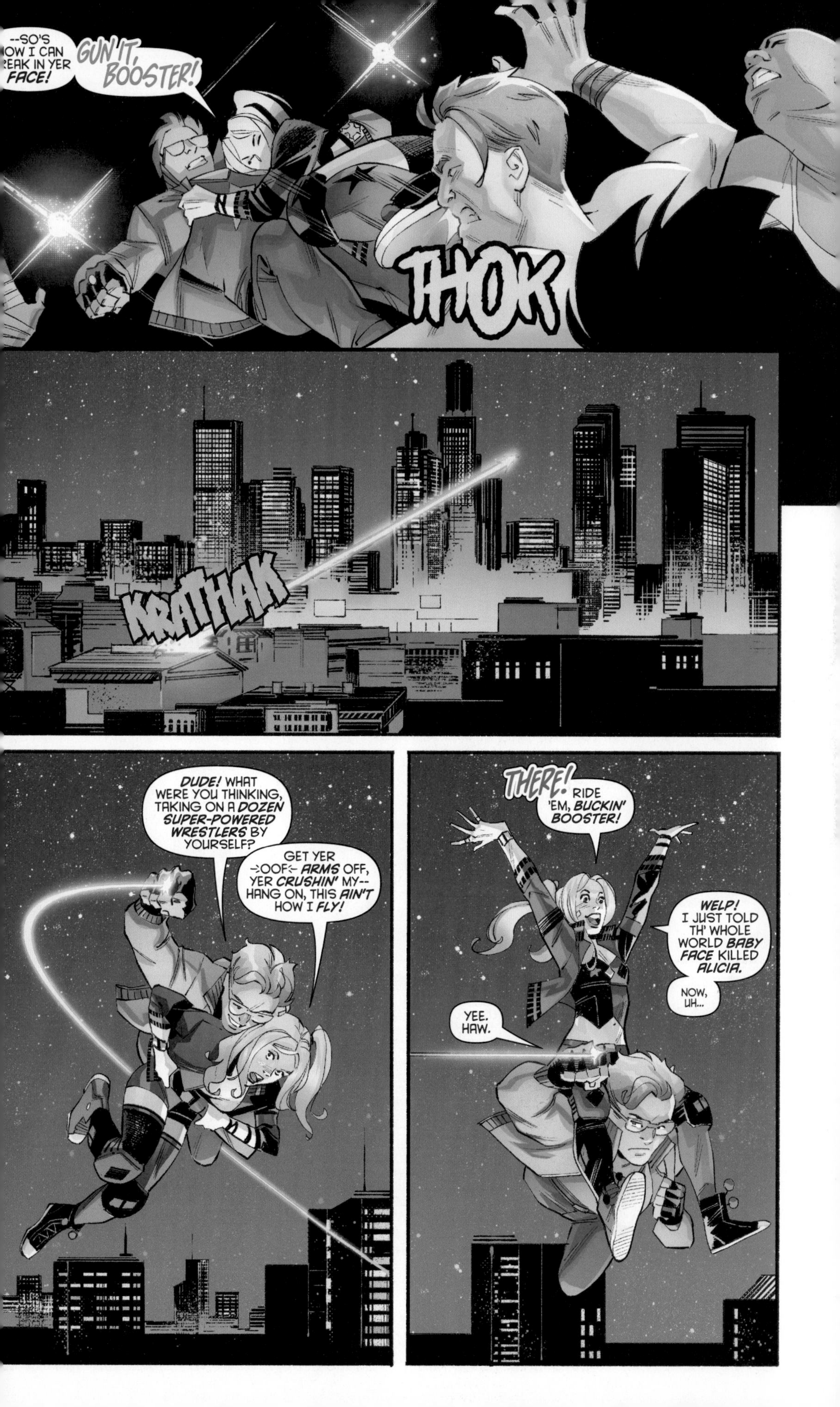
--SO'S
OW I CAN
EAK IN YER
FACE!
GUN IT, BOOSTER!
THOK
KRATHAK
DUDE! WHAT WERE YOU THINKING, TAKING ON A DOZEN SUPER-POWERED WRESTLERS BY YOURSELF?
GET YER --OOF-- ARMS OFF, YER CRUSHIN' MY-- HANG ON, THIS AIN'T HOW I FLY!
THERE! RIDE 'EM, BUCKIN' BOOSTER!
WELP! I JUST TOLD TH' WHOLE WORLD BABY FACE KILLED ALICIA.
NOW, UH...
YEE. HAW.

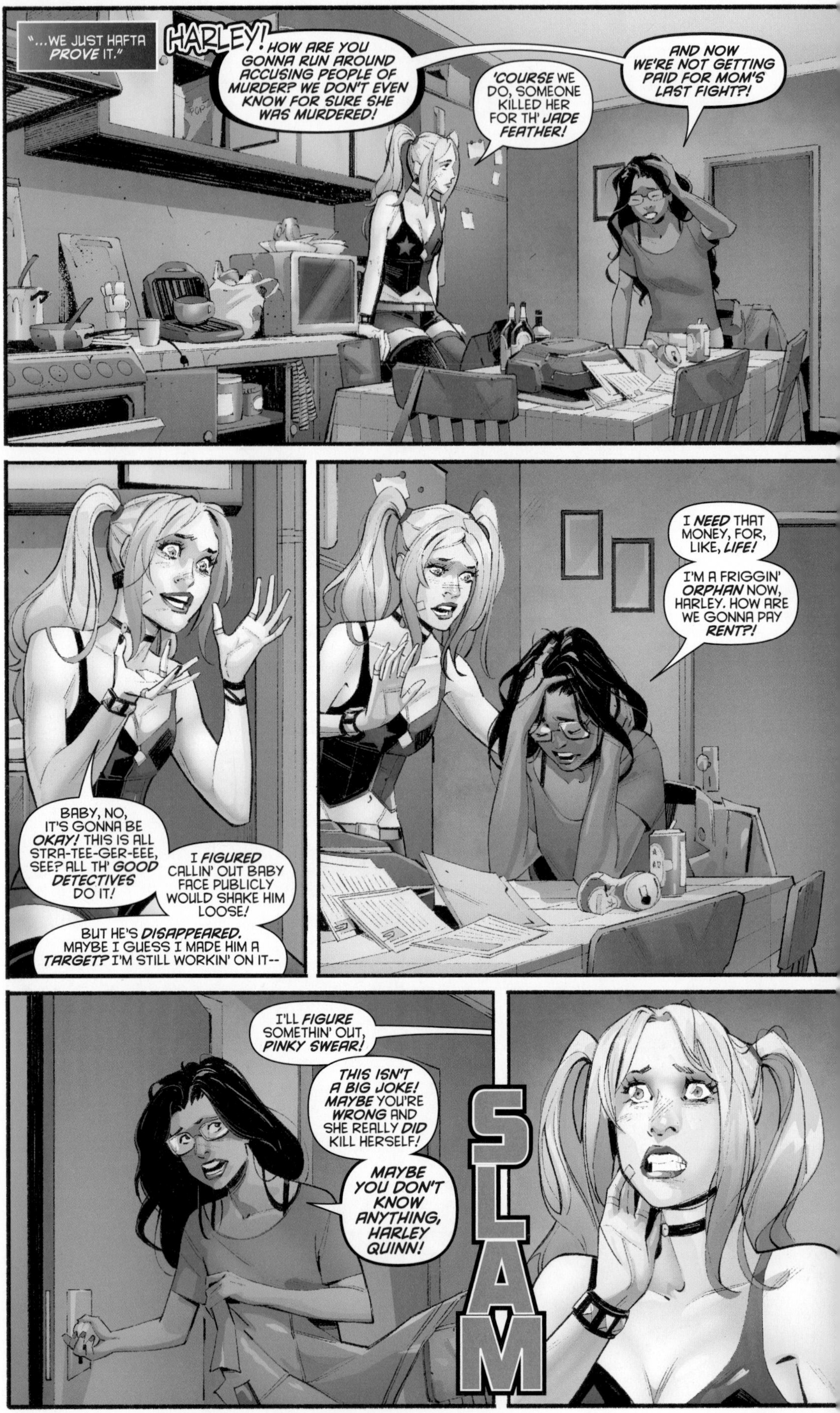
"...WE JUST HAFTA PROVE IT."
HARLEY! HOW ARE YOU GONNA RUN AROUND ACCUSING PEOPLE OF MURDER? WE DON'T EVEN KNOW FOR SURE SHE WAS MURDERED!
'COURSE WE DO, SOMEONE KILLED HER FOR TH' JADE FEATHER!
AND NOW WE'RE NOT GETTING PAID FOR MOM'S LAST FIGHT?!
I NEED THAT MONEY, FOR, LIKE, LIFE!
I'M A FRIGGIN' ORPHAN NOW, HARLEY. HOW ARE WE GONNA PAY RENT?!
BABY, NO, IT'S GONNA BE OKAY! THIS IS ALL STRA-TEE-GER-EEE, SEE? ALL TH' GOOD DETECTIVES DO IT!
I FIGURED CALLIN' OUT BABY FACE PUBLICLY WOULD SHAKE HIM LOOSE!
BUT HE'S DISAPPEARED. MAYBE I GUESS I MADE HIM A TARGET? I'M STILL WORKIN' ON IT--
I'LL FIGURE SOMETHIN' OUT, PINKY SWEAR!
THIS ISN'T A BIG JOKE! MAYBE YOU'RE WRONG AND SHE REALLY DID KILL HERSELF!
MAYBE YOU DON'T KNOW ANYTHING, HARLEY QUINN!
SLAM

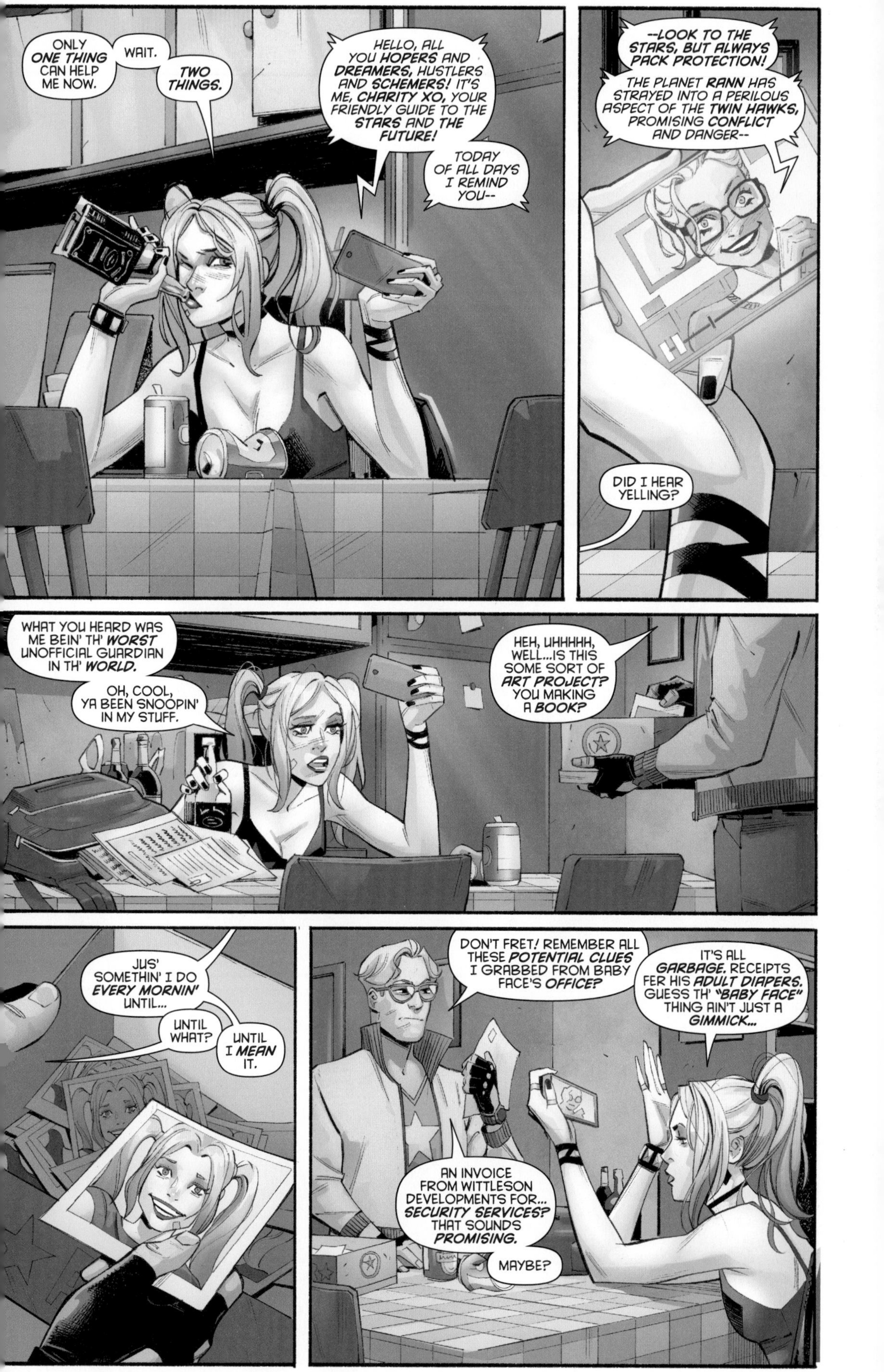
ONLY ONE THING CAN HELP ME NOW.
WAIT.
TWO THINGS.
HELLO, ALL YOU HOPERS AND DREAMERS, HUSTLERS AND SCHEMERS! IT'S ME, CHARITY XO, YOUR FRIENDLY GUIDE TO THE STARS AND THE FUTURE!
TODAY OF ALL DAYS I REMIND YOU--
--LOOK TO THE STARS, BUT ALWAYS PACK PROTECTION!
THE PLANET RANN HAS STRAYED INTO A PERILOUS ASPECT OF THE TWIN HAWKS, PROMISING CONFLICT AND DANGER--
DID I HEAR YELLING?
WHAT YOU HEARD WAS ME BEIN' TH' WORST UNOFFICIAL GUARDIAN IN TH' WORLD.
OH, COOL, YA BEEN SNOOPIN' IN MY STUFF.
HEH, UHHHHH, WELL...IS THIS SOME SORT OF ART PROJECT? YOU MAKING A BOOK?
JUS' SOMETHIN' I DO EVERY MORNIN' UNTIL...
UNTIL WHAT?
UNTIL I MEAN IT.
DON'T FRET! REMEMBER ALL THESE POTENTIAL CLUES I GRABBED FROM BABY FACE'S OFFICE?
IT'S ALL GARBAGE. RECEIPTS FER HIS ADULT DIAPERS. GUESS TH' "BABY FACE" THING AIN'T JUST A GIMMICK...
AN INVOICE FROM WITTLESON DEVELOPMENTS FOR... SECURITY SERVICES? THAT SOUNDS PROMISING.
MAYBE?

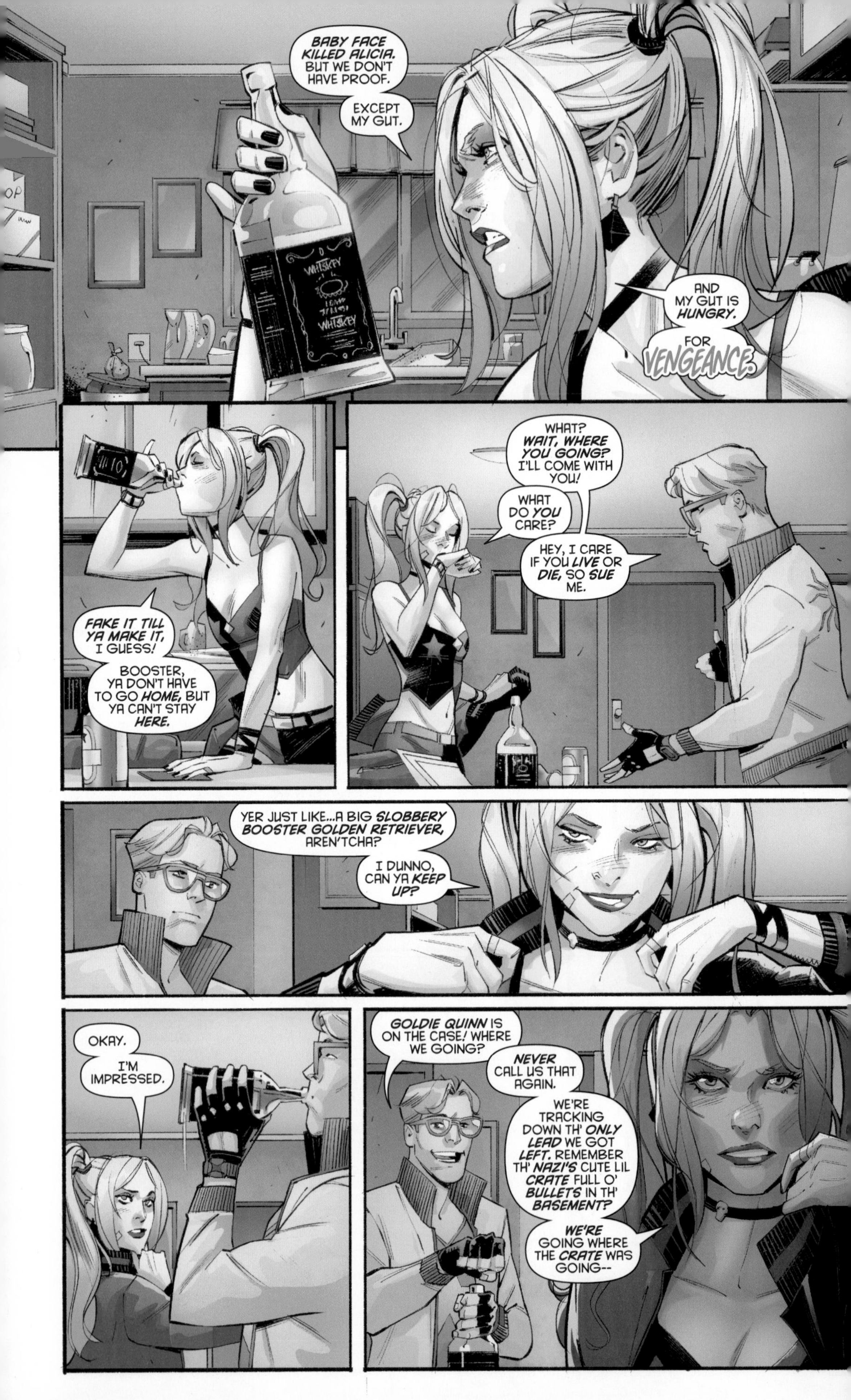

BABY FACE KILLED ALICIA. BUT WE DON'T HAVE PROOF.
EXCEPT MY GUT.
AND MY GUT IS HUNGRY.
FOR VENGEANCE.
WHISKEY
FAKE IT TILL YA MAKE IT, I GUESS!
BOOSTER, YA DON'T HAVE TO GO HOME, BUT YA CAN'T STAY HERE.
WHAT? WAIT, WHERE YOU GOING? I'LL COME WITH YOU!
WHAT DO YOU CARE?
HEY, I CARE IF YOU LIVE OR DIE, SO SUE ME.
YER JUST LIKE...A BIG SLOBBERY BOOSTER GOLDEN RETRIEVER, AREN'TCHA?
I DUNNO, CAN YA KEEP UP?
OKAY.
I'M IMPRESSED.
GOLDIE QUINN IS ON THE CASE! WHERE WE GOING?
NEVER CALL US THAT AGAIN.
WE'RE TRACKING DOWN TH' ONLY LEAD WE GOT LEFT. REMEMBER TH' NAZI'S CUTE LIL CRATE FULL O' BULLETS IN TH' BASEMENT?
WE'RE GOING WHERE THE CRATE WAS GOING--

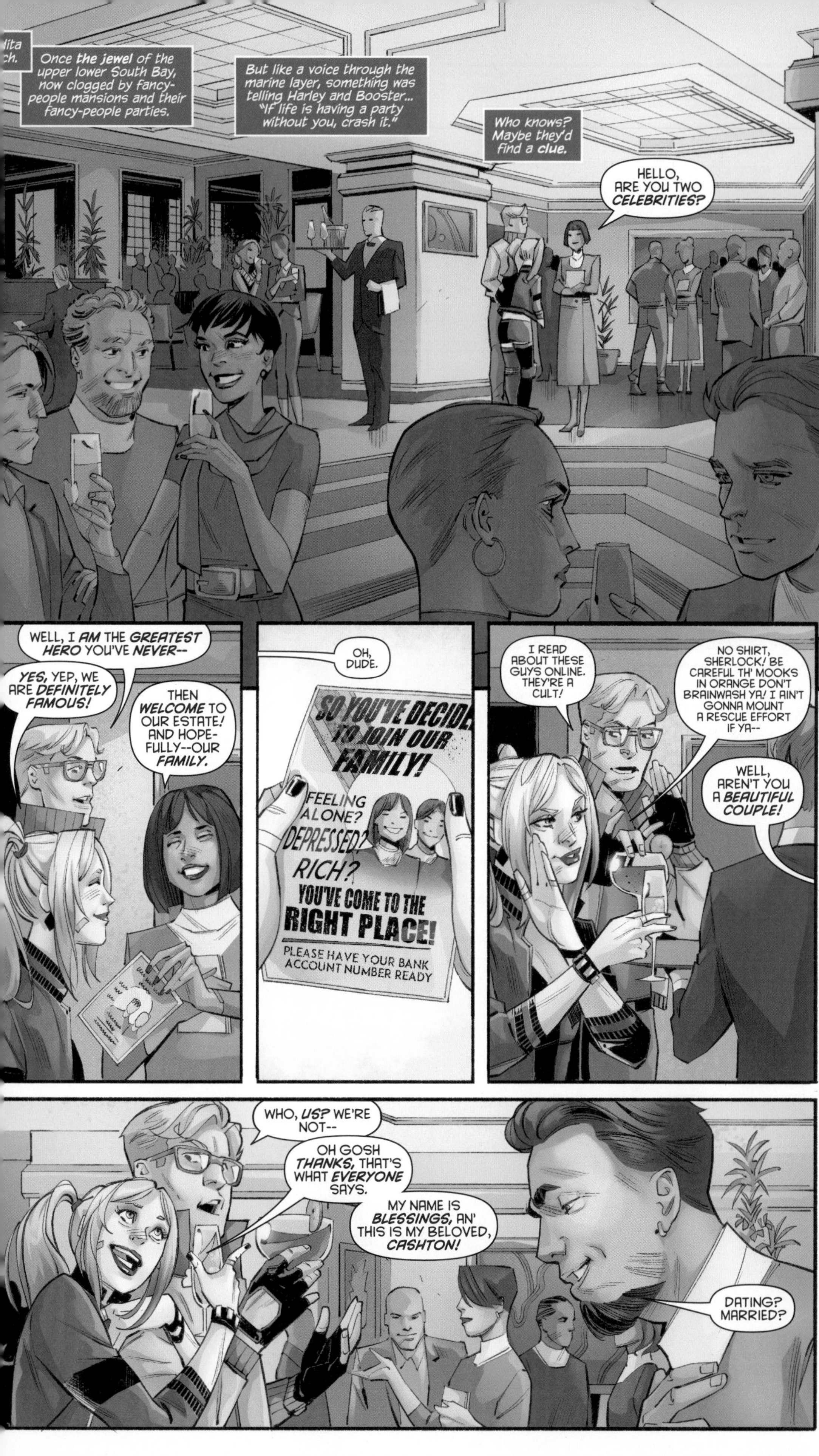

Once the jewel of the upper lower South Bay, now clogged by fancy-people mansions and their fancy-people parties.
But like a voice through the marine layer, something was telling Harley and Booster... "If life is having a party without you, crash it."
Who knows? Maybe they'd find a clue.
HELLO, ARE YOU TWO CELEBRITIES?
WELL, I AM THE GREATEST HERO YOU'VE NEVER--
YES, YEP, WE ARE DEFINITELY FAMOUS!
THEN WELCOME TO OUR ESTATE! AND HOPE-FULLY--OUR FAMILY.
OH, DUDE.
SO YOU'VE DECIDE TO JOIN OUR FAMILY!
FEELING ALONE? DEPRESSED? RICH?
YOU'VE COME TO THE RIGHT PLACE!
PLEASE HAVE YOUR BANK ACCOUNT NUMBER READY
I READ ABOUT THESE GUYS ONLINE. THEY'RE A CULT!
NO SHIRT, SHERLOCK! BE CAREFUL TH' MOOKS IN ORANGE DON'T BRAINWASH YA! I AIN'T GONNA MOUNT A RESCUE EFFORT IF YA--
WELL, AREN'T YOU A BEAUTIFUL COUPLE!
WHO, US? WE'RE NOT--
OH GOSH THANKS, THAT'S WHAT EVERYONE SAYS.
MY NAME IS BLESSINGS, AN' THIS IS MY BELOVED, CASHTON!
DATING? MARRIED?

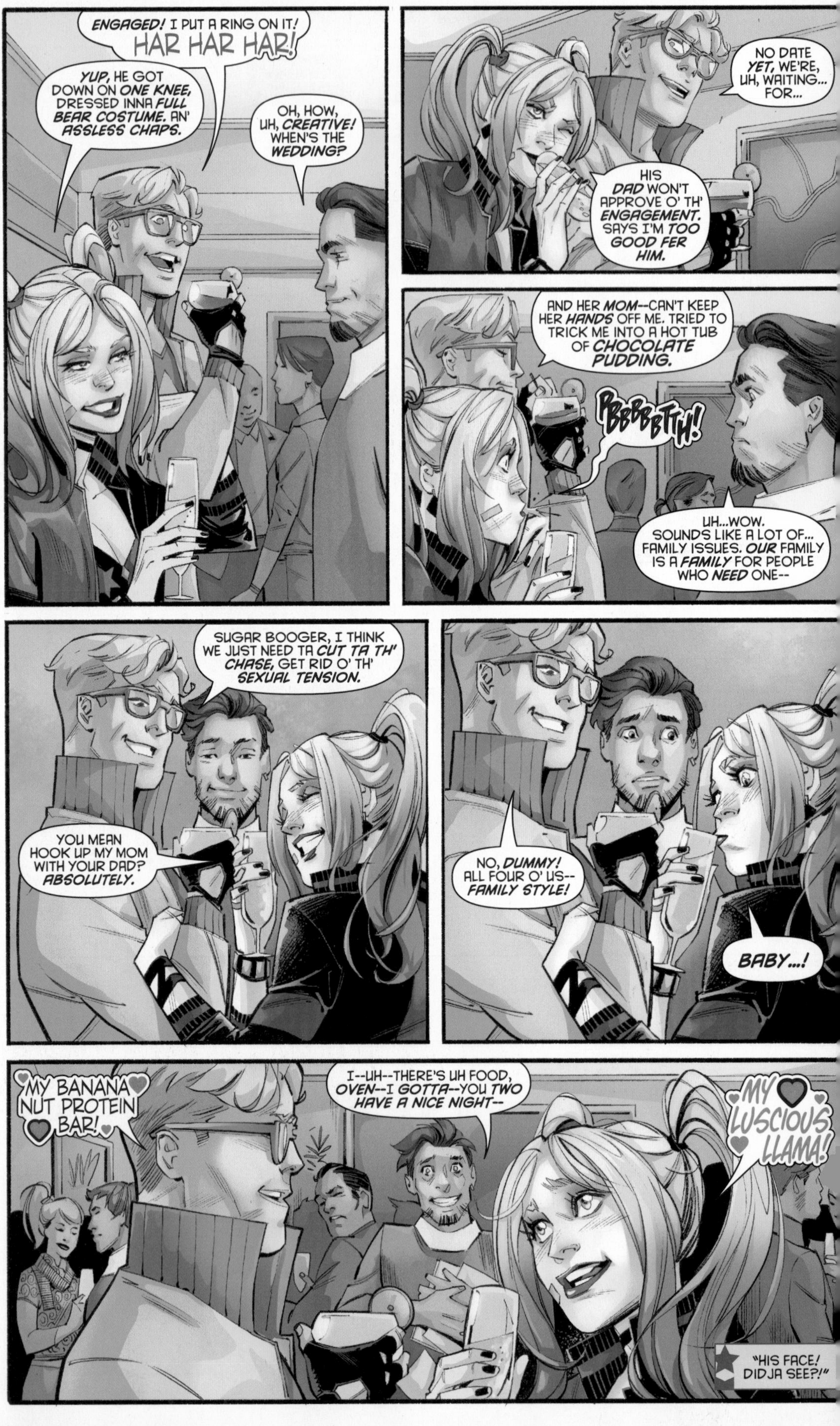

ENGAGED! I PUT A RING ON IT! HAR HAR HAR!
YUP, HE GOT DOWN ON ONE KNEE, DRESSED INNA FULL BEAR COSTUME. AN' ASSLESS CHAPS.
OH, HOW, UH, CREATIVE! WHEN'S THE WEDDING?
NO DATE YET, WE'RE, UH, WAITING... FOR...
HIS DAD WON'T APPROVE O' TH' ENGAGEMENT. SAYS I'M TOO GOOD FER HIM.
AND HER MOM--CAN'T KEEP HER HANDS OFF ME. TRIED TO TRICK ME INTO A HOT TUB OF CHOCOLATE PUDDING.
PBBBBBTTH!
UH...WOW. SOUNDS LIKE A LOT OF... FAMILY ISSUES. OUR FAMILY IS A FAMILY FOR PEOPLE WHO NEED ONE--
SUGAR BOOGER, I THINK WE JUST NEED TA CUT TA TH' CHASE, GET RID O' TH' SEXUAL TENSION.
YOU MEAN HOOK UP MY MOM WITH YOUR DAD? ABSOLUTELY.
NO, DUMMY! ALL FOUR O' US--FAMILY STYLE!
BABY...!
MY BANANA NUT PROTEIN BAR!
I--UH--THERE'S UH FOOD, OVEN--I GOTTA--YOU TWO HAVE A NICE NIGHT--
MY LUSCIOUS LLAMA!
"HIS FACE! DIDJA SEE?!"

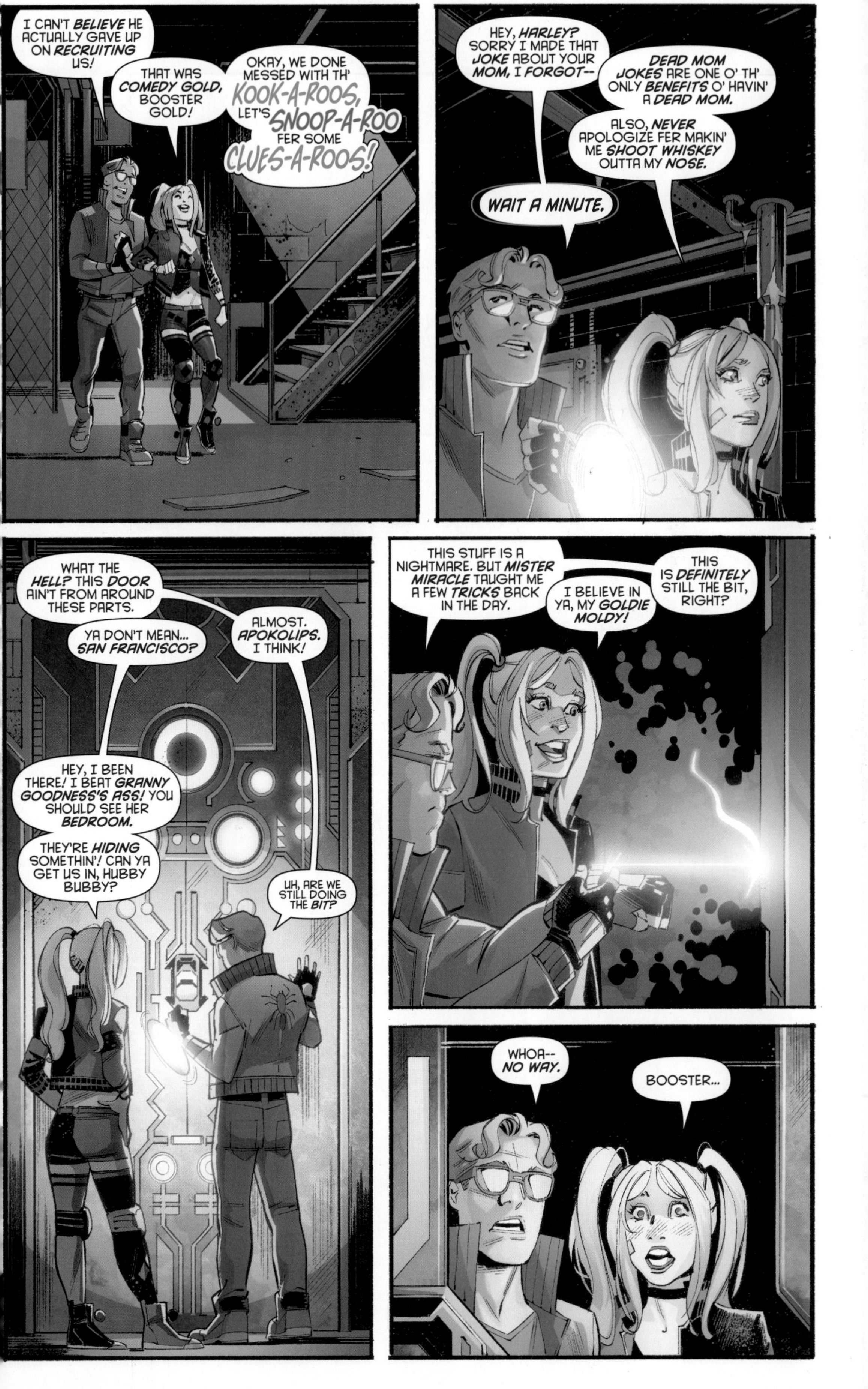

I CAN'T BELIEVE HE ACTUALLY GAVE UP ON RECRUITING US!
THAT WAS COMEDY GOLD, BOOSTER GOLD!
OKAY, WE DONE MESSED WITH TH' KOOK-A-ROOS, LET'S SNOOP-A-ROO FER SOME CLUES-A-ROOS!
HEY, HARLEY? SORRY I MADE THAT JOKE ABOUT YOUR MOM, I FORGOT--
DEAD MOM JOKES ARE ONE O' TH' ONLY BENEFITS O' HAVIN' A DEAD MOM.
ALSO, NEVER APOLOGIZE FER MAKIN' ME SHOOT WHISKEY OUTTA MY NOSE.
WAIT A MINUTE.
WHAT THE HELL? THIS DOOR AIN'T FROM AROUND THESE PARTS.
YA DON'T MEAN... SAN FRANCISCO?
ALMOST. APOKOLIPS. I THINK!
HEY, I BEEN THERE! I BEAT GRANNY GOODNESS'S ASS! YOU SHOULD SEE HER BEDROOM.
THEY'RE HIDING SOMETHIN'! CAN YA GET US IN, HUBBY BUBBY?
UH, ARE WE STILL DOING THE BIT?
THIS STUFF IS A NIGHTMARE. BUT MISTER MIRACLE TAUGHT ME A FEW TRICKS BACK IN THE DAY.
I BELIEVE IN YA, MY GOLDIE MOLDY!
THIS IS DEFINITELY STILL THE BIT, RIGHT?
WHOA-- NO WAY.
BOOSTER...

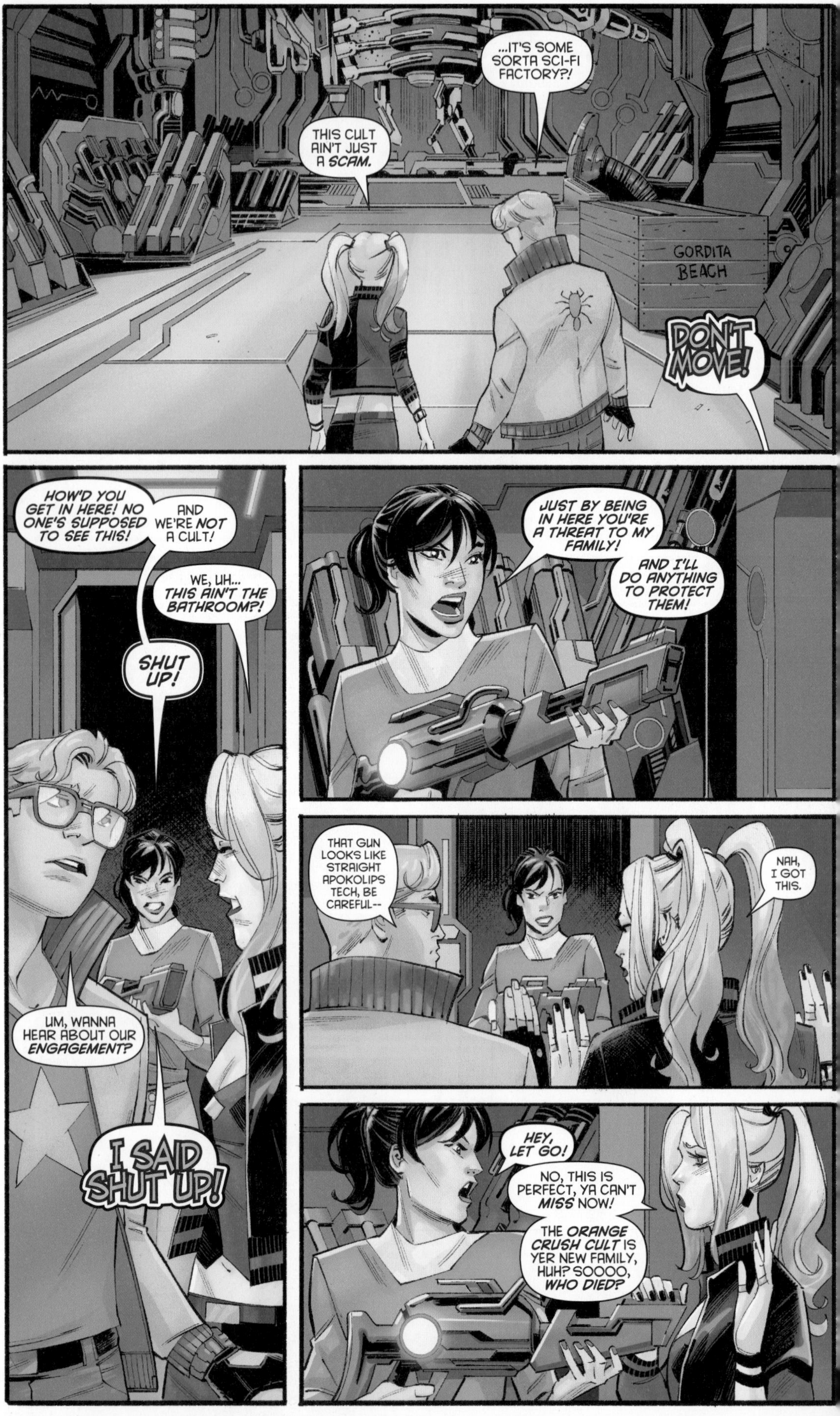
...IT'S SOME SORTA SCI-FI FACTORY?!
THIS CULT AIN'T JUST A SCAM.
GORDITA BEACH
DON'T MOVE!
HOW'D YOU GET IN HERE! NO ONE'S SUPPOSED TO SEE THIS!
AND WE'RE NOT A CULT!
WE, UH... THIS AIN'T THE BATHROOM?!
SHUT UP!
UM, WANNA HEAR ABOUT OUR ENGAGEMENT?
I SAID SHUT UP!
JUST BY BEING IN HERE YOU'RE A THREAT TO MY FAMILY!
AND I'LL DO ANYTHING TO PROTECT THEM!
THAT GUN LOOKS LIKE STRAIGHT APOKOLIPS TECH, BE CAREFUL--
NAH, I GOT THIS.
HEY, LET GO!
NO, THIS IS PERFECT, YA CAN'T MISS NOW!
THE ORANGE CRUSH CULT IS YER NEW FAMILY, HUH? SOOOO, WHO DIED?

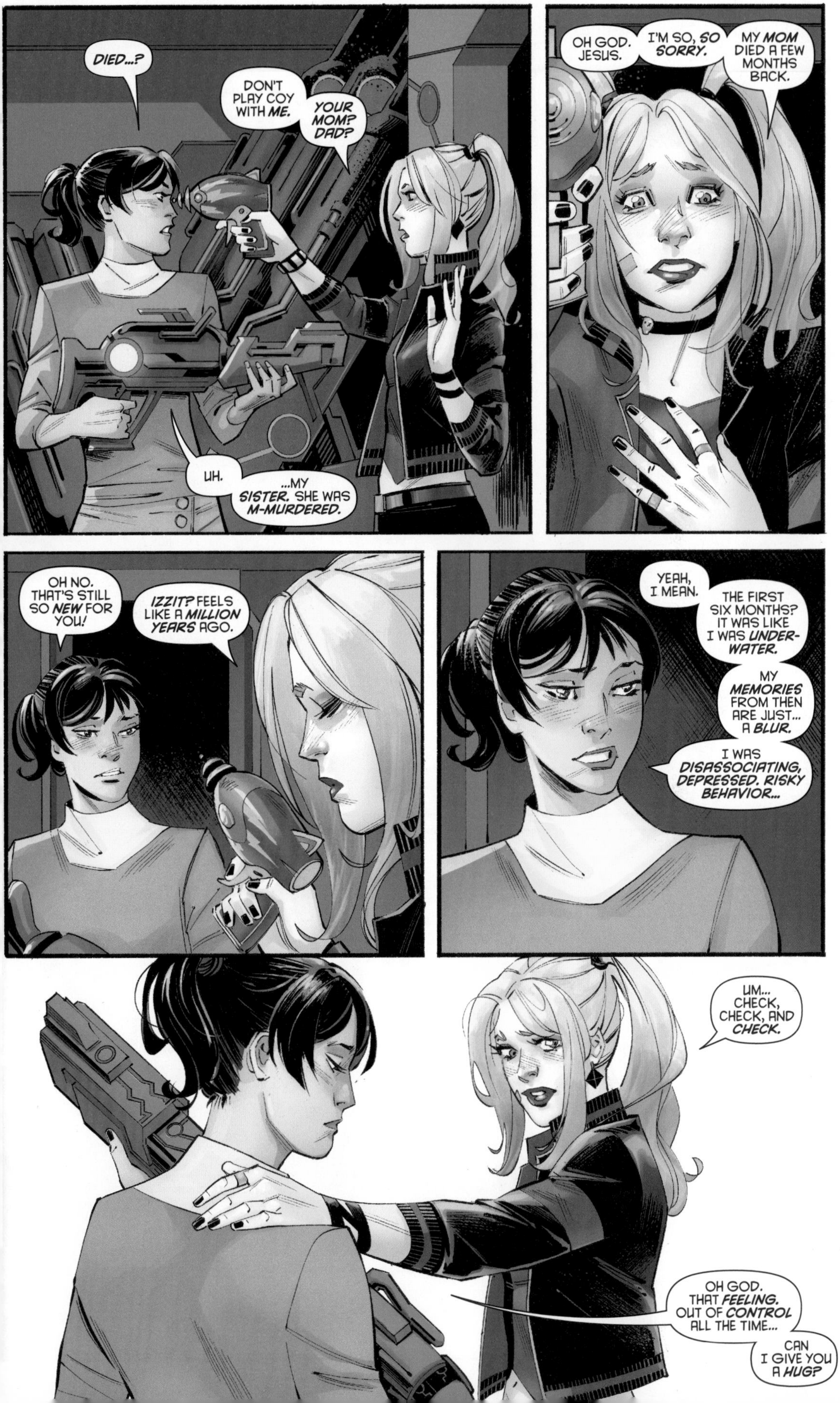
DIED...?
DON'T PLAY COY WITH ME.
YOUR MOM? DAD?
UH.
...MY SISTER. SHE WAS M-MURDERED.
OH GOD. JESUS.
I'M SO, SO SORRY.
MY MOM DIED A FEW MONTHS BACK.
OH NO. THAT'S STILL SO NEW FOR YOU!
IZZIT? FEELS LIKE A MILLION YEARS AGO.
YEAH, I MEAN.
THE FIRST SIX MONTHS? IT WAS LIKE I WAS UNDER-WATER.
MY MEMORIES FROM THEN ARE JUST... A BLUR.
I WAS DISASSOCIATING, DEPRESSED. RISKY BEHAVIOR...
UM... CHECK, CHECK, AND CHECK.
OH GOD. THAT FEELING. OUT OF CONTROL ALL THE TIME...
CAN I GIVE YOU A HUG?

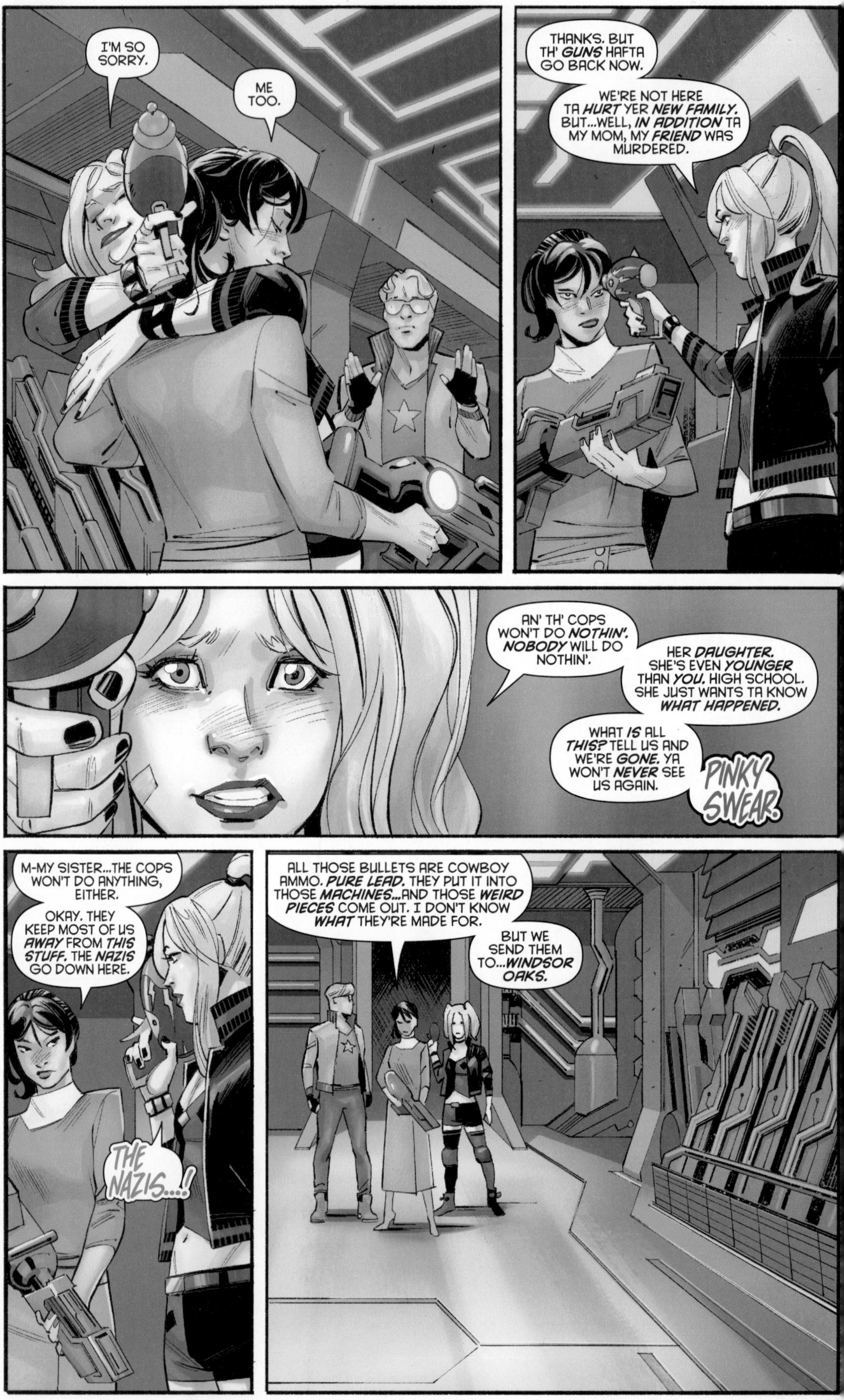

I'M SO SORRY.
ME TOO.
THANKS. BUT TH' GUNS HAFTA GO BACK NOW.
WE'RE NOT HERE TA HURT YER NEW FAMILY. BUT...WELL, IN ADDITION TA MY MOM, MY FRIEND WAS MURDERED.
AN' TH' COPS WON'T DO NOTHIN'. NOBODY WILL DO NOTHIN'.
HER DAUGHTER. SHE'S EVEN YOUNGER THAN YOU. HIGH SCHOOL. SHE JUST WANTS TA KNOW WHAT HAPPENED.
WHAT IS ALL THIS? TELL US AND WE'RE GONE. YA WON'T NEVER SEE US AGAIN.
PINKY SWEAR.
M-MY SISTER...THE COPS WON'T DO ANYTHING, EITHER.
OKAY. THEY KEEP MOST OF US AWAY FROM THIS STUFF. THE NAZIS GO DOWN HERE.
THE NAZIS...!
ALL THOSE BULLETS ARE COWBOY AMMO. PURE LEAD. THEY PUT IT INTO THOSE MACHINES...AND THOSE WEIRD PIECES COME OUT. I DON'T KNOW WHAT THEY'RE MADE FOR.
BUT WE SEND THEM TO...WINDSOR OAKS.

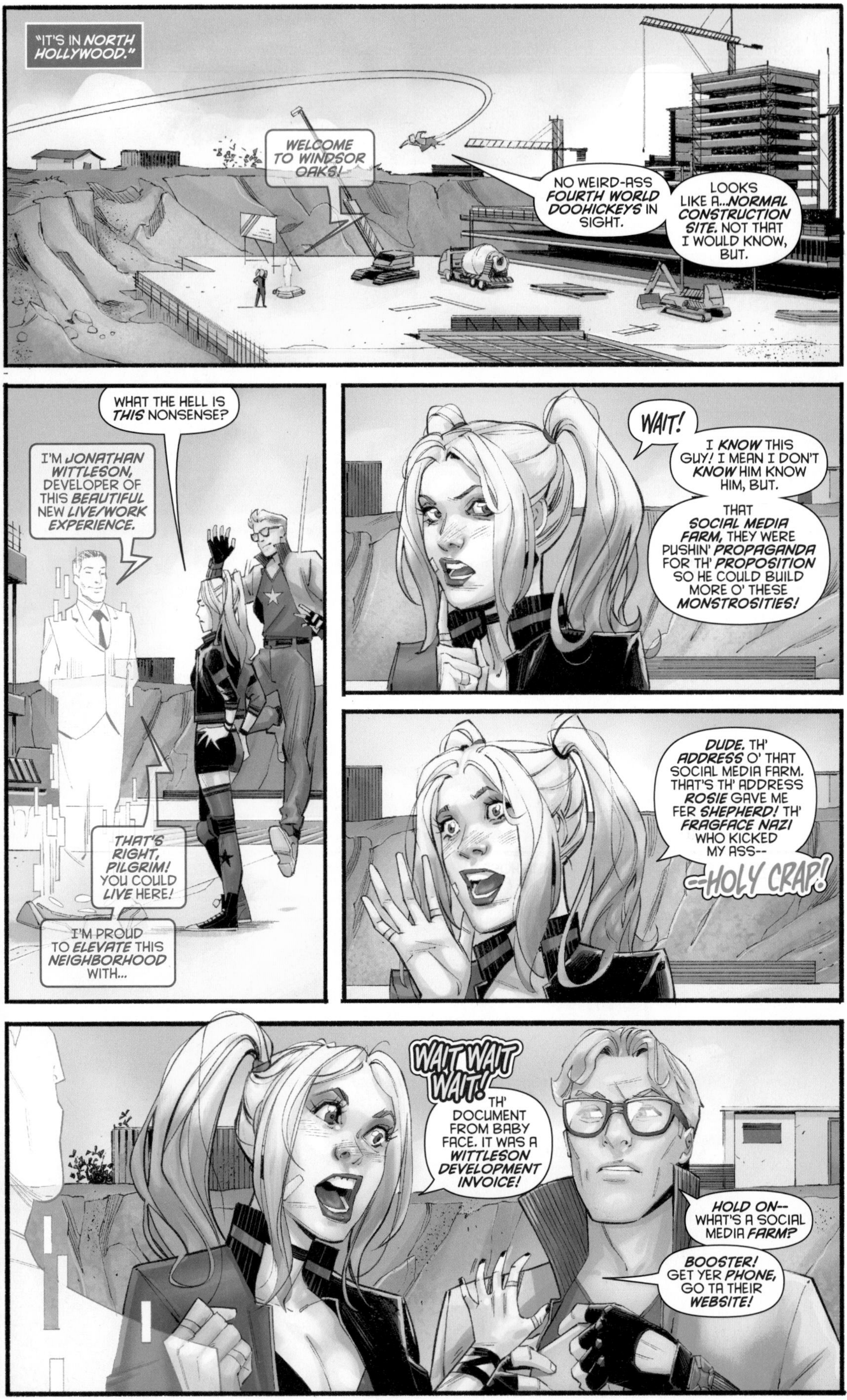

"IT'S IN NORTH HOLLYWOOD."
WELCOME TO WINDSOR OAKS!
NO WEIRD-ASS FOURTH WORLD DOOHICKEYS IN SIGHT.
LOOKS LIKE A...NORMAL CONSTRUCTION SITE. NOT THAT I WOULD KNOW, BUT.
WHAT THE HELL IS THIS NONSENSE?
I'M JONATHAN WITTLESON, DEVELOPER OF THIS BEAUTIFUL NEW LIVE/WORK EXPERIENCE.
THAT'S RIGHT, PILGRIM! YOU COULD LIVE HERE!
I'M PROUD TO ELEVATE THIS NEIGHBORHOOD WITH...
WAIT!
I KNOW THIS GUY! I MEAN I DON'T KNOW HIM KNOW HIM, BUT.
THAT SOCIAL MEDIA FARM, THEY WERE PUSHIN' PROPAGANDA FOR TH' PROPOSITION SO HE COULD BUILD MORE O' THESE MONSTROSITIES!
DUDE. TH' ADDRESS O' THAT SOCIAL MEDIA FARM. THAT'S TH' ADDRESS ROSIE GAVE ME FER SHEPHERD! TH' FRAGFACE NAZI WHO KICKED MY ASS--
--HOLY CRAP!
WAIT WAIT WAIT!
TH' DOCUMENT FROM BABY FACE. IT WAS A WITTLESON DEVELOPMENT INVOICE!
HOLD ON-- WHAT'S A SOCIAL MEDIA FARM?
BOOSTER! GET YER PHONE, GO TA THEIR WEBSITE!

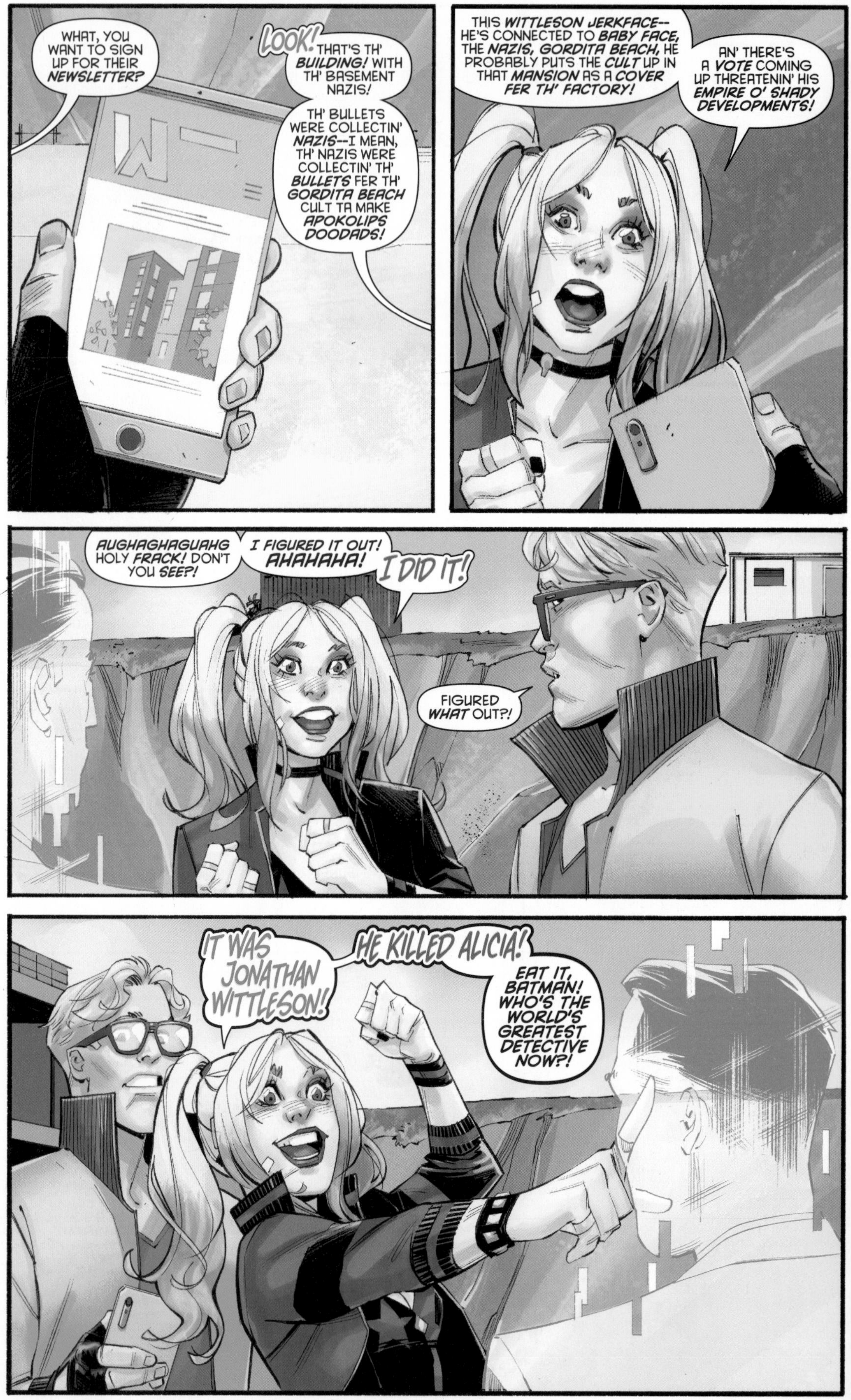
WHAT, YOU WANT TO SIGN UP FOR THEIR NEWSLETTER?
LOOK!
THAT'S TH' BUILDING! WITH TH' BASEMENT NAZIS!
TH' BULLETS WERE COLLECTIN' NAZIS--I MEAN, TH' NAZIS WERE COLLECTIN' TH' BULLETS FER TH' GORDITA BEACH CULT TA MAKE APOKOLIPS DOODADS!
THIS WITTLESON JERKFACE-- HE'S CONNECTED TO BABY FACE, THE NAZIS, GORDITA BEACH, HE PROBABLY PUTS THE CULT UP IN THAT MANSION AS A COVER FER TH' FACTORY!
AN' THERE'S A VOTE COMING UP THREATENIN' HIS EMPIRE O' SHADY DEVELOPMENTS!
AUGHAGHAGUAHG HOLY FRACK! DON'T YOU SEE?!
I FIGURED IT OUT! AHAHAHA!
I DID IT!
FIGURED WHAT OUT?!
IT WAS JONATHAN WITTLESON!
HE KILLED ALICIA!
EAT IT, BATMAN! WHO'S THE WORLD'S GREATEST DETECTIVE NOW?!

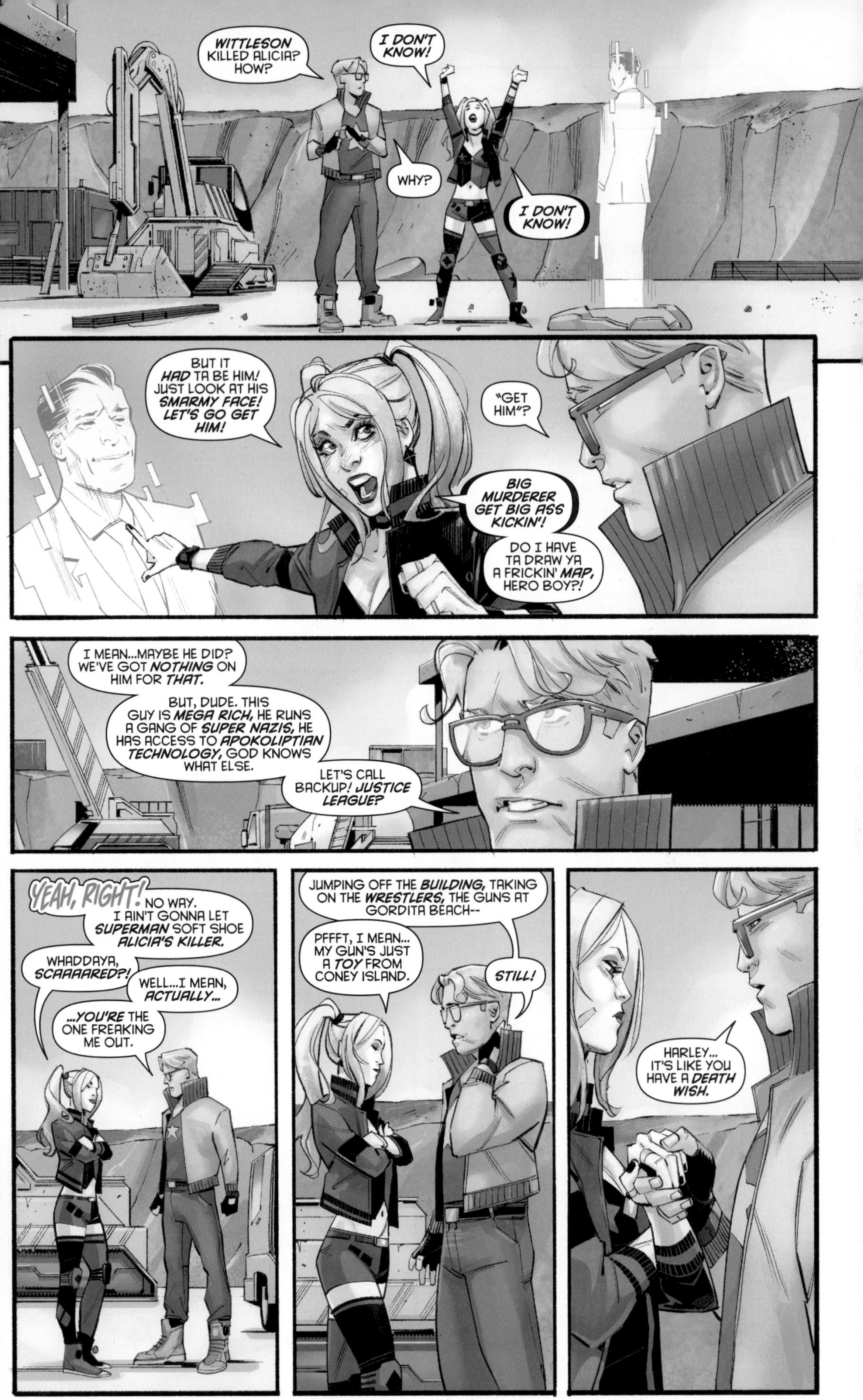
WITTLESON KILLED ALICIA? HOW?
I DON'T KNOW!
WHY?
I DON'T KNOW!
BUT IT HAD TA BE HIM! JUST LOOK AT HIS SMARMY FACE! LET'S GO GET HIM!
"GET HIM"?
BIG MURDERER GET BIG ASS KICKIN'!
DO I HAVE TA DRAW YA A FRICKIN' MAP, HERO BOY?!
I MEAN...MAYBE HE DID? WE'VE GOT NOTHING ON HIM FOR THAT.
BUT, DUDE. THIS GUY IS MEGA RICH, HE RUNS A GANG OF SUPER NAZIS, HE HAS ACCESS TO APOKOLIPTIAN TECHNOLOGY, GOD KNOWS WHAT ELSE.
LET'S CALL BACKUP! JUSTICE LEAGUE?
YEAH, RIGHT! NO WAY. I AIN'T GONNA LET SUPERMAN SOFT SHOE ALICIA'S KILLER.
WHADDAYA, SCAAAARED?!
WELL...I MEAN, ACTUALLY...
...YOU'RE THE ONE FREAKING ME OUT.
JUMPING OFF THE BUILDING, TAKING ON THE WRESTLERS, THE GUNS AT GORDITA BEACH--
PFFFT, I MEAN... MY GUN'S JUST A TOY FROM CONEY ISLAND.
STILL!
HARLEY... IT'S LIKE YOU HAVE A DEATH WISH.

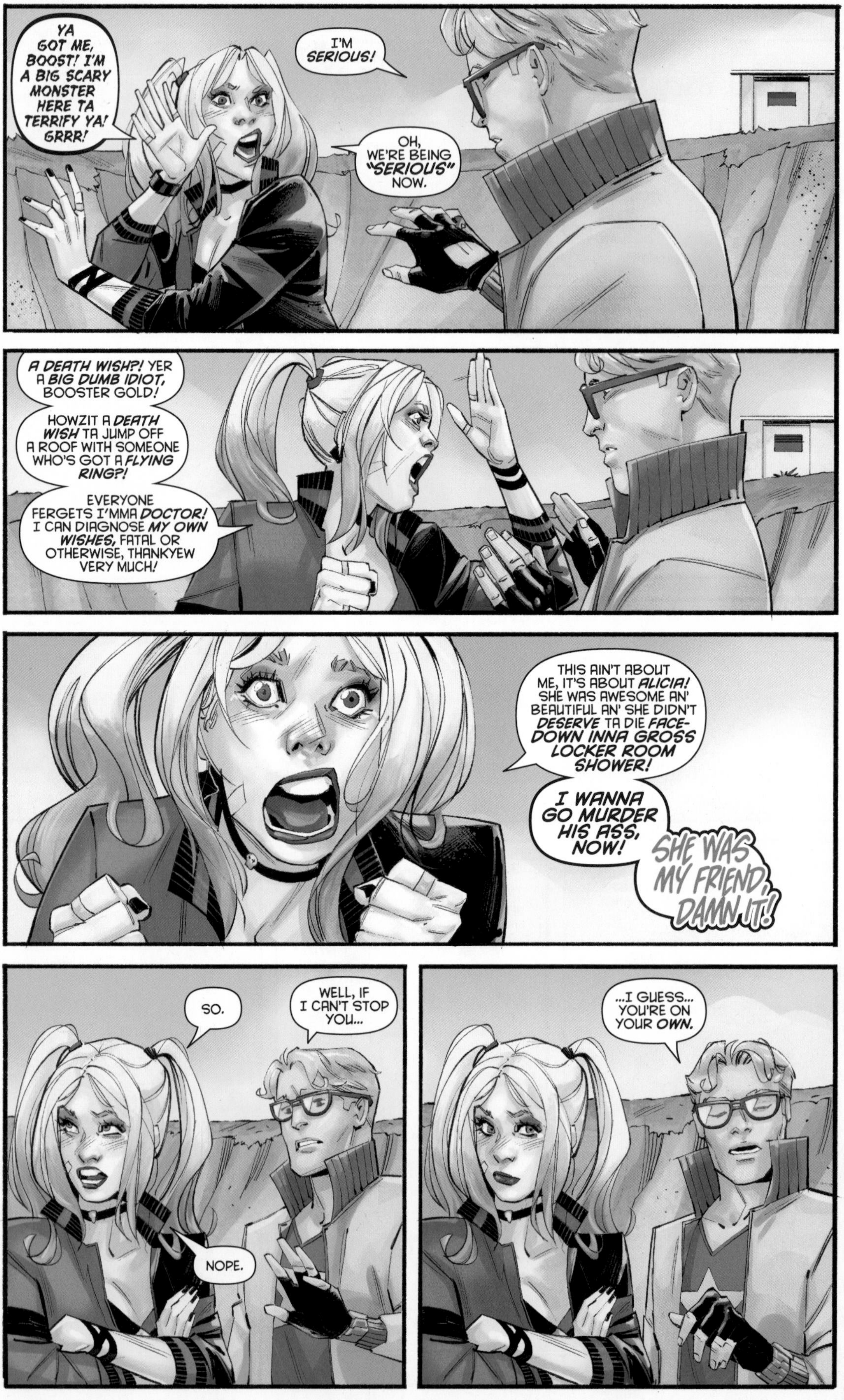

YA GOT ME, BOOST! I'M A BIG SCARY MONSTER HERE TA TERRIFY YA! GRRR!
I'M SERIOUS!
OH, WE'RE BEING "SERIOUS" NOW.
A DEATH WISH?! YER A BIG DUMB IDIOT, BOOSTER GOLD!
HOWZIT A DEATH WISH TA JUMP OFF A ROOF WITH SOMEONE WHO'S GOT A FLYING RING?!
EVERYONE FERGETS I'MMA DOCTOR! I CAN DIAGNOSE MY OWN WISHES, FATAL OR OTHERWISE, THANKYEW VERY MUCH!
THIS AIN'T ABOUT ME, IT'S ABOUT ALICIA! SHE WAS AWESOME AN' BEAUTIFUL AN' SHE DIDN'T DESERVE TA DIE FACE-DOWN INNA GROSS LOCKER ROOM SHOWER!
I WANNA GO MURDER HIS ASS, NOW!
SHE WAS MY FRIEND, DAMN IT!
SO.
WELL, IF I CAN'T STOP YOU...
NOPE.
...I GUESS... YOU'RE ON YOUR OWN.

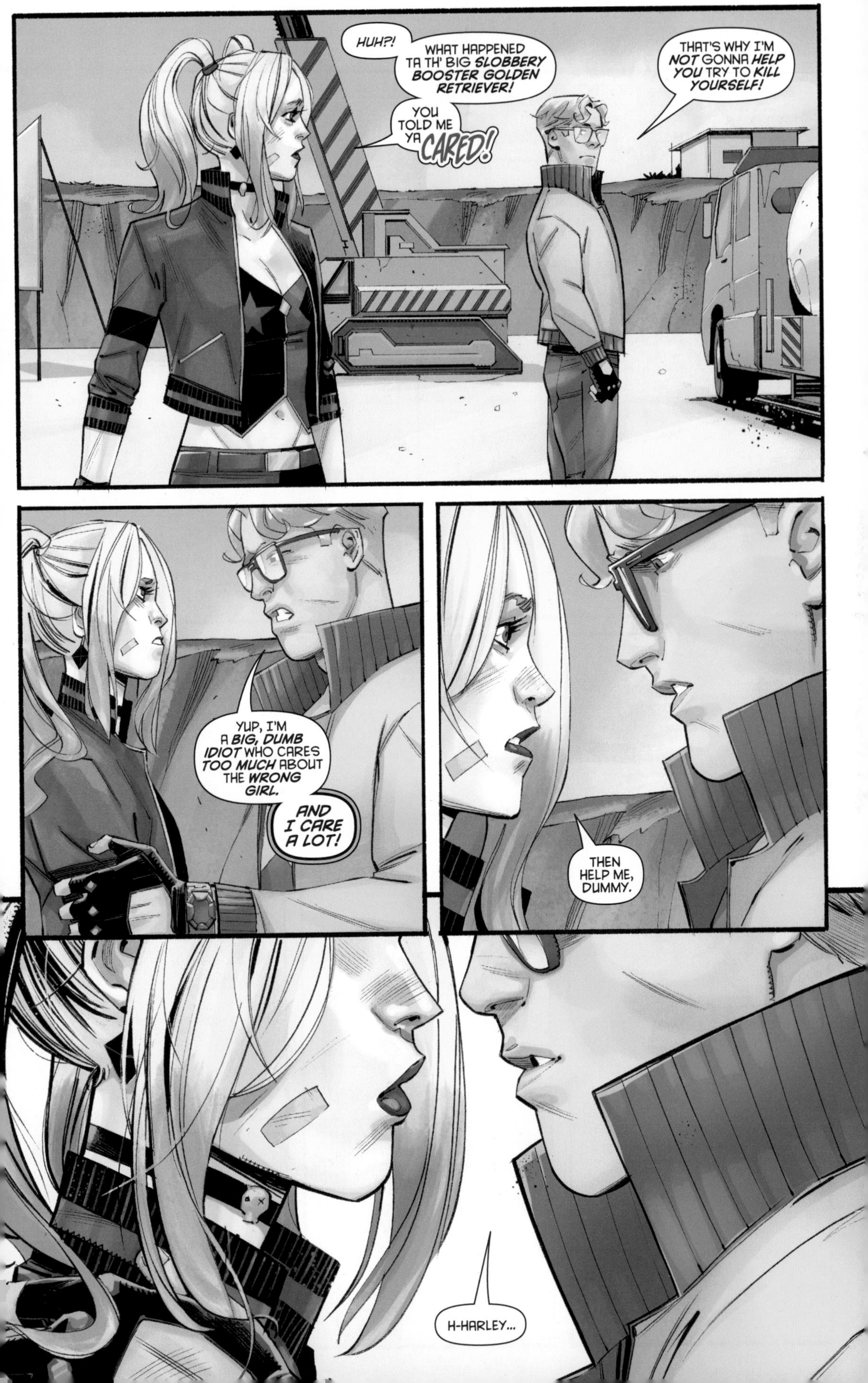
HUH?!
WHAT HAPPENED TA TH' BIG SLOBBERY BOOSTER GOLDEN RETRIEVER!
YOU TOLD ME YA CARED!
THAT'S WHY I'M NOT GONNA HELP YOU TRY TO KILL YOURSELF!
YUP, I'M A BIG, DUMB IDIOT WHO CARES TOO MUCH ABOUT THE WRONG GIRL.
AND I CARE A LOT!
THEN HELP ME, DUMMY.
H-HARLEY...

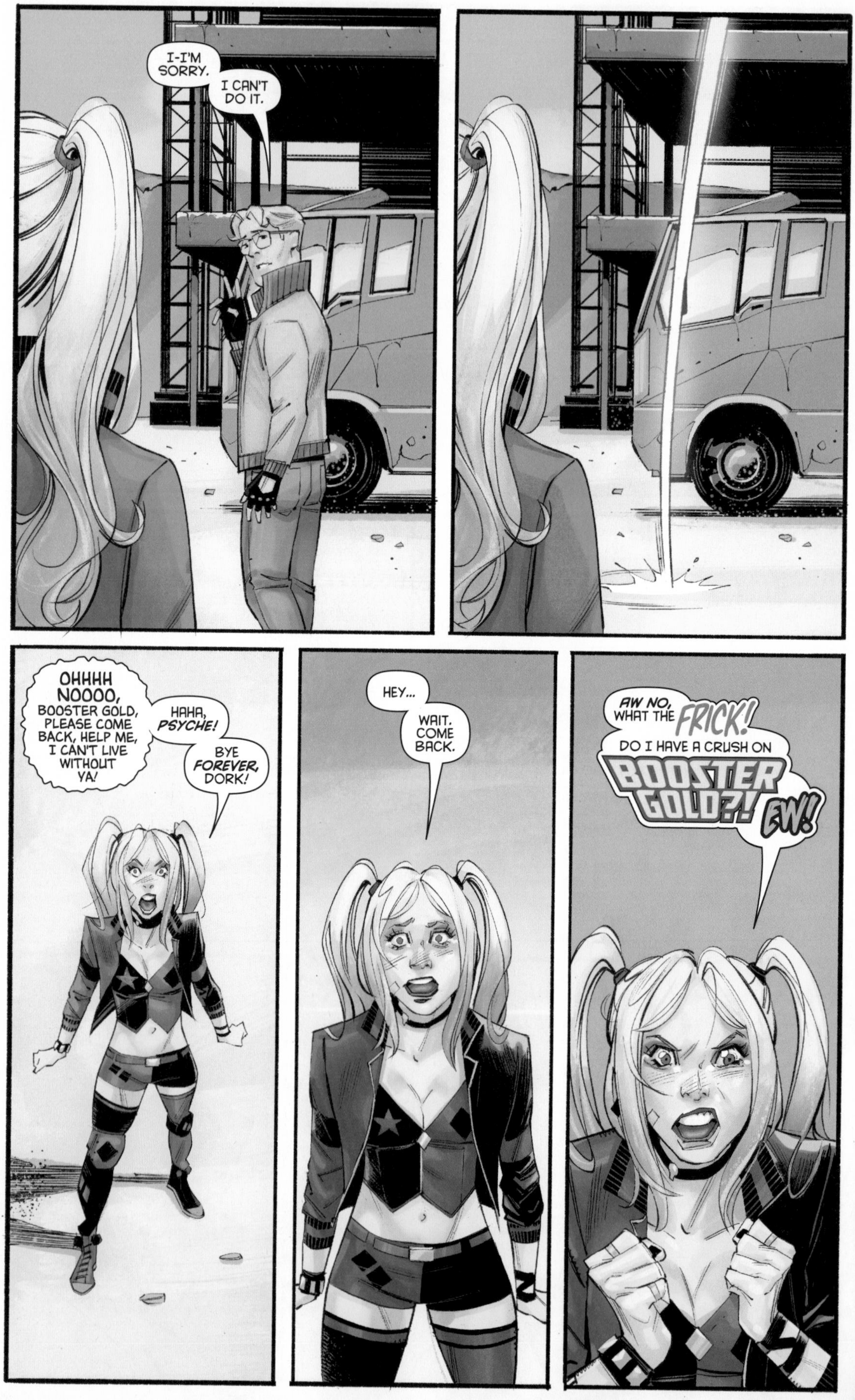
I-I'M SORRY.
I CAN'T DO IT.
OHHHH NOOOO, BOOSTER GOLD, PLEASE COME BACK, HELP ME, I CAN'T LIVE WITHOUT YA!
HAHA, *PSYCHE!*
BYE *FOREVER,* DORK!
HEY...
WAIT. COME BACK.
AW NO, WHAT THE FRICK!
DO I HAVE A CRUSH ON BOOSTER GOLD?! EW!!

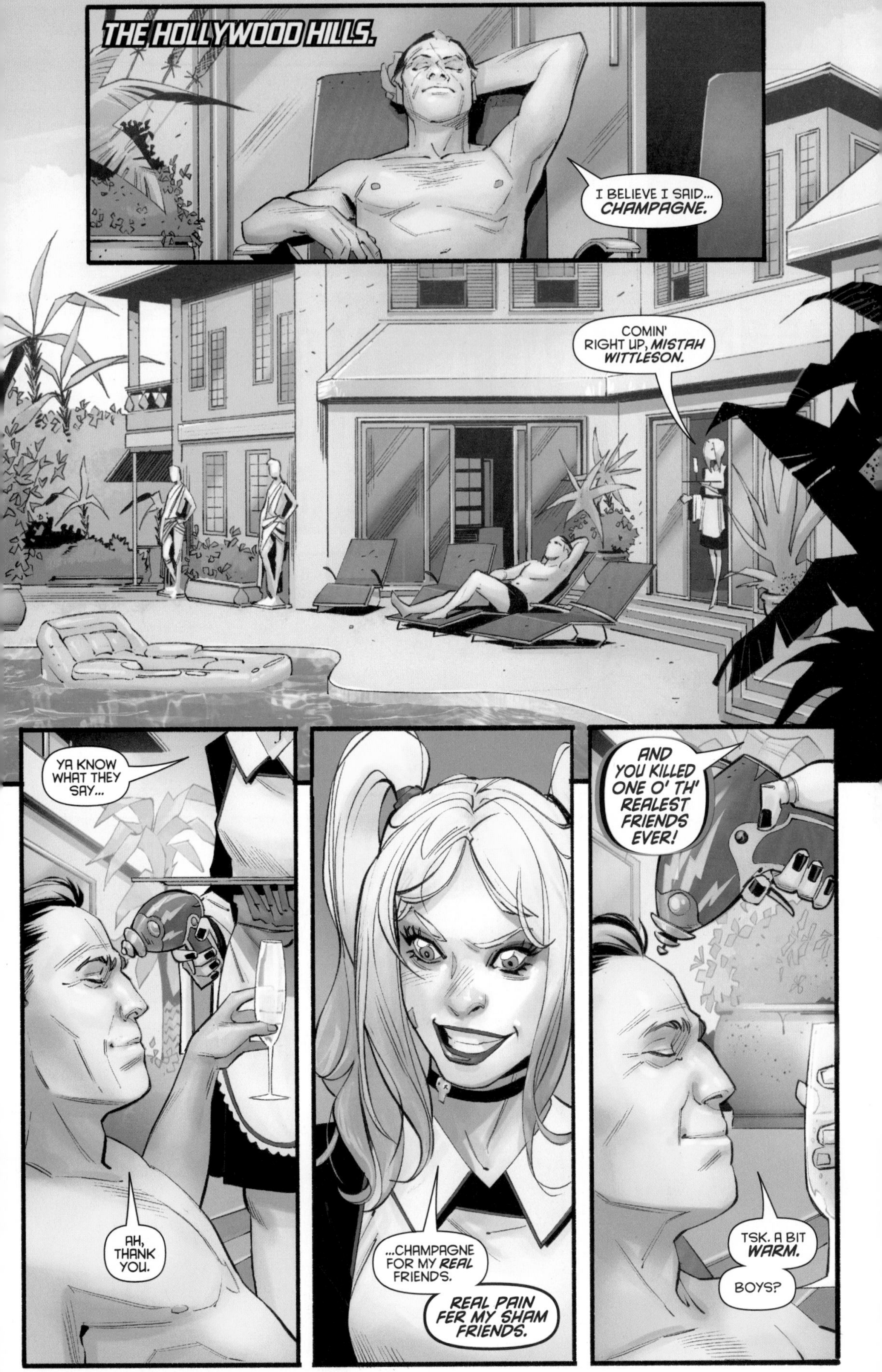
THE HOLLYWOOD HILLS.
I BELIEVE I SAID... CHAMPAGNE.
COMIN' RIGHT UP, MISTAH WITTLESON.
YA KNOW WHAT THEY SAY...
AH, THANK YOU.
...CHAMPAGNE FOR MY REAL FRIENDS.
REAL PAIN FER MY SHAM FRIENDS.
AND YOU KILLED ONE O' TH' REALEST FRIENDS EVER!
TSK. A BIT WARM.
BOYS?

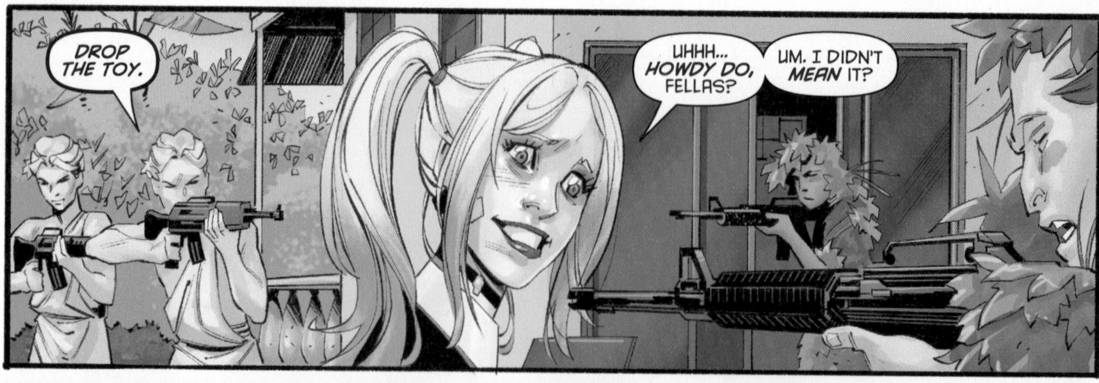

DROP THE TOY.
UHHH... HOWDY DO, FELLAS?
UM. I DIDN'T MEAN IT?

CALIFORNIA OR DEATH

CHAPTER 3 THE GOLD COAST

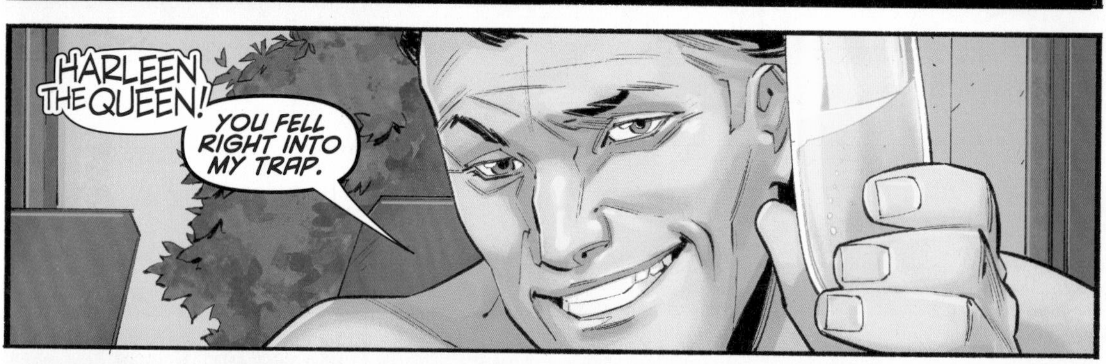

HARLEEN THE QUEEN!
YOU FELL RIGHT INTO MY TRAP.

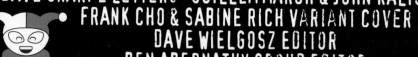

SAM HUMPHRIES WRITER ABEL ARTIST HI-FI COLORS
DAVE SHARPE LETTERS GUILLEM MARCH & JOHN KALISZ COVER
FRANK CHO & SABINE RICH VARIANT COVER
DAVE WIELGOSZ EDITOR
BEN ABERNATHY GROUP EDITOR
HARLEY QUINN CREATED BY PAUL DINI & BRUCE TIMM
BOOSTER GOLD CREATED BY DAN JURGENS

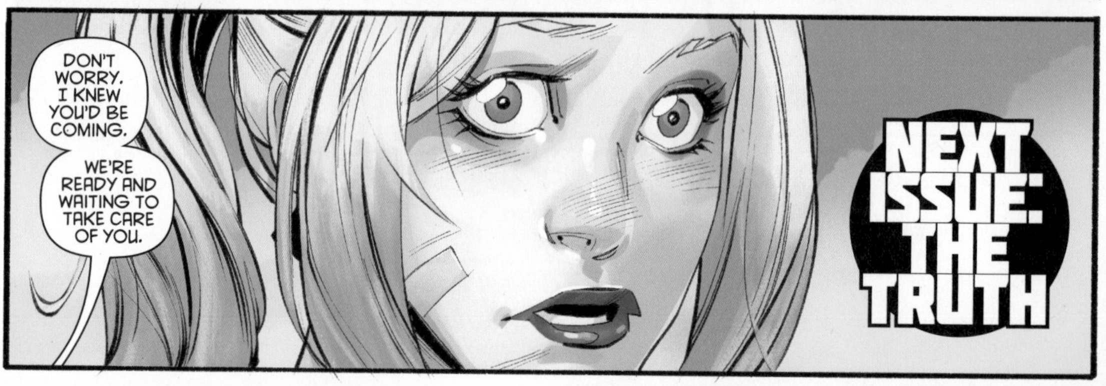

DON'T WORRY. I KNEW YOU'D BE COMING.
WE'RE READY AND WAITING TO TAKE CARE OF YOU.
NEXT ISSUE: THE TRUTH

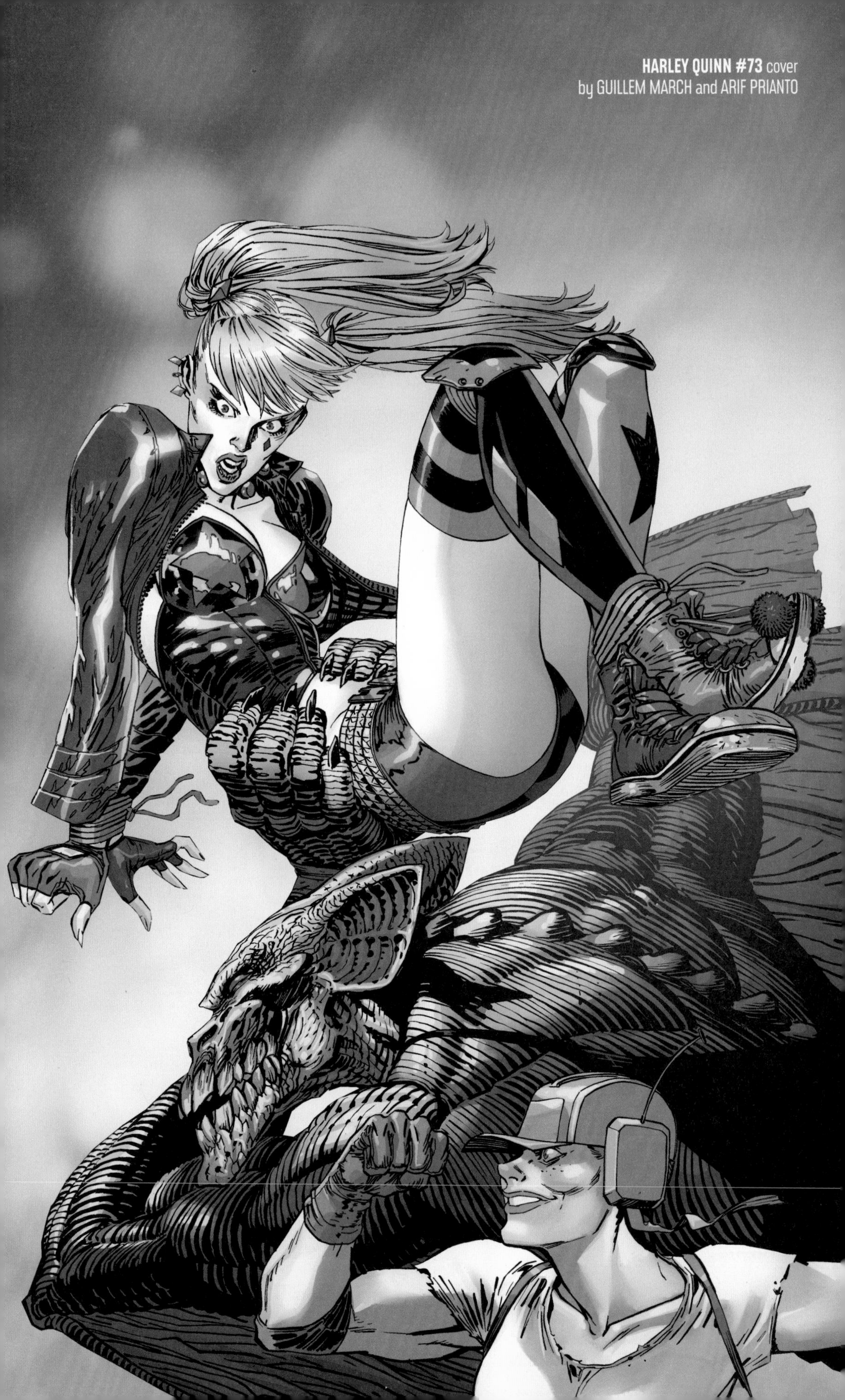

HARLEY QUINN #73 cover
by GUILLEM MARCH and ARIF PRIANTO

HARLEY QUINN #73 variant cover by FRANK CHO and SABINE RICH

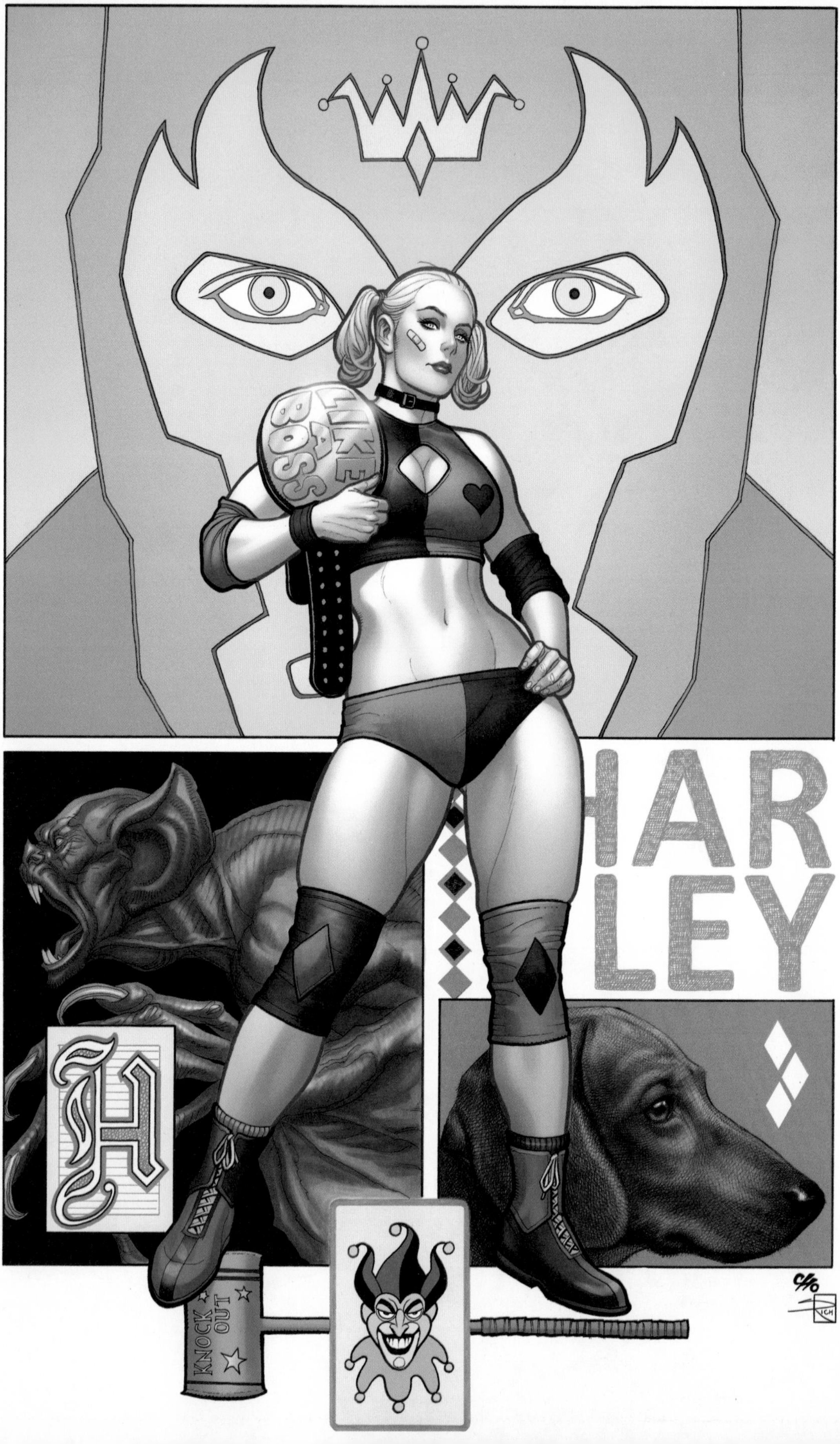
LIKE A BOSS
HAR
LEY
H
KNOCK OUT
CHO
RICH

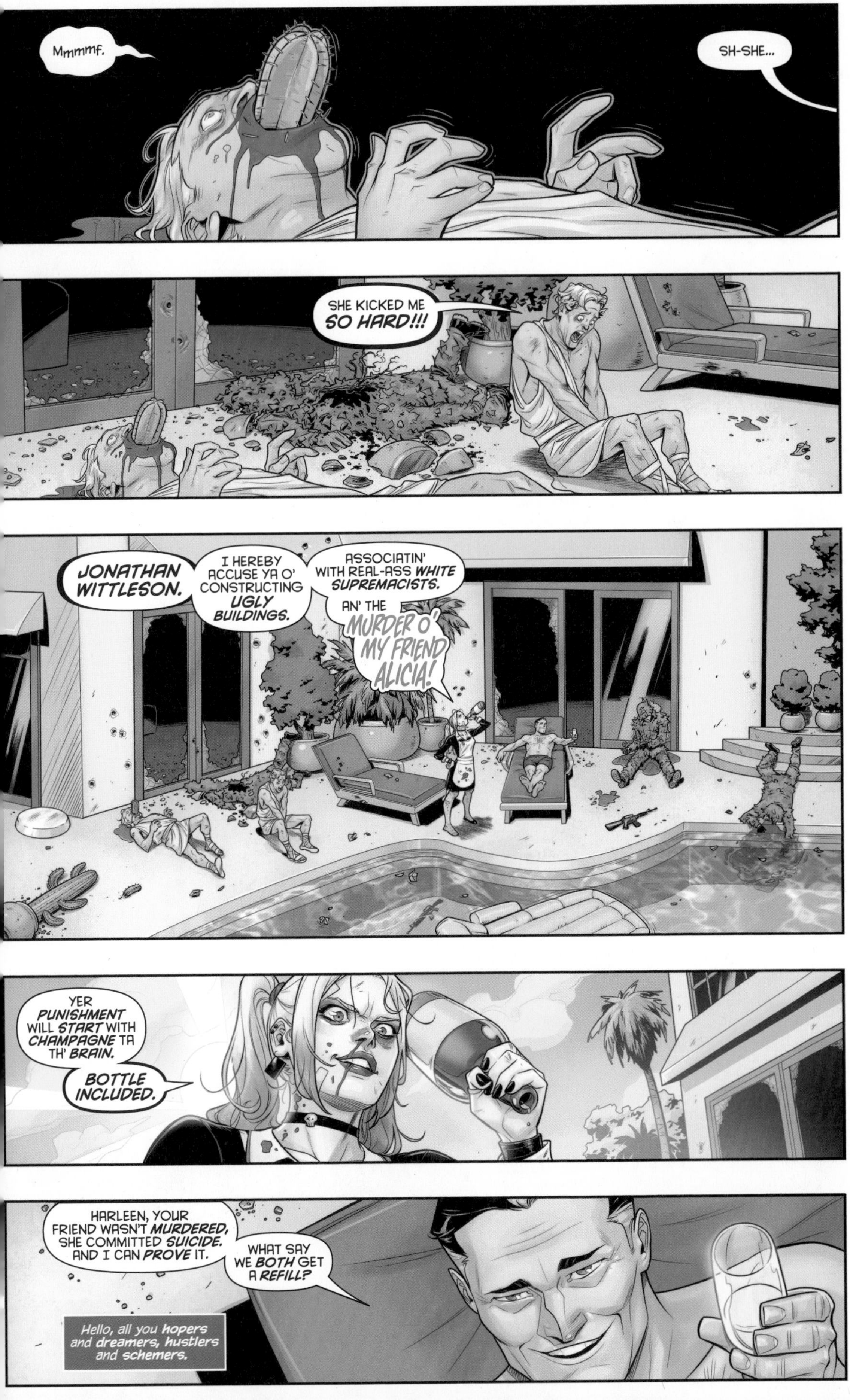
Mmmmf.
SH-SHE...
SHE KICKED ME SO HARD!!!
JONATHAN WITTLESON.
I HEREBY ACCUSE YA O' CONSTRUCTING UGLY BUILDINGS.
ASSOCIATIN' WITH REAL-ASS WHITE SUPREMACISTS.
AN' THE MURDER O' MY FRIEND ALICIA!
YER PUNISHMENT WILL START WITH CHAMPAGNE TA TH' BRAIN.
BOTTLE INCLUDED.
HARLEEN, YOUR FRIEND WASN'T MURDERED, SHE COMMITTED SUICIDE. AND I CAN PROVE IT.
WHAT SAY WE BOTH GET A REFILL?
Hello, all you hopers and dreamers, hustlers and schemers.

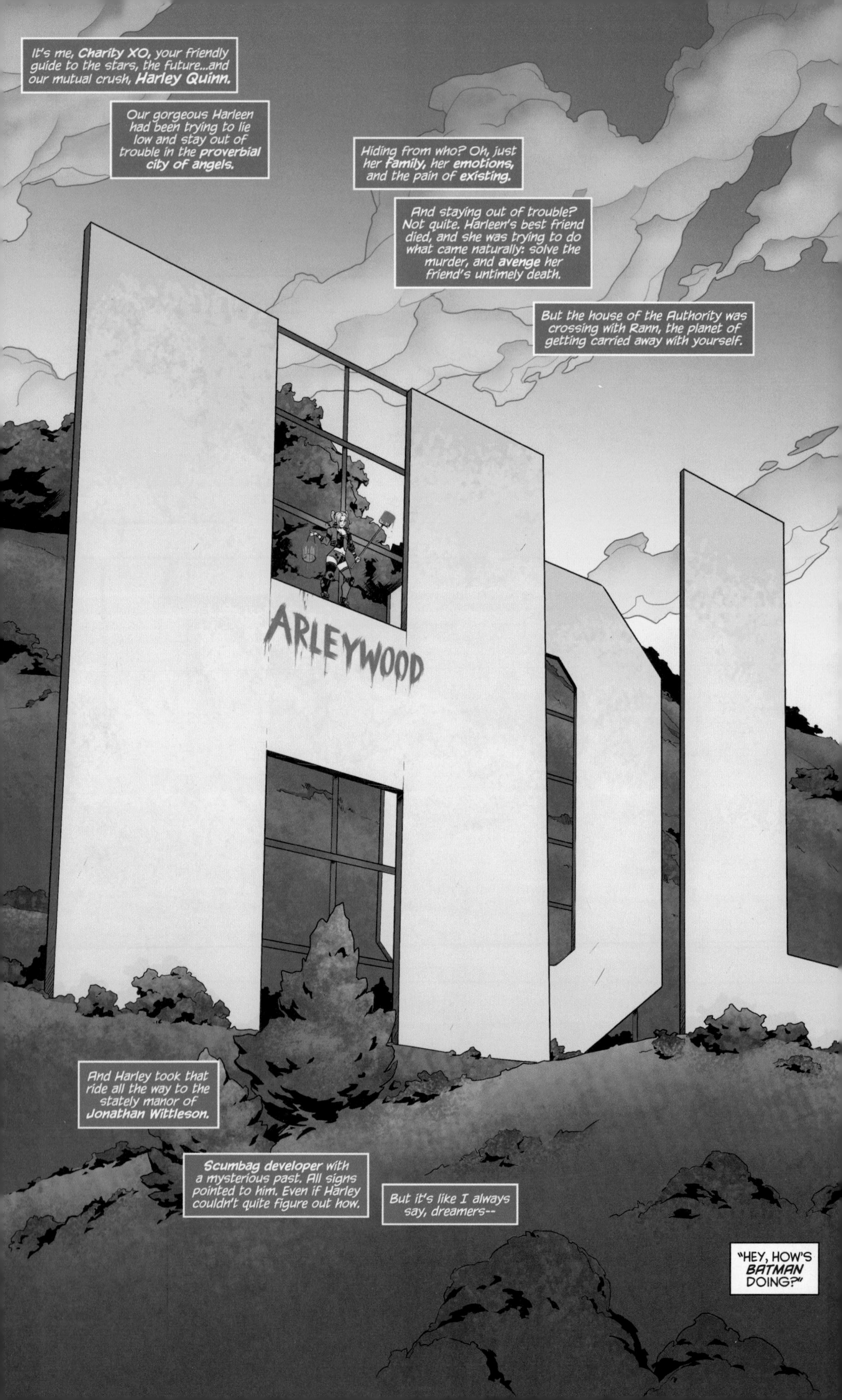
It's me, Charity XO, your friendly guide to the stars, the future...and our mutual crush, Harley Quinn.
Our gorgeous Harleen had been trying to lie low and stay out of trouble in the proverbial city of angels.
Hiding from who? Oh, just her family, her emotions, and the pain of existing.
And staying out of trouble? Not quite. Harleen's best friend died, and she was trying to do what came naturally: solve the murder, and avenge her friend's untimely death.
But the house of the Authority was crossing with Rann, the planet of getting carried away with yourself.
ARLEYWOOD
And Harley took that ride all the way to the stately manor of Jonathan Wittleson.
Scumbag developer with a mysterious past. All signs pointed to him. Even if Harley couldn't quite figure out how.
But it's like I always say, dreamers--
"HEY, HOW'S BATMAN DOING?"

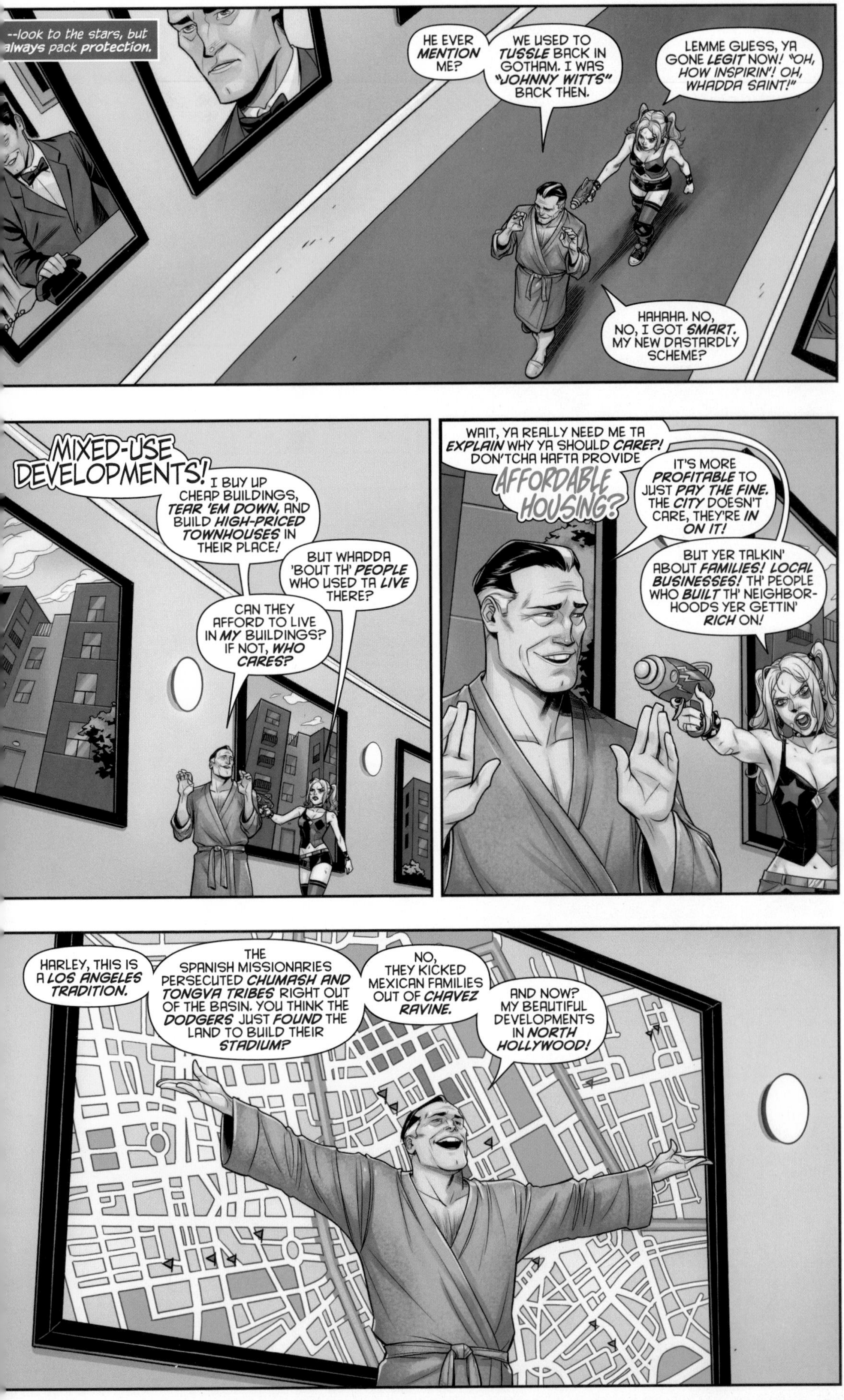
--look to the stars, but always pack protection.
HE EVER MENTION ME?
WE USED TO TUSSLE BACK IN GOTHAM. I WAS "JOHNNY WITTS" BACK THEN.
LEMME GUESS, YA GONE LEGIT NOW! "OH, HOW INSPIRIN'! OH, WHADDA SAINT!"
HAHAHA. NO, NO, I GOT SMART. MY NEW DASTARDLY SCHEME?
MIXED-USE DEVELOPMENTS!
I BUY UP CHEAP BUILDINGS, TEAR 'EM DOWN, AND BUILD HIGH-PRICED TOWNHOUSES IN THEIR PLACE!
BUT WHADDA 'BOUT TH' PEOPLE WHO USED TA LIVE THERE?
CAN THEY AFFORD TO LIVE IN MY BUILDINGS? IF NOT, WHO CARES?
WAIT, YA REALLY NEED ME TA EXPLAIN WHY YA SHOULD CARE?! DON'TCHA HAFTA PROVIDE AFFORDABLE HOUSING?
IT'S MORE PROFITABLE TO JUST PAY THE FINE. THE CITY DOESN'T CARE, THEY'RE IN ON IT!
BUT YER TALKIN' ABOUT FAMILIES! LOCAL BUSINESSES! TH' PEOPLE WHO BUILT TH' NEIGHBOR-HOODS YER GETTIN' RICH ON!
HARLEY, THIS IS A LOS ANGELES TRADITION.
THE SPANISH MISSIONARIES PERSECUTED CHUMASH AND TONGVA TRIBES RIGHT OUT OF THE BASIN. YOU THINK THE DODGERS JUST FOUND THE LAND TO BUILD THEIR STADIUM?
NO, THEY KICKED MEXICAN FAMILIES OUT OF CHAVEZ RAVINE.
AND NOW? MY BEAUTIFUL DEVELOPMENTS IN NORTH HOLLYWOOD!

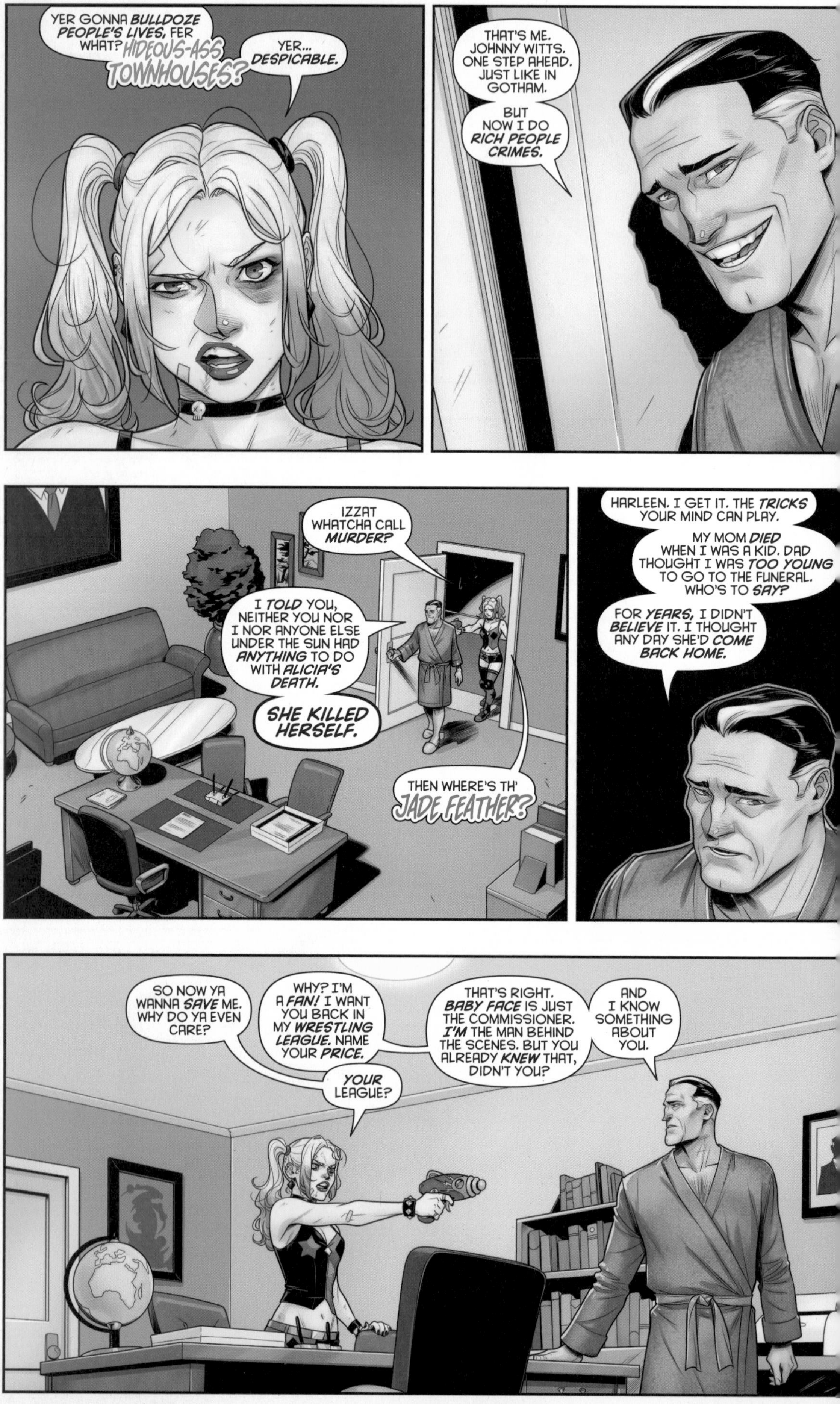

YER GONNA BULLDOZE PEOPLE'S LIVES, FER WHAT? HIDEOUS-ASS TOWNHOUSES?
YER... DESPICABLE.
THAT'S ME. JOHNNY WITTS. ONE STEP AHEAD. JUST LIKE IN GOTHAM.
BUT NOW I DO RICH PEOPLE CRIMES.
IZZAT WHATCHA CALL MURDER?
I TOLD YOU, NEITHER YOU NOR I NOR ANYONE ELSE UNDER THE SUN HAD ANYTHING TO DO WITH ALICIA'S DEATH.
SHE KILLED HERSELF.
THEN WHERE'S TH' JADE FEATHER?
HARLEEN. I GET IT. THE TRICKS YOUR MIND CAN PLAY.
MY MOM DIED WHEN I WAS A KID. DAD THOUGHT I WAS TOO YOUNG TO GO TO THE FUNERAL. WHO'S TO SAY?
FOR YEARS, I DIDN'T BELIEVE IT. I THOUGHT ANY DAY SHE'D COME BACK HOME.
SO NOW YA WANNA SAVE ME. WHY DO YA EVEN CARE?
WHY? I'M A FAN! I WANT YOU BACK IN MY WRESTLING LEAGUE. NAME YOUR PRICE.
YOUR LEAGUE?
THAT'S RIGHT. BABY FACE IS JUST THE COMMISSIONER. I'M THE MAN BEHIND THE SCENES. BUT YOU ALREADY KNEW THAT, DIDN'T YOU?
AND I KNOW SOMETHING ABOUT YOU.

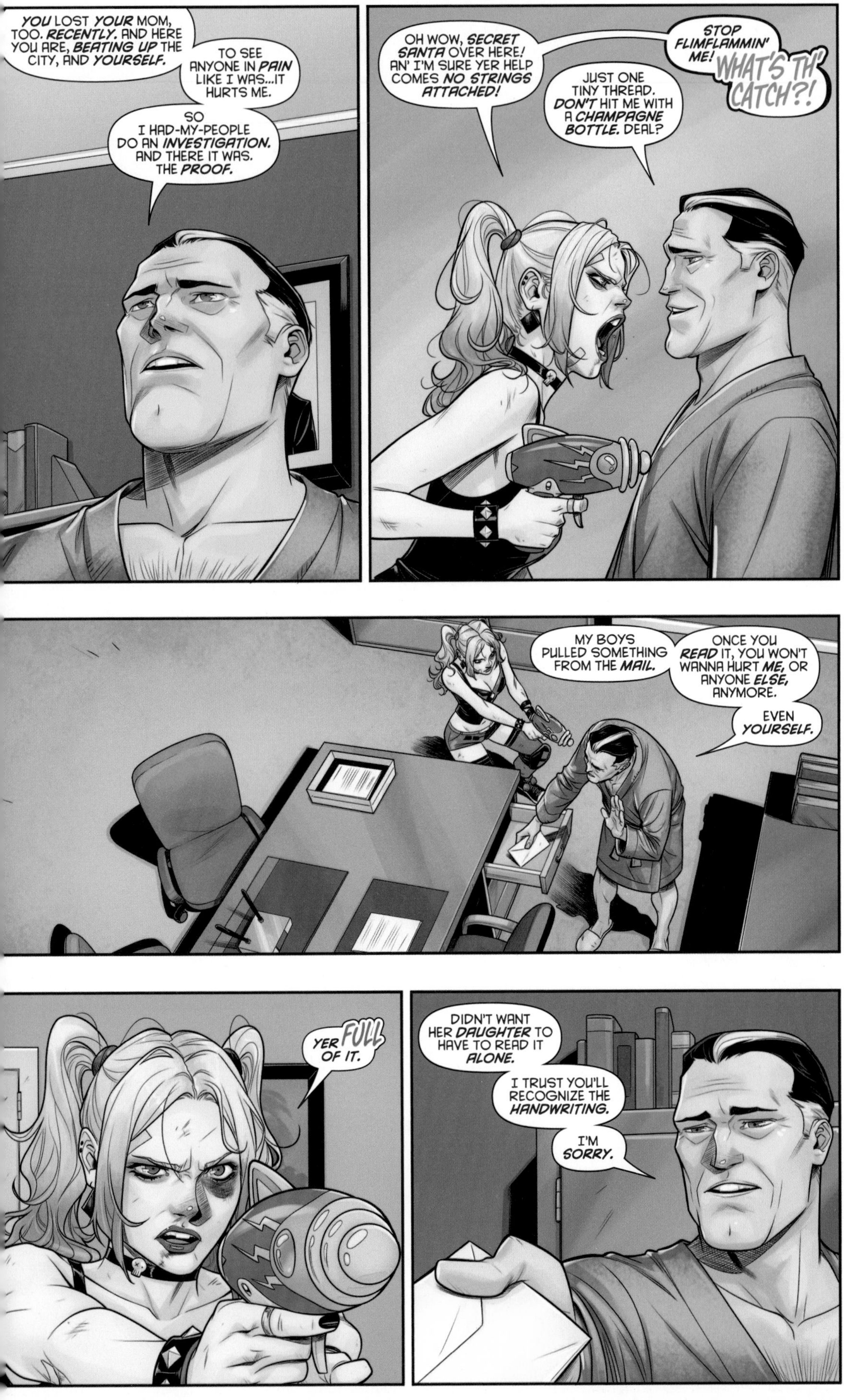
YOU LOST YOUR MOM, TOO. RECENTLY. AND HERE YOU ARE, BEATING UP THE CITY, AND YOURSELF.
TO SEE ANYONE IN PAIN LIKE I WAS...IT HURTS ME.
SO I HAD-MY-PEOPLE DO AN INVESTIGATION. AND THERE IT WAS. THE PROOF.
OH WOW, SECRET SANTA OVER HERE! AN' I'M SURE YER HELP COMES NO STRINGS ATTACHED!
STOP FLIMFLAMMIN' ME! WHAT'S TH' CATCH?!
JUST ONE TINY THREAD. DON'T HIT ME WITH A CHAMPAGNE BOTTLE. DEAL?
MY BOYS PULLED SOMETHING FROM THE MAIL.
ONCE YOU READ IT, YOU WON'T WANNA HURT ME, OR ANYONE ELSE, ANYMORE.
EVEN YOURSELF.
YER FULL OF IT.
DIDN'T WANT HER DAUGHTER TO HAVE TO READ IT ALONE.
I TRUST YOU'LL RECOGNIZE THE HANDWRITING.
I'M SORRY.

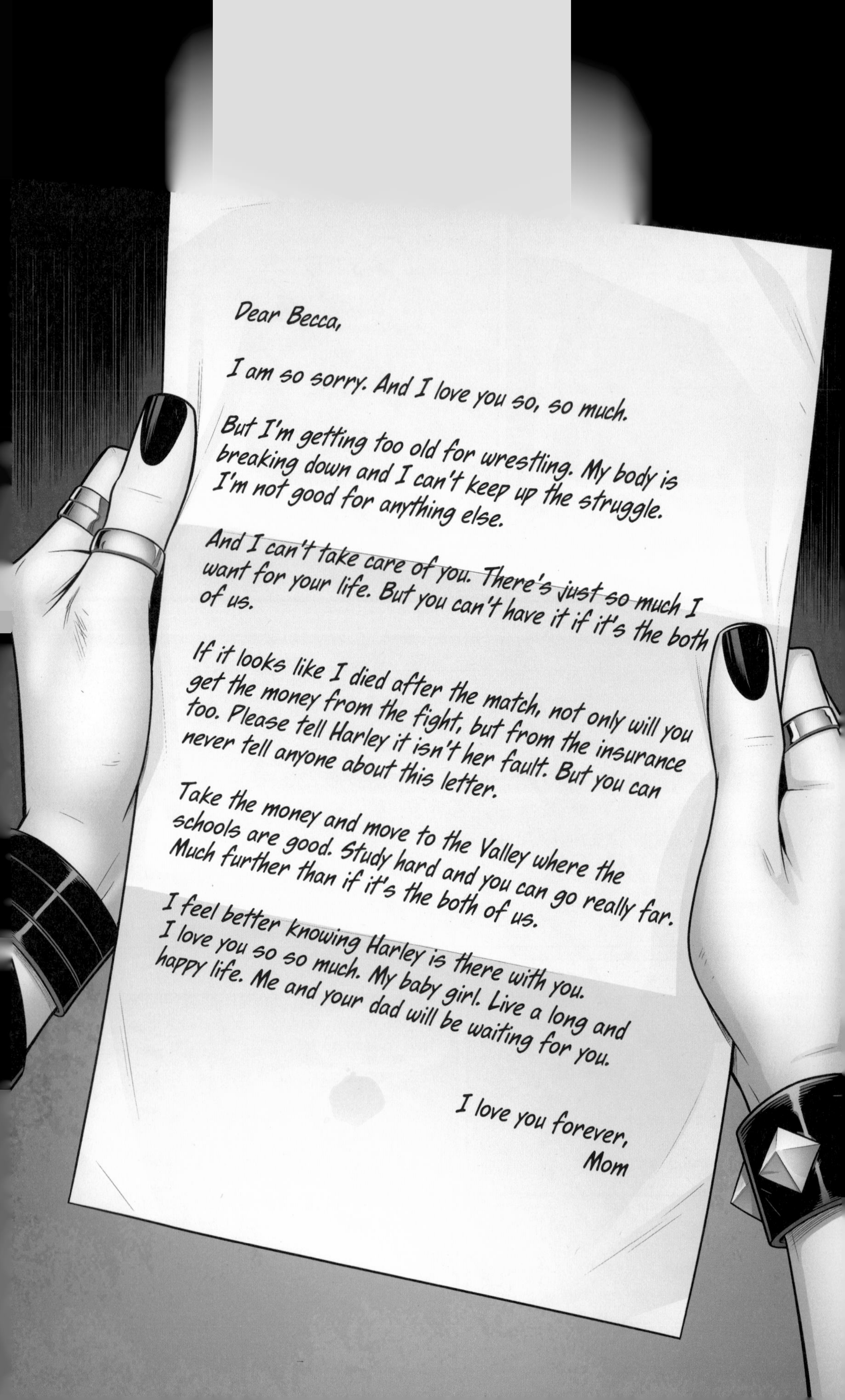
Dear Becca,
I am so sorry. And I love you so, so much.
But I'm getting too old for wrestling. My body is breaking down and I can't keep up the struggle. I'm not good for anything else.
And I can't take care of you. There's just so much I want for your life. But you can't have it if it's the both of us.
If it looks like I died after the match, not only will you get the money from the fight, but from the insurance too. Please tell Harley it isn't her fault. But you can never tell anyone about this letter.
Take the money and move to the Valley where the schools are good. Study hard and you can go really far. Much further than if it's the both of us.
I feel better knowing Harley is there with you. I love you so so much. My baby girl. Live a long and happy life. Me and your dad will be waiting for you.
I love you forever,
Mom

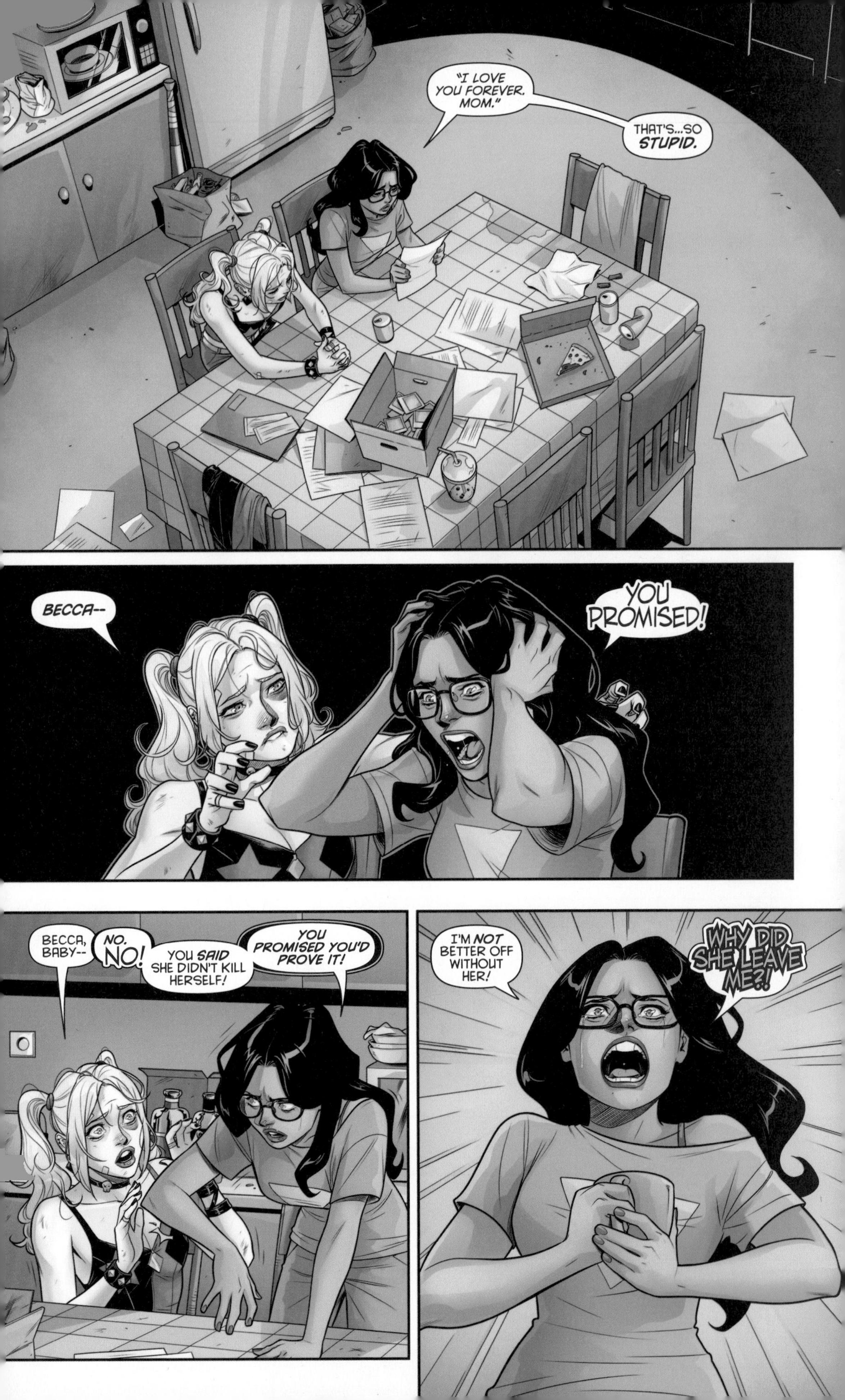
"I LOVE YOU FOREVER. MOM."
THAT'S...SO STUPID.
BECCA--
YOU PROMISED!
BECCA, BABY--
NO. NO!
YOU SAID SHE DIDN'T KILL HERSELF!
YOU PROMISED YOU'D PROVE IT!
I'M NOT BETTER OFF WITHOUT HER!
WHY DID SHE LEAVE ME?!

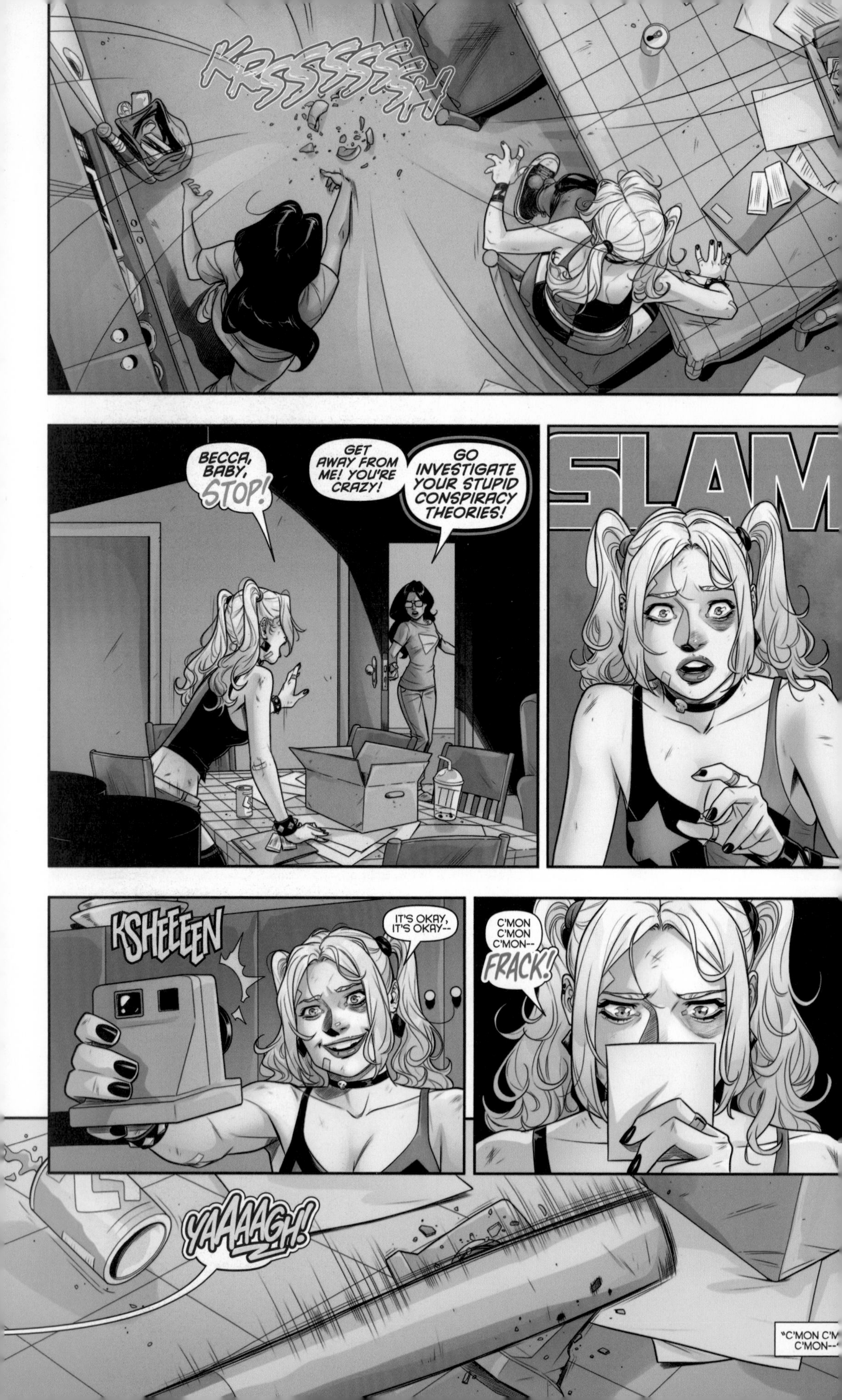
KRSSSSSSH
BECCA, BABY, STOP!
GET AWAY FROM ME! YOU'RE CRAZY!
GO INVESTIGATE YOUR STUPID CONSPIRACY THEORIES!
SLAM
KSHEEEEN
IT'S OKAY, IT'S OKAY--
C'MON C'MON C'MON--
FRACK!
YAAAAGH!
"C'MON C'M
C'MON--

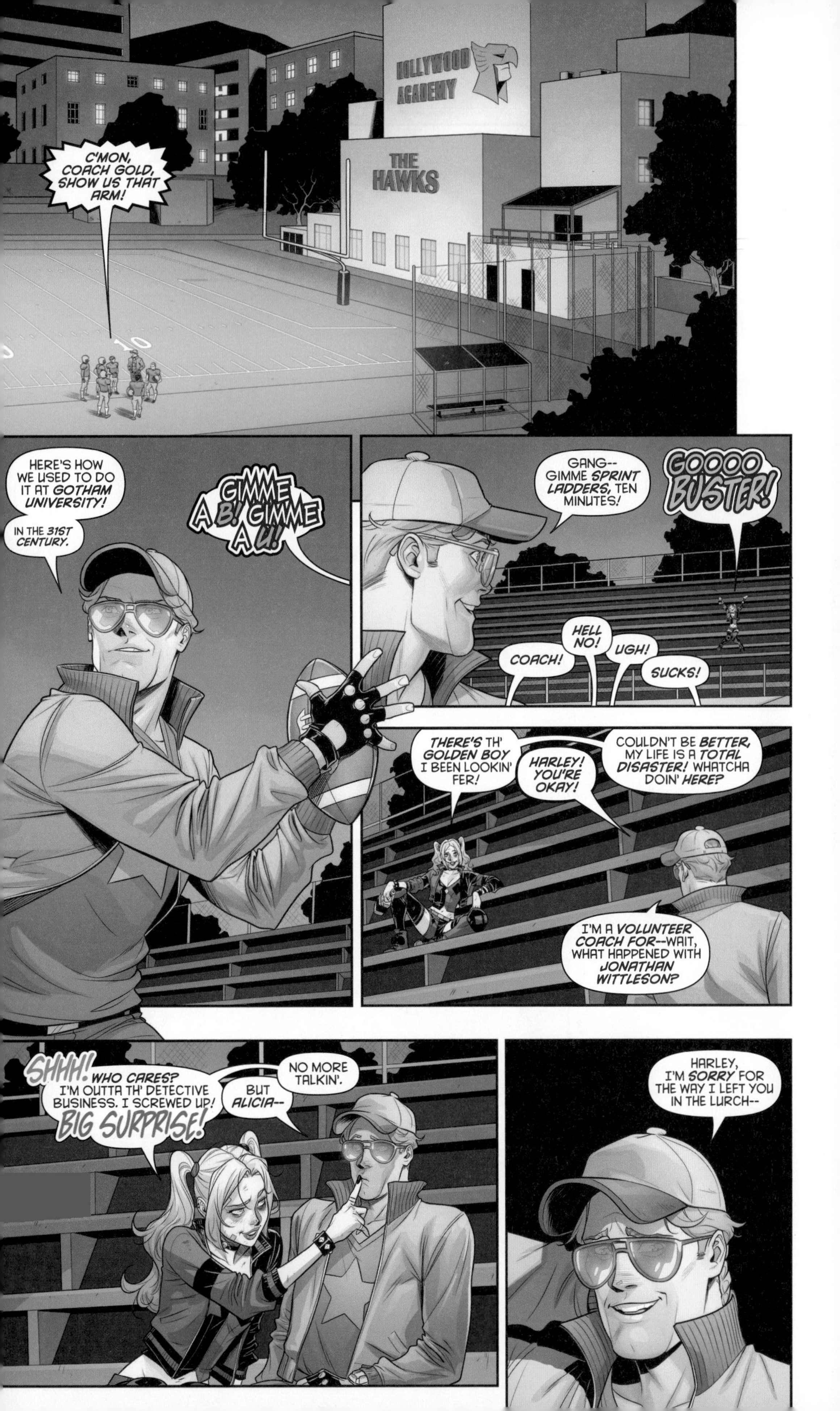
HOLLYWOOD ACADEMY
THE HAWKS
C'MON, COACH GOLD, SHOW US THAT ARM!
10
HERE'S HOW WE USED TO DO IT AT GOTHAM UNIVERSITY!
IN THE 31ST CENTURY.
GIMME A B! GIMME A U!
GANG-- GIMME SPRINT LADDERS, TEN MINUTES!
GOOOO BUSTER!
COACH!
HELL NO!
UGH!
SUCKS!
THERE'S TH' GOLDEN BOY I BEEN LOOKIN' FER!
HARLEY! YOU'RE OKAY!
COULDN'T BE BETTER, MY LIFE IS A TOTAL DISASTER! WHATCHA DOIN' HERE?
I'M A VOLUNTEER COACH FOR--WAIT, WHAT HAPPENED WITH JONATHAN WITTLESON?
SHHH! WHO CARES? I'M OUTTA TH' DETECTIVE BUSINESS. I SCREWED UP! BIG SURPRISE!
BUT ALICIA--
NO MORE TALKIN'.
HARLEY, I'M SORRY FOR THE WAY I LEFT YOU IN THE LURCH--

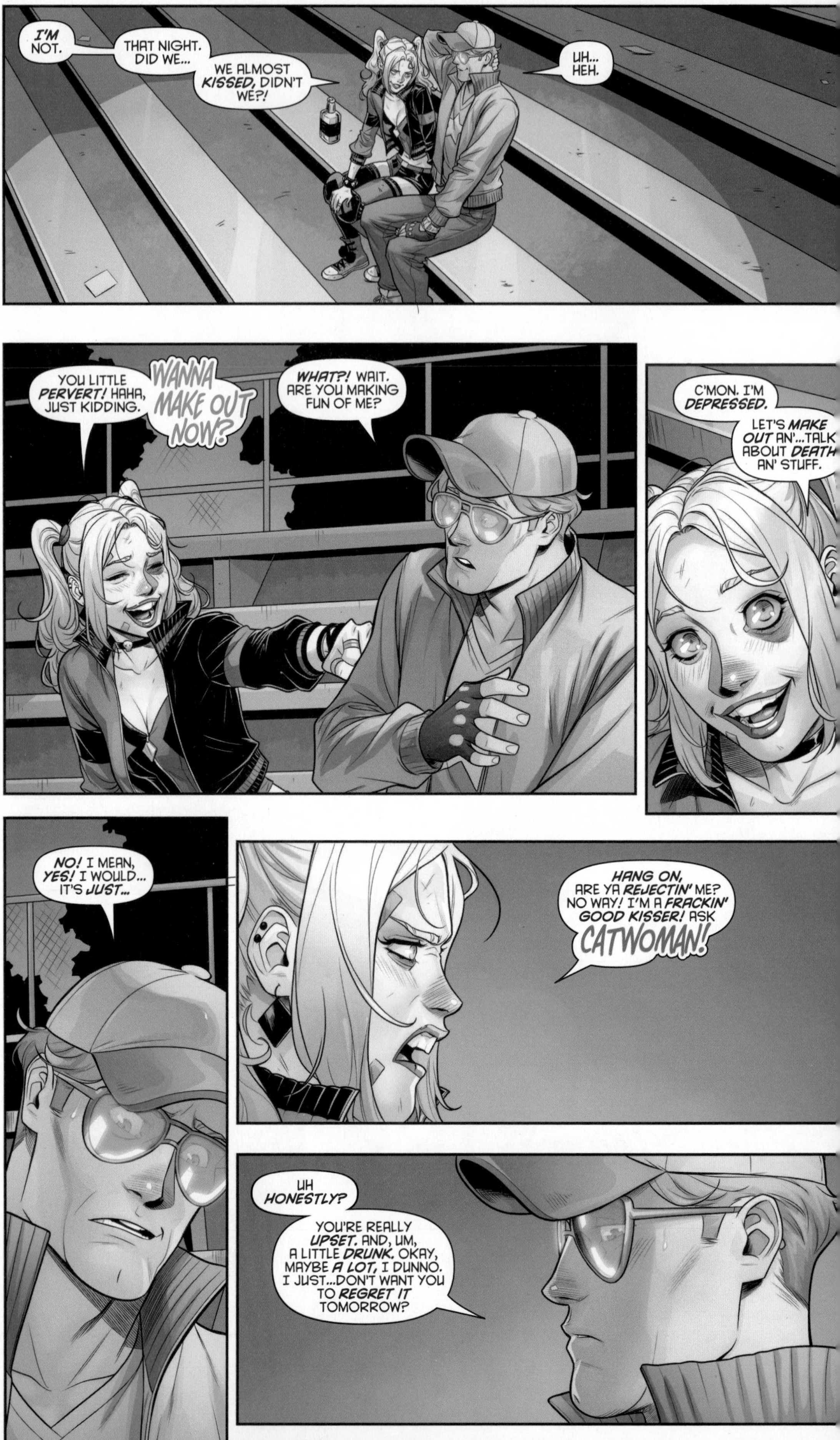
I'M NOT.
THAT NIGHT. DID WE...
WE ALMOST KISSED, DIDN'T WE?!
UH... HEH.
YOU LITTLE PERVERT! HAHA, JUST KIDDING.
WANNA MAKE OUT NOW?
WHAT?! WAIT. ARE YOU MAKING FUN OF ME?
C'MON. I'M DEPRESSED.
LET'S MAKE OUT AN'...TALK ABOUT DEATH AN' STUFF.
NO! I MEAN, YES! I WOULD... IT'S JUST...
HANG ON, ARE YA REJECTIN' ME? NO WAY! I'M A FRACKIN' GOOD KISSER! ASK CATWOMAN!
UH HONESTLY?
YOU'RE REALLY UPSET. AND, UM, A LITTLE DRUNK. OKAY, MAYBE A LOT, I DUNNO. I JUST...DON'T WANT YOU TO REGRET IT TOMORROW?

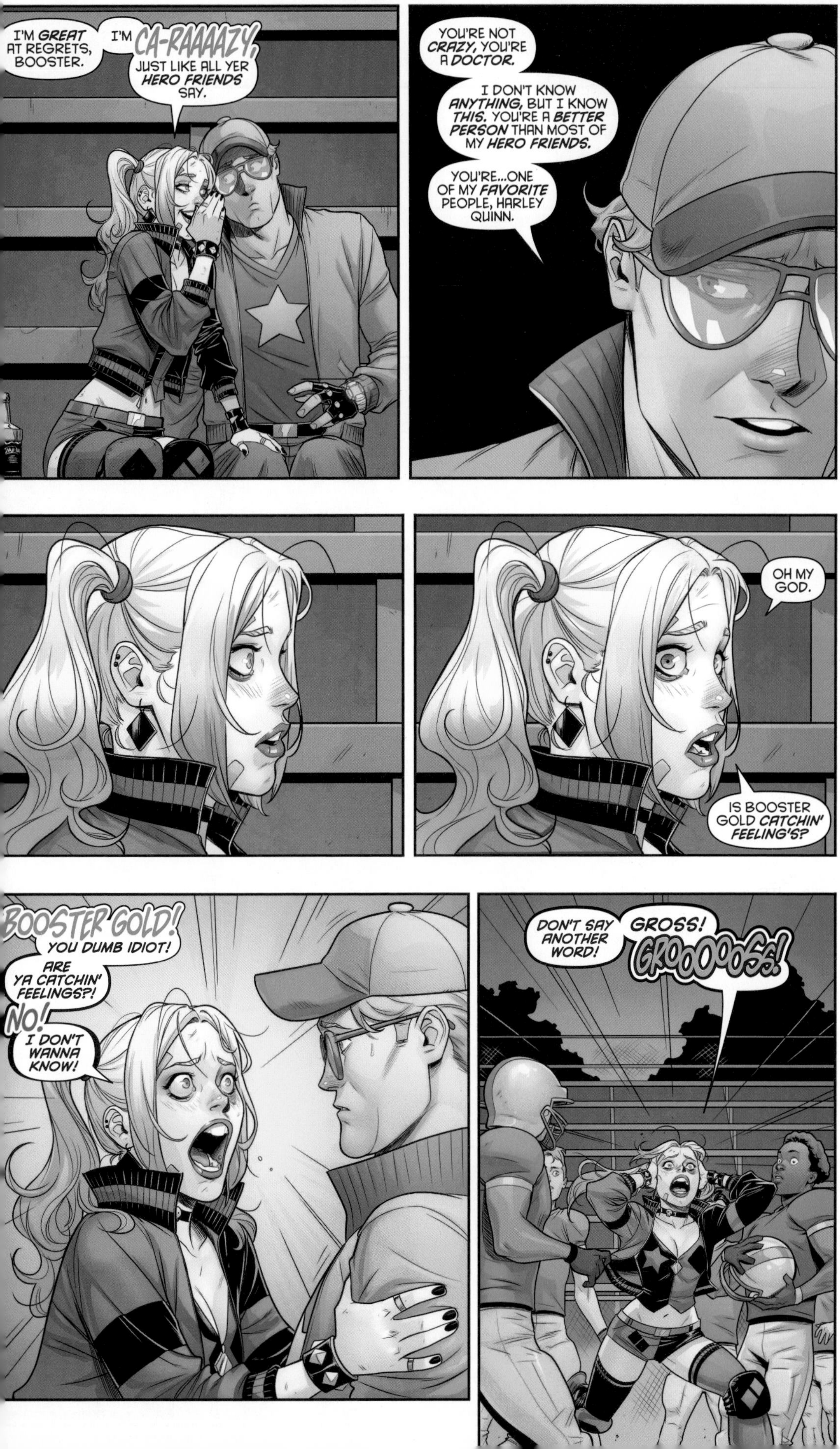
I'M GREAT AT REGRETS, BOOSTER.
I'M CA-RAAAAZY, JUST LIKE ALL YER HERO FRIENDS SAY.
YOU'RE NOT CRAZY, YOU'RE A DOCTOR.
I DON'T KNOW ANYTHING, BUT I KNOW THIS. YOU'RE A BETTER PERSON THAN MOST OF MY HERO FRIENDS.
YOU'RE...ONE OF MY FAVORITE PEOPLE, HARLEY QUINN.
OH MY GOD.
IS BOOSTER GOLD CATCHIN' FEELING'S?
BOOSTER GOLD! YOU DUMB IDIOT!
ARE YA CATCHIN' FEELINGS?!
NO! I DON'T WANNA KNOW!
DON'T SAY ANOTHER WORD!
GROSS! GROOOOOSS!

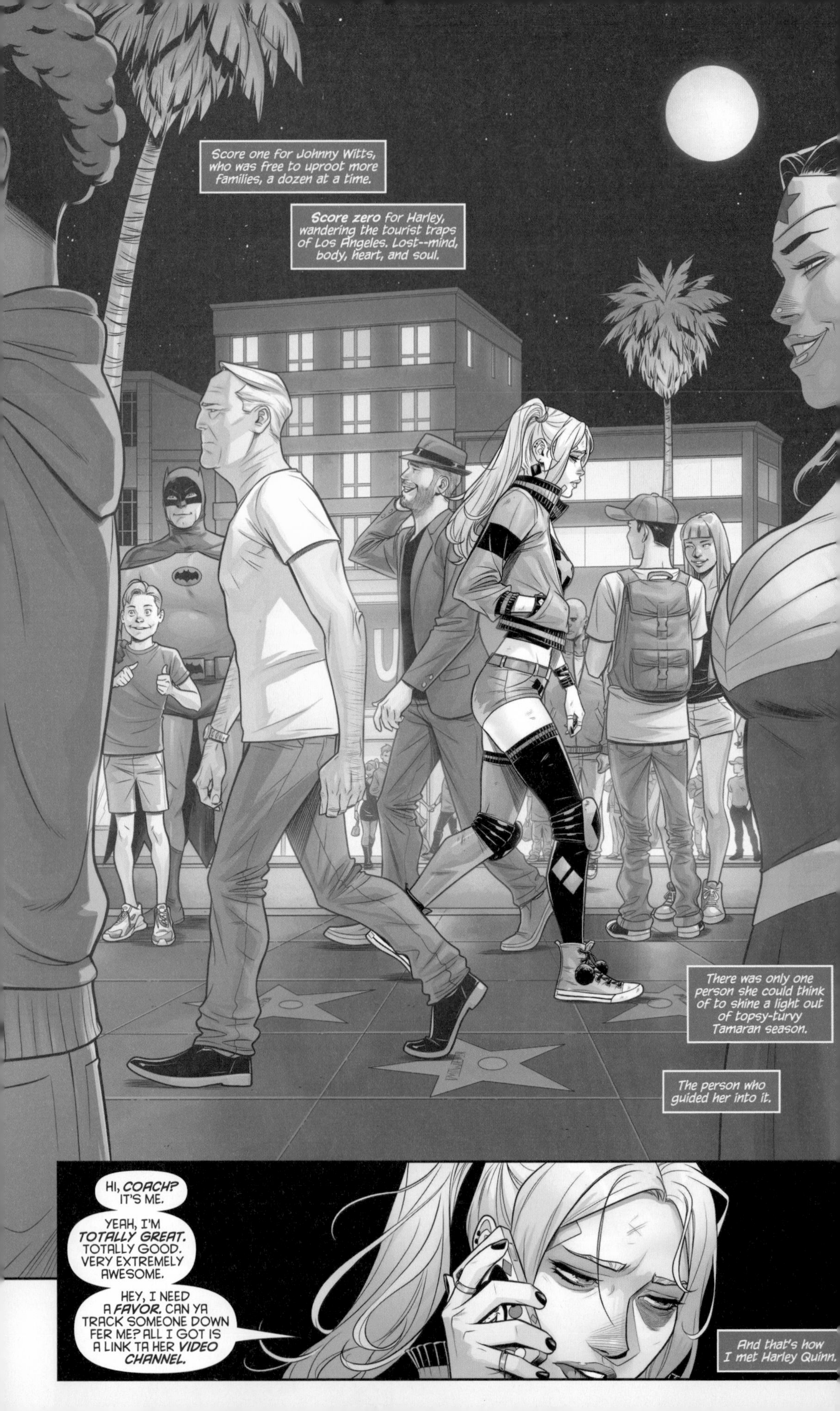

Score one for Johnny Witts, who was free to uproot more families, a dozen at a time.
Score zero for Harley, wandering the tourist traps of Los Angeles. Lost--mind, body, heart, and soul.
There was only one person she could think of to shine a light out of topsy-turvy Tamaran season.
The person who guided her into it.
HI, COACH? IT'S ME.
YEAH, I'M TOTALLY GREAT. TOTALLY GOOD. VERY EXTREMELY AWESOME.
HEY, I NEED A FAVOR. CAN YA TRACK SOMEONE DOWN FER ME? ALL I GOT IS A LINK TA HER VIDEO CHANNEL.
And that's how I met Harley Quinn.

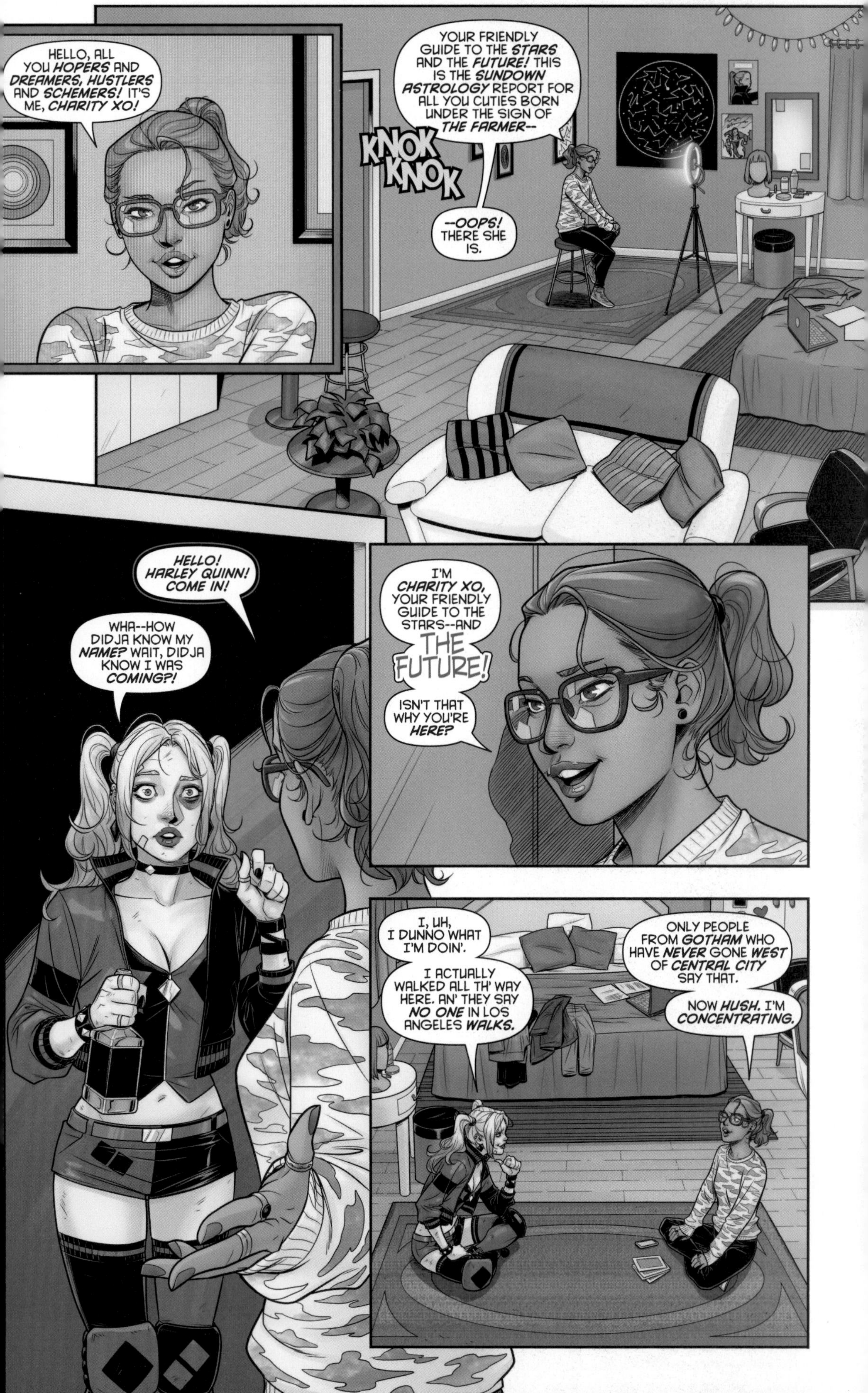

HELLO, ALL YOU HOPERS AND DREAMERS, HUSTLERS AND SCHEMERS! IT'S ME, CHARITY XO!
YOUR FRIENDLY GUIDE TO THE STARS AND THE FUTURE! THIS IS THE SUNDOWN ASTROLOGY REPORT FOR ALL YOU CUTIES BORN UNDER THE SIGN OF THE FARMER--
KNOK KNOK
--OOPS! THERE SHE IS.
HELLO! HARLEY QUINN! COME IN!
WHA--HOW DIDJA KNOW MY NAME? WAIT, DIDJA KNOW I WAS COMING?!
I'M CHARITY XO, YOUR FRIENDLY GUIDE TO THE STARS--AND THE FUTURE!
ISN'T THAT WHY YOU'RE HERE?
I, UH, I DUNNO WHAT I'M DOIN'.
I ACTUALLY WALKED ALL TH' WAY HERE. AN' THEY SAY NO ONE IN LOS ANGELES WALKS.
ONLY PEOPLE FROM GOTHAM WHO HAVE NEVER GONE WEST OF CENTRAL CITY SAY THAT.
NOW HUSH. I'M CONCENTRATING.

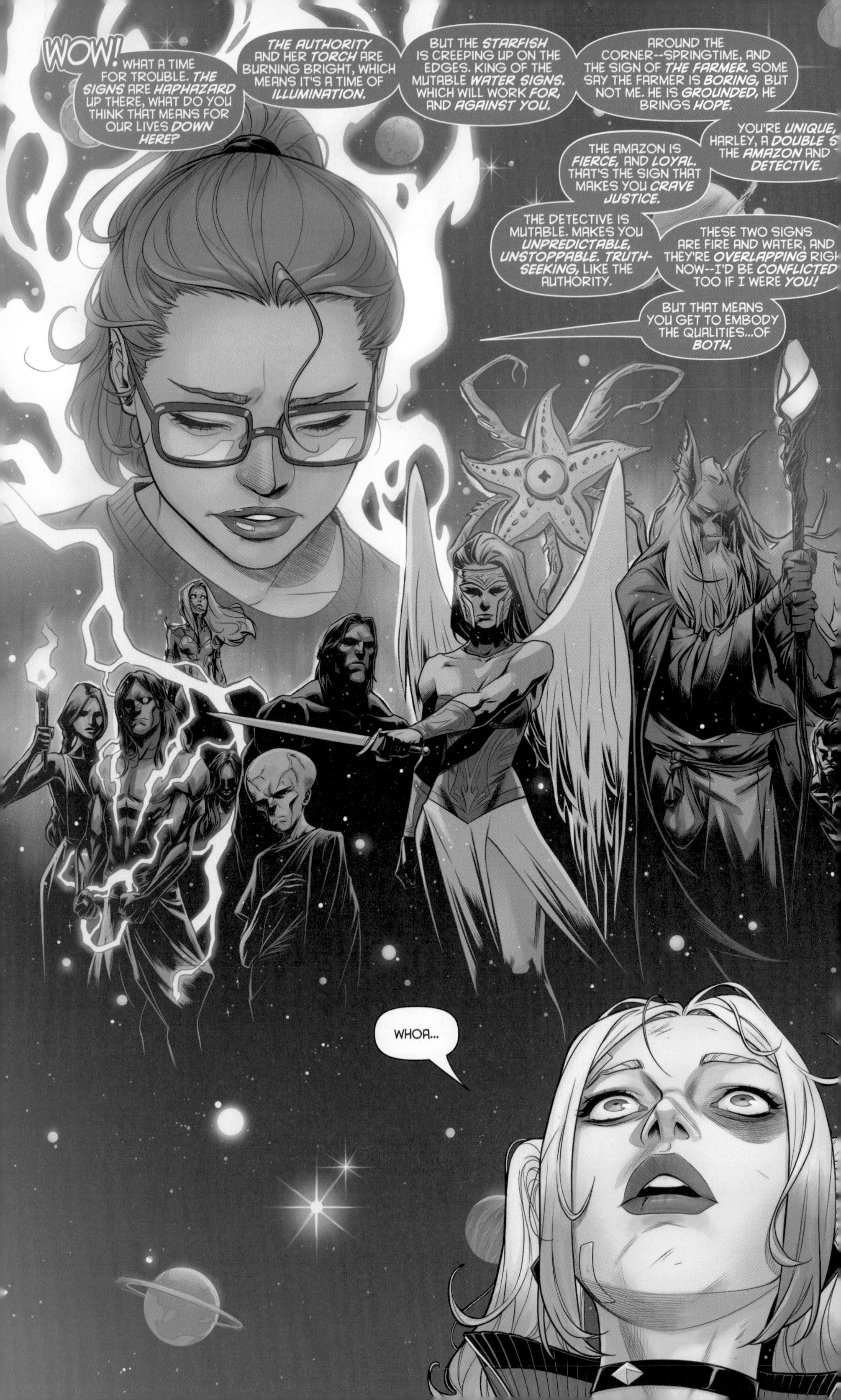
WOW! WHAT A TIME FOR TROUBLE. THE SIGNS ARE HAPHAZARD UP THERE, WHAT DO YOU THINK THAT MEANS FOR OUR LIVES DOWN HERE?
THE AUTHORITY AND HER TORCH ARE BURNING BRIGHT, WHICH MEANS IT'S A TIME OF ILLUMINATION.
BUT THE STARFISH IS CREEPING UP ON THE EDGES. KING OF THE MUTABLE WATER SIGNS. WHICH WILL WORK FOR, AND AGAINST YOU.
AROUND THE CORNER--SPRINGTIME, AND THE SIGN OF THE FARMER. SOME SAY THE FARMER IS BORING, BUT NOT ME. HE IS GROUNDED, HE BRINGS HOPE.
YOU'RE UNIQUE, HARLEY, A DOUBLE S THE AMAZON AND DETECTIVE.
THE AMAZON IS FIERCE, AND LOYAL. THAT'S THE SIGN THAT MAKES YOU CRAVE JUSTICE.
THE DETECTIVE IS MUTABLE. MAKES YOU UNPREDICTABLE, UNSTOPPABLE. TRUTH-SEEKING, LIKE THE AUTHORITY.
THESE TWO SIGNS ARE FIRE AND WATER, AND THEY'RE OVERLAPPING RIGH NOW--I'D BE CONFLICTED TOO IF I WERE YOU!
BUT THAT MEANS YOU GET TO EMBODY THE QUALITIES...OF BOTH.
WHOA...

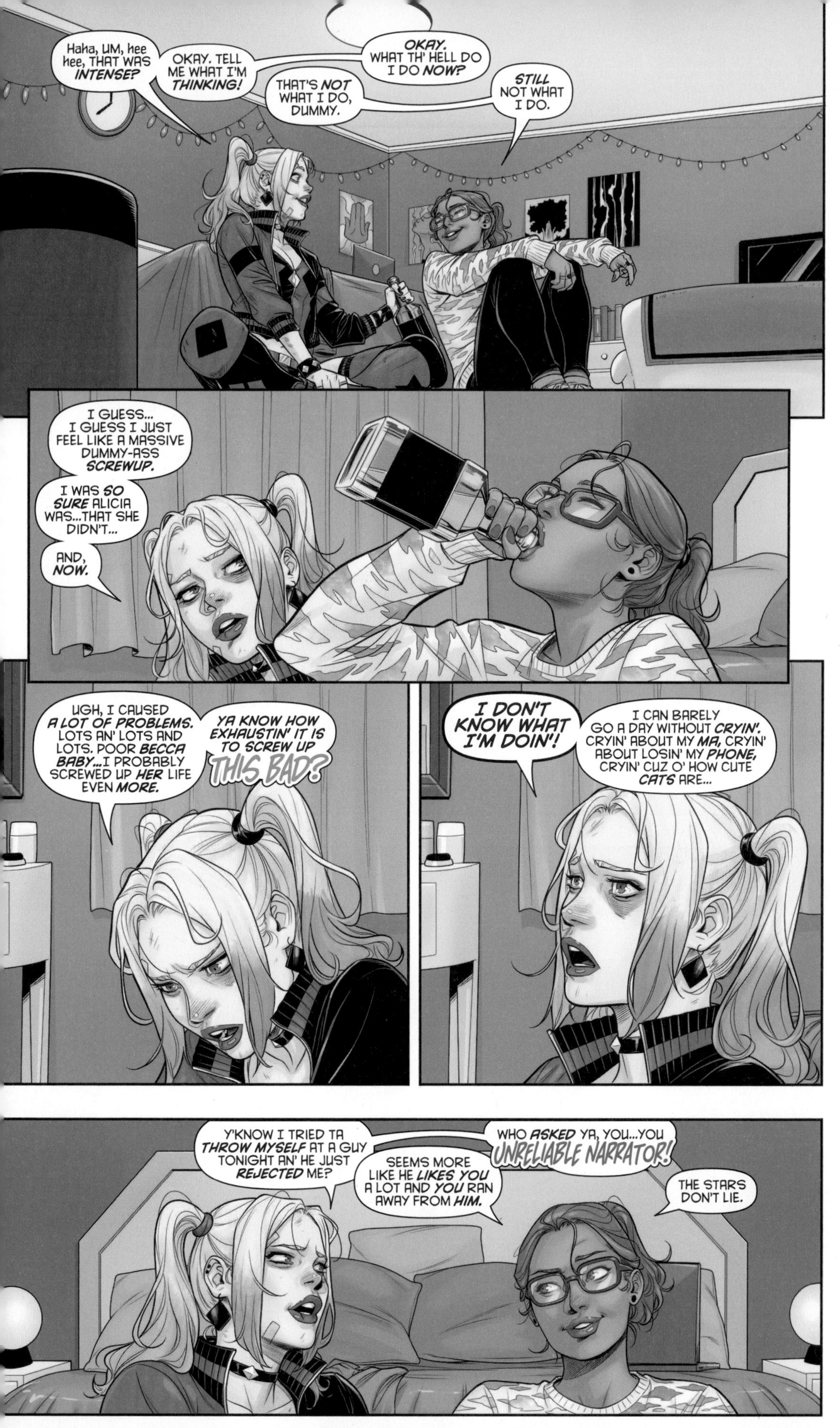
Haha, UM, hee hee, THAT WAS INTENSE?
OKAY. TELL ME WHAT I'M THINKING!
THAT'S NOT WHAT I DO, DUMMY.
OKAY. WHAT TH' HELL DO I DO NOW?
STILL NOT WHAT I DO.
I GUESS... I GUESS I JUST FEEL LIKE A MASSIVE DUMMY-ASS SCREWUP.
I WAS SO SURE ALICIA WAS...THAT SHE DIDN'T...
AND, NOW.
UGH, I CAUSED A LOT OF PROBLEMS. LOTS AN' LOTS AND LOTS. POOR BECCA BABY...I PROBABLY SCREWED UP HER LIFE EVEN MORE.
YA KNOW HOW EXHAUSTIN' IT IS TO SCREW UP THIS BAD?
I DON'T KNOW WHAT I'M DOIN'!
I CAN BARELY GO A DAY WITHOUT CRYIN'. CRYIN' ABOUT MY MA, CRYIN' ABOUT LOSIN' MY PHONE, CRYIN' CUZ O' HOW CUTE CATS ARE...
Y'KNOW I TRIED TA THROW MYSELF AT A GUY TONIGHT AN' HE JUST REJECTED ME?
SEEMS MORE LIKE HE LIKES YOU A LOT AND YOU RAN AWAY FROM HIM.
WHO ASKED YA, YOU...YOU UNRELIABLE NARRATOR!
THE STARS DON'T LIE.

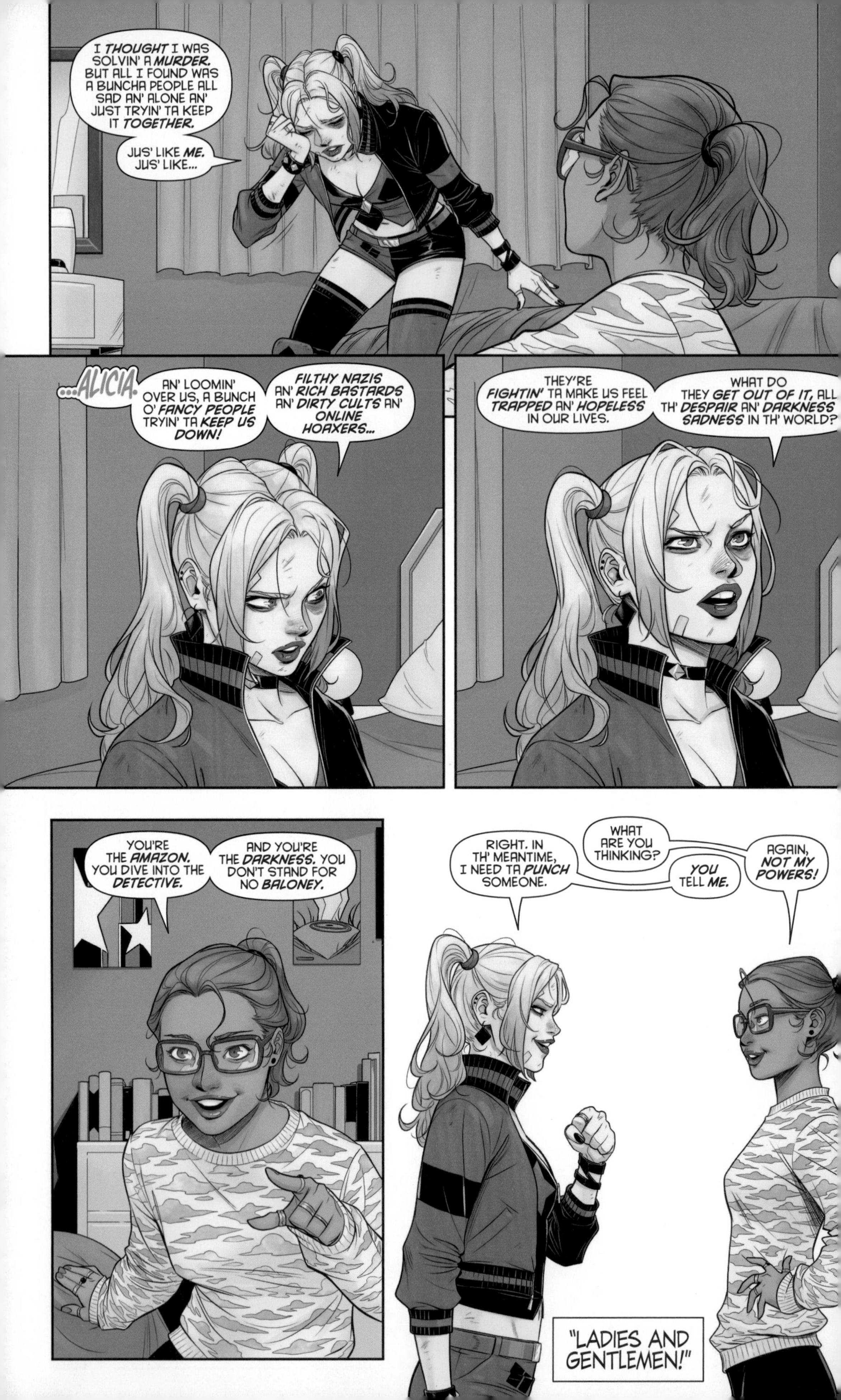
I THOUGHT I WAS SOLVIN' A MURDER. BUT ALL I FOUND WAS A BUNCHA PEOPLE ALL SAD AN' ALONE AN' JUST TRYIN' TA KEEP IT TOGETHER.
JUS' LIKE ME. JUS' LIKE...
...ALICIA.
AN' LOOMIN' OVER US, A BUNCH O' FANCY PEOPLE TRYIN' TA KEEP US DOWN!
FILTHY NAZIS AN' RICH BASTARDS AN' DIRTY CULTS AN' ONLINE HOAXERS...
THEY'RE FIGHTIN' TA MAKE US FEEL TRAPPED AN' HOPELESS IN OUR LIVES.
WHAT DO THEY GET OUT OF IT, ALL TH' DESPAIR AN' DARKNESS SADNESS IN TH' WORLD?
YOU'RE THE AMAZON. YOU DIVE INTO THE DETECTIVE.
AND YOU'RE THE DARKNESS. YOU DON'T STAND FOR NO BALONEY.
RIGHT. IN TH' MEANTIME, I NEED TA PUNCH SOMEONE.
WHAT ARE YOU THINKING?
YOU TELL ME.
AGAIN, NOT MY POWERS!
"LADIES AND GENTLEMEN!"

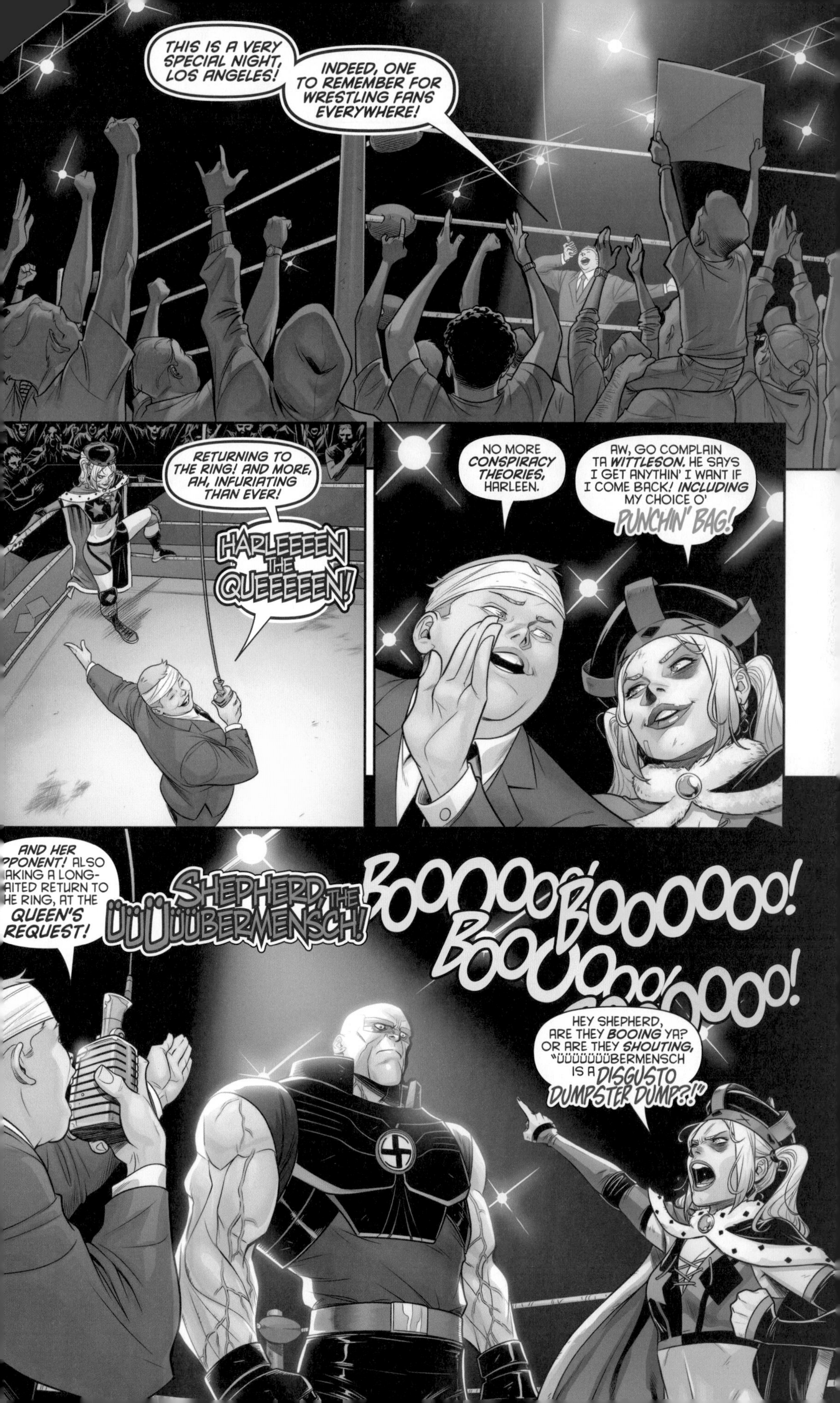
THIS IS A VERY SPECIAL NIGHT, LOS ANGELES!
INDEED, ONE TO REMEMBER FOR WRESTLING FANS EVERYWHERE!
RETURNING TO THE RING! AND MORE, AH, INFURIATING THAN EVER!
HARLEEEEN THE QUEEEEEEN!
NO MORE CONSPIRACY THEORIES, HARLEEN.
AW, GO COMPLAIN TA WITTLESON. HE SAYS I GET ANYTHIN' I WANT IF I COME BACK! INCLUDING MY CHOICE O' PUNCHIN' BAG!
AND HER PPONENT! ALSO AKING A LONG-AITED RETURN TO HE RING, AT THE QUEEN'S REQUEST!
SHEPHERD, THE ÜÜÜüüüBERMENSCH!
BOOOOOO! BOOOOOOO! BOOOOOO! BOOOOOOO!
HEY SHEPHERD, ARE THEY BOOING YA? OR ARE THEY SHOUTING, "ÜÜÜÜÜÜÜBERMENSCH IS A DISGUSTO DUMPSTER DUMP?!"

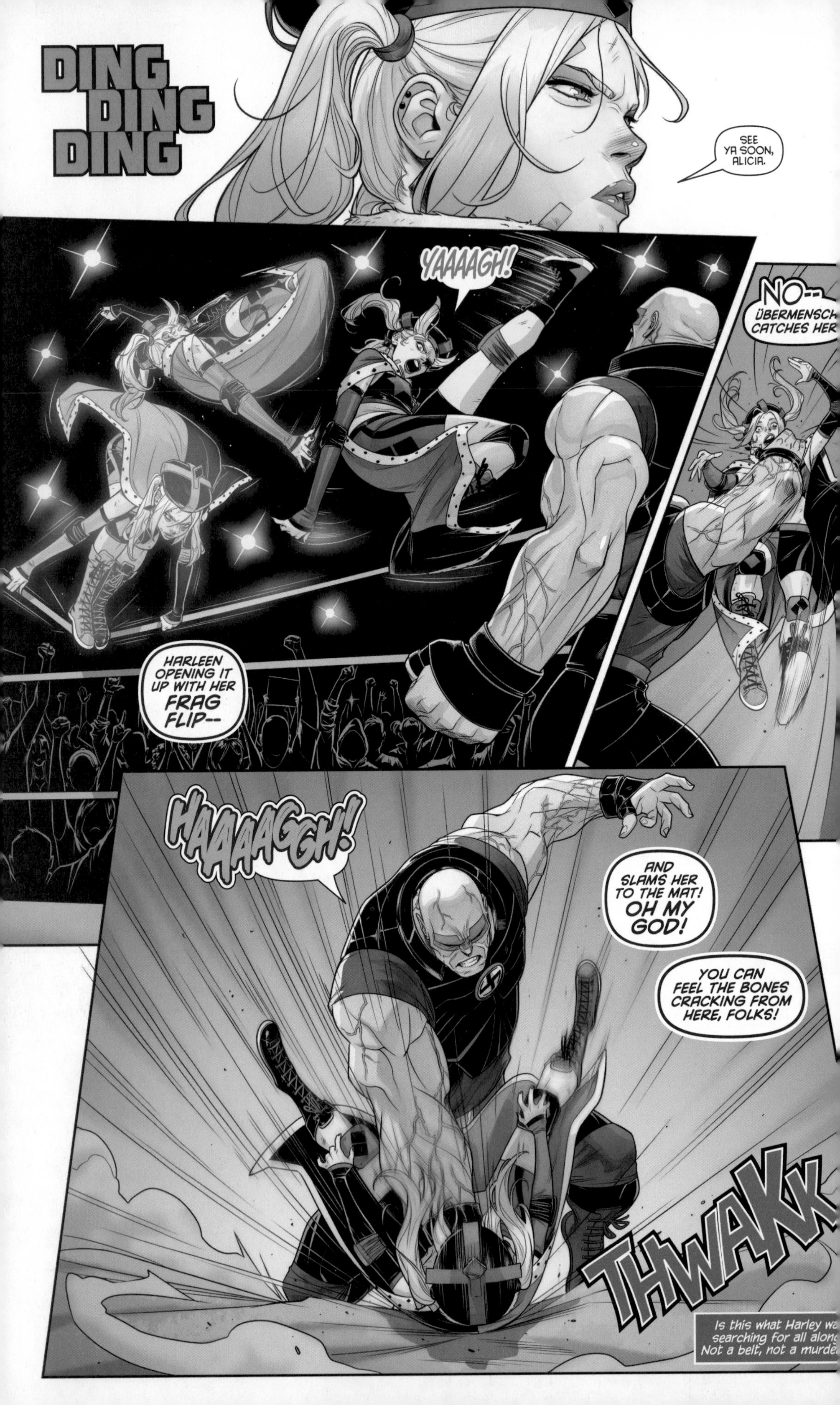
DING DING DING
SEE YA SOON, ALICIA.
YAAAAGH!
HARLEEN OPENING IT UP WITH HER FRAG FLIP--
NO--
ÜBERMENSCH CATCHES HER
HAAAAGGH!
AND SLAMS HER TO THE MAT! OH MY GOD!
YOU CAN FEEL THE BONES CRACKING FROM HERE, FOLKS!
THWAKK
Is this what Harley wa
searching for all along
Not a belt, not a murde

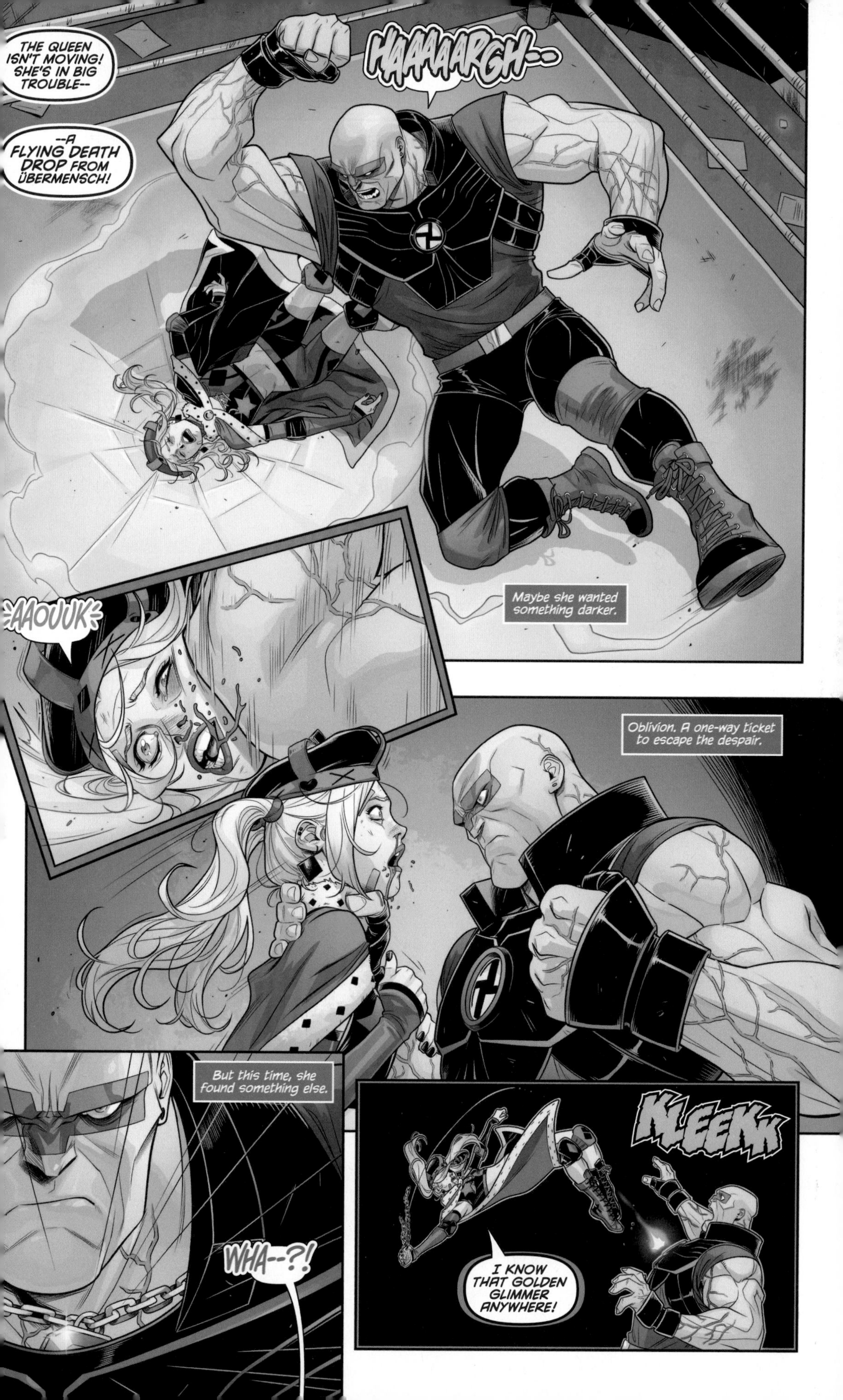
THE QUEEN ISN'T MOVING! SHE'S IN BIG TROUBLE--
HAAAAARGH--
--A FLYING DEATH DROP FROM ÜBERMENSCH!
Maybe she wanted something darker.
AAOUUK
Oblivion. A one-way ticket to escape the despair.
But this time, she found something else.
WHA--?!
KLEEKK
I KNOW THAT GOLDEN GLIMMER ANYWHERE!

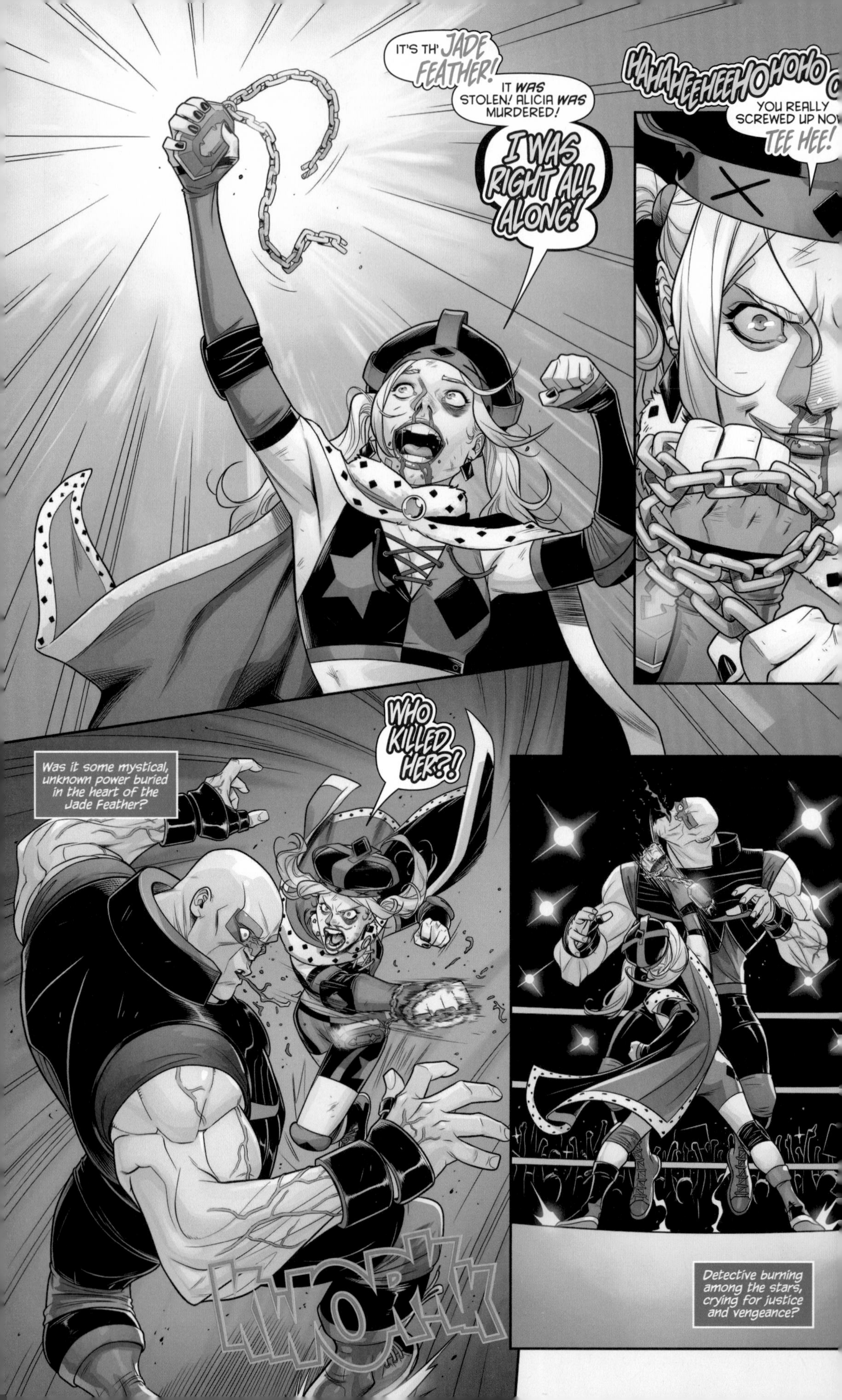
IT'S TH' JADE FEATHER!
IT WAS STOLEN! ALICIA WAS MURDERED!
I WAS RIGHT ALL ALONG!
HAHAHEEHEEHOHOHO
YOU REALLY SCREWED UP NOW
TEE HEE!
Was it some mystical, unknown power buried in the heart of the Jade Feather?
WHO KILLED HER?!
KWORKK
Detective burning among the stars, crying for justice and vengeance?

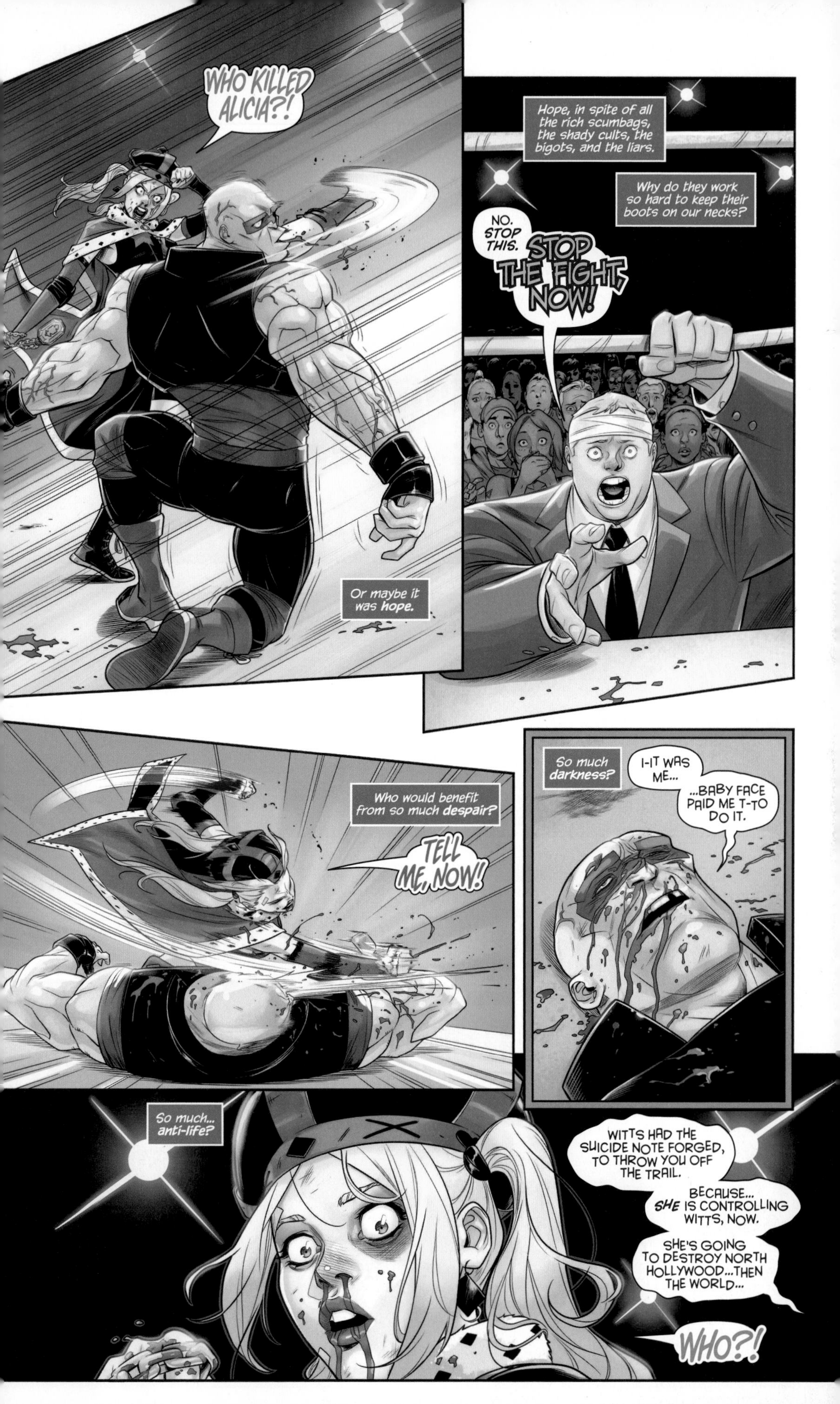
WHO KILLED ALICIA?!
Or maybe it was hope.
Hope, in spite of all the rich scumbags, the shady cults, the bigots, and the liars.
Why do they work so hard to keep their boots on our necks?
NO. STOP THIS.
STOP THE FIGHT, NOW!
Who would benefit from so much despair?
TELL ME, NOW!
So much darkness?
I-IT WAS ME...
...BABY FACE PAID ME T-TO DO IT.
So much... anti-life?
WITTS HAD THE SUICIDE NOTE FORGED, TO THROW YOU OFF THE TRAIL.
BECAUSE... SHE IS CONTROLLING WITTS, NOW.
SHE'S GOING TO DESTROY NORTH HOLLYWOOD...THEN THE WORLD...
WHO?!

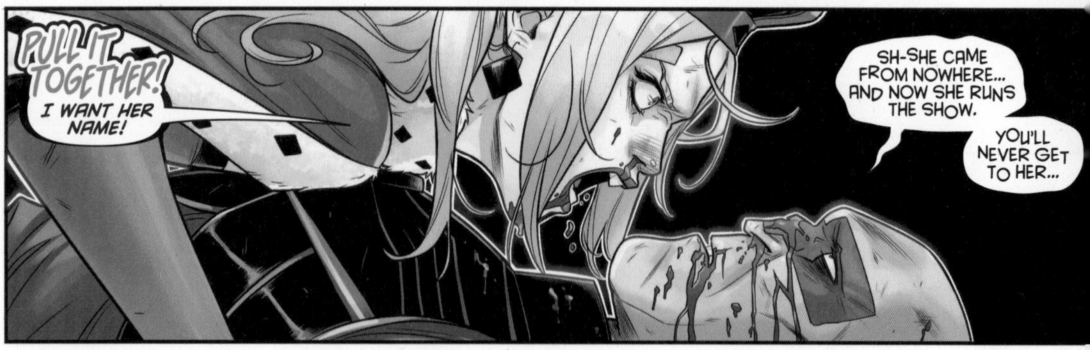
PULL IT TOGETHER!
I WANT HER NAME!
SH-SHE CAME FROM NOWHERE... AND NOW SHE RUNS THE SHOW.
YOU'LL NEVER GET TO HER...

CALIFORNIA OR DEATH

CHAPTER 4 LOST AND FOUND

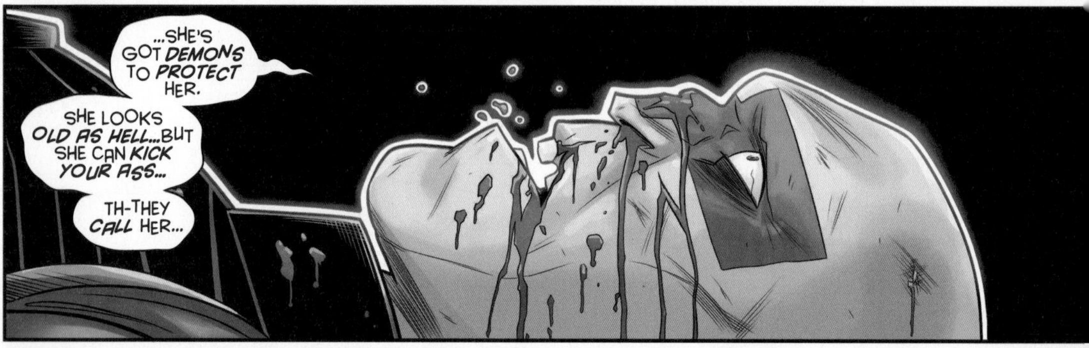
...SHE'S GOT DEMONS TO PROTECT HER.
SHE LOOKS OLD AS HELL...BUT SHE CAN KICK YOUR ASS...
TH-THEY CALL HER...

SAM HUMPHRIES WRITER SAMI BASRI ARTIST HI-FI COLORS
DAVE SHARPE LETTERS GUILLEM MARCH & ROMUL FAJARDO JR. COVER
FRANK CHO & SABINE RICH VARIANT COVER
DAVE WIELGOSZ EDITOR
BEN ABERNATHY GROUP EDITOR
HARLEY QUINN CREATED BY PAUL DINI & BRUCE TIMM

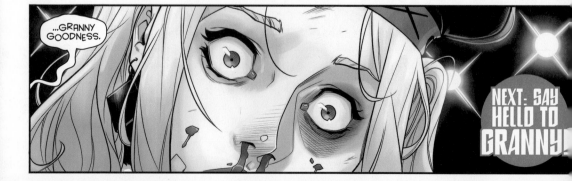

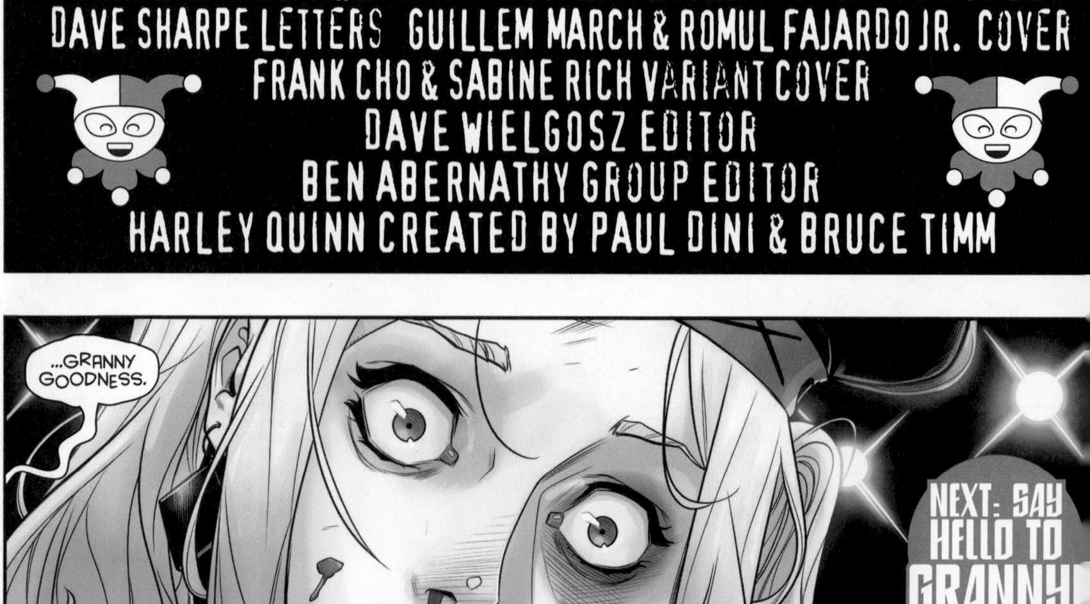
...GRANNY GOODNESS.
NEXT: SAY HELLO TO GRANNY!

HARLEY QUINN #74 cover
by GUILLEM MARCH and ARIF PRIANTO

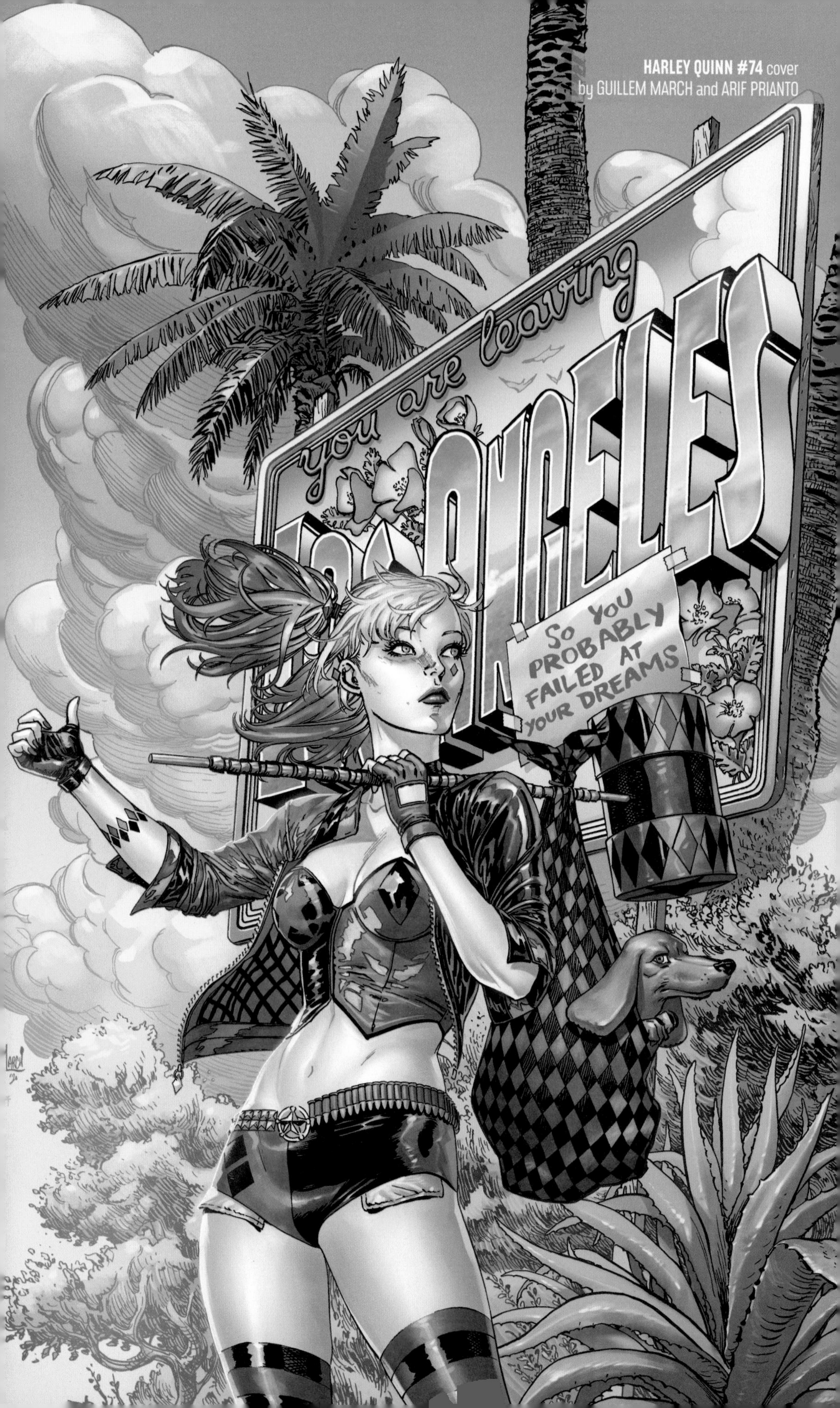
you are leaving
SO YOU PROBABLY FAILED AT YOUR DREAMS

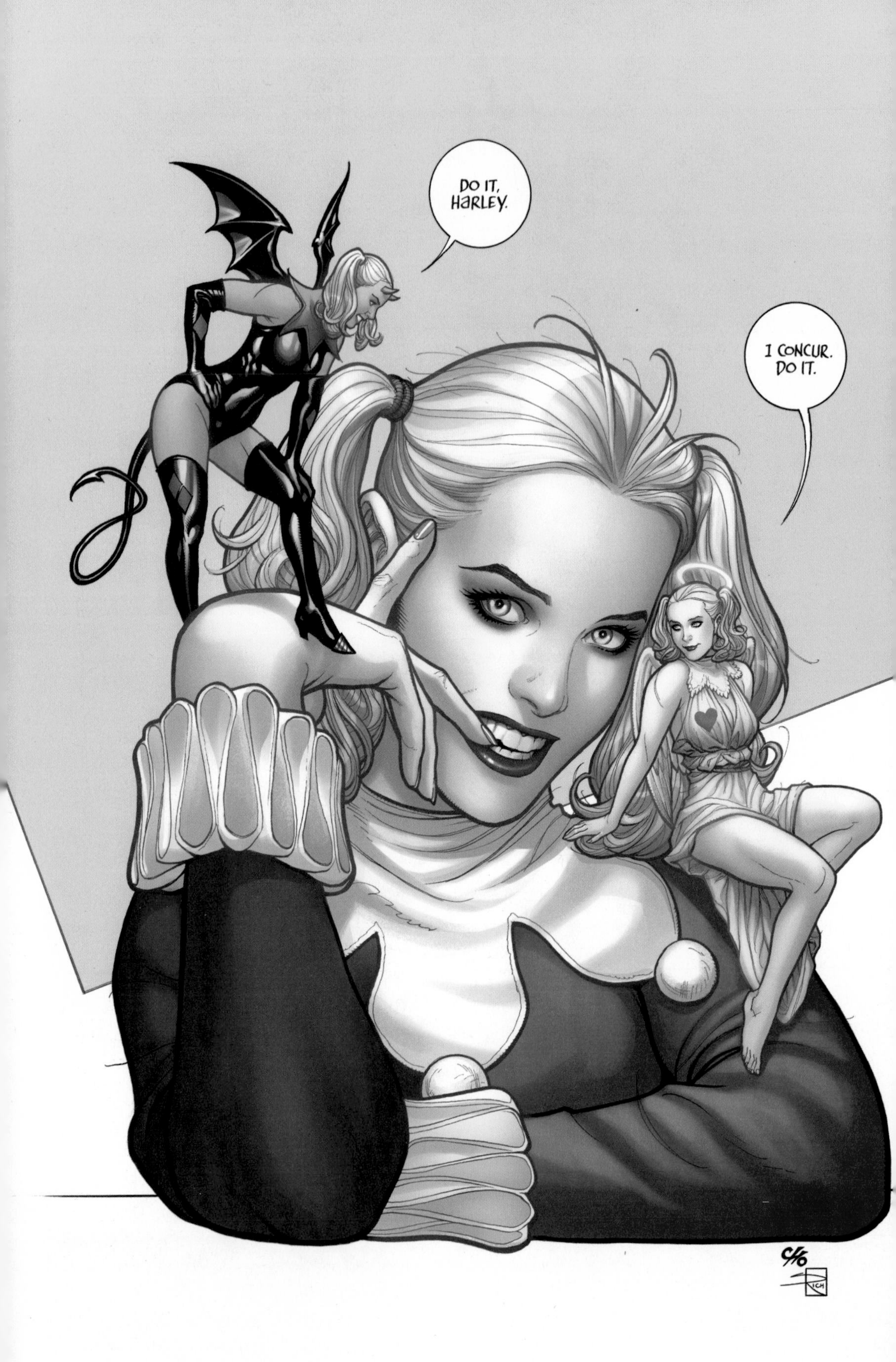
DO IT, HARLEY.
I CONCUR. DO IT.

HARLEY QUINN #74 variant cover
by FRANK CHO and SABINE RICH

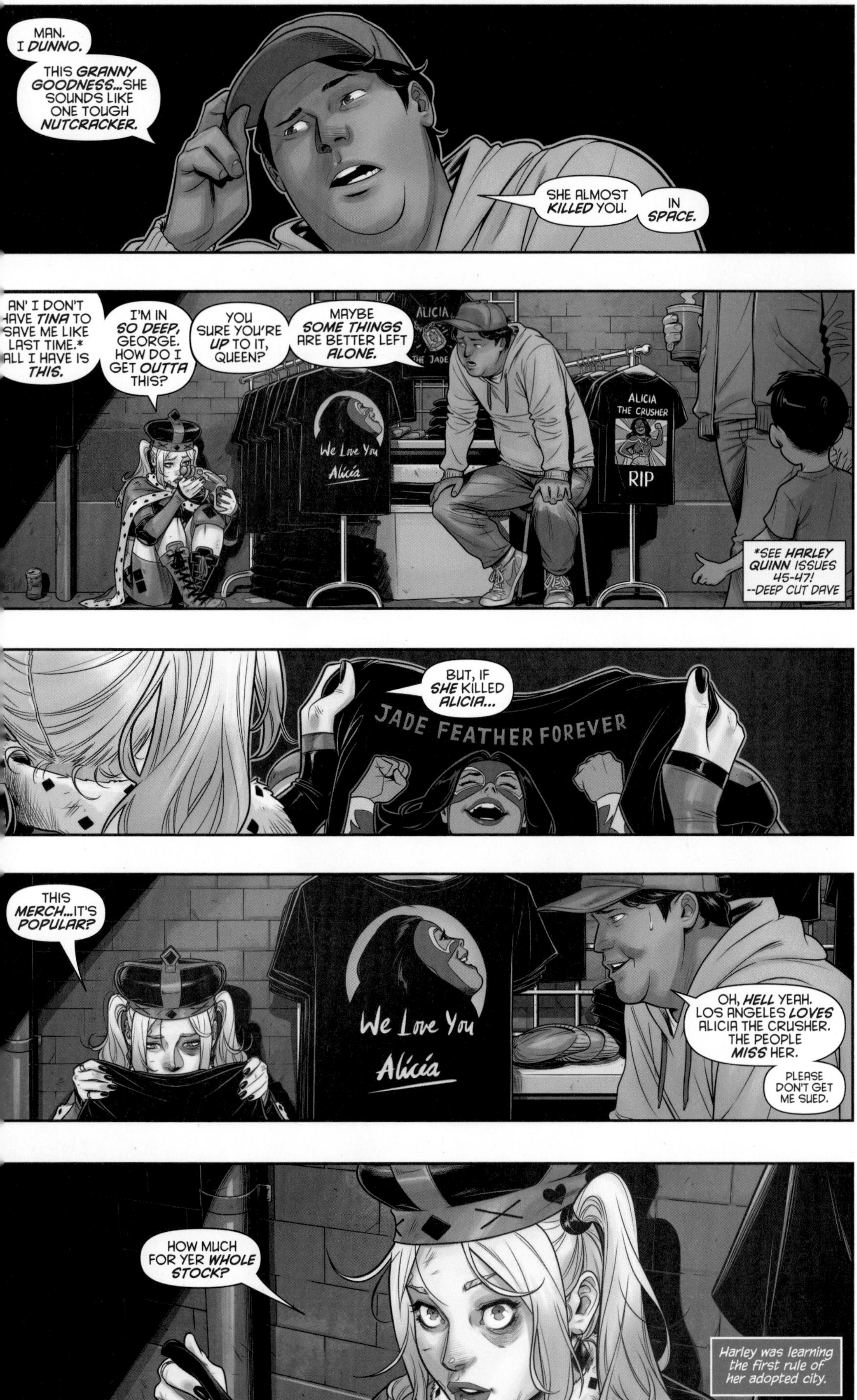
MAN. I DUNNO.
THIS GRANNY GOODNESS...SHE SOUNDS LIKE ONE TOUGH NUTCRACKER.
SHE ALMOST KILLED YOU.
IN SPACE.
AN' I DON'T HAVE TINA TO SAVE ME LIKE LAST TIME.* ALL I HAVE IS THIS.
I'M IN SO DEEP, GEORGE. HOW DO I GET OUTTA THIS?
YOU SURE YOU'RE UP TO IT, QUEEN?
MAYBE SOME THINGS ARE BETTER LEFT ALONE.
ALICIA THE JADE
We Love You Alicia
ALICIA THE CRUSHER RIP
*SEE HARLEY QUINN ISSUES 45-47! --DEEP CUT DAVE
BUT, IF SHE KILLED ALICIA...
JADE FEATHER FOREVER
THIS MERCH...IT'S POPULAR?
We Love You Alicia
OH, HELL YEAH. LOS ANGELES LOVES ALICIA THE CRUSHER. THE PEOPLE MISS HER.
PLEASE DON'T GET ME SUED.
HOW MUCH FOR YER WHOLE STOCK?
Harley was learning the first rule of her adopted city.

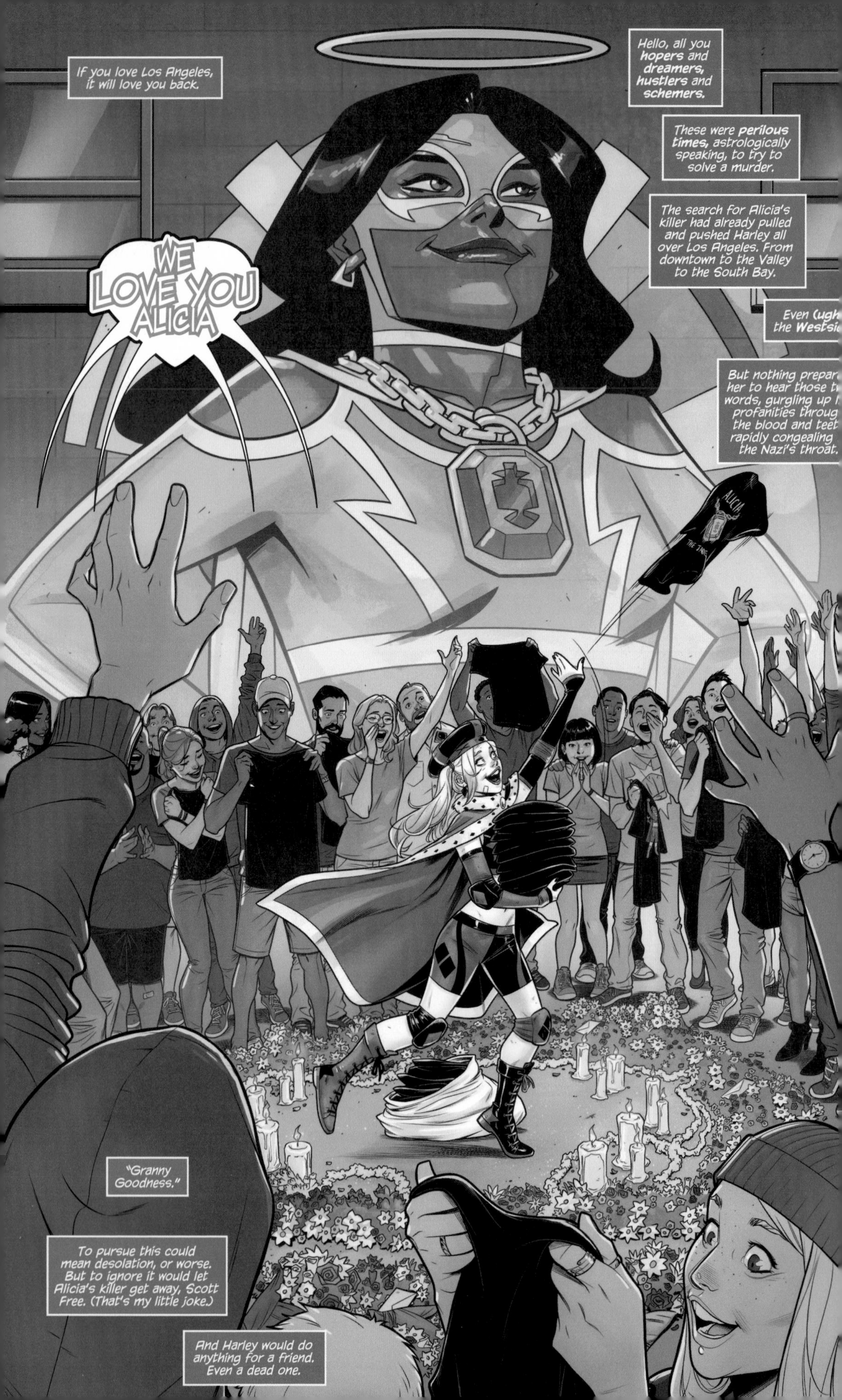
If you love Los Angeles, it will love you back.
Hello, all you hopers and dreamers, hustlers and schemers.
These were perilous times, astrologically speaking, to try to solve a murder.
The search for Alicia's killer had already pulled and pushed Harley all over Los Angeles. From downtown to the Valley to the South Bay.
WE LOVE YOU ALICIA
"Granny Goodness."
To pursue this could mean desolation, or worse. But to ignore it would let Alicia's killer get away, Scott Free. (That's my little joke.)
And Harley would do anything for a friend. Even a dead one.

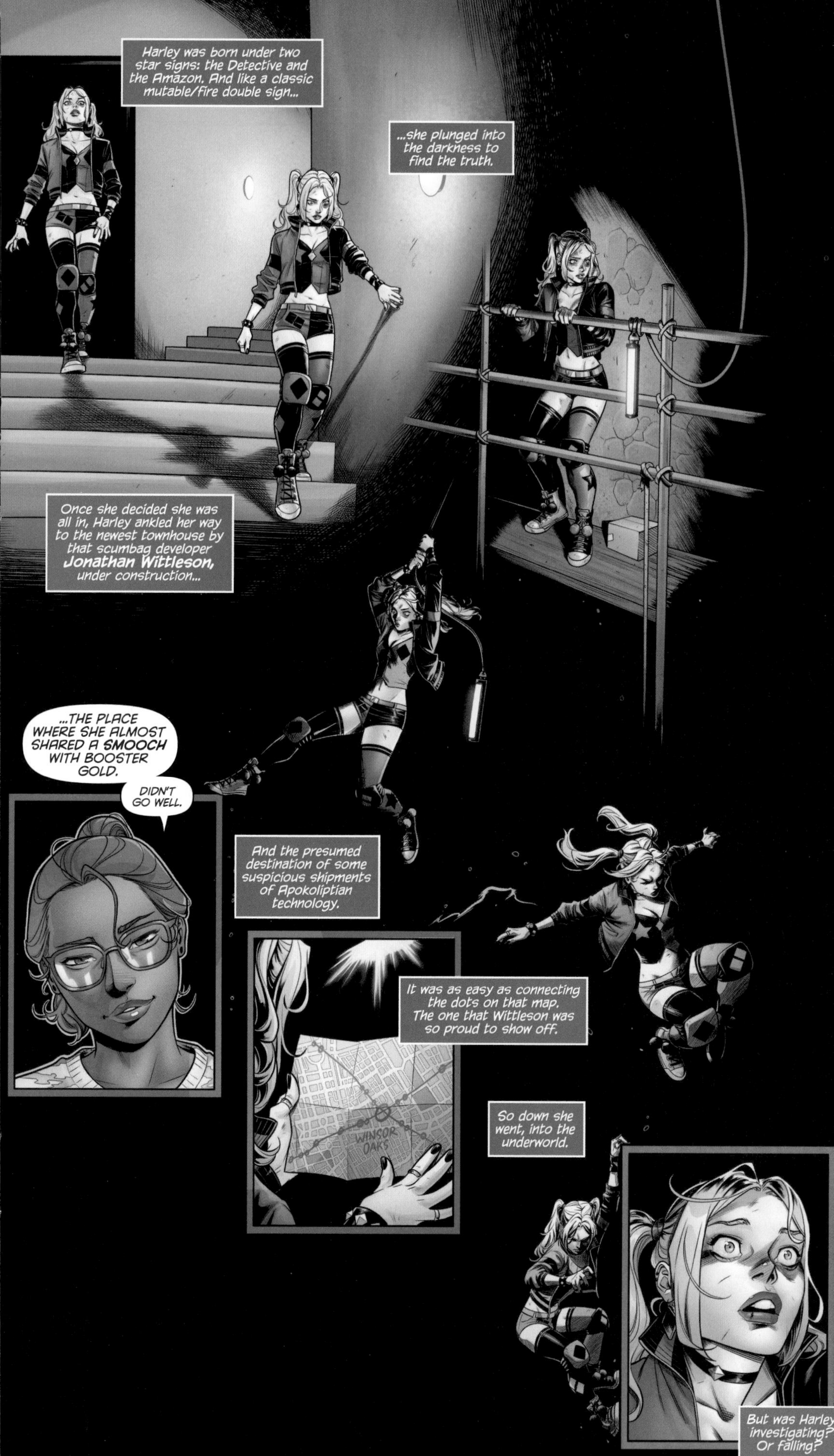
Harley was born under two star signs: the Detective and the Amazon. And like a classic mutable/fire double sign...
...she plunged into the darkness to find the truth.
Once she decided she was all in, Harley ankled her way to the newest townhouse by that scumbag developer Jonathan Wittleson, under construction...
...THE PLACE WHERE SHE ALMOST SHARED A SMOOCH WITH BOOSTER GOLD.
DIDN'T GO WELL.
And the presumed destination of some suspicious shipments of Apokoliptian technology.
It was as easy as connecting the dots on that map. The one that Wittleson was so proud to show off.
WINSOR OAKS
So down she went, into the underworld.
But was Harley investigating? Or falling?

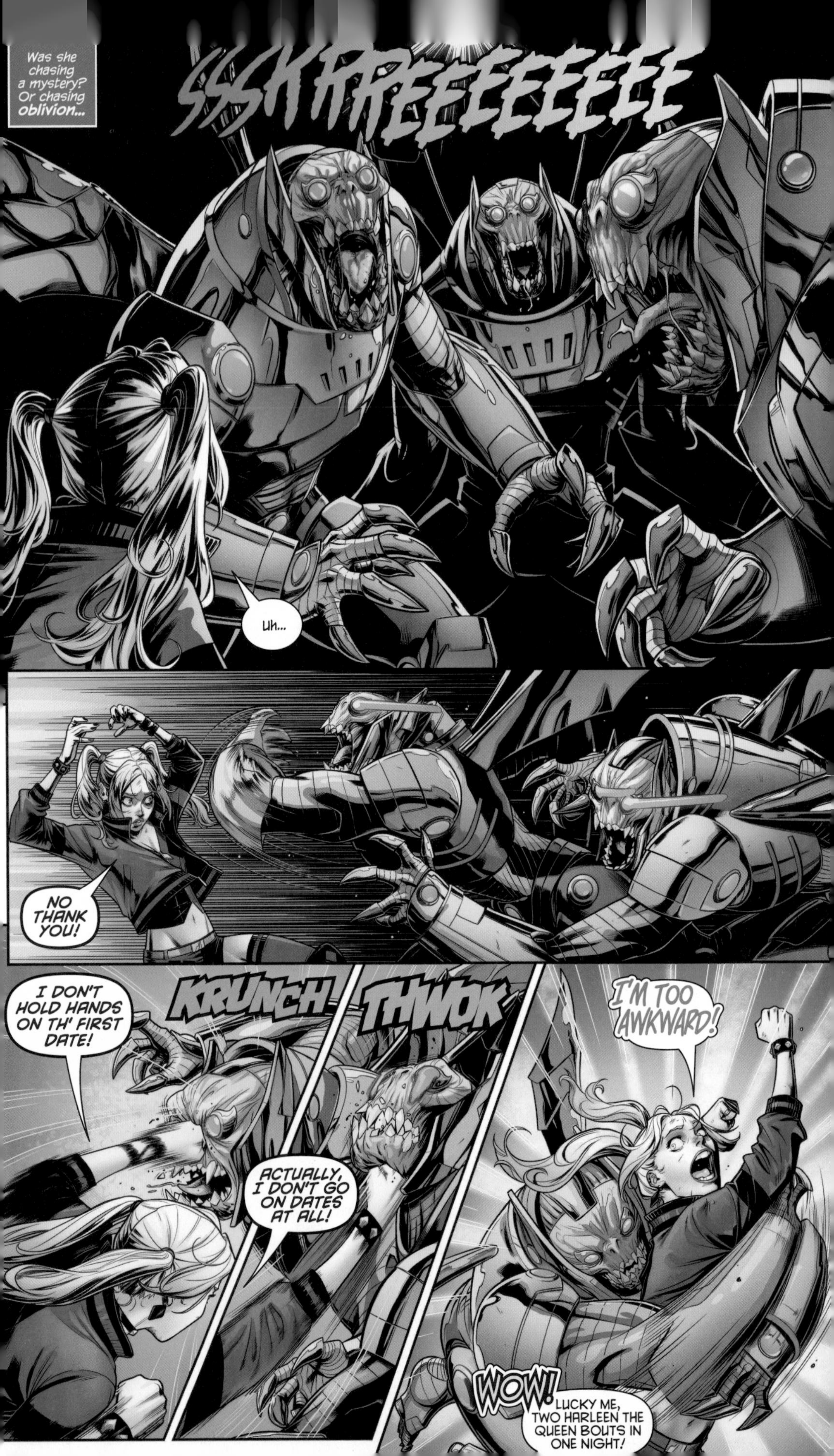

Was she chasing a mystery? Or chasing **oblivion...**
SSSKRREEEEEEEEE
uh...
NO THANK YOU!
I DON'T HOLD HANDS ON TH' FIRST DATE!
KRUNCH
THWOK
ACTUALLY, I DON'T GO ON DATES AT ALL!
I'M TOO AWKWARD!
WOW!
LUCKY ME, TWO HARLEEN THE QUEEN BOUTS IN ONE NIGHT!

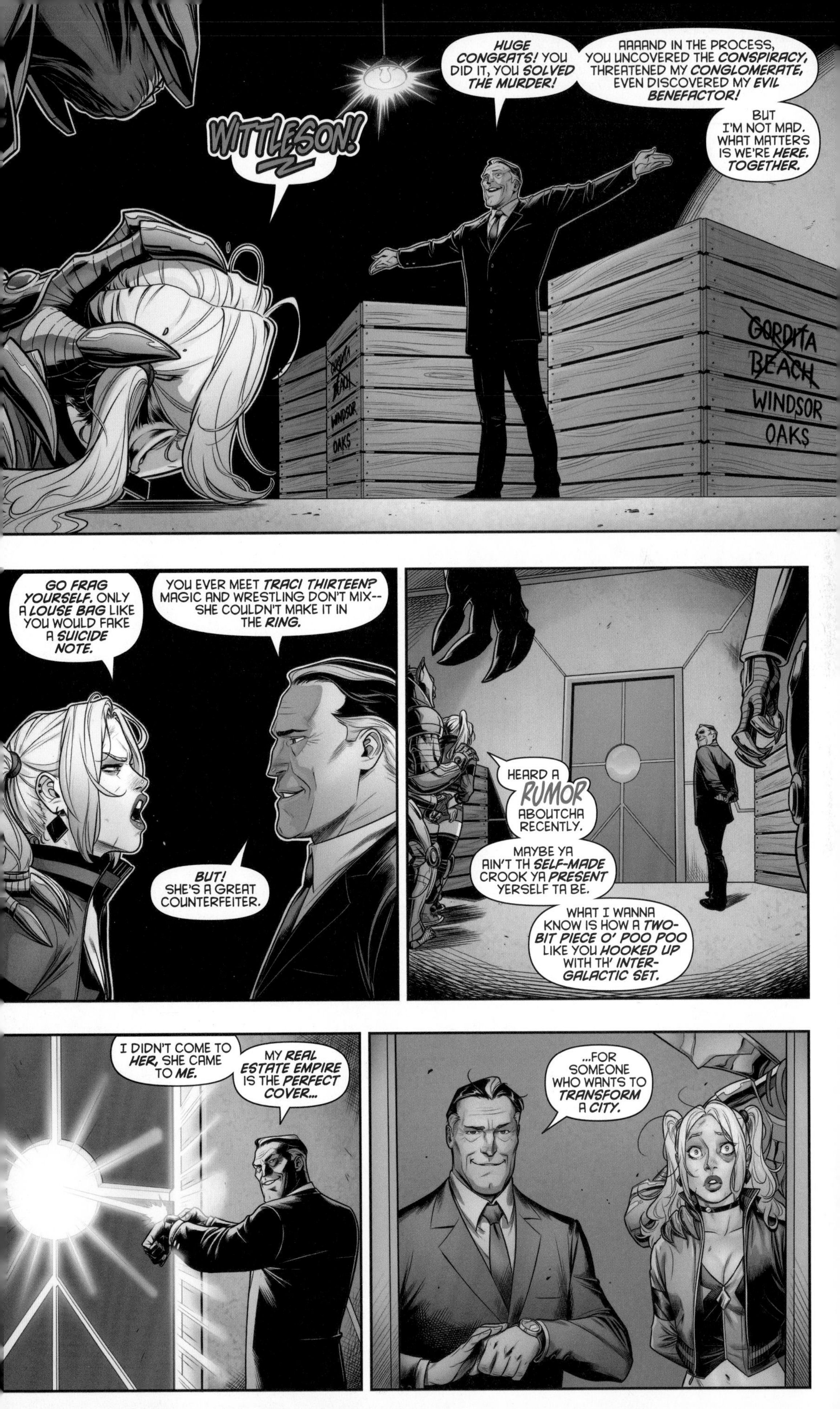
WITTLESON!
HUGE CONGRATS! YOU DID IT, YOU SOLVED THE MURDER!
AAAAND IN THE PROCESS, YOU UNCOVERED THE CONSPIRACY, THREATENED MY CONGLOMERATE, EVEN DISCOVERED MY EVIL BENEFACTOR!
BUT I'M NOT MAD. WHAT MATTERS IS WE'RE HERE. TOGETHER.
GORDITA BEACH
WINDSOR OAKS
GORDITA BEACH
WINDSOR OAKS
GO FRAG YOURSELF. ONLY A LOUSE BAG LIKE YOU WOULD FAKE A SUICIDE NOTE.
YOU EVER MEET TRACI THIRTEEN? MAGIC AND WRESTLING DON'T MIX-- SHE COULDN'T MAKE IT IN THE RING.
BUT! SHE'S A GREAT COUNTERFEITER.
HEARD A RUMOR ABOUTCHA RECENTLY.
MAYBE YA AIN'T TH SELF-MADE CROOK YA PRESENT YERSELF TA BE.
WHAT I WANNA KNOW IS HOW A TWO-BIT PIECE O' POO POO LIKE YOU HOOKED UP WITH TH' INTER-GALACTIC SET.
I DIDN'T COME TO HER, SHE CAME TO ME.
MY REAL ESTATE EMPIRE IS THE PERFECT COVER...
...FOR SOMEONE WHO WANTS TO TRANSFORM A CITY.

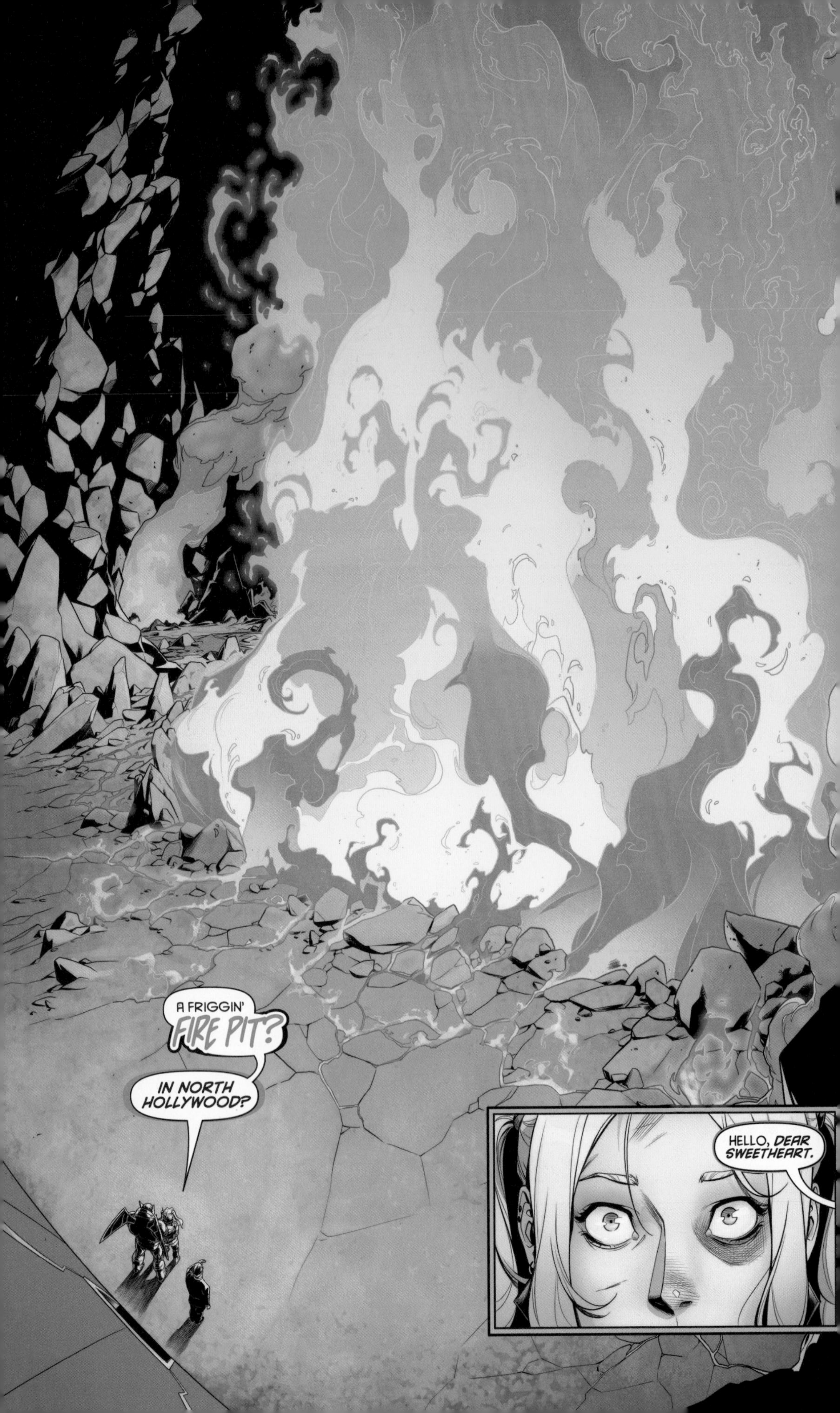
A FRIGGIN' FIRE PIT?
IN NORTH HOLLYWOOD?
HELLO, DEAR SWEETHEART.

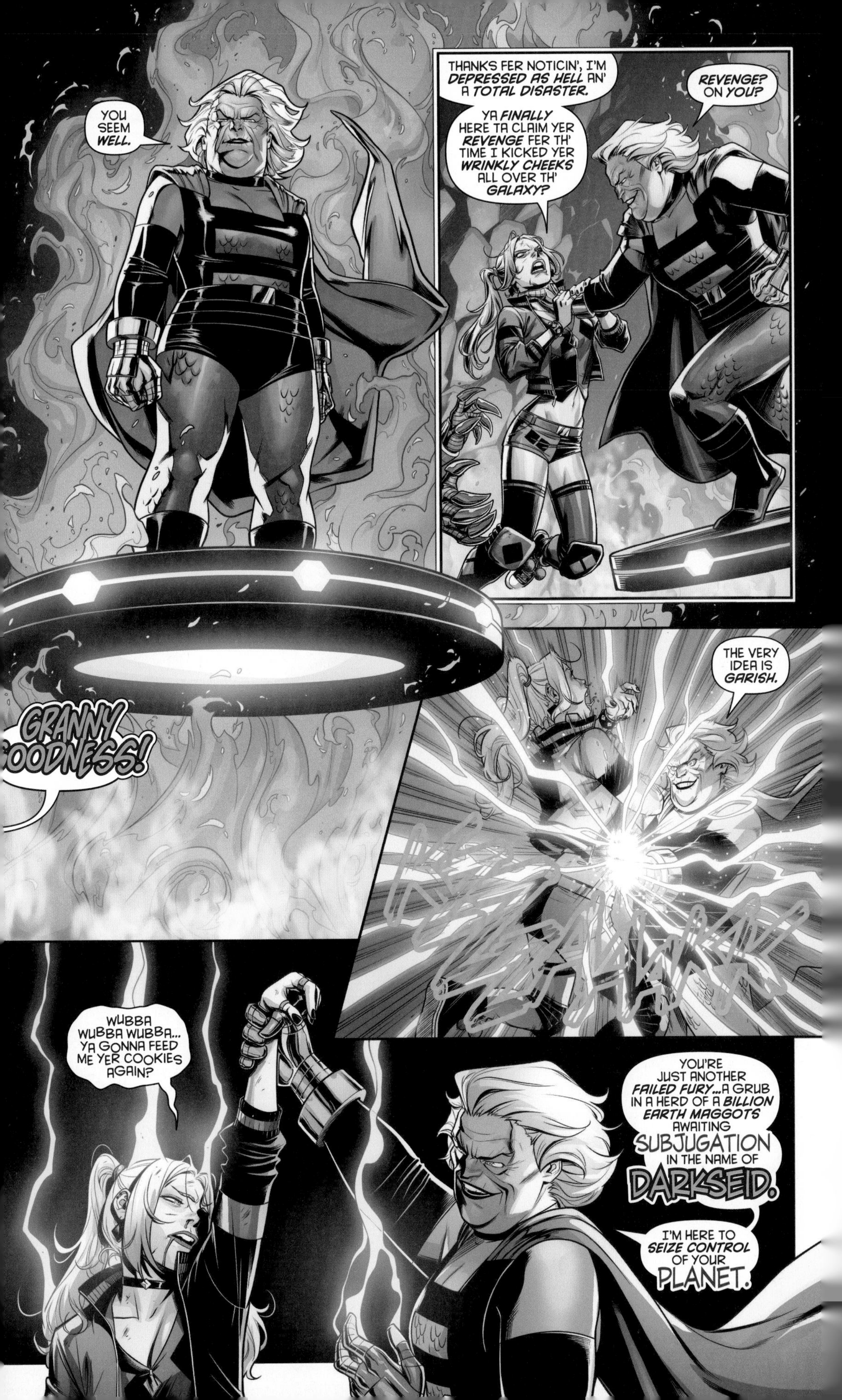
YOU SEEM WELL.
GRANNY GOODNESS!
THANKS FER NOTICIN', I'M DEPRESSED AS HELL AN' A TOTAL DISASTER.
YA FINALLY HERE TA CLAIM YER REVENGE FER TH' TIME I KICKED YER WRINKLY CHEEKS ALL OVER TH' GALAXY?
REVENGE? ON YOU?
THE VERY IDEA IS GARISH.
WUBBA WUBBA WUBBA... YA GONNA FEED ME YER COOKIES AGAIN?
YOU'RE JUST ANOTHER FAILED FURY...A GRUB IN A HERD OF A BILLION EARTH MAGGOTS AWAITING SUBJUGATION IN THE NAME OF DARKSEID.
I'M HERE TO SEIZE CONTROL OF YOUR PLANET.

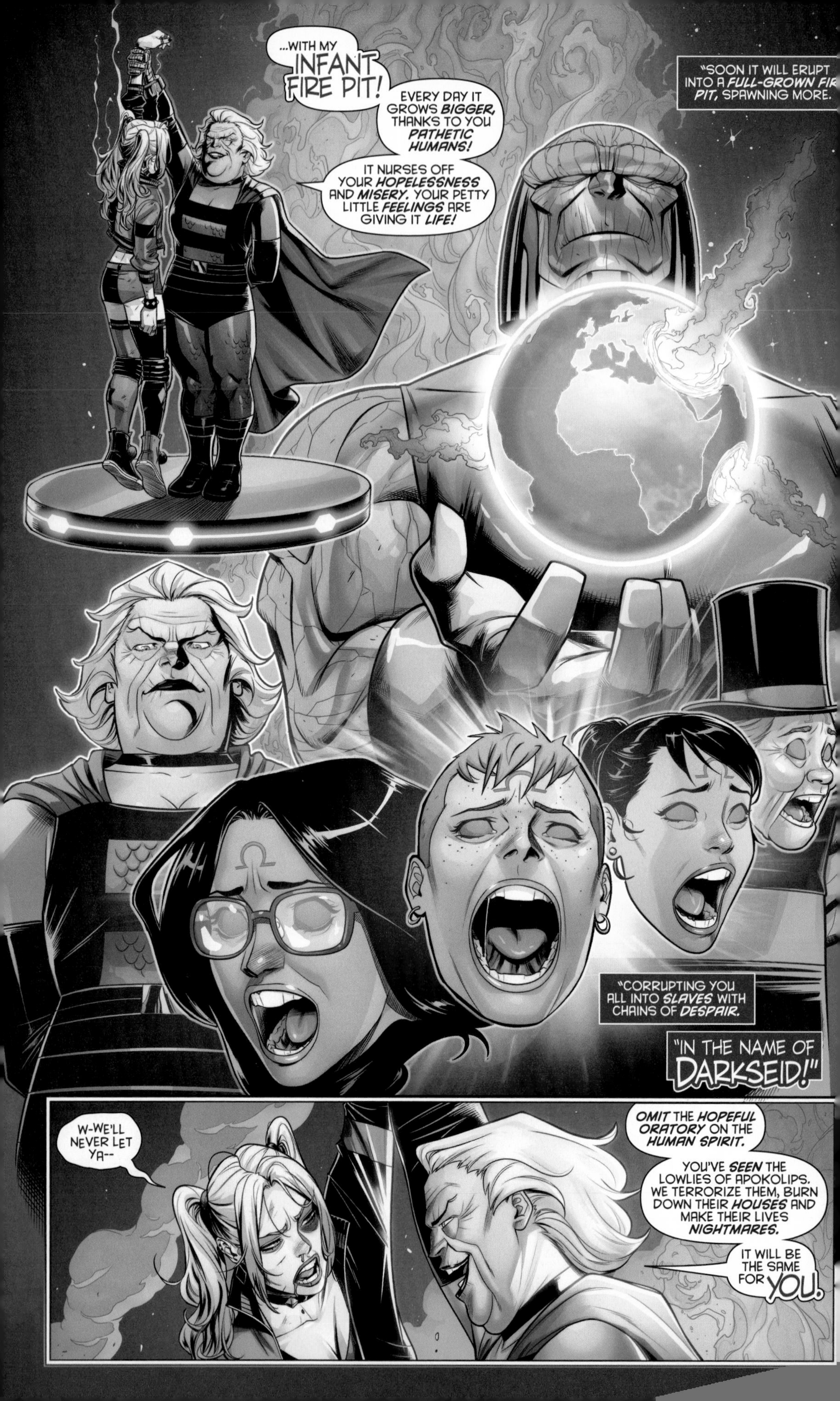

...WITH MY INFANT FIRE PIT!
EVERY DAY IT GROWS BIGGER, THANKS TO YOU PATHETIC HUMANS!
IT NURSES OFF YOUR HOPELESSNESS AND MISERY. YOUR PETTY LITTLE FEELINGS ARE GIVING IT LIFE!
"SOON IT WILL ERUPT INTO A FULL-GROWN FIR PIT, SPAWNING MORE.
"CORRUPTING YOU ALL INTO SLAVES WITH CHAINS OF DESPAIR.
"IN THE NAME OF DARKSEID!"
W-WE'LL NEVER LET YA--
OMIT THE HOPEFUL ORATORY ON THE HUMAN SPIRIT.
YOU'VE SEEN THE LOWLIES OF APOKOLIPS. WE TERRORIZE THEM, BURN DOWN THEIR HOUSES AND MAKE THEIR LIVES NIGHTMARES.
IT WILL BE THE SAME FOR YOU.

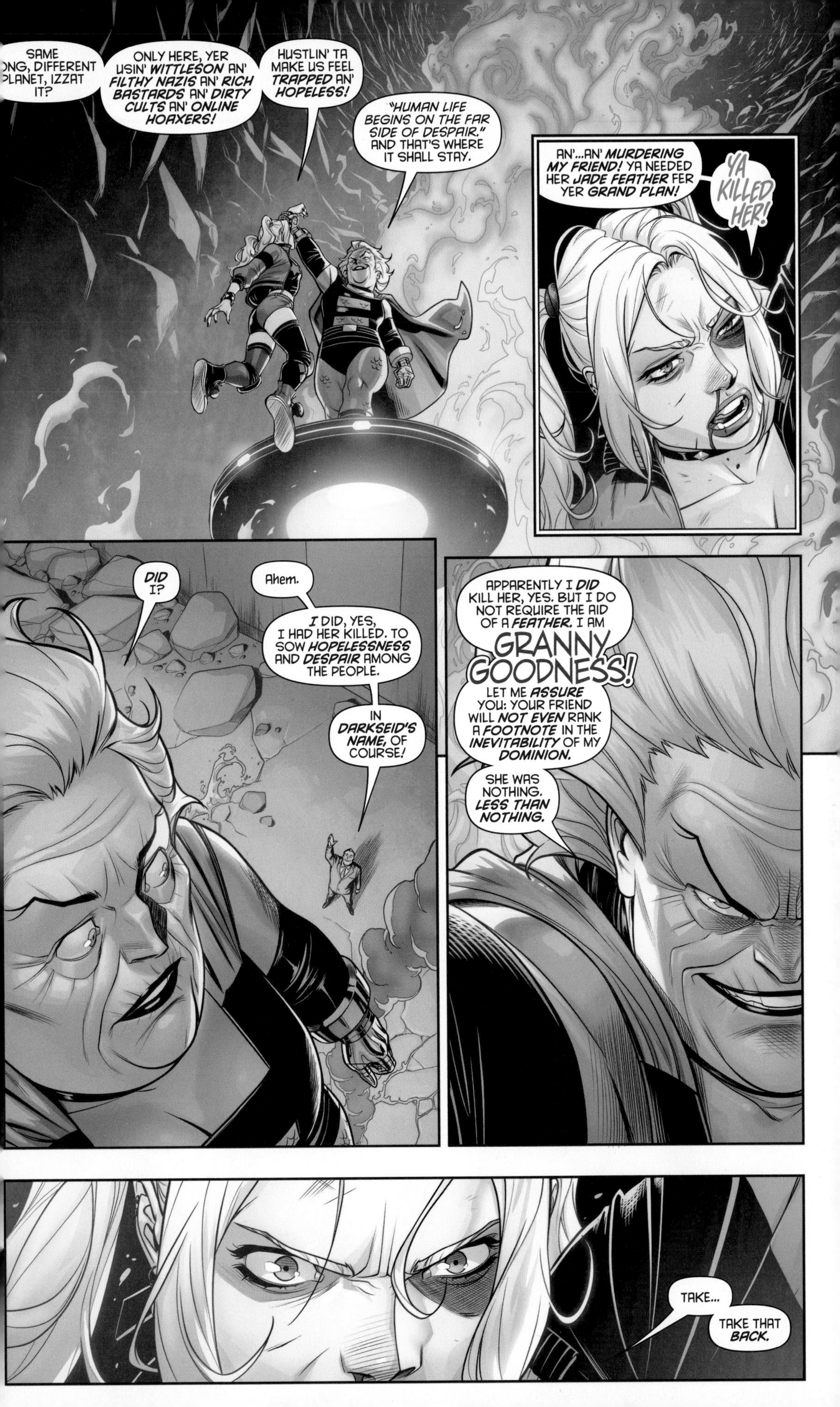
SAME
ONG, DIFFERENT
PLANET, IZZAT
IT?
ONLY HERE, YER USIN' WITTLESON AN' FILTHY NAZIS AN' RICH BASTARDS AN' DIRTY CULTS AN' ONLINE HOAXERS!
HUSTLIN' TA MAKE US FEEL TRAPPED AN' HOPELESS!
"HUMAN LIFE BEGINS ON THE FAR SIDE OF DESPAIR." AND THAT'S WHERE IT SHALL STAY.
AN'...AN' MURDERING MY FRIEND! YA NEEDED HER JADE FEATHER FER YER GRAND PLAN!
YA KILLED HER!
DID I?
Ahem.
I DID, YES, I HAD HER KILLED. TO SOW HOPELESSNESS AND DESPAIR AMONG THE PEOPLE.
IN DARKSEID'S NAME, OF COURSE!
APPARENTLY I DID KILL HER, YES. BUT I DO NOT REQUIRE THE AID OF A FEATHER. I AM
GRANNY GOODNESS!
LET ME ASSURE YOU: YOUR FRIEND WILL NOT EVEN RANK A FOOTNOTE IN THE INEVITABILITY OF MY DOMINION.
SHE WAS NOTHING. LESS THAN NOTHING.
TAKE...
TAKE THAT BACK.

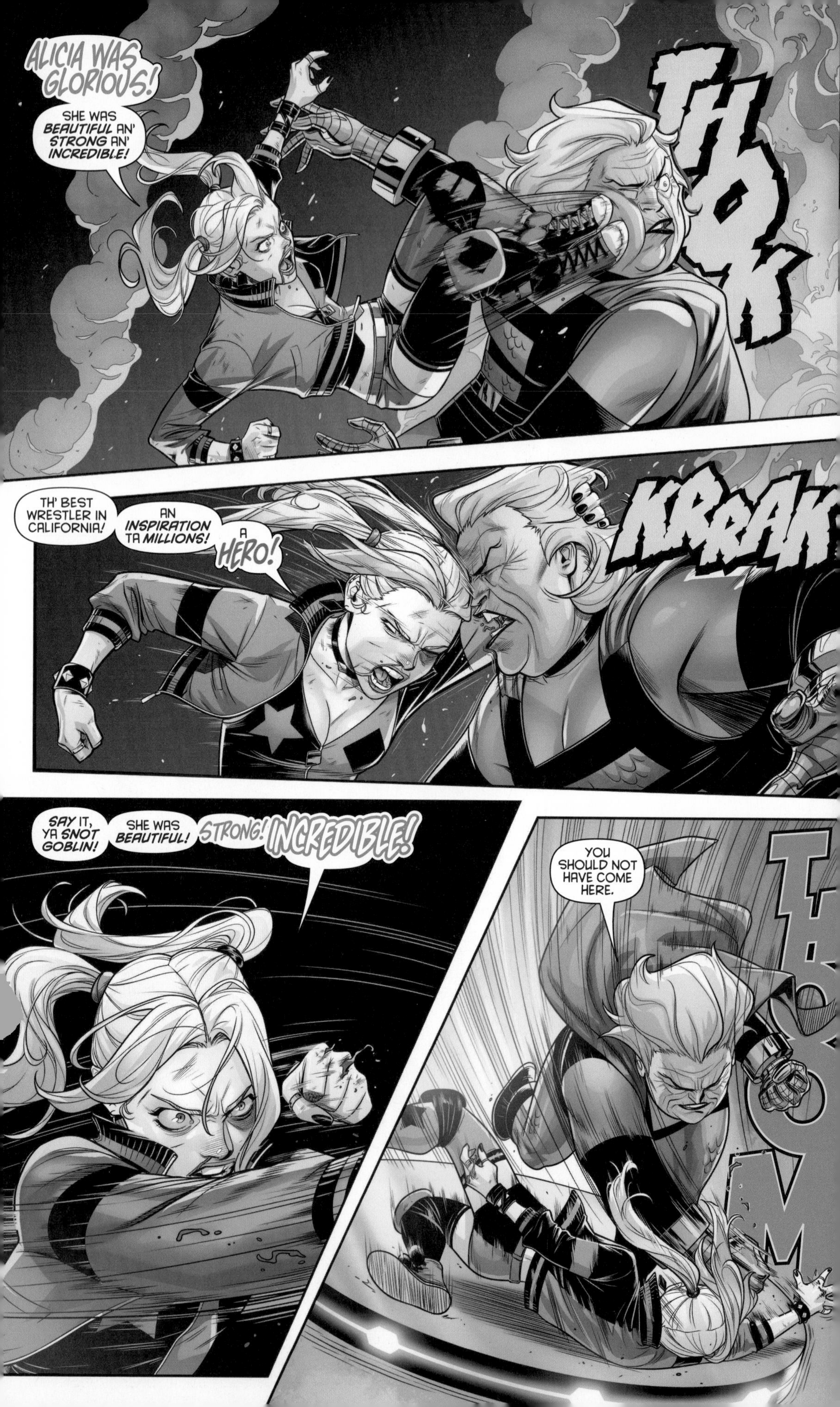

ALICIA WAS GLORIOUS!
SHE WAS BEAUTIFUL AN' STRONG AN' INCREDIBLE!
THOK
TH' BEST WRESTLER IN CALIFORNIA!
AN INSPIRATION TA MILLIONS!
A HERO!
KRRAK
SAY IT, YA SNOT GOBLIN!
SHE WAS BEAUTIFUL!
STRONG!
INCREDIBLE!
YOU SHOULD NOT HAVE COME HERE.

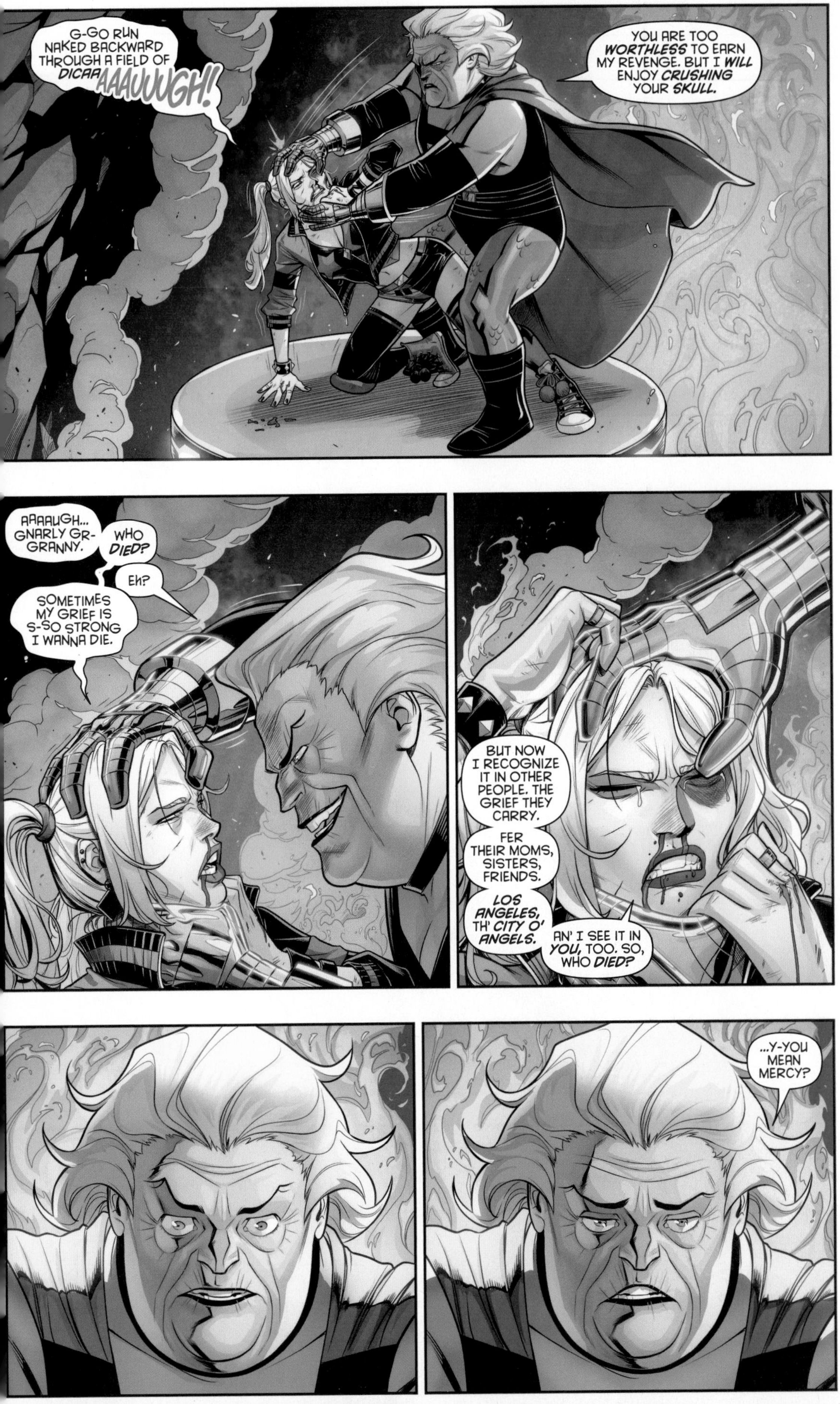
G-GO RUN NAKED BACKWARD THROUGH A FIELD OF DICAAAAAUUUGH!
YOU ARE TOO WORTHLESS TO EARN MY REVENGE. BUT I WILL ENJOY CRUSHING YOUR SKULL.
AAAAUGH... GNARLY GR-GRANNY.
WHO DIED?
EH?
SOMETIMES MY GRIEF IS S-SO STRONG I WANNA DIE.
BUT NOW I RECOGNIZE IT IN OTHER PEOPLE. THE GRIEF THEY CARRY.
FER THEIR MOMS, SISTERS, FRIENDS.
LOS ANGELES, TH' CITY O' ANGELS.
AN' I SEE IT IN YOU, TOO. SO, WHO DIED?
...Y-YOU MEAN MERCY?

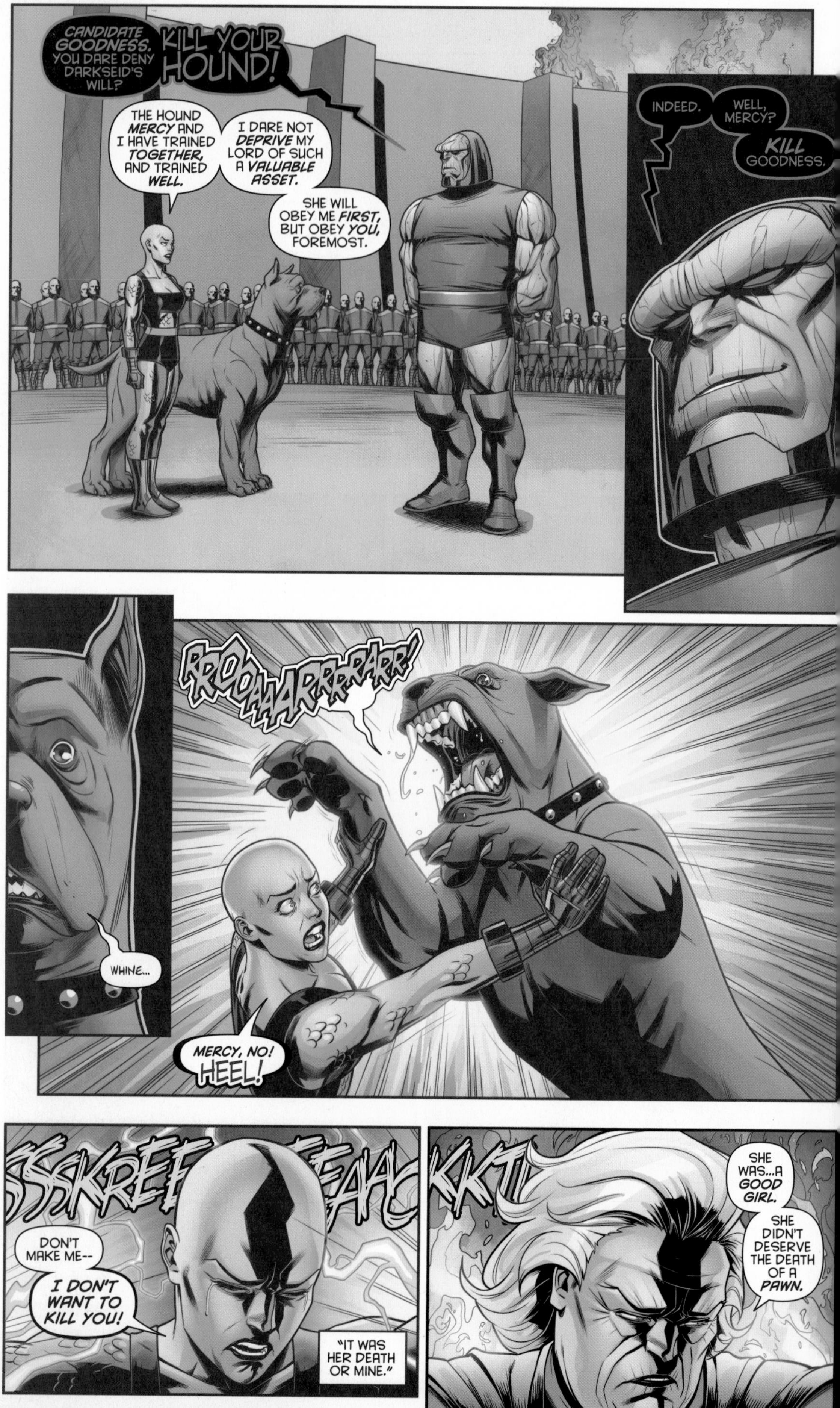
CANDIDATE GOODNESS. YOU DARE DENY DARKSEID'S WILL?
KILL YOUR HOUND!
THE HOUND MERCY AND I HAVE TRAINED TOGETHER, AND TRAINED WELL.
I DARE NOT DEPRIVE MY LORD OF SUCH A VALUABLE ASSET.
SHE WILL OBEY ME FIRST, BUT OBEY YOU, FOREMOST.
INDEED.
WELL, MERCY?
KILL GOODNESS.
WHINE...
RROOAAARRRRARR!
MERCY, NO! HEEL!
SSSKREEEEEAACKKT!
DON'T MAKE ME--
I DON'T WANT TO KILL YOU!
"IT WAS HER DEATH OR MINE."
SHE WAS...A GOOD GIRL.
SHE DIDN'T DESERVE THE DEATH OF A PAWN.

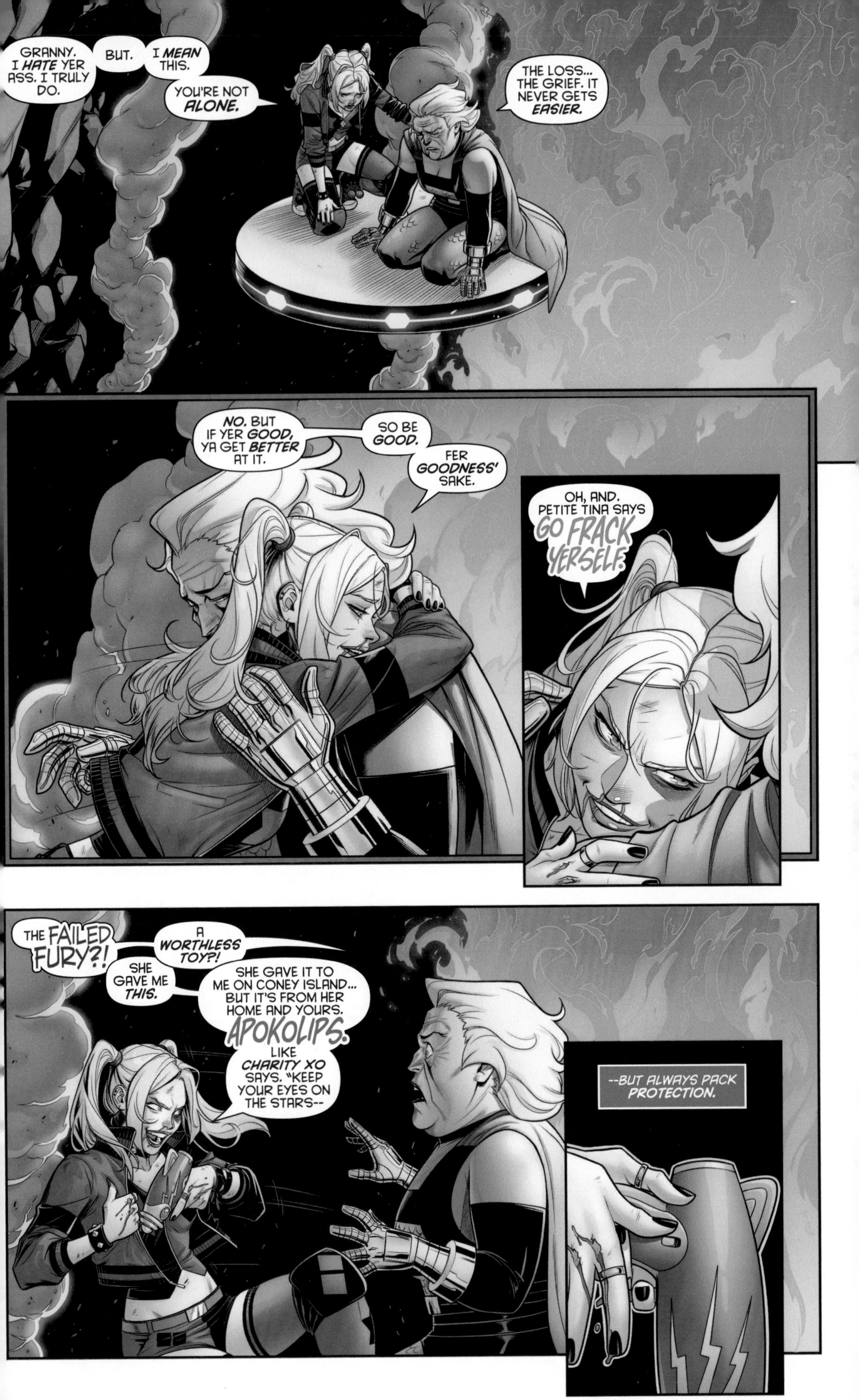

GRANNY. I HATE YER ASS. I TRULY DO.
BUT.
I MEAN THIS.
YOU'RE NOT ALONE.
THE LOSS... THE GRIEF. IT NEVER GETS EASIER.
NO. BUT IF YER GOOD, YA GET BETTER AT IT.
SO BE GOOD.
FER GOODNESS' SAKE.
OH, AND. PETITE TINA SAYS GO FRACK YERSELF.
THE FAILED FURY?!
A WORTHLESS TOY?!
SHE GAVE ME THIS.
SHE GAVE IT TO ME ON CONEY ISLAND... BUT IT'S FROM HER HOME AND YOURS. APOKOLIPS.
LIKE CHARITY XO SAYS. "KEEP YOUR EYES ON THE STARS--
--BUT ALWAYS PACK PROTECTION.

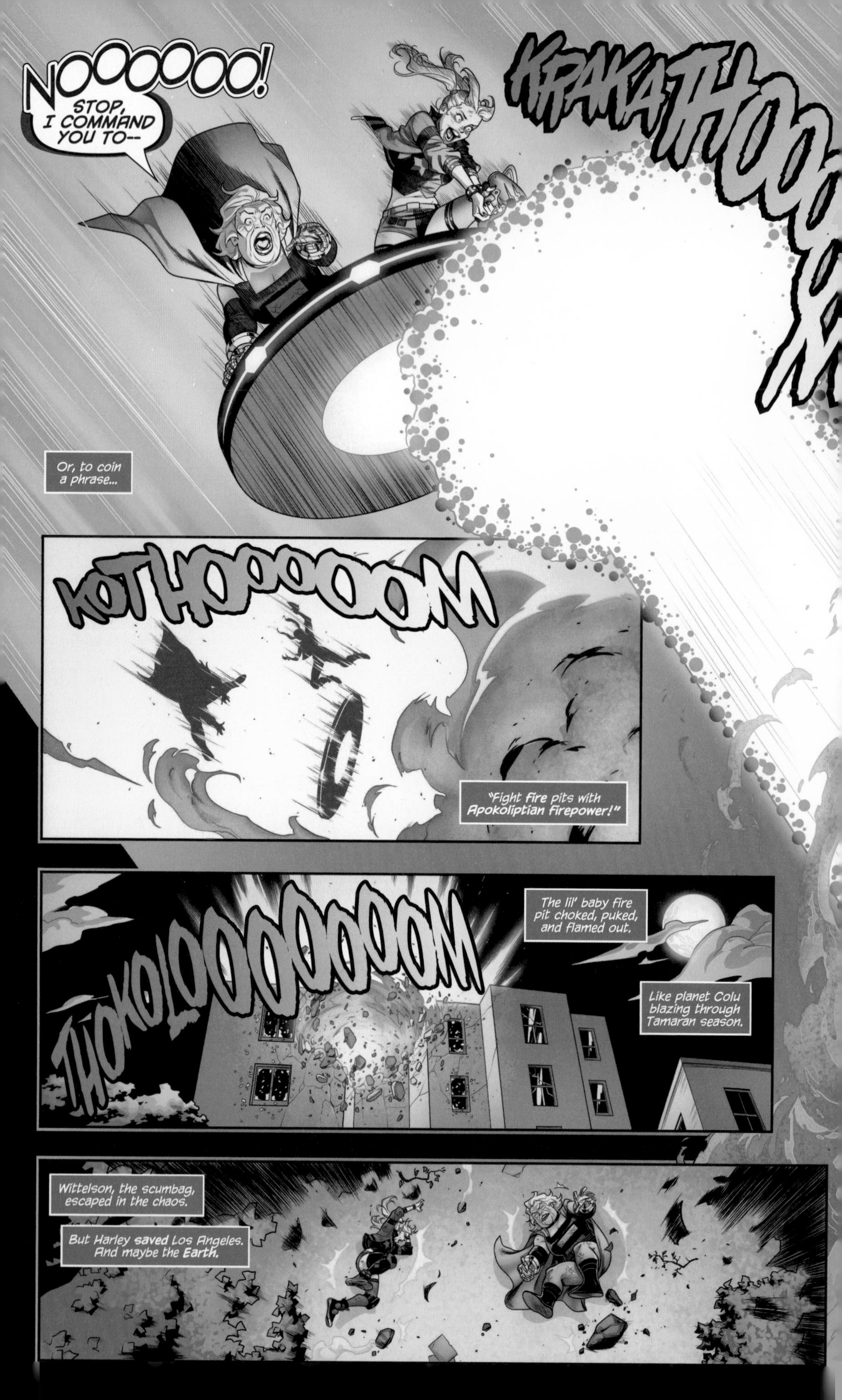
NOOOOOOO!
STOP, I COMMAND YOU TO--
KRAKATHOOOOM
Or, to coin a phrase...
KOTHOOOOOOM
"Fight fire pits with Apokoliptian firepower!"
THOKOLOOOOOOOOM
The lil' baby fire pit choked, puked, and flamed out.
Like planet Colu blazing through Tamaran season.
Wittelson, the scumbag, escaped in the chaos.
But Harley saved Los Angeles. And maybe the Earth.

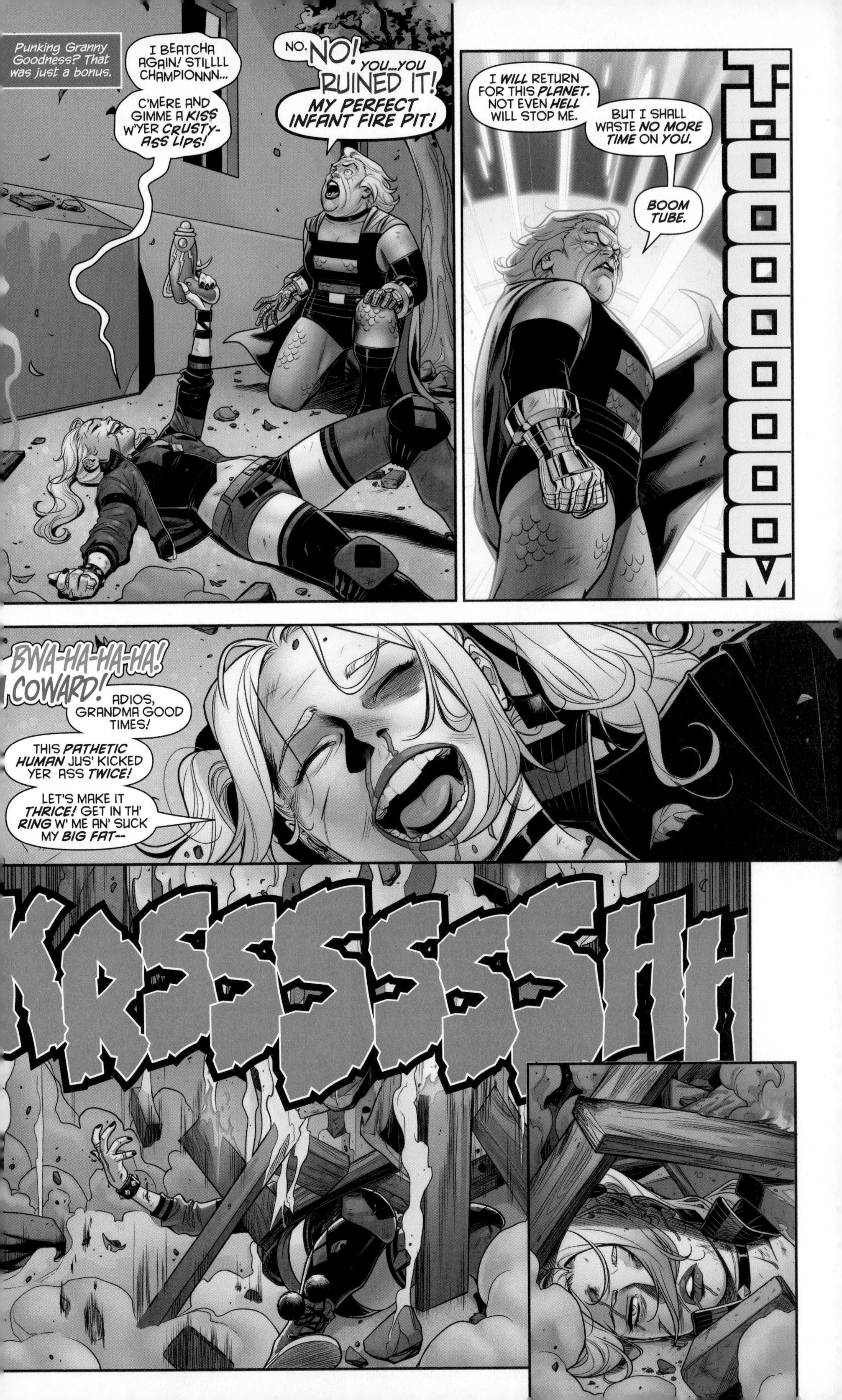

Punking Granny Goodness? That was just a bonus.
I BEATCHA AGAIN! STILLLL CHAMPIONNN...
C'MERE AND GIMME A KISS W'YER CRUSTY-ASS LIPS!
NO.
NO!
YOU...YOU RUINED IT!
MY PERFECT INFANT FIRE PIT!
I WILL RETURN FOR THIS PLANET. NOT EVEN HELL WILL STOP ME.
BUT I SHALL WASTE NO MORE TIME ON YOU.
BOOM TUBE.
THOOOOOOOOM
BWA-HA-HA-HA! COWARD!
ADIOS, GRANDMA GOOD TIMES!
THIS PATHETIC HUMAN JUS' KICKED YER ASS TWICE!
LET'S MAKE IT THRICE! GET IN TH' RING W' ME AN' SUCK MY BIG FAT--
KRSSSSSSHH

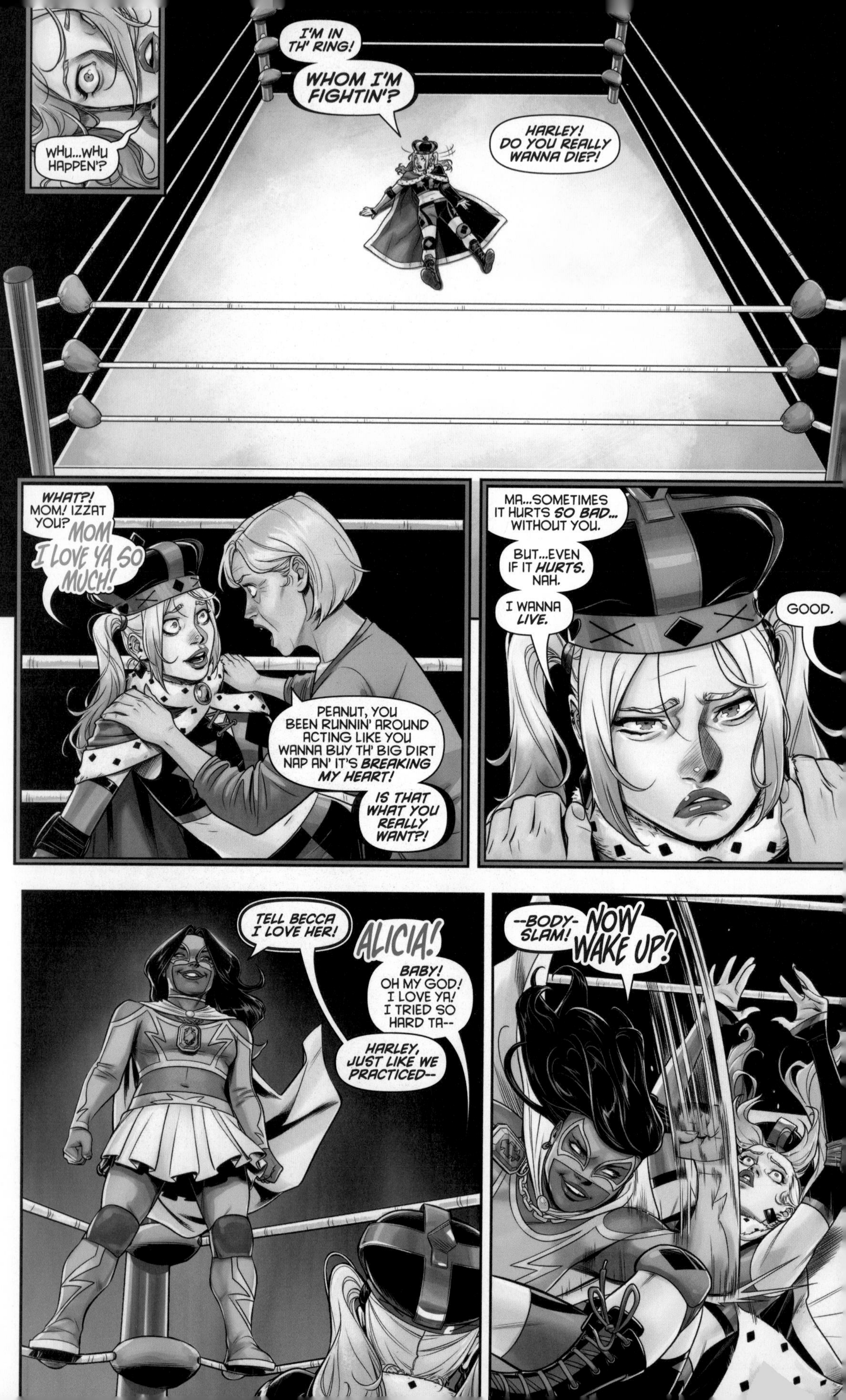
WHU...WHU HAPPEN'?
I'M IN TH' RING!
WHOM I'M FIGHTIN'?
HARLEY! DO YOU REALLY WANNA DIE?!
WHAT?! MOM! IZZAT YOU?
MOM I LOVE YA SO MUCH!
PEANUT, YOU BEEN RUNNIN' AROUND ACTING LIKE YOU WANNA BUY TH' BIG DIRT NAP AN' IT'S BREAKING MY HEART!
IS THAT WHAT YOU REALLY WANT?!
MA...SOMETIMES IT HURTS SO BAD... WITHOUT YOU.
BUT...EVEN IF IT HURTS. NAH.
I WANNA LIVE.
GOOD.
TELL BECCA I LOVE HER!
ALICIA!
BABY! OH MY GOD! I LOVE YA! I TRIED SO HARD TA--
HARLEY, JUST LIKE WE PRACTICED--
--BODY-SLAM!
NOW WAKE UP!

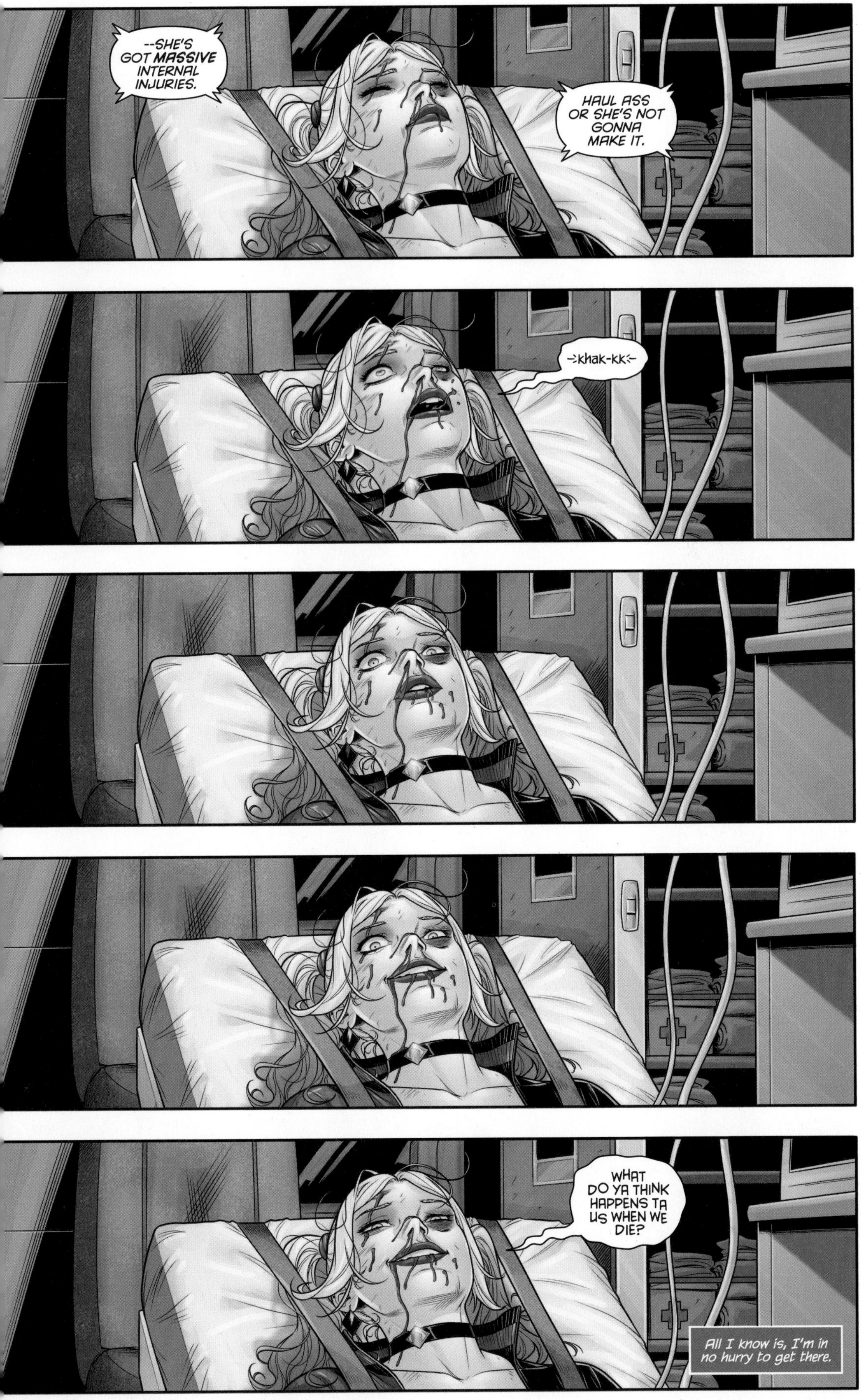
--SHE'S GOT **MASSIVE** INTERNAL INJURIES.
HAUL ASS OR SHE'S NOT GONNA MAKE IT.
-khak-kk-
WHAT DO YA THINK HAPPENS TA US WHEN WE DIE?
All I know is, I'm in no hurry to get there.

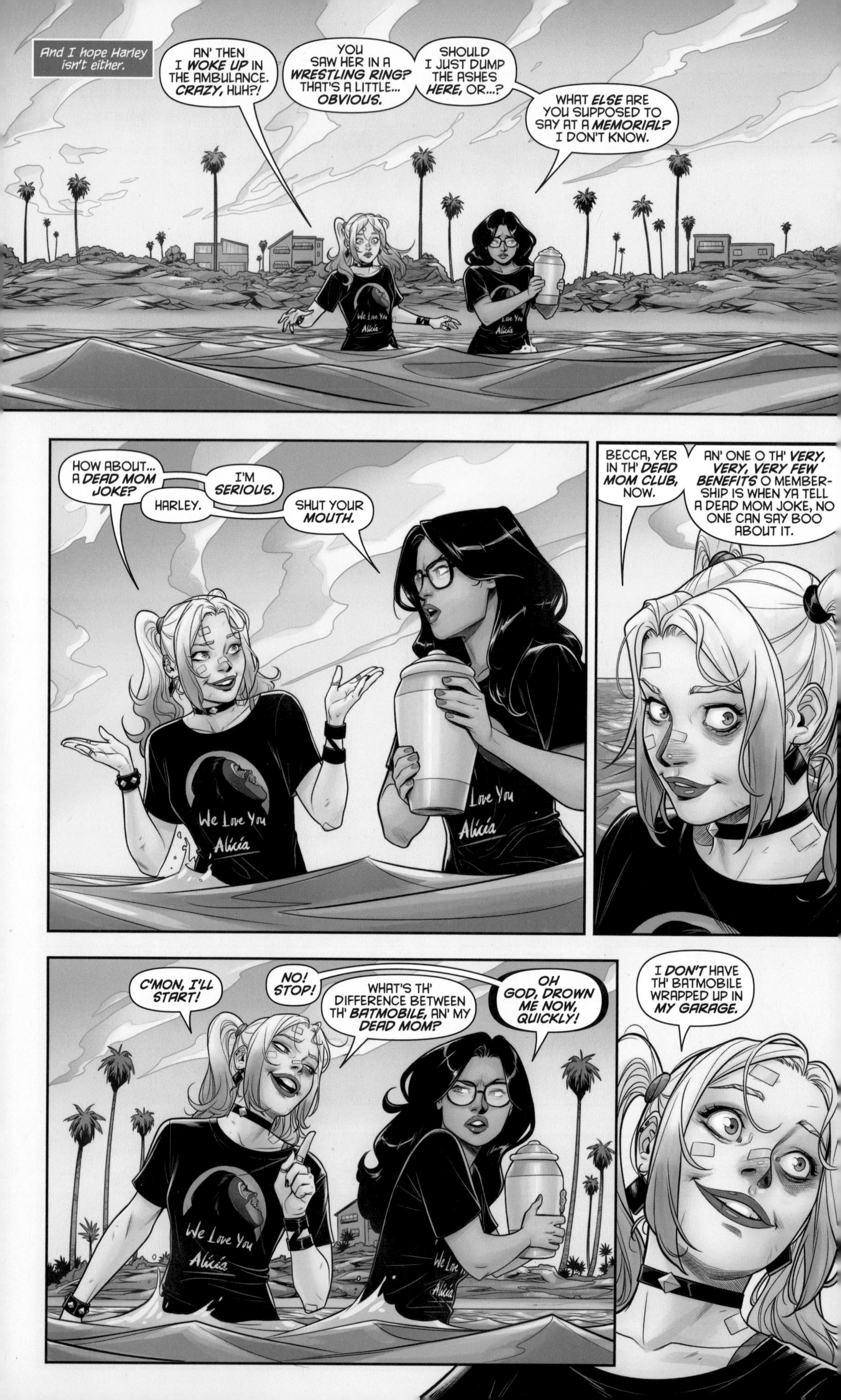
And I hope Harley isn't either.
AN' THEN I WOKE UP IN THE AMBULANCE. CRAZY, HUH?!
YOU SAW HER IN A WRESTLING RING? THAT'S A LITTLE... OBVIOUS.
SHOULD I JUST DUMP THE ASHES HERE, OR...?
WHAT ELSE ARE YOU SUPPOSED TO SAY AT A MEMORIAL? I DON'T KNOW.
We Love You Alicia
HOW ABOUT... A DEAD MOM JOKE?
I'M SERIOUS.
HARLEY.
SHUT YOUR MOUTH.
We Love You Alicia
BECCA, YER IN TH' DEAD MOM CLUB, NOW.
AN' ONE O TH' VERY, VERY, VERY FEW BENEFITS O MEMBER-SHIP IS WHEN YA TELL A DEAD MOM JOKE, NO ONE CAN SAY BOO ABOUT IT.
C'MON, I'LL START!
NO! STOP!
WHAT'S TH' DIFFERENCE BETWEEN TH' BATMOBILE, AN' MY DEAD MOM?
OH GOD, DROWN ME NOW, QUICKLY!
We Love You Alicia
I DON'T HAVE TH' BATMOBILE WRAPPED UP IN MY GARAGE.

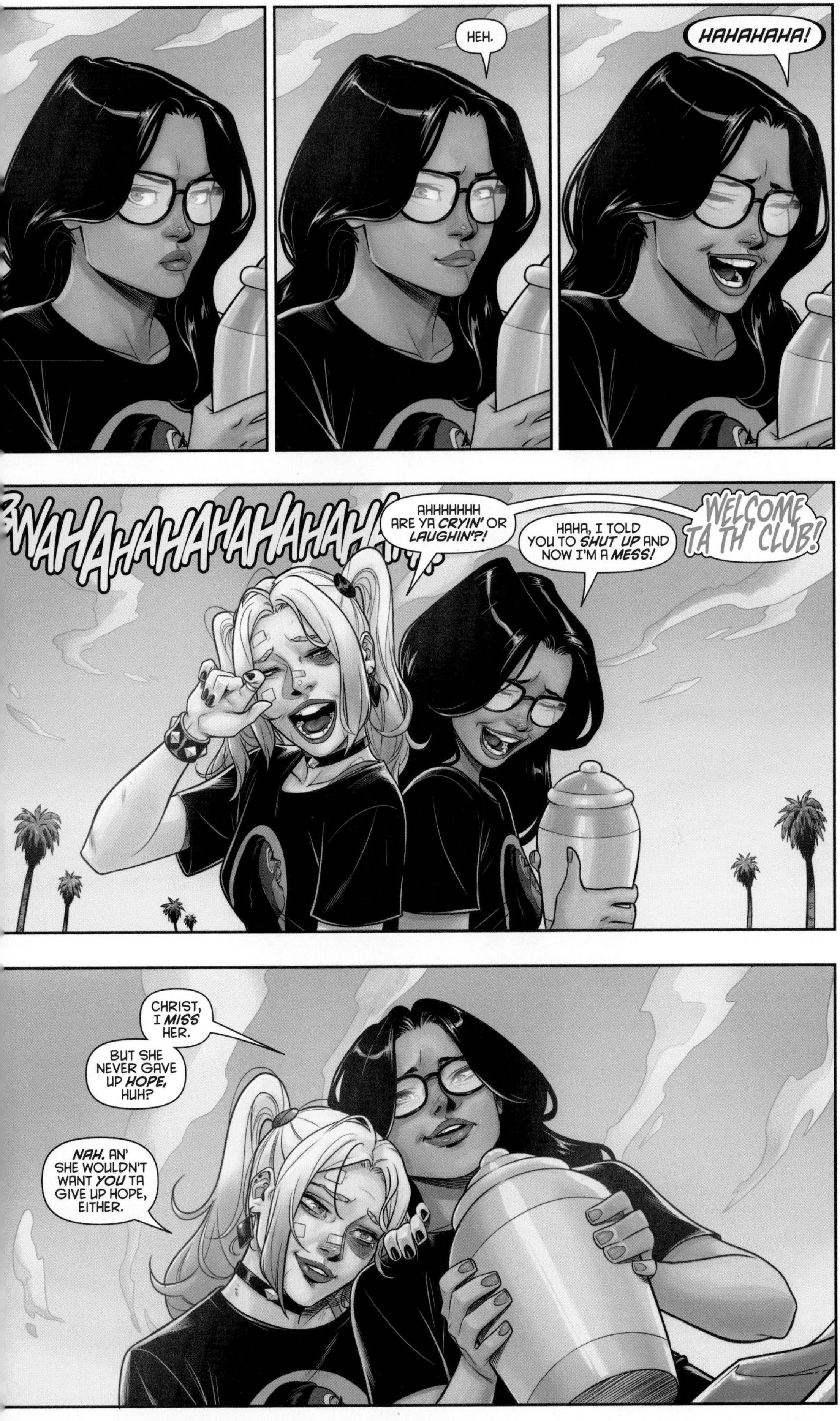
HEH.
HAHAHAHA!
WAHAHAHAHAHAHAHAHAHA
AHHHHHHH ARE YA CRYIN' OR LAUGHIN'?!
HAHA, I TOLD YOU TO SHUT UP AND NOW I'M A MESS!
WELCOME TA TH' CLUB!
CHRIST, I MISS HER.
BUT SHE NEVER GAVE UP HOPE, HUH?
NAH. AN' SHE WOULDN'T WANT YOU TA GIVE UP HOPE, EITHER.

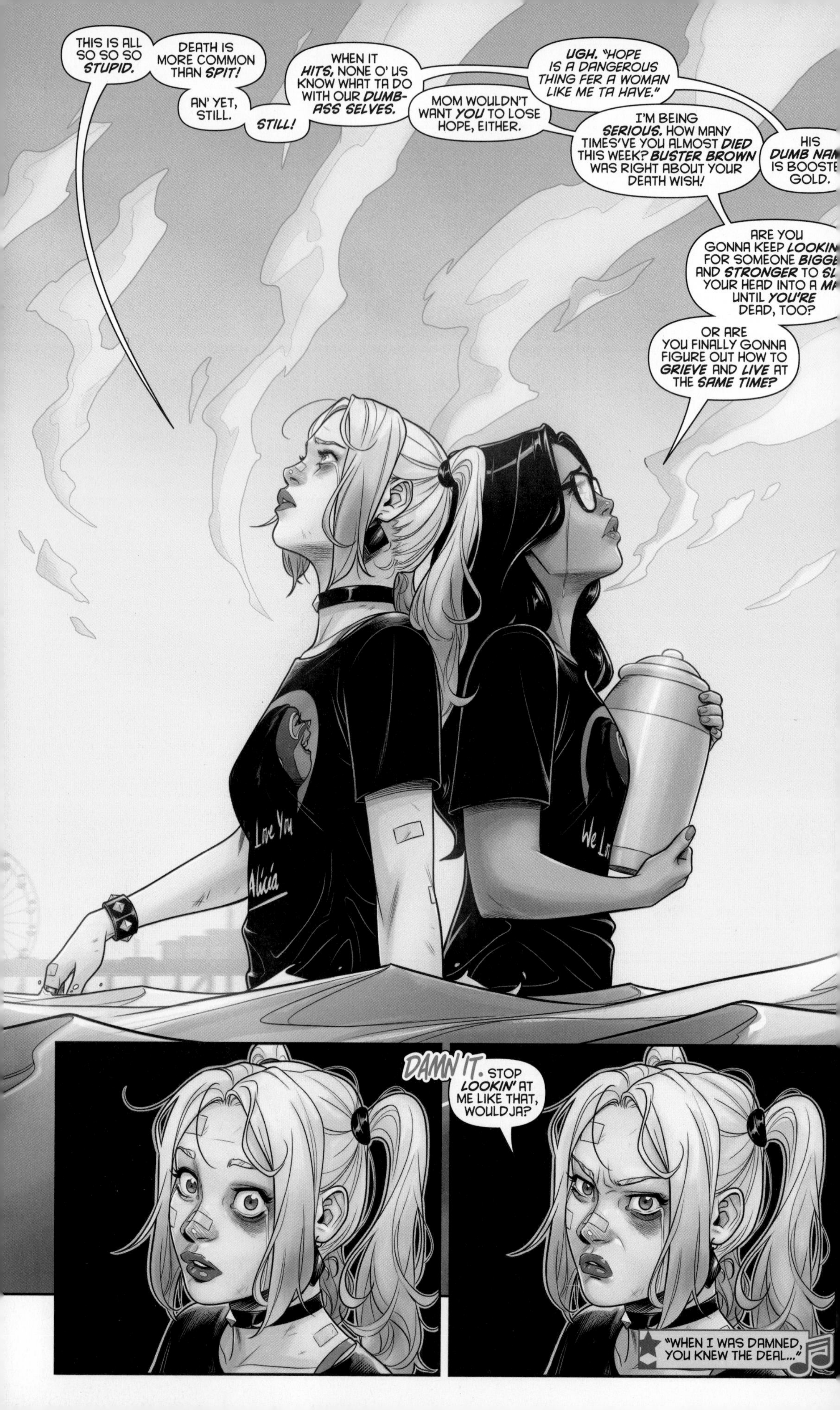
THIS IS ALL SO SO SO *STUPID.*
DEATH IS MORE COMMON THAN *SPIT!*
AN' YET, STILL.
STILL!
WHEN IT *HITS,* NONE O' US KNOW WHAT TA DO WITH OUR *DUMB-ASS SELVES.*
MOM WOULDN'T WANT *YOU* TO LOSE HOPE, EITHER.
UGH. "HOPE IS A DANGEROUS THING FER A WOMAN LIKE ME TA HAVE."
I'M BEING *SERIOUS.* HOW MANY TIMES'VE YOU ALMOST *DIED* THIS WEEK? *BUSTER BROWN* WAS RIGHT ABOUT YOUR DEATH WISH!
HIS *DUMB NAM* IS BOOSTE GOLD.
ARE YOU GONNA KEEP *LOOKIN* FOR SOMEONE *BIGGE* AND *STRONGER* TO *SL* YOUR HEAD INTO A *M* UNTIL *YOU'RE* DEAD, TOO?
OR ARE YOU FINALLY GONNA FIGURE OUT HOW TO *GRIEVE* AND *LIVE* AT THE *SAME TIME?*
DAMN IT. STOP *LOOKIN'* AT ME LIKE THAT, WOULDJA?
"WHEN I WAS DAMNED, YOU KNEW THE DEAL..."

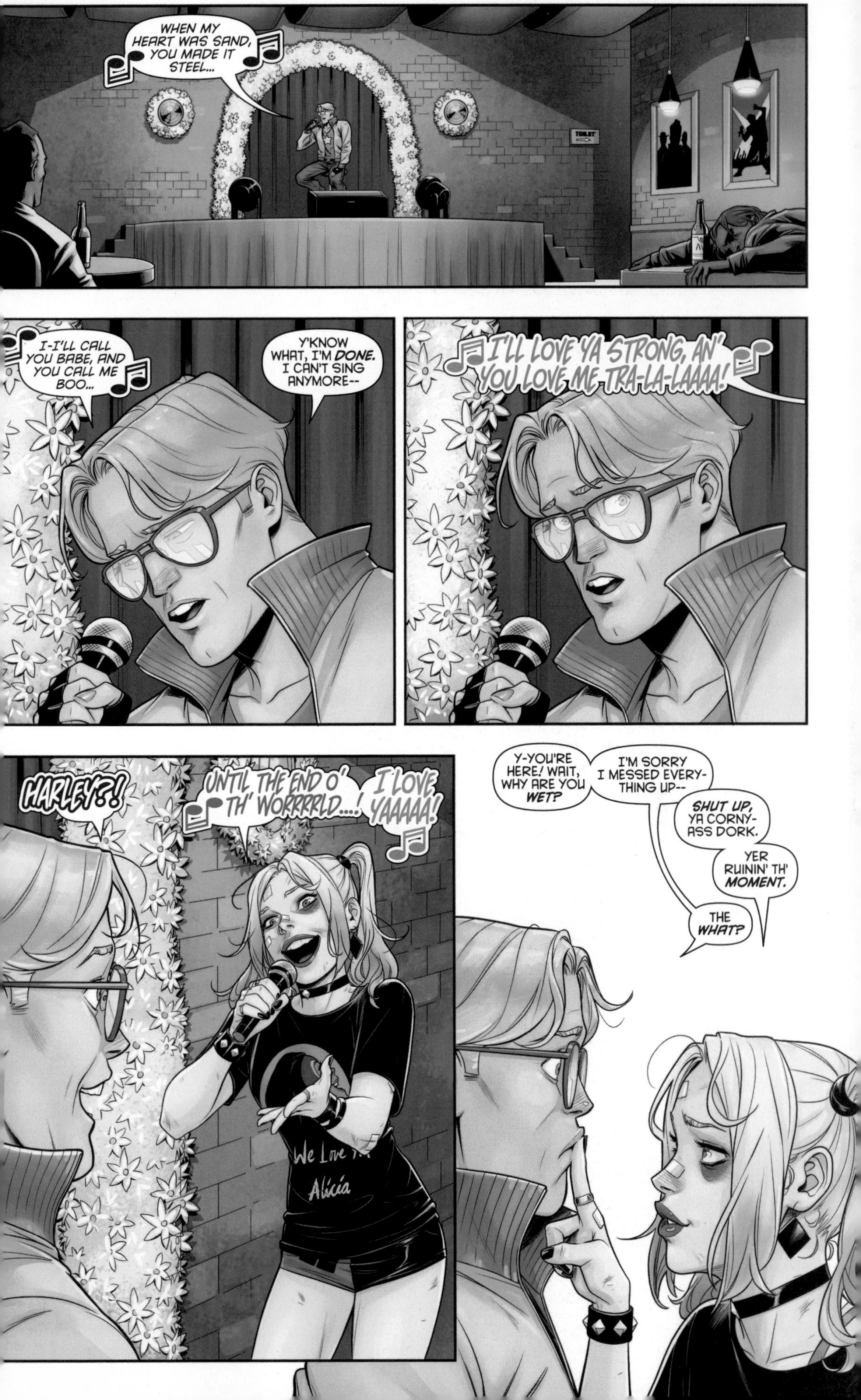
WHEN MY HEART WAS SAND, YOU MADE IT STEEL...
I-I'LL CALL YOU BABE, AND YOU CALL ME BOO...
Y'KNOW WHAT, I'M DONE. I CAN'T SING ANYMORE--
I'LL LOVE YA STRONG, AN' YOU LOVE ME TRA-LA-LAAAA!
CHARLEY?!
UNTIL THE END O' TH' WORRRRLD...!
I LOVE YAAAAA!
Y-YOU'RE HERE! WAIT, WHY ARE YOU WET?
I'M SORRY I MESSED EVERY-THING UP--
SHUT UP, YA CORNY-ASS DORK.
YER RUININ' TH' MOMENT.
THE WHAT?

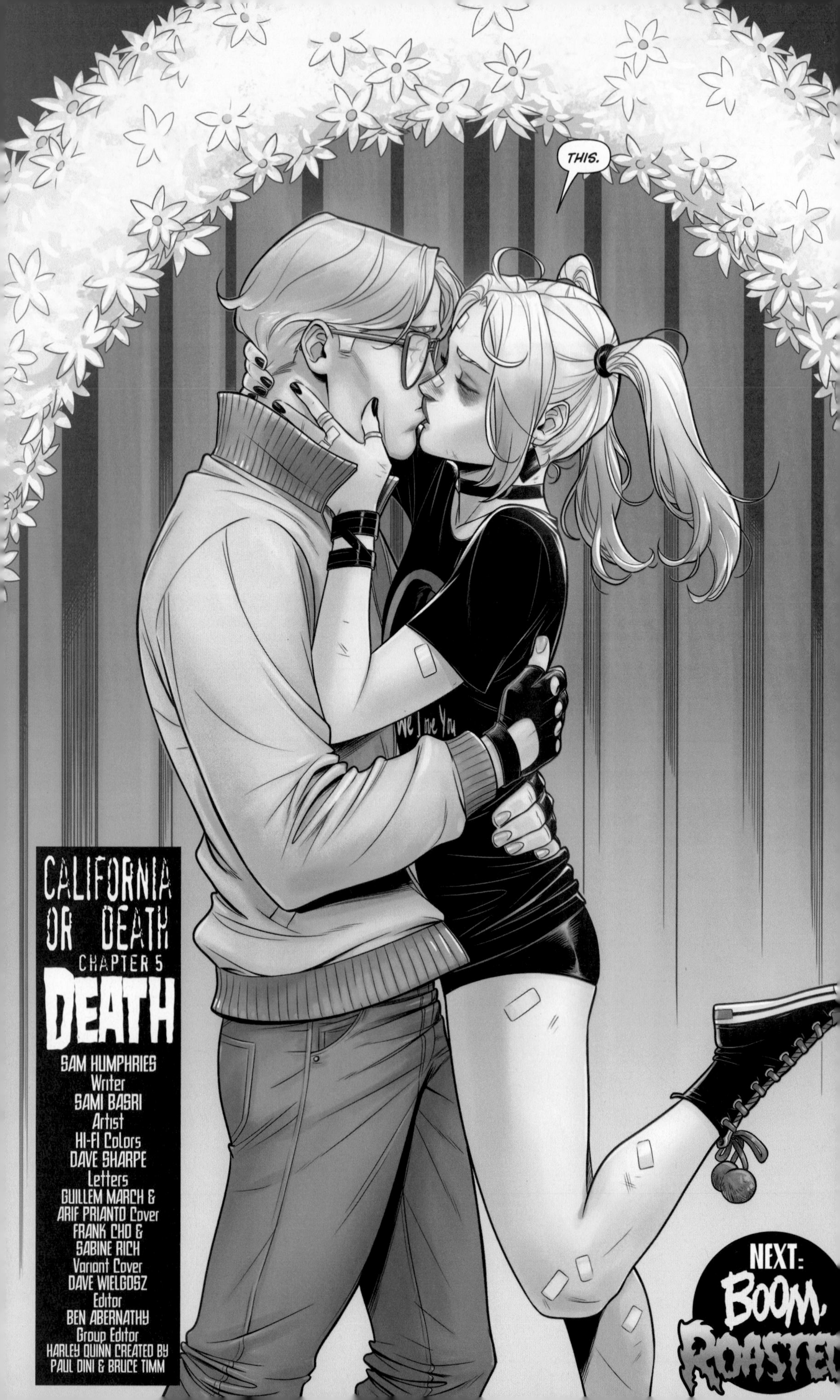
THIS.
We Love You
CALIFORNIA OR DEATH
CHAPTER 5
DEATH
SAM HUMPHRIES Writer
SAMI BASRI Artist
HI-FI Colors
DAVE SHARPE Letters
GUILLEM MARCH & ARIF PRIANTO Cover
FRANK CHO & SABINE RICH Variant Cover
DAVE WIELGOSZ Editor
BEN ABERNATHY Group Editor
HARLEY QUINN CREATED BY PAUL DINI & BRUCE TIMM
NEXT: BOOM ROASTED

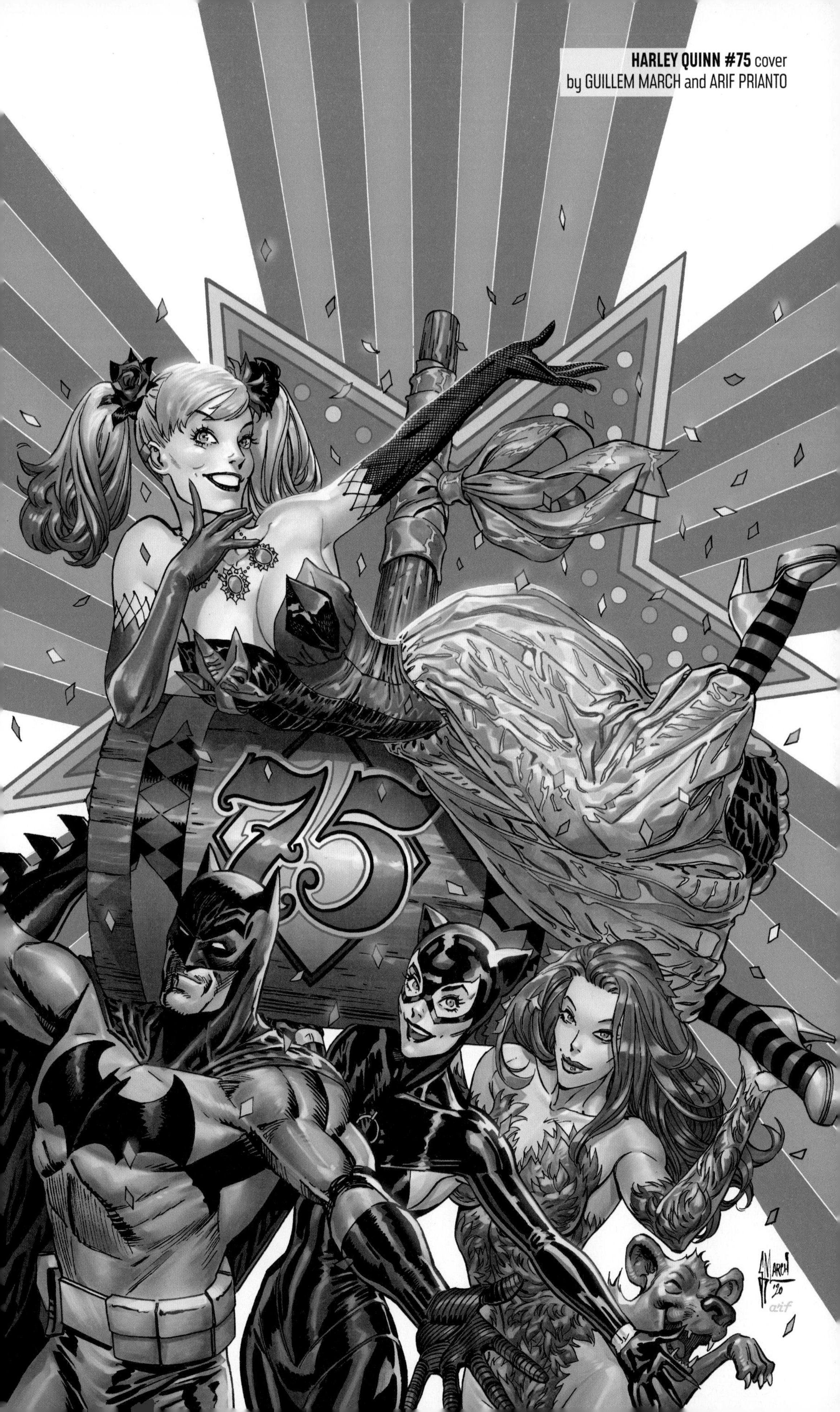
75

HARLEY QUINN #75 cover
by GUILLEM MARCH and ARIF PRIANTO

HARLEY QUINN #75 variant cover
by FRANK CHO and SABINE RICH

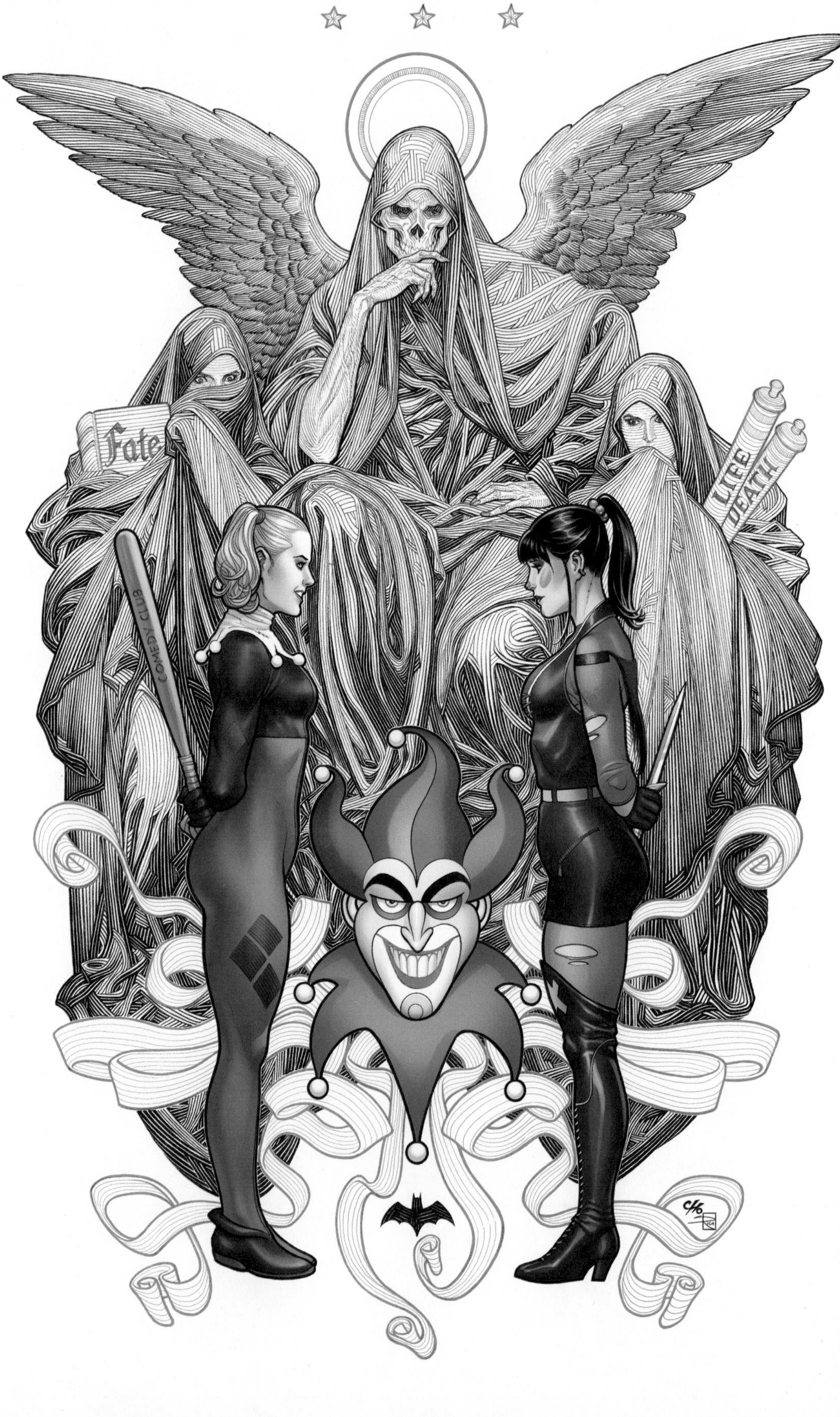
Fate
LIFE
DEATH
COMEDY CLUB

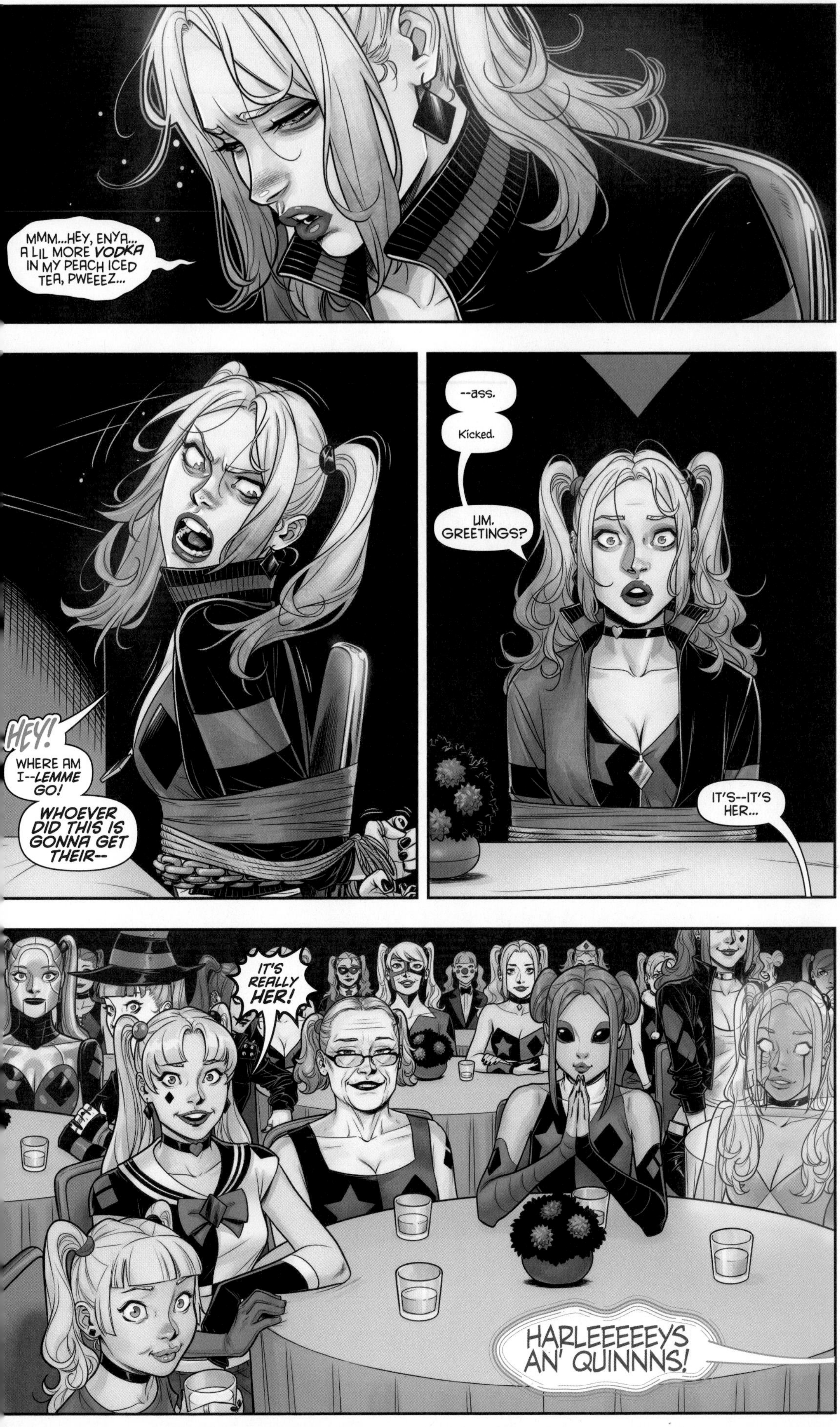

MMM...HEY, ENYA... A LIL MORE VODKA IN MY PEACH ICED TEA, PWEEEZ...
HEY!
WHERE AM I--LEMME GO!
WHOEVER DID THIS IS GONNA GET THEIR--
--ass.
Kicked.
UM. GREETINGS?
IT'S--IT'S HER...
IT'S REALLY HER!
HARLEEEEEYS AN' QUINNNS!

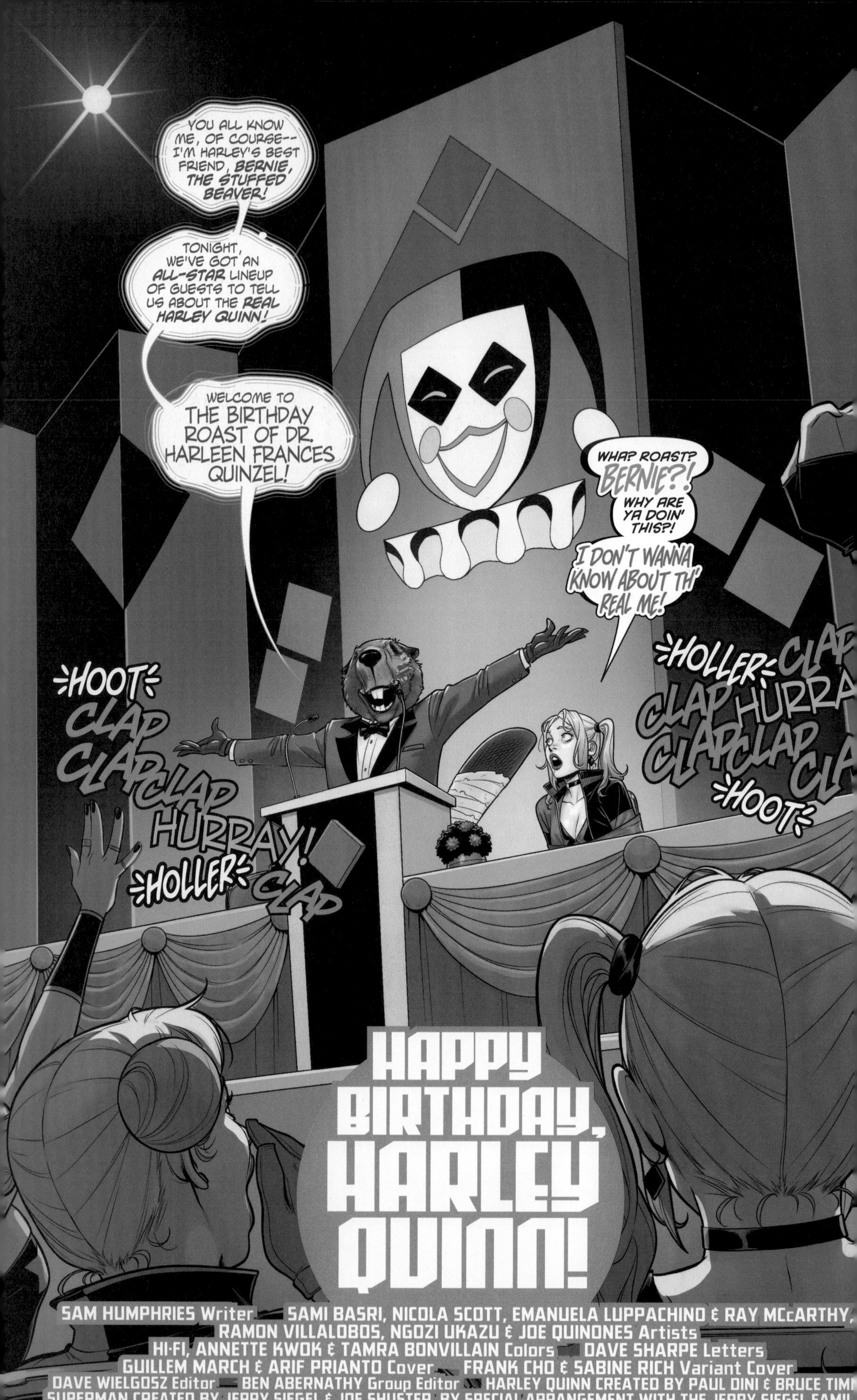

YOU ALL KNOW ME, OF COURSE-- I'M HARLEY'S BEST FRIEND, BERNIE, THE STUFFED BEAVER!
TONIGHT, WE'VE GOT AN ALL-STAR LINEUP OF GUESTS TO TELL US ABOUT THE REAL HARLEY QUINN!
WELCOME TO THE BIRTHDAY ROAST OF DR. HARLEEN FRANCES QUINZEL!
WHA? ROAST? BERNIE?! WHY ARE YA DOIN' THIS?!
I DON'T WANNA KNOW ABOUT TH' REAL ME!
HOOT CLAP CLAP CLAP HURRAY! HOLLER CLAP
HOLLER CLAP CLAP HURRA CLAP CLAP CLA HOOT
HAPPY BIRTHDAY, HARLEY QUINN!
SAM HUMPHRIES Writer SAMI BASRI, NICOLA SCOTT, EMANUELA LUPPACHINO & RAY McCARTHY, RAMON VILLALOBOS, NGOZI UKAZU & JOE QUINONES Artists
HI-FI, ANNETTE KWOK & TAMRA BONVILLAIN Colors DAVE SHARPE Letters
GUILLEM MARCH & ARIF PRIANTO Cover FRANK CHO & SABINE RICH Variant Cover
DAVE WIELGOSZ Editor BEN ABERNATHY Group Editor HARLEY QUINN CREATED BY PAUL DINI & BRUCE TIMM
SUPERMAN CREATED BY JERRY SIEGEL & JOE SHUSTER. BY SPECIAL ARRANGEMENT WITH THE JERRY SIEGEL FAMIL

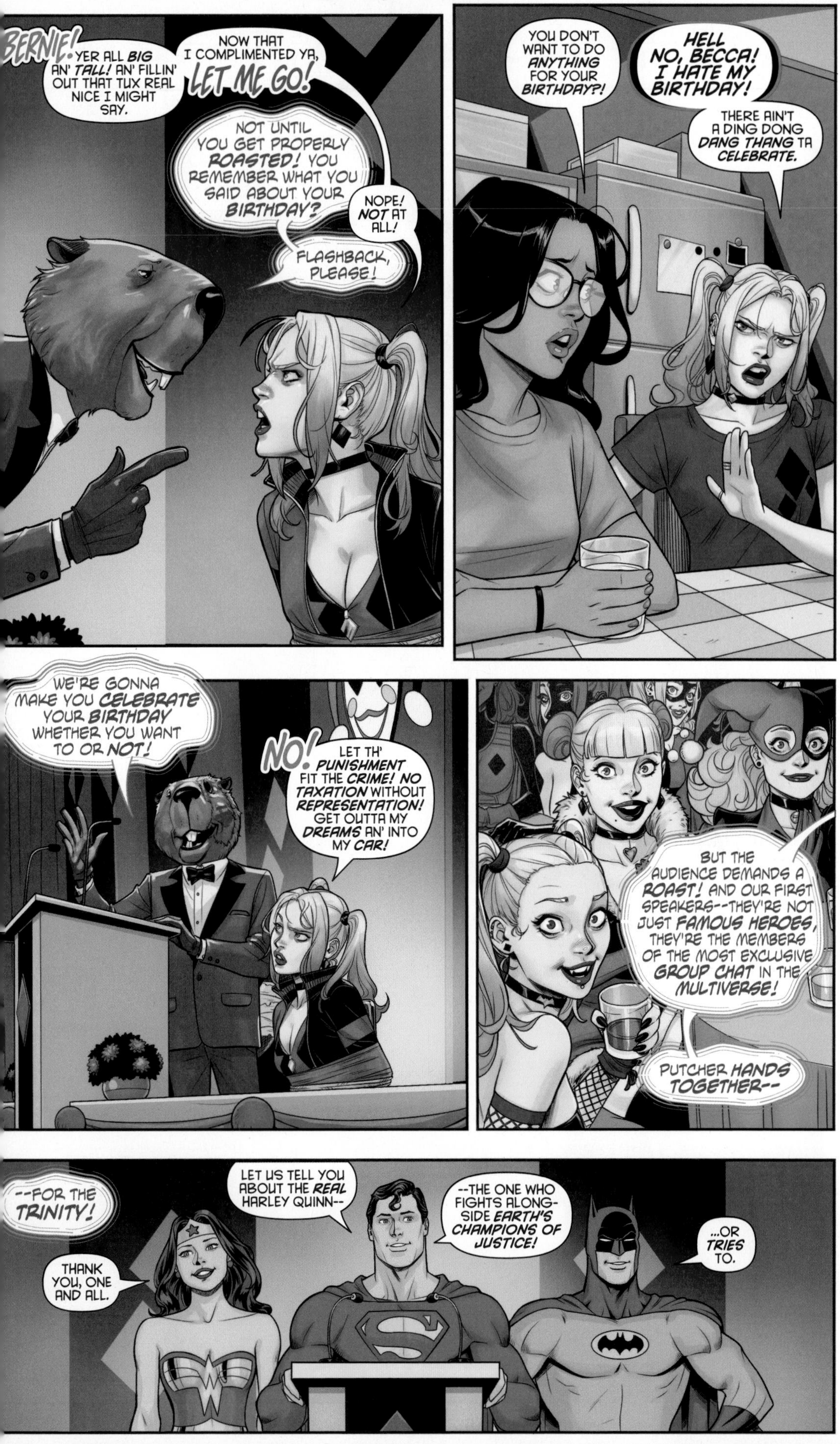
BERNIE!
YER ALL BIG AN' TALL! AN' FILLIN' OUT THAT TUX REAL NICE I MIGHT SAY.
NOW THAT I COMPLIMENTED YA, LET ME GO!
NOT UNTIL YOU GET PROPERLY ROASTED! YOU REMEMBER WHAT YOU SAID ABOUT YOUR BIRTHDAY?
NOPE! NOT AT ALL!
FLASHBACK, PLEASE!
YOU DON'T WANT TO DO ANYTHING FOR YOUR BIRTHDAY?!
HELL NO, BECCA! I HATE MY BIRTHDAY!
THERE AIN'T A DING DONG DANG THANG TA CELEBRATE.
WE'RE GONNA MAKE YOU CELEBRATE YOUR BIRTHDAY WHETHER YOU WANT TO OR NOT!
NO!
LET TH' PUNISHMENT FIT THE CRIME! NO TAXATION WITHOUT REPRESENTATION! GET OUTTA MY DREAMS AN' INTO MY CAR!
BUT THE AUDIENCE DEMANDS A ROAST! AND OUR FIRST SPEAKERS--THEY'RE NOT JUST FAMOUS HEROES, THEY'RE THE MEMBERS OF THE MOST EXCLUSIVE GROUP CHAT IN THE MULTIVERSE!
PUTCHER HANDS TOGETHER--
--FOR THE TRINITY!
THANK YOU, ONE AND ALL.
LET US TELL YOU ABOUT THE REAL HARLEY QUINN--
--THE ONE WHO FIGHTS ALONGSIDE EARTH'S CHAMPIONS OF JUSTICE!
...OR TRIES TO.

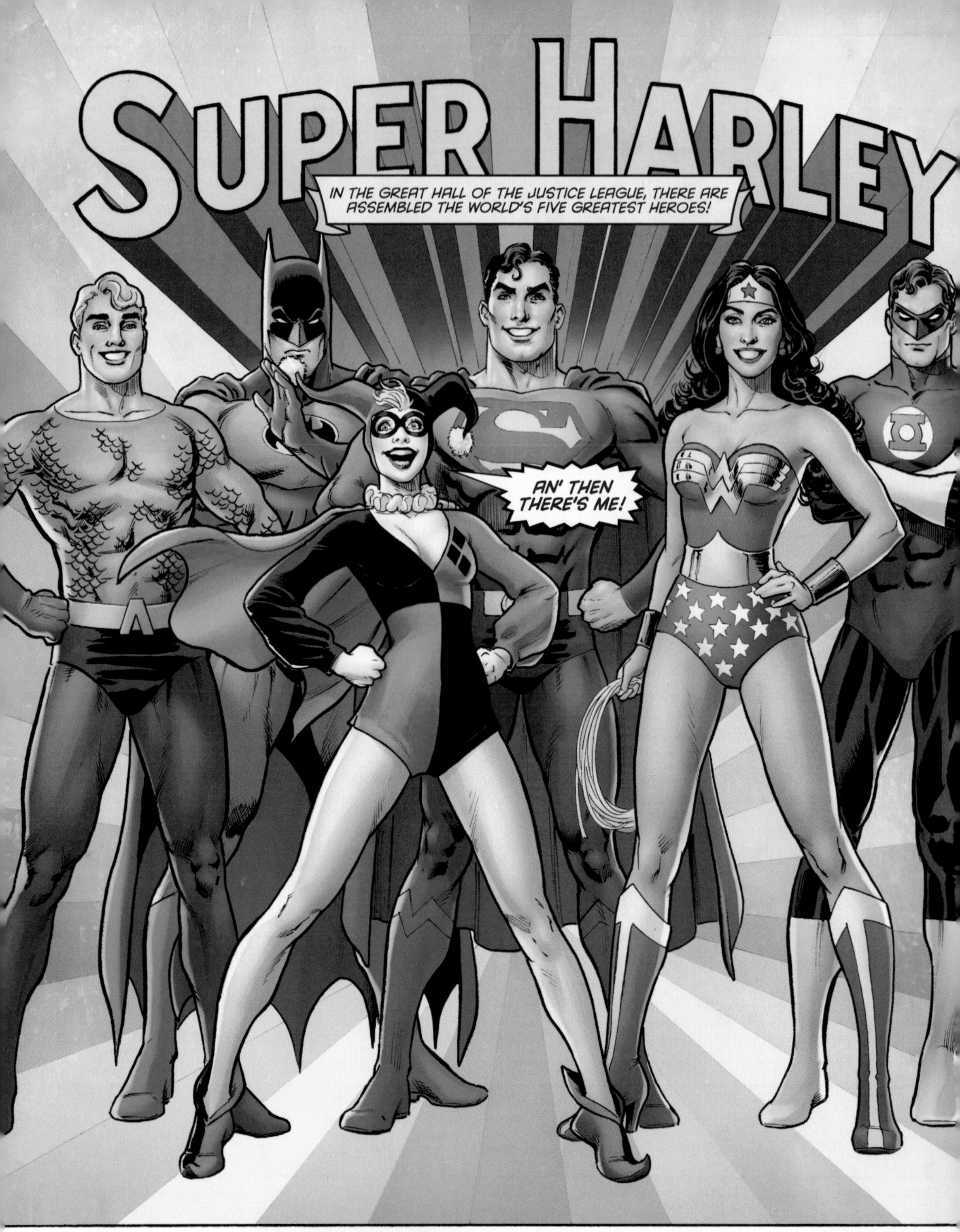
SUPER HARLEY
IN THE GREAT HALL OF THE JUSTICE LEAGUE, THERE ARE ASSEMBLED THE WORLD'S FIVE GREATEST HEROES!
AN' THEN THERE'S ME!

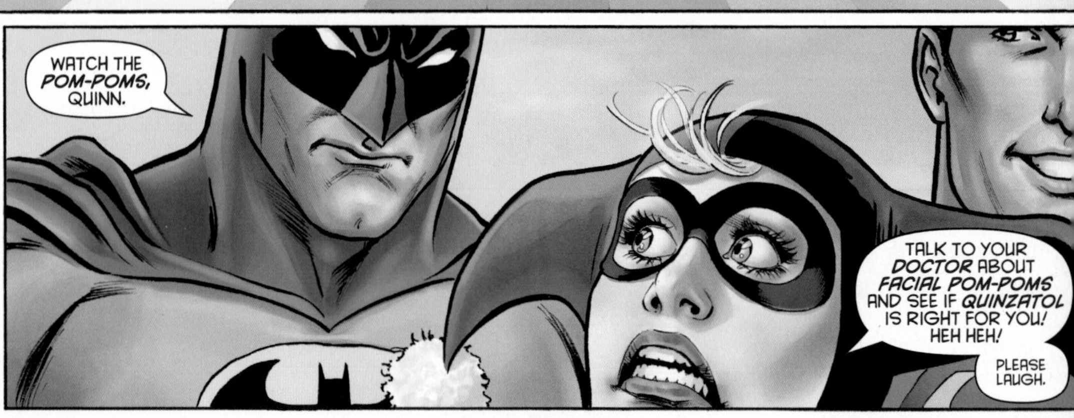
WATCH THE POM-POMS, QUINN.
TALK TO YOUR DOCTOR ABOUT FACIAL POM-POMS AND SEE IF QUINZATOL IS RIGHT FOR YOU! HEH HEH!
PLEASE LAUGH.

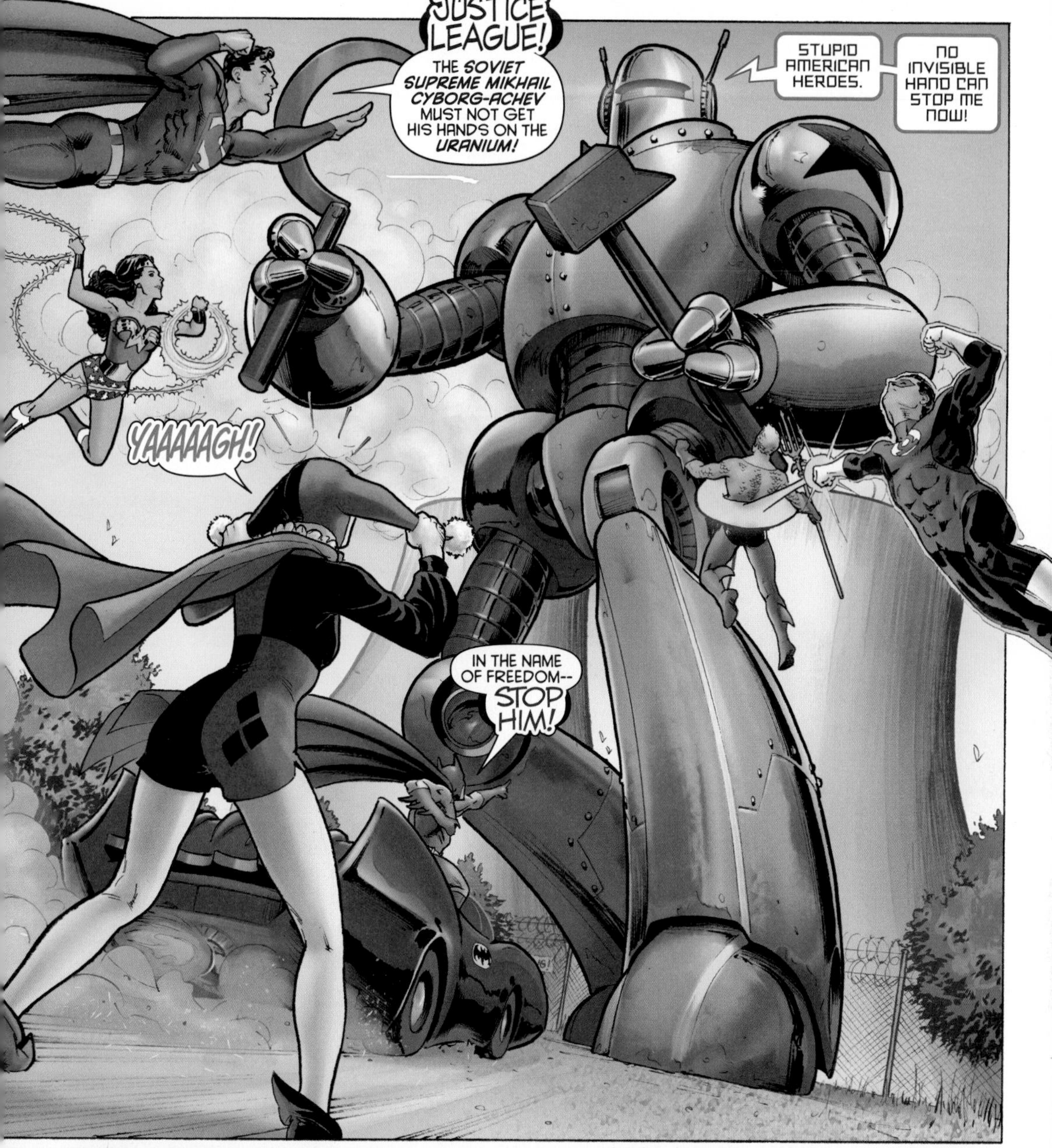
JUSTICE LEAGUE!
THE SOVIET SUPREME MIKHAIL CYBORG-ACHEV MUST NOT GET HIS HANDS ON THE URANIUM!
STUPID AMERICAN HEROES.
NO INVISIBLE HAND CAN STOP ME NOW!
YAAAAAGH!
IN THE NAME OF FREEDOM-- STOP HIM!

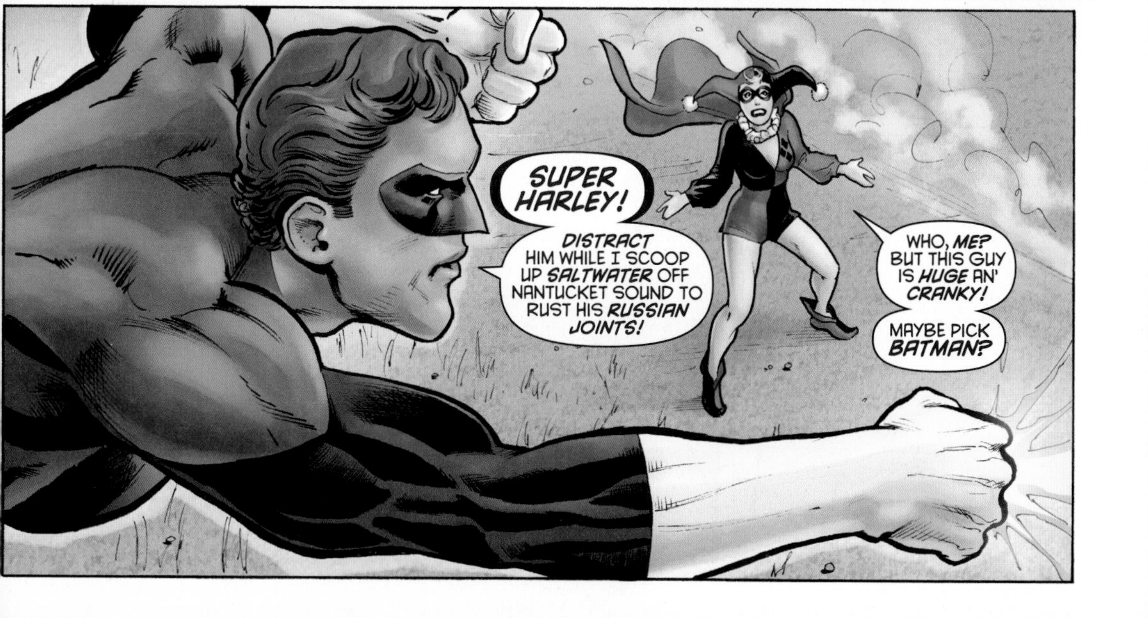
SUPER HARLEY!
DISTRACT HIM WHILE I SCOOP UP SALTWATER OFF NANTUCKET SOUND TO RUST HIS RUSSIAN JOINTS!
WHO, ME? BUT THIS GUY IS HUGE AN' CRANKY!
MAYBE PICK BATMAN?

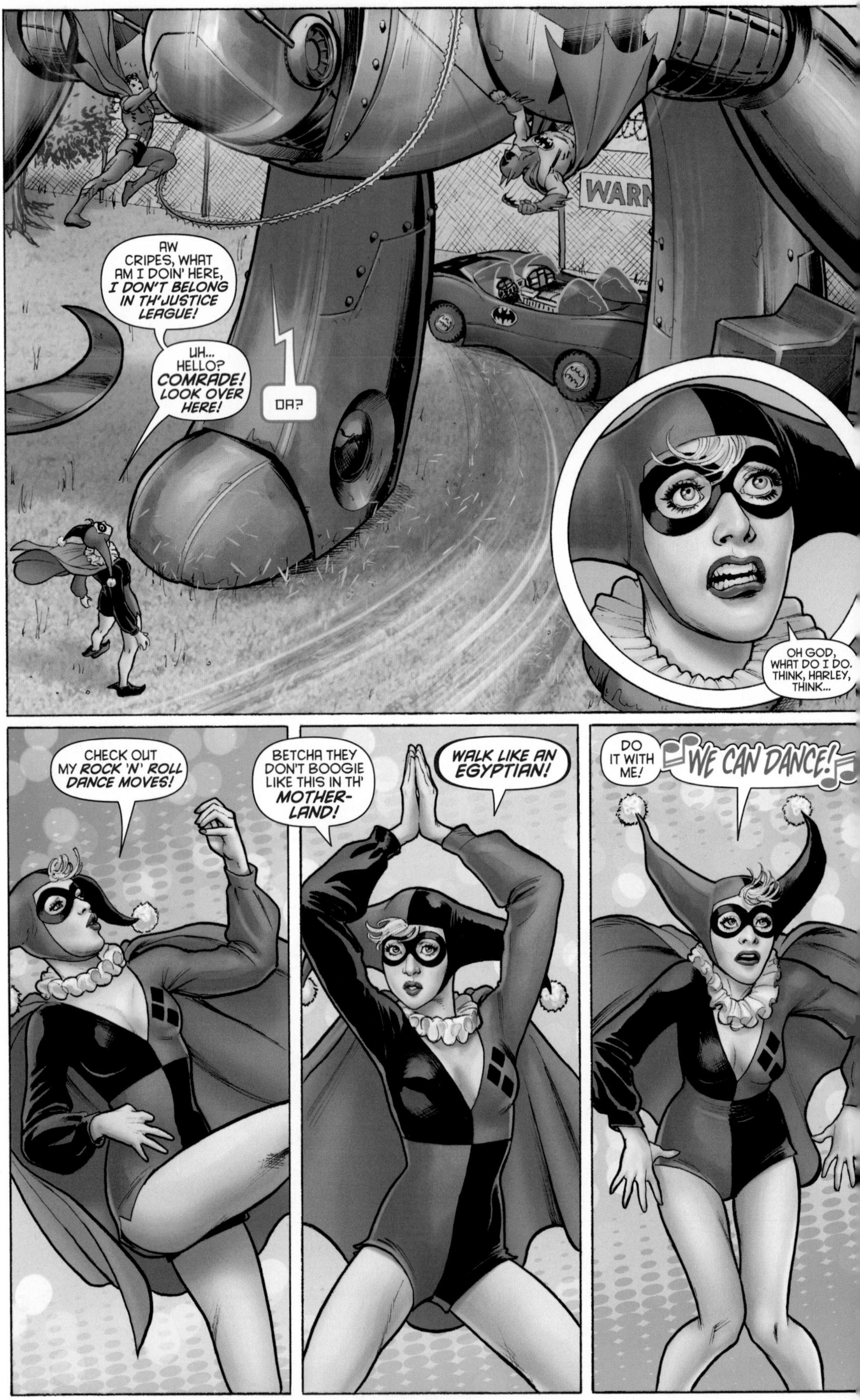
WARN
AW CRIPES, WHAT AM I DOIN' HERE, I DON'T BELONG IN TH' JUSTICE LEAGUE!
UH... HELLO? COMRADE! LOOK OVER HERE!
DA?
OH GOD, WHAT DO I DO. THINK, HARLEY, THINK...
CHECK OUT MY ROCK 'N' ROLL DANCE MOVES!
BETCHA THEY DON'T BOOGIE LIKE THIS IN TH' MOTHER-LAND!
WALK LIKE AN EGYPTIAN!
DO IT WITH ME!
WE CAN DANCE!

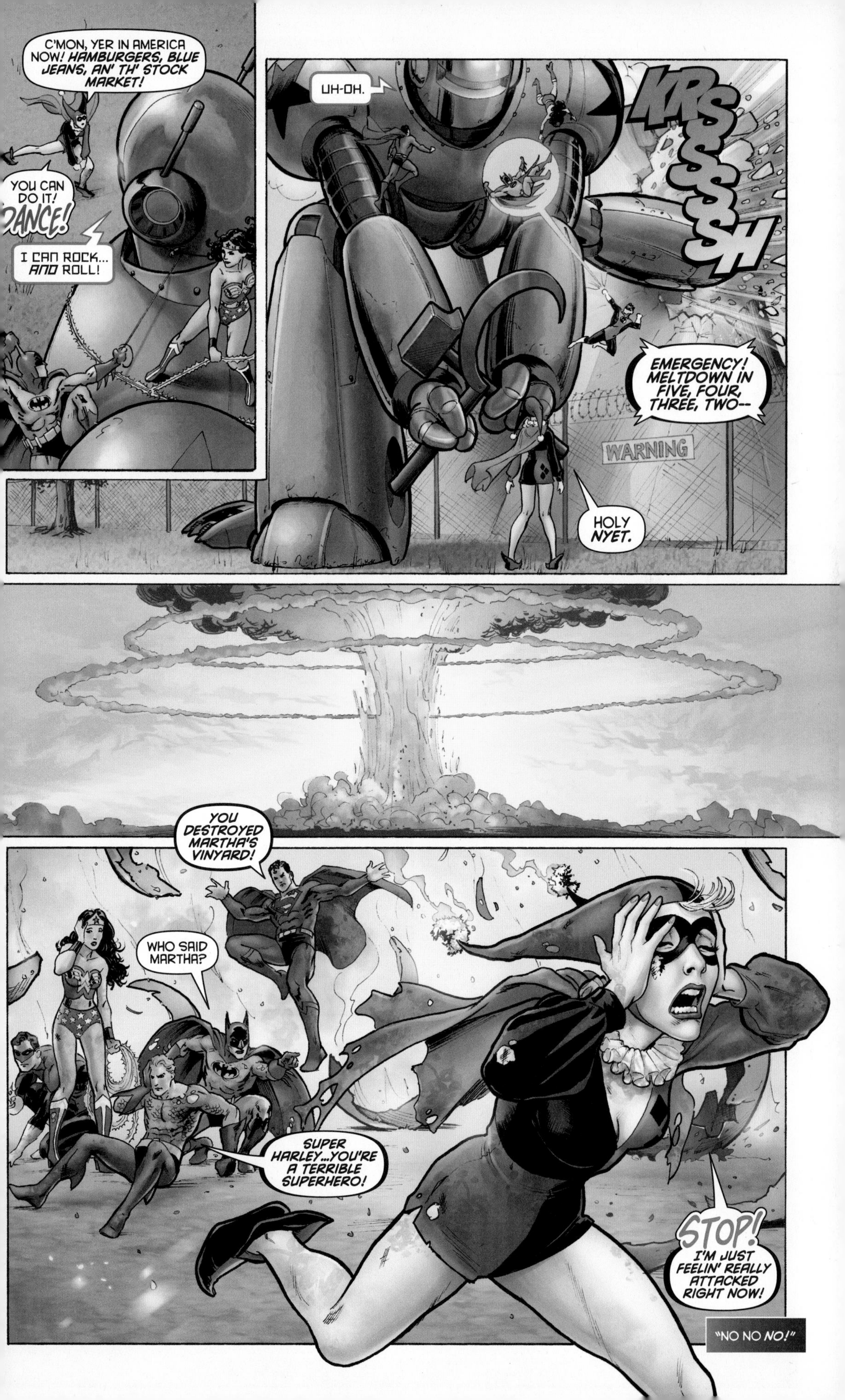
C'MON, YER IN AMERICA NOW! HAMBURGERS, BLUE JEANS, AN' TH' STOCK MARKET!
YOU CAN DO IT! DANCE!
I CAN ROCK... AND ROLL!
UH-OH.
KRSSSSH
EMERGENCY! MELTDOWN IN FIVE, FOUR, THREE, TWO--
WARNING
HOLY NYET.
YOU DESTROYED MARTHA'S VINYARD!
WHO SAID MARTHA?
SUPER HARLEY...YOU'RE A TERRIBLE SUPERHERO!
STOP! I'M JUST FEELIN' REALLY ATTACKED RIGHT NOW!
"NO NO NO!"

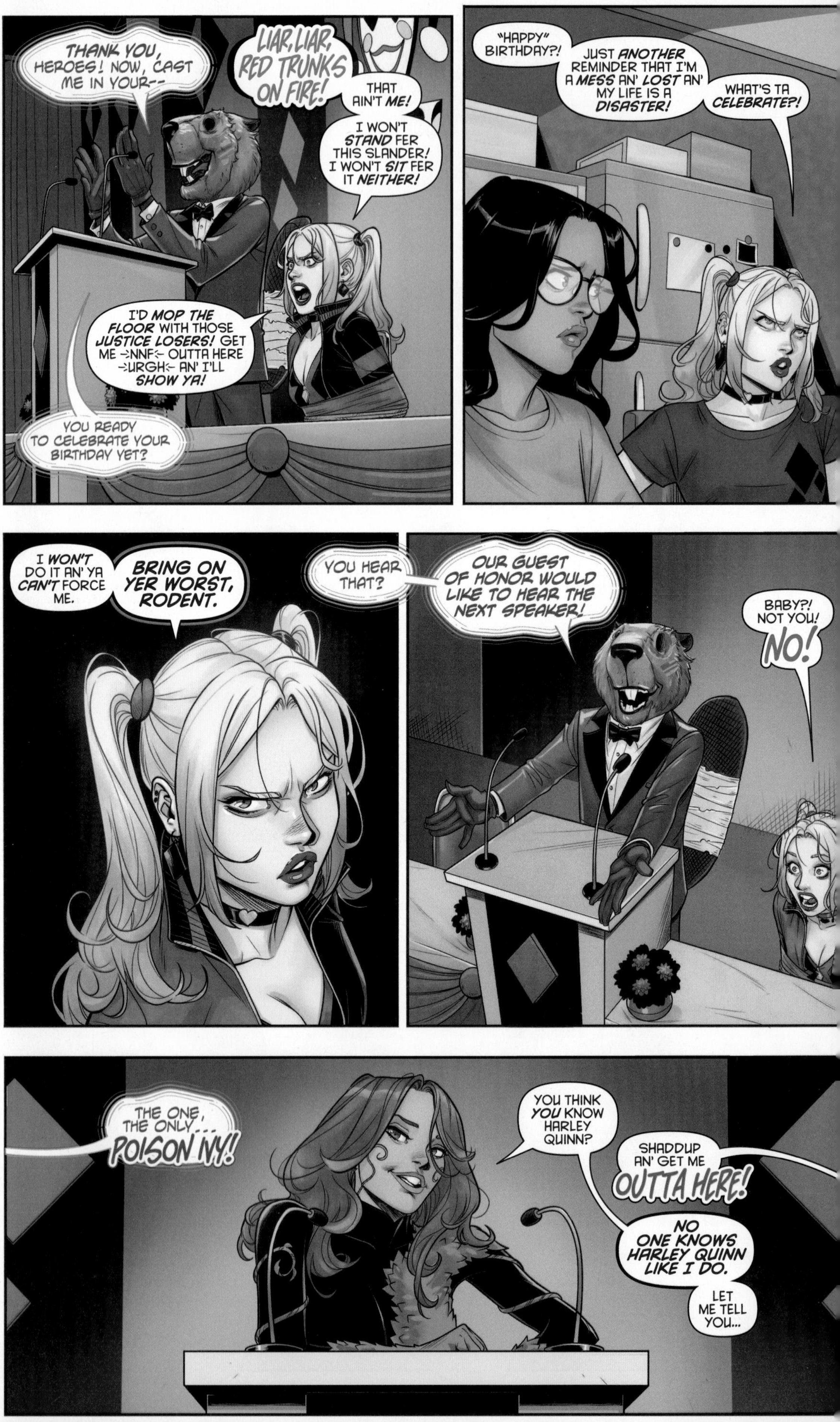
THANK YOU, HEROES! NOW, CAST ME IN YOUR--
LIAR, LIAR, RED TRUNKS ON FIRE!
THAT AIN'T ME!
I WON'T STAND FER THIS SLANDER! I WON'T SIT FER IT NEITHER!
I'D MOP THE FLOOR WITH THOSE JUSTICE LOSERS! GET ME ->NNF<- OUTTA HERE ->URGH<- AN' I'LL SHOW YA!
YOU READY TO CELEBRATE YOUR BIRTHDAY YET?
"HAPPY" BIRTHDAY?!
JUST ANOTHER REMINDER THAT I'M A MESS AN' LOST AN' MY LIFE IS A DISASTER!
WHAT'S TA CELEBRATE?!
I WON'T DO IT AN' YA CAN'T FORCE ME.
BRING ON YER WORST, RODENT.
YOU HEAR THAT?
OUR GUEST OF HONOR WOULD LIKE TO HEAR THE NEXT SPEAKER!
BABY?! NOT YOU! NO!
THE ONE, THE ONLY... POISON IVY!
YOU THINK YOU KNOW HARLEY QUINN?
SHADDUP AN' GET ME OUTTA HERE!
NO ONE KNOWS HARLEY QUINN LIKE I DO.
LET ME TELL YOU...

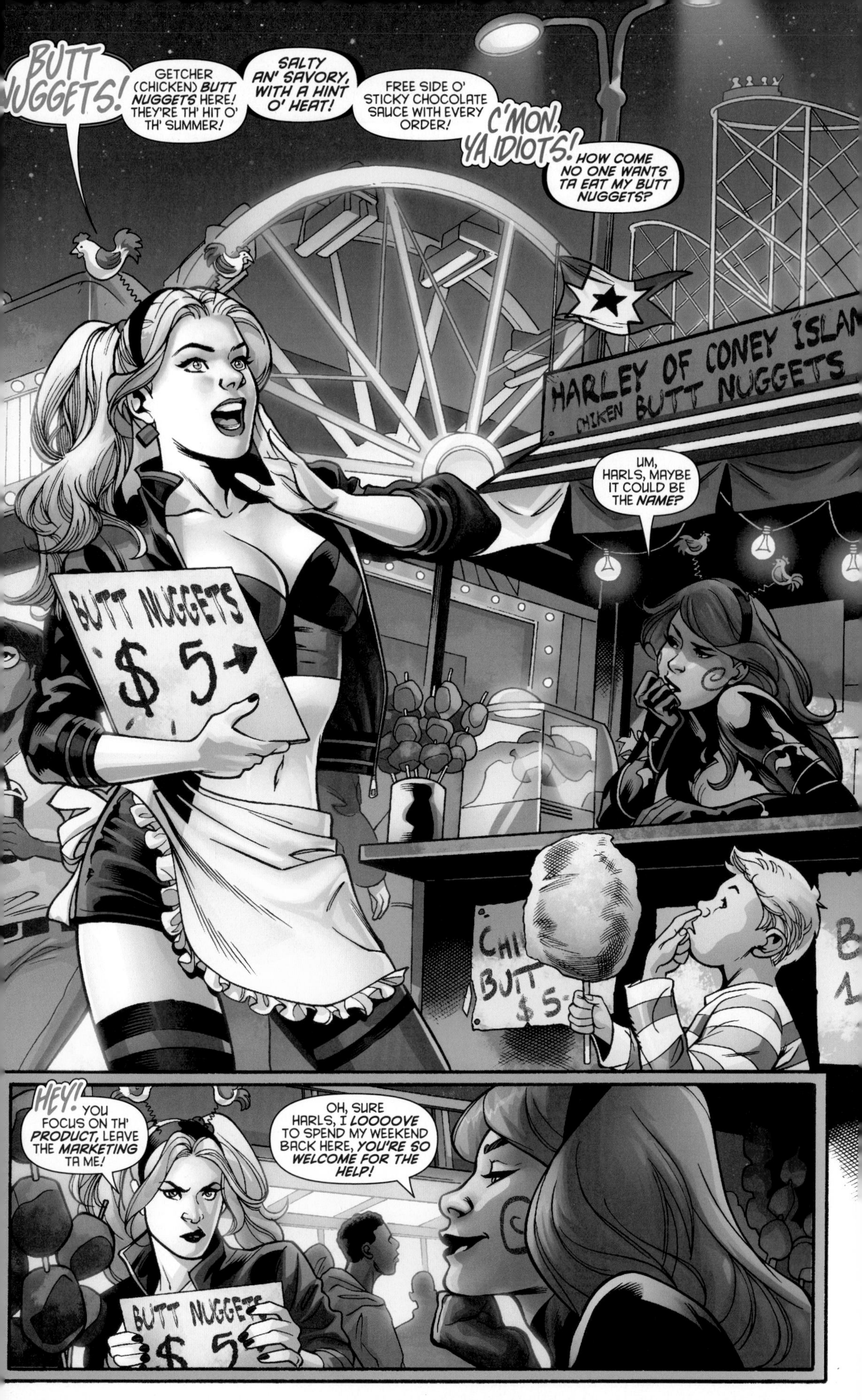
BUTT NUGGETS!
GETCHER (CHICKEN) BUTT NUGGETS HERE! THEY'RE TH' HIT O' TH' SUMMER!
SALTY AN' SAVORY, WITH A HINT O' HEAT!
FREE SIDE O' STICKY CHOCOLATE SAUCE WITH EVERY ORDER!
C'MON, YA IDIOTS!
HOW COME NO ONE WANTS TA EAT MY BUTT NUGGETS?
HARLEY OF CONEY ISLAN
CHIKEN BUTT NUGGETS
UM, HARLS, MAYBE IT COULD BE THE NAME?
BUTT NUGGETS
$ 5
HEY! YOU FOCUS ON TH' PRODUCT, LEAVE THE MARKETING TA ME!
OH, SURE HARLS, I LOOOOVE TO SPEND MY WEEKEND BACK HERE, YOU'RE SO WELCOME FOR THE HELP!

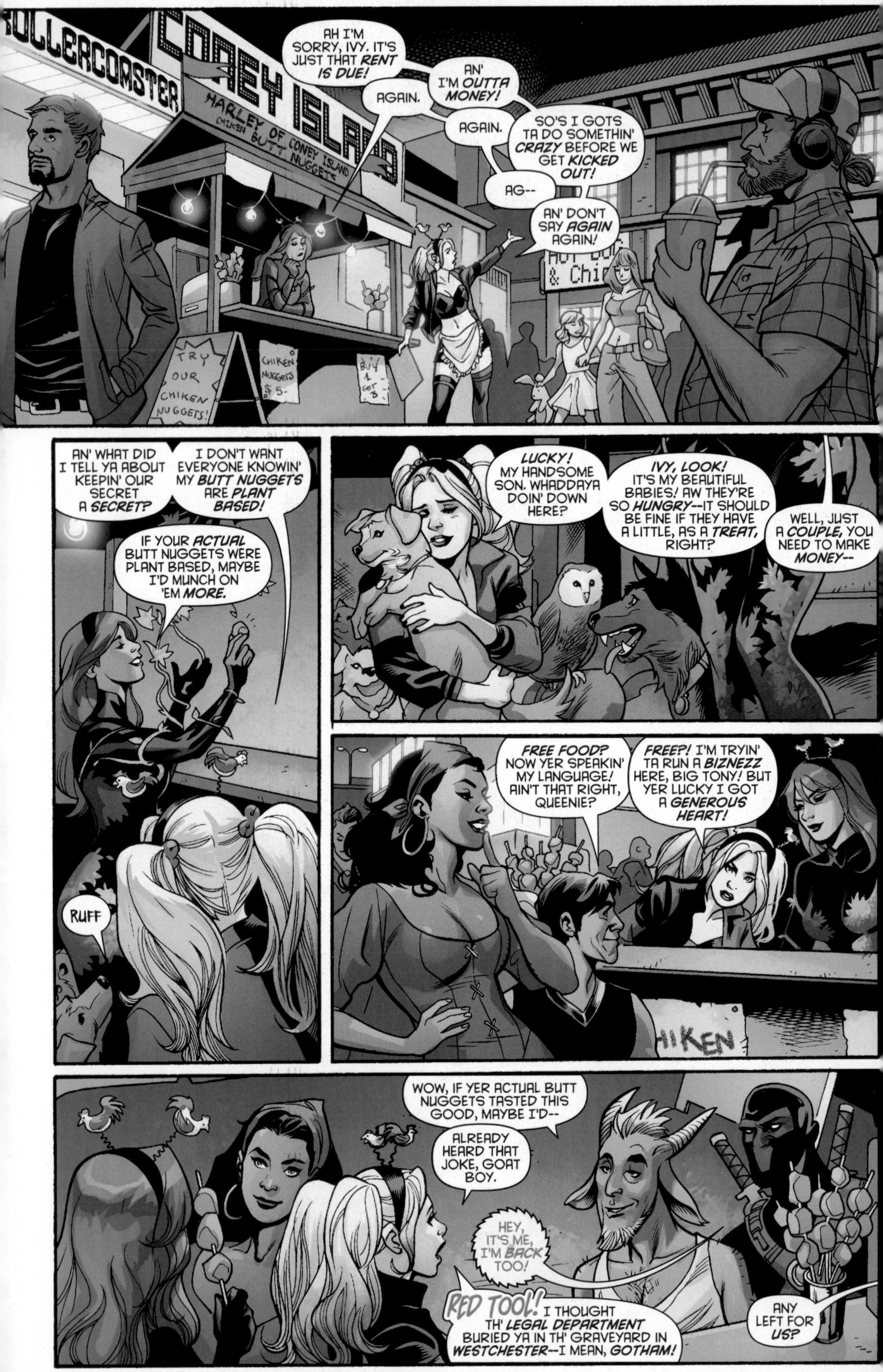
ROLLERCOASTER
CONEY ISLAND
HARLEY OF CONEY ISLAND CHIKEN BUTT NUGGETS
AH I'M SORRY, IVY. IT'S JUST THAT RENT IS DUE!
AN' I'M OUTTA MONEY!
AGAIN.
AGAIN.
SO'S I GOTS TA DO SOMETHIN' CRAZY BEFORE WE GET KICKED OUT!
AG--
AN' DON'T SAY AGAIN AGAIN!
& Chi
TRY OUR CHIKEN NUGGETS!
CHIKEN NUGGETS $5-
BUY 1 GET 3
AN' WHAT DID I TELL YA ABOUT KEEPIN' OUR SECRET A SECRET?
I DON'T WANT EVERYONE KNOWIN' MY BUTT NUGGETS ARE PLANT BASED!
IF YOUR ACTUAL BUTT NUGGETS WERE PLANT BASED, MAYBE I'D MUNCH ON 'EM MORE.
RUFF
LUCKY! MY HANDSOME SON. WHADDAYA DOIN' DOWN HERE?
IVY, LOOK! IT'S MY BEAUTIFUL BABIES! AW THEY'RE SO HUNGRY--IT SHOULD BE FINE IF THEY HAVE A LITTLE, AS A TREAT, RIGHT?
WELL, JUST A COUPLE, YOU NEED TO MAKE MONEY--
FREE FOOD? NOW YER SPEAKIN' MY LANGUAGE! AIN'T THAT RIGHT, QUEENIE?
FREE?! I'M TRYIN' TA RUN A BIZNEZZ HERE, BIG TONY! BUT YER LUCKY I GOT A GENEROUS HEART!
HIKEN
WOW, IF YER ACTUAL BUTT NUGGETS TASTED THIS GOOD, MAYBE I'D--
ALREADY HEARD THAT JOKE, GOAT BOY.
HEY, IT'S ME, I'M BACK TOO!
RED TOOL! I THOUGHT TH' LEGAL DEPARTMENT BURIED YA IN TH' GRAVEYARD IN WESTCHESTER--I MEAN, GOTHAM!
ANY LEFT FOR US?

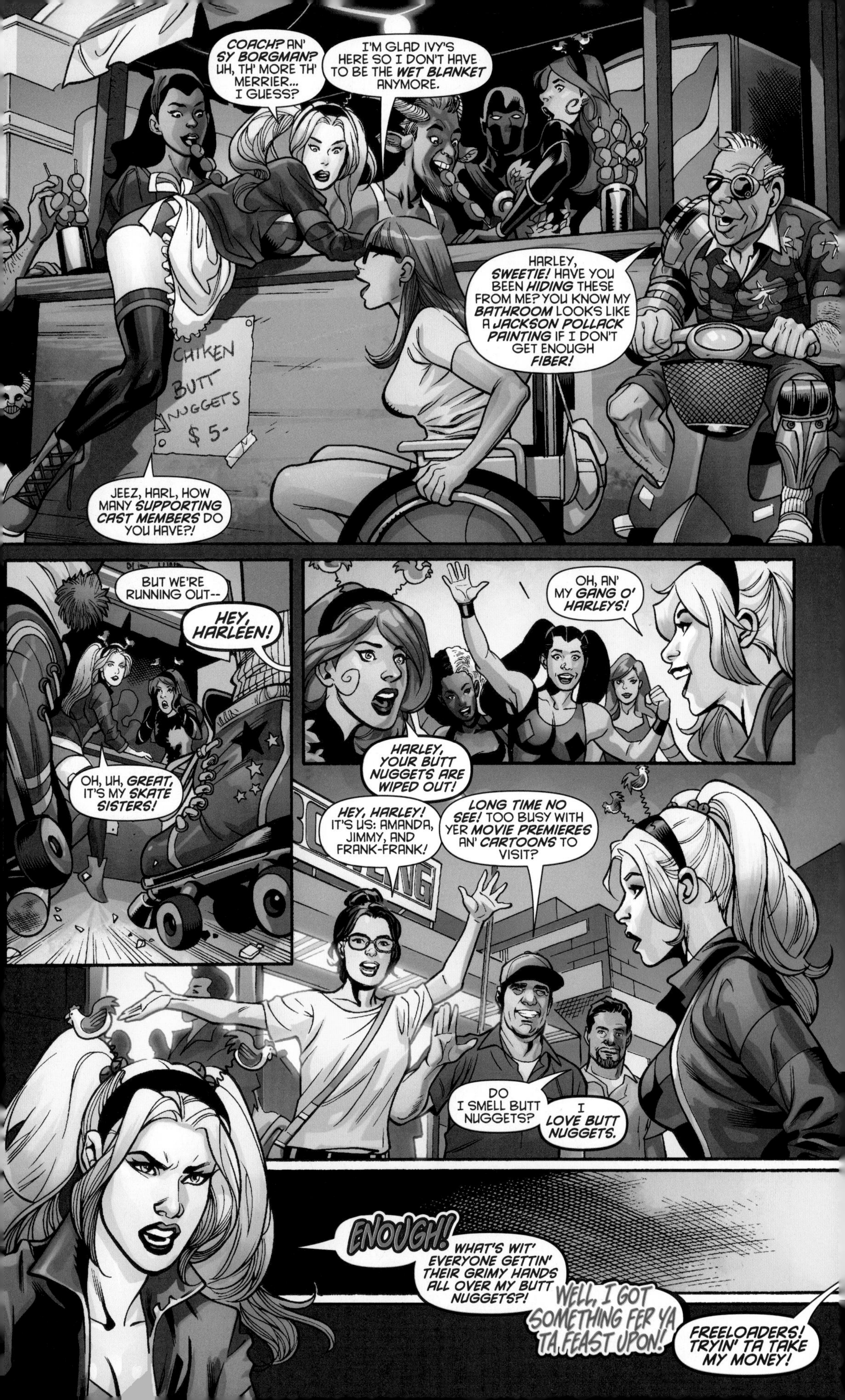
COACH? AN' SY BORGMAN? UH, TH' MORE TH' MERRIER... I GUESS?
I'M GLAD IVY'S HERE SO I DON'T HAVE TO BE THE WET BLANKET ANYMORE.
HARLEY, SWEETIE! HAVE YOU BEEN HIDING THESE FROM ME? YOU KNOW MY BATHROOM LOOKS LIKE A JACKSON POLLACK PAINTING IF I DON'T GET ENOUGH FIBER!
CHIKEN BUTT NUGGETS $ 5-
JEEZ, HARL, HOW MANY SUPPORTING CAST MEMBERS DO YOU HAVE?!
BUT WE'RE RUNNING OUT--
HEY, HARLEEN!
OH, UH, GREAT, IT'S MY SKATE SISTERS!
OH, AN' MY GANG O' HARLEYS!
HARLEY, YOUR BUTT NUGGETS ARE WIPED OUT!
HEY, HARLEY! IT'S US: AMANDA, JIMMY, AND FRANK-FRANK!
LONG TIME NO SEE! TOO BUSY WITH YER MOVIE PREMIERES AN' CARTOONS TO VISIT?
DO I SMELL BUTT NUGGETS?
I LOVE BUTT NUGGETS.
ENOUGH!
WHAT'S WIT' EVERYONE GETTIN' THEIR GRIMY HANDS ALL OVER MY BUTT NUGGETS?!
WELL, I GOT SOMETHING FER YA TA FEAST UPON!
FREELOADERS! TRYIN' TA TAKE MY MONEY!

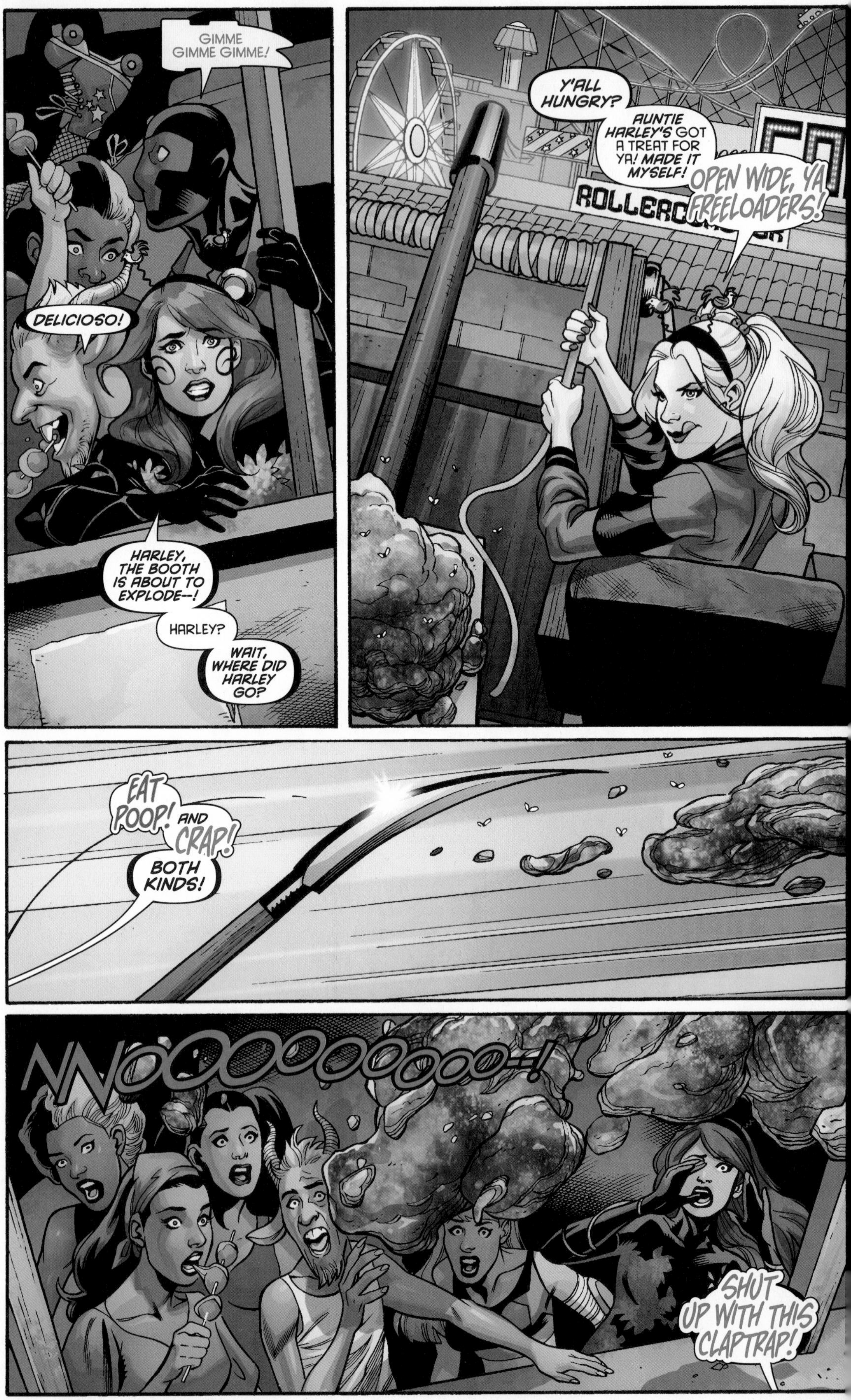
GIMME GIMME GIMME!
DELICIOSO!
HARLEY, THE BOOTH IS ABOUT TO EXPLODE--!
HARLEY?
WAIT, WHERE DID HARLEY GO?
Y'ALL HUNGRY?
AUNTIE HARLEY'S GOT A TREAT FOR YA! MADE IT MYSELF!
OPEN WIDE, YA FREELOADERS!
EAT POOP! AND CRAP!
BOTH KINDS!
NNOOOOOOOOOOOO--!
SHUT UP WITH THIS CLAPTRAP!

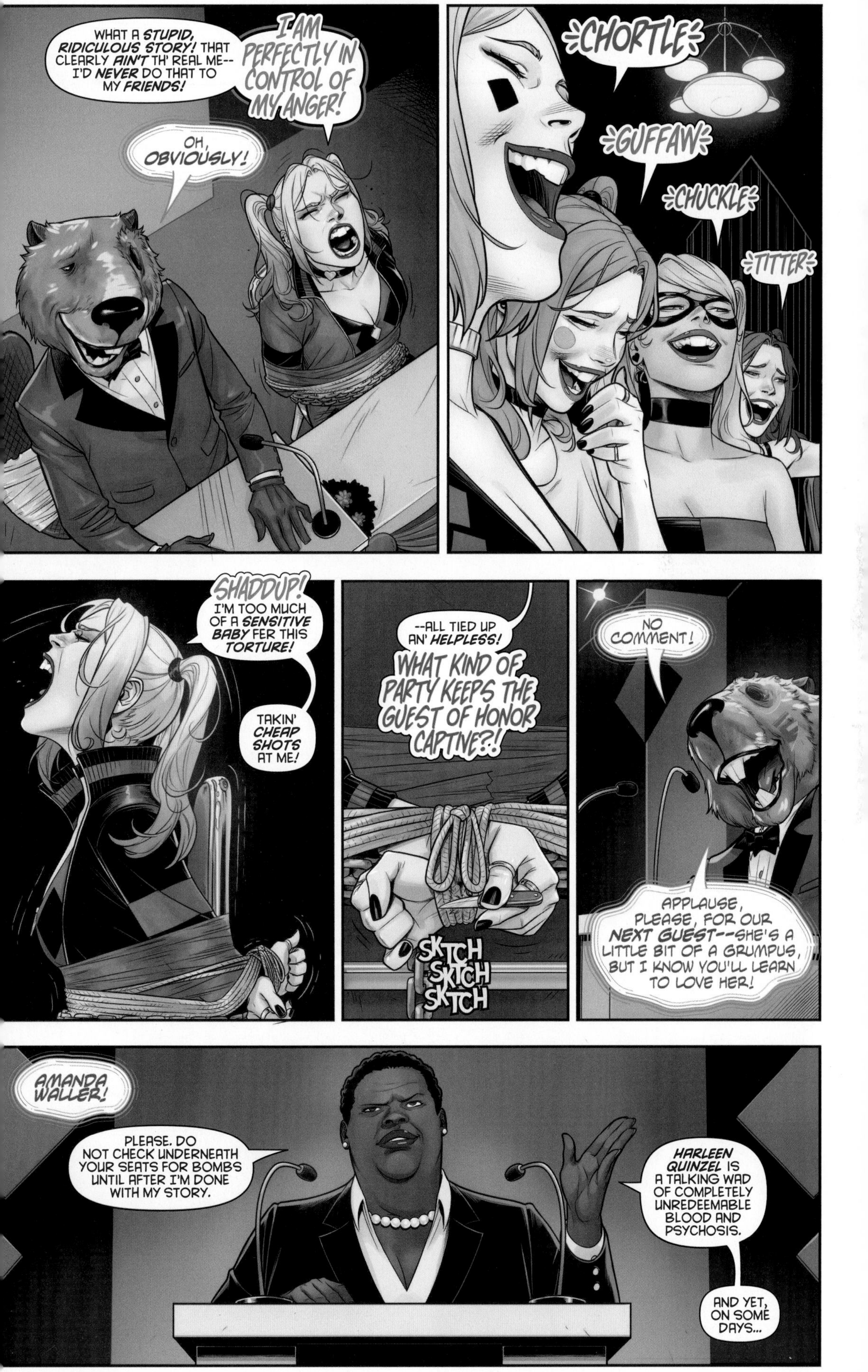

WHAT A STUPID, RIDICULOUS STORY! THAT CLEARLY AIN'T TH' REAL ME-- I'D NEVER DO THAT TO MY FRIENDS!
I AM PERFECTLY IN CONTROL OF MY ANGER!
OH, OBVIOUSLY!
CHORTLE
GUFFAW
CHUCKLE
TITTER
SHADDUP! I'M TOO MUCH OF A SENSITIVE BABY FER THIS TORTURE!
TAKIN' CHEAP SHOTS AT ME!
--ALL TIED UP AN' HELPLESS!
WHAT KIND OF PARTY KEEPS THE GUEST OF HONOR CAPTIVE?!
SKTCH SKTCH SKTCH
NO COMMENT!
APPLAUSE, PLEASE, FOR OUR NEXT GUEST--SHE'S A LITTLE BIT OF A GRUMPUS, BUT I KNOW YOU'LL LEARN TO LOVE HER!
AMANDA WALLER!
PLEASE. DO NOT CHECK UNDERNEATH YOUR SEATS FOR BOMBS UNTIL AFTER I'M DONE WITH MY STORY.
HARLEEN QUINZEL IS A TALKING WAD OF COMPLETELY UNREDEEMABLE BLOOD AND PSYCHOSIS.
AND YET, ON SOME DAYS...

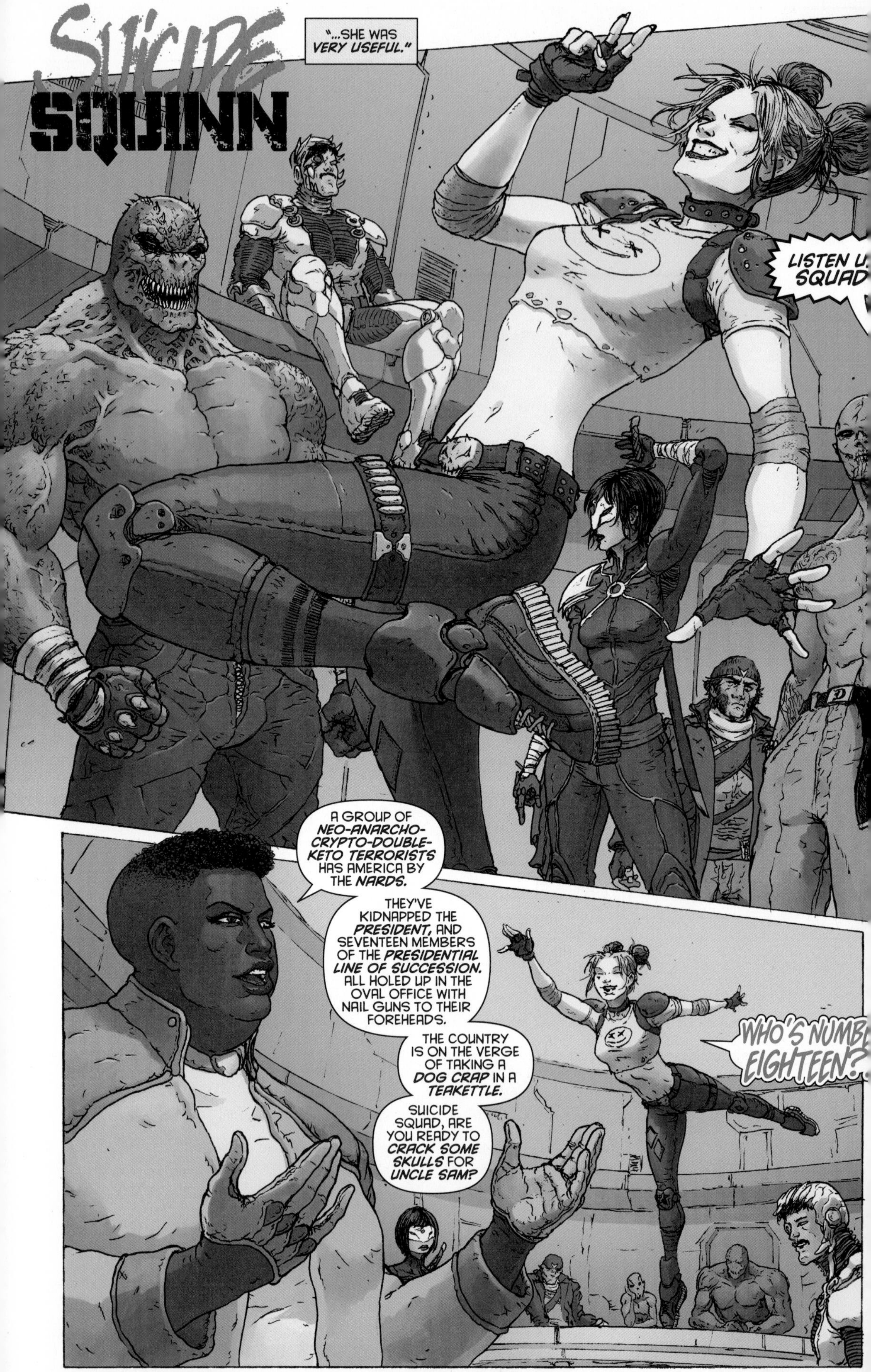

SUICIDE SQUINN
"...SHE WAS VERY USEFUL."
LISTEN U... SQUAD
A GROUP OF NEO-ANARCHO-CRYPTO-DOUBLE-KETO TERRORISTS HAS AMERICA BY THE NARDS.
THEY'VE KIDNAPPED THE PRESIDENT, AND SEVENTEEN MEMBERS OF THE PRESIDENTIAL LINE OF SUCCESSION. ALL HOLED UP IN THE OVAL OFFICE WITH NAIL GUNS TO THEIR FOREHEADS.
THE COUNTRY IS ON THE VERGE OF TAKING A DOG CRAP IN A TEAKETTLE.
SUICIDE SQUAD, ARE YOU READY TO CRACK SOME SKULLS FOR UNCLE SAM?
WHO'S NUMB... EIGHTEEN?

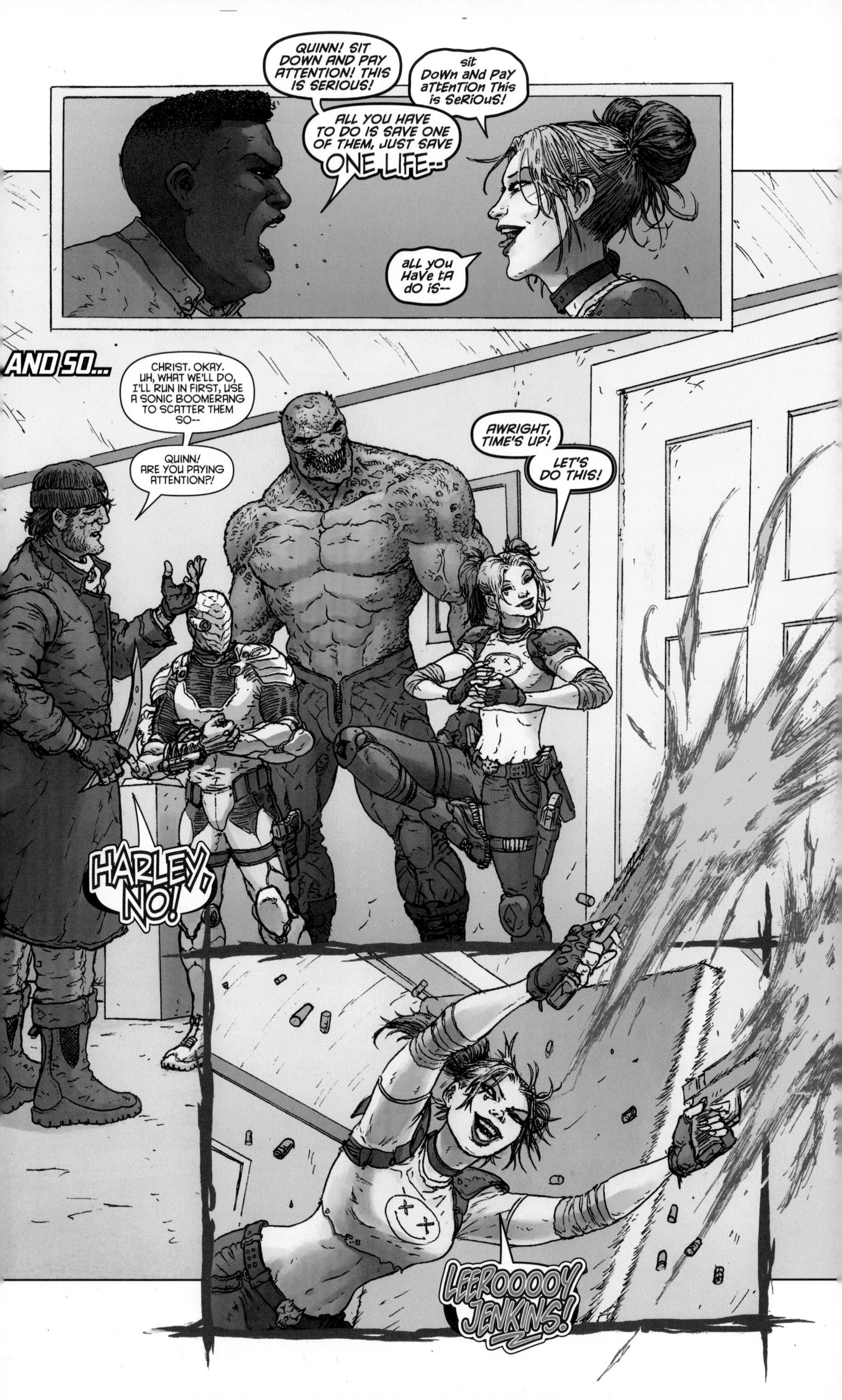

QUINN! SIT DOWN AND PAY ATTENTION! THIS IS SERIOUS!
sit DoWn aNd Pay aTTEnTIOn This is SeRIOuS!
ALL YOU HAVE TO DO IS SAVE ONE OF THEM, JUST SAVE ONE LIFE--
aLL yOu HaVe tA dO iS--
AND SO...
CHRIST. OKAY. UH, WHAT WE'LL DO, I'LL RUN IN FIRST, USE A SONIC BOOMERANG TO SCATTER THEM SO--
QUINN! ARE YOU PAYING ATTENTION?!
AWRIGHT, TIME'S UP!
LET'S DO THIS!
HARLEY, NO!
LEEROOOOOY JENKINS!

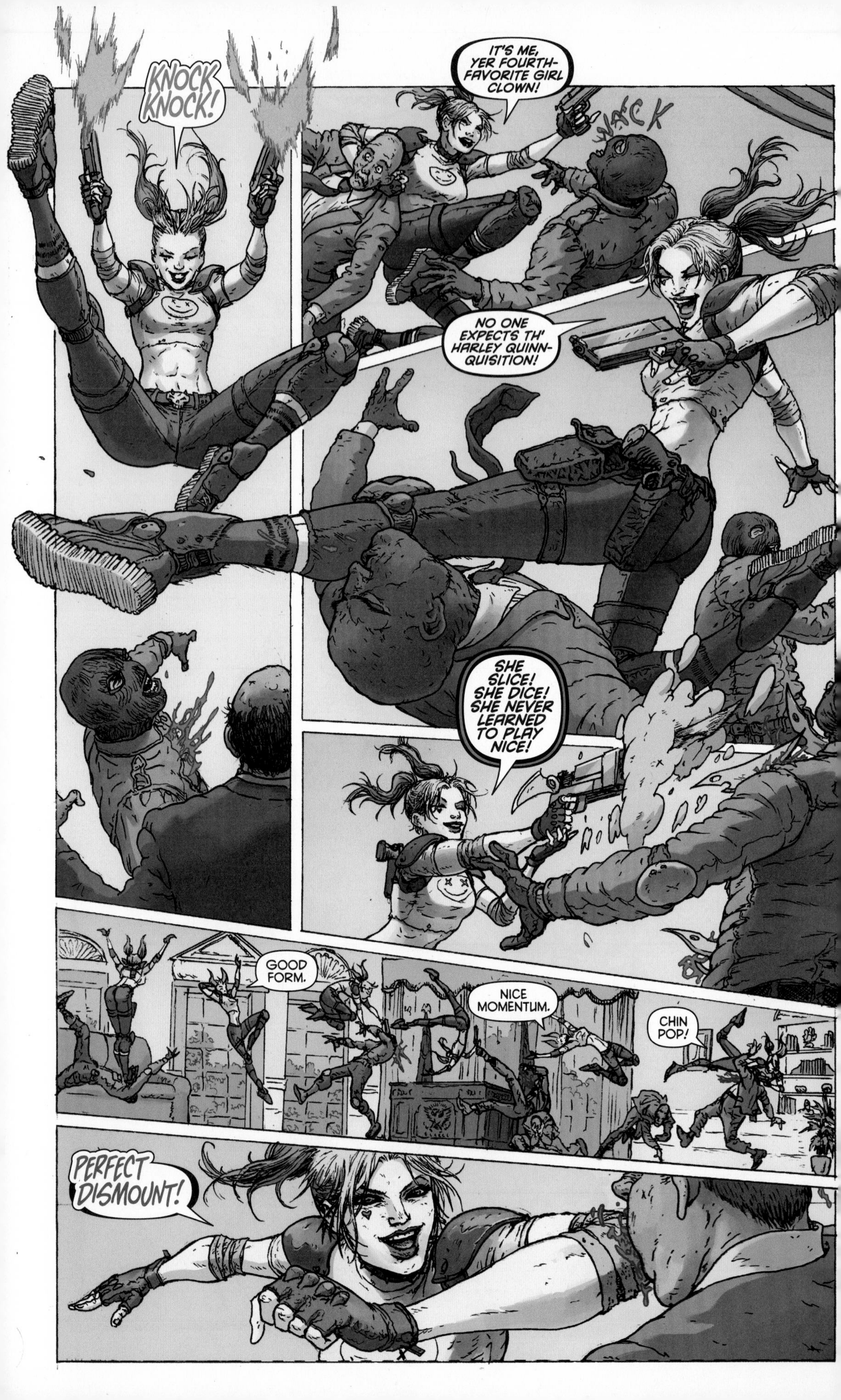
KNOCK KNOCK!
IT'S ME, YER FOURTH-FAVORITE GIRL CLOWN!
WACK
NO ONE EXPECTS TH' HARLEY QUINN-QUISITION!
SHE SLICE! SHE DICE! SHE NEVER LEARNED TO PLAY NICE!
GOOD FORM.
NICE MOMENTUM.
CHIN POP!
PERFECT DISMOUNT!

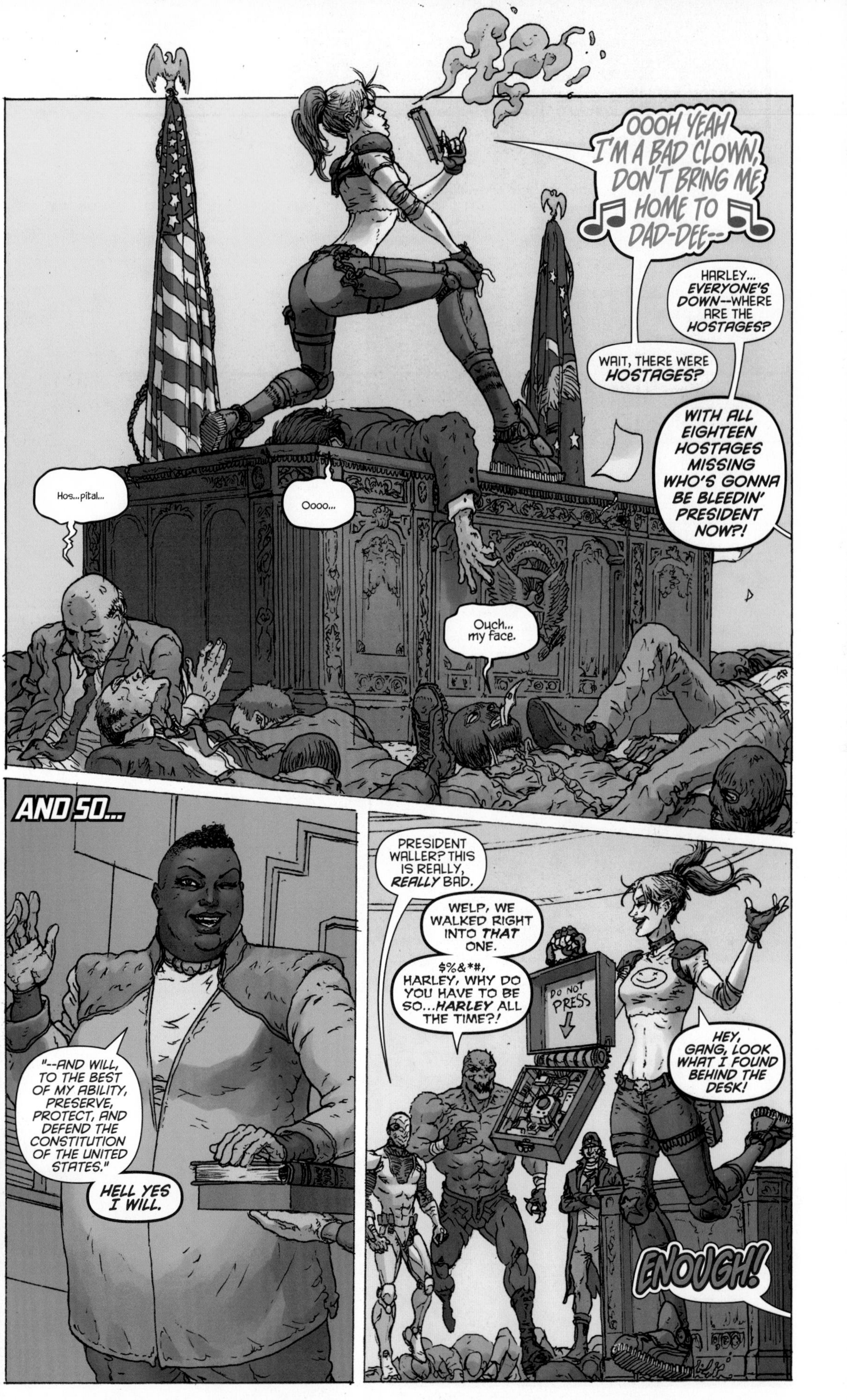
OOOH YEAH I'M A BAD CLOWN, DON'T BRING ME HOME TO DAD-DEE--
HARLEY... EVERYONE'S DOWN--WHERE ARE THE HOSTAGES?
WAIT, THERE WERE HOSTAGES?
WITH ALL EIGHTEEN HOSTAGES MISSING WHO'S GONNA BE BLEEDIN' PRESIDENT NOW?!
Hos...pital...
Oooo...
Ouch... my face.
AND SO...
"--AND WILL, TO THE BEST OF MY ABILITY, PRESERVE, PROTECT, AND DEFEND THE CONSTITUTION OF THE UNITED STATES."
HELL YES I WILL.
PRESIDENT WALLER? THIS IS REALLY, REALLY BAD.
WELP, WE WALKED RIGHT INTO THAT ONE.
$%&*#, HARLEY, WHY DO YOU HAVE TO BE SO...HARLEY ALL THE TIME?!
DO NOT PRESS
HEY, GANG, LOOK WHAT I FOUND BEHIND THE DESK!
ENOUGH!

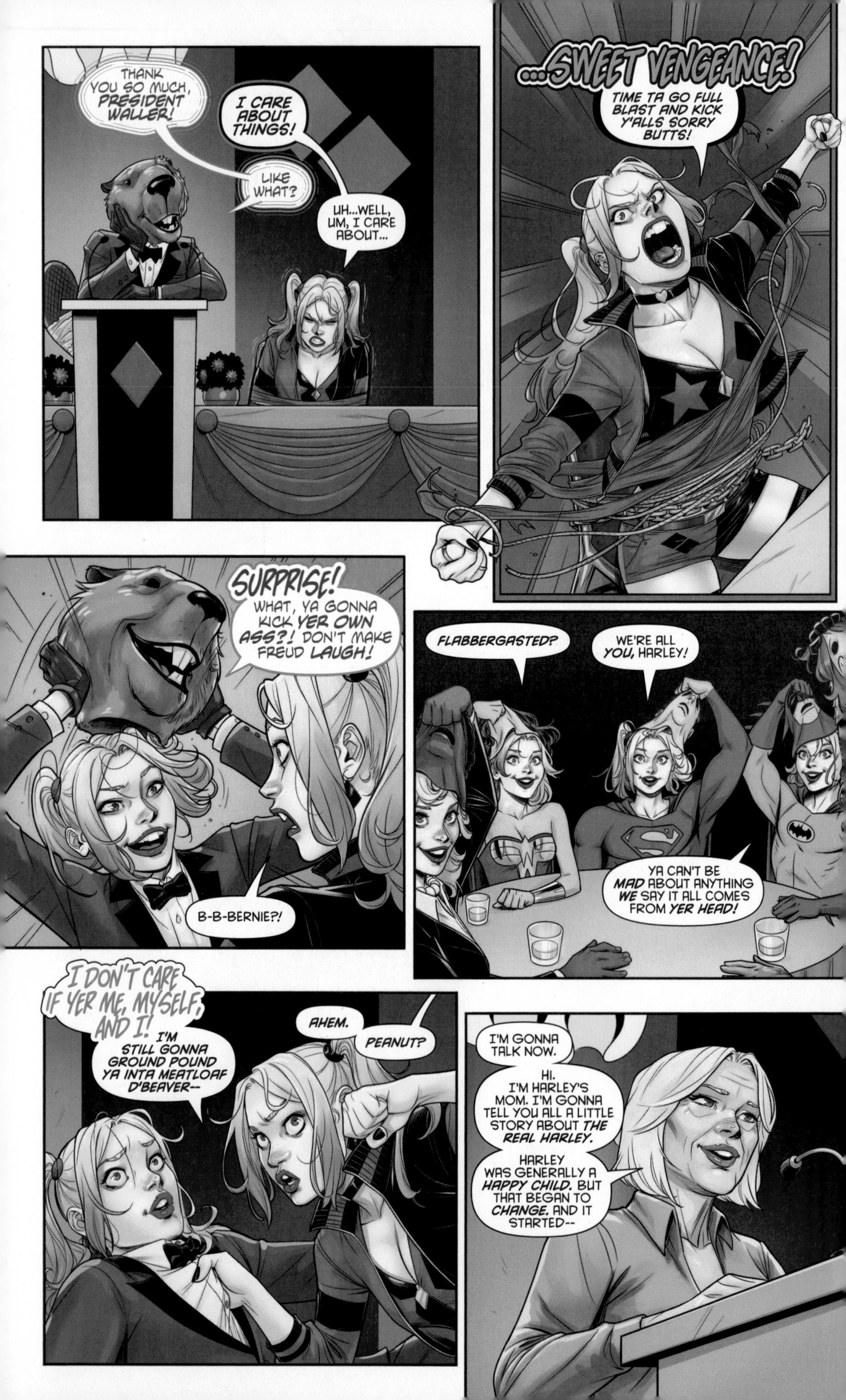
THANK YOU SO MUCH, PRESIDENT WALLER!
I CARE ABOUT THINGS!
LIKE WHAT?
UH...WELL, UM, I CARE ABOUT...
...SWEET VENGEANCE!
TIME TA GO FULL BLAST AND KICK Y'ALLS SORRY BUTTS!
SURPRISE!
WHAT, YA GONNA KICK YER OWN ASS?! DON'T MAKE FREUD LAUGH!
B-B-BERNIE?!
FLABBERGASTED?
WE'RE ALL YOU, HARLEY!
YA CAN'T BE MAD ABOUT ANYTHING WE SAY IT ALL COMES FROM YER HEAD!
I DON'T CARE IF YER ME, MYSELF, AND I!
I'M STILL GONNA GROUND POUND YA INTA MEATLOAF D'BEAVER--
AHEM.
PEANUT?
I'M GONNA TALK NOW.
HI. I'M HARLEY'S MOM. I'M GONNA TELL YOU ALL A LITTLE STORY ABOUT THE REAL HARLEY.
HARLEY WAS GENERALLY A HAPPY CHILD. BUT THAT BEGAN TO CHANGE. AND IT STARTED--

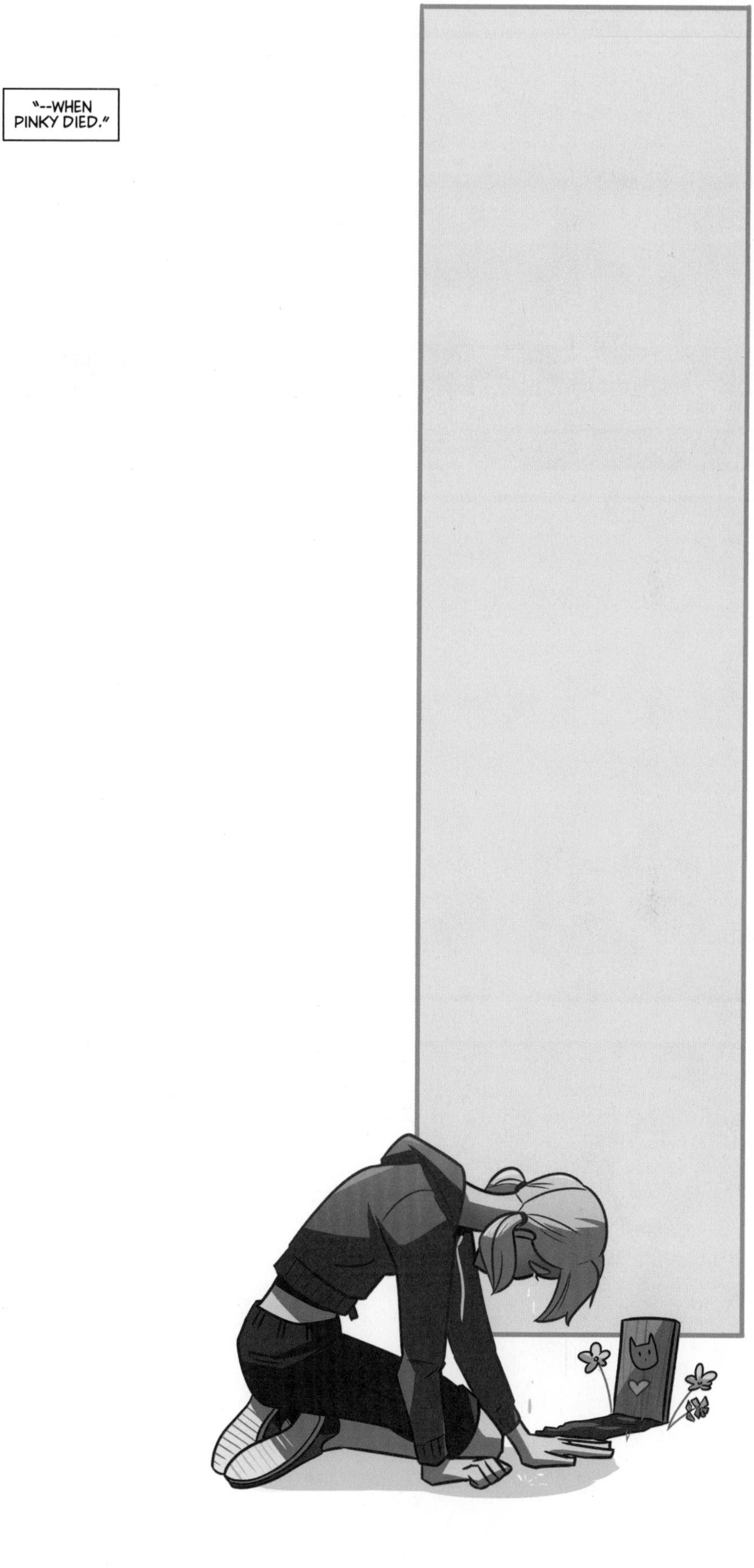

"--WHEN PINKY DIED."

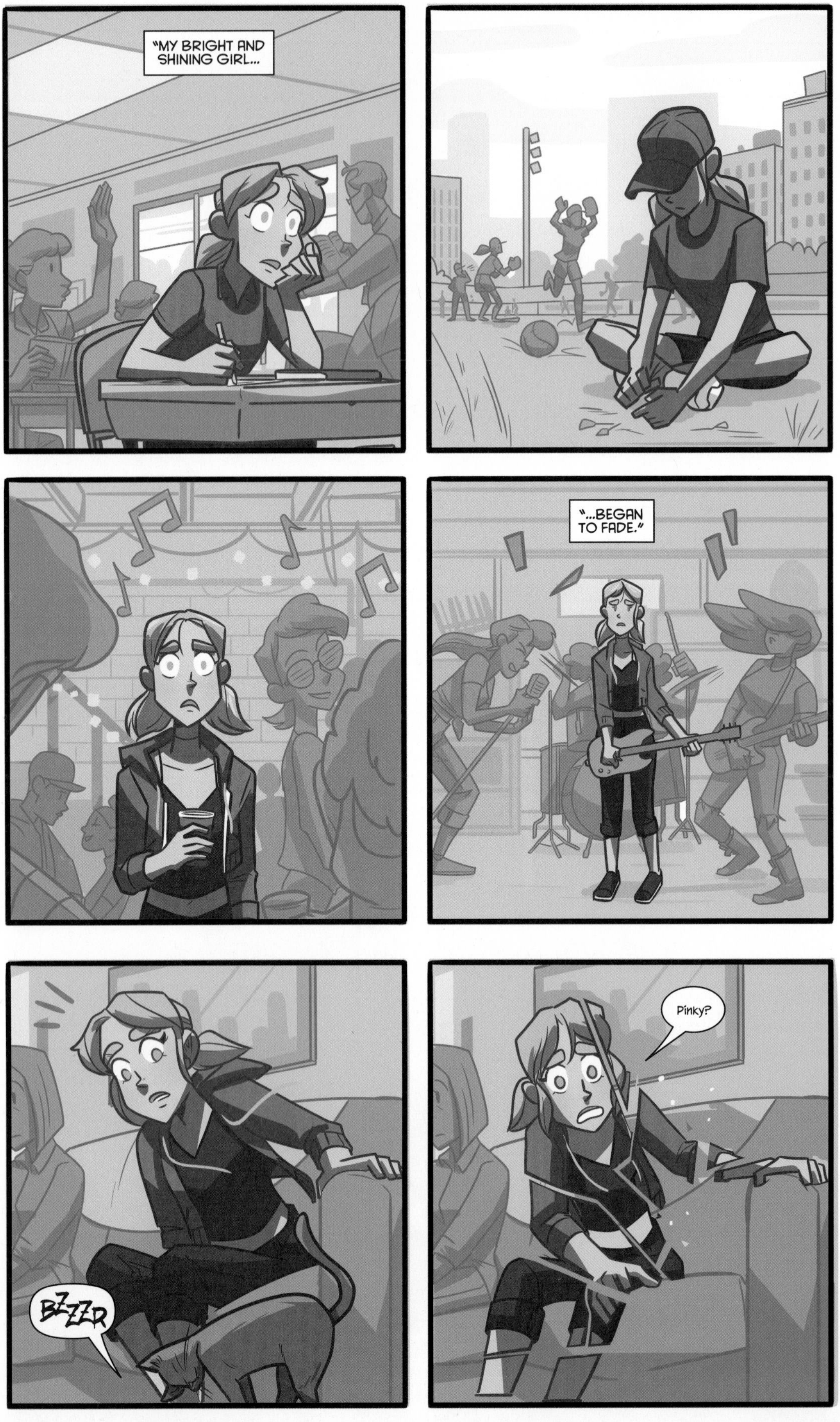
"MY BRIGHT AND SHINING GIRL...
"...BEGAN TO FADE."
BZZZD
Pinky?

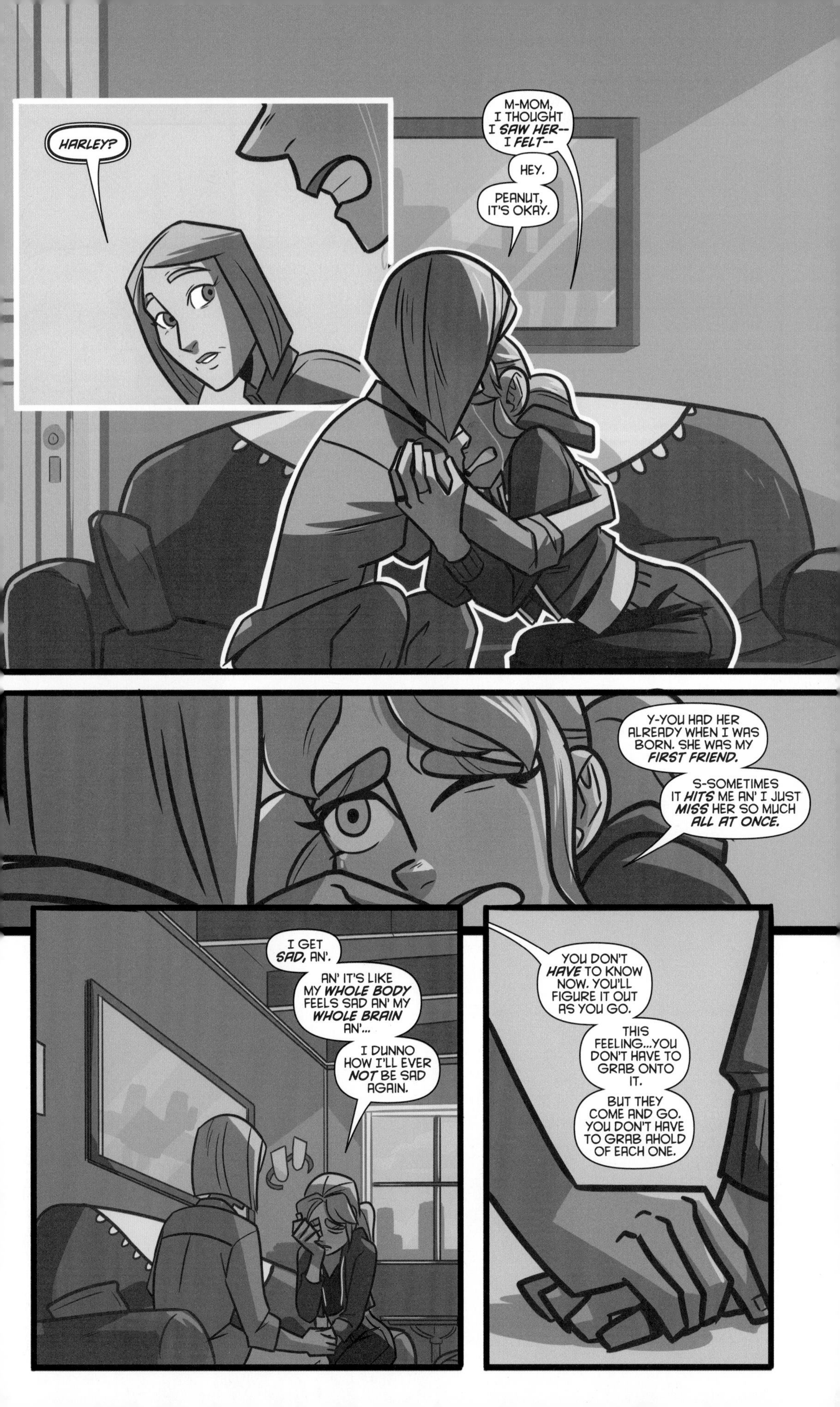
HARLEY?
M-MOM, I THOUGHT I SAW HER-- I FELT--
HEY.
PEANUT, IT'S OKAY.
Y-YOU HAD HER ALREADY WHEN I WAS BORN. SHE WAS MY FIRST FRIEND.
S-SOMETIMES IT HITS ME AN' I JUST MISS HER SO MUCH ALL AT ONCE.
I GET SAD, AN'.
AN' IT'S LIKE MY WHOLE BODY FEELS SAD AN' MY WHOLE BRAIN AN'...
I DUNNO HOW I'LL EVER NOT BE SAD AGAIN.
YOU DON'T HAVE TO KNOW NOW. YOU'LL FIGURE IT OUT AS YOU GO.
THIS FEELING...YOU DON'T HAVE TO GRAB ONTO IT.
BUT THEY COME AND GO. YOU DON'T HAVE TO GRAB AHOLD OF EACH ONE.

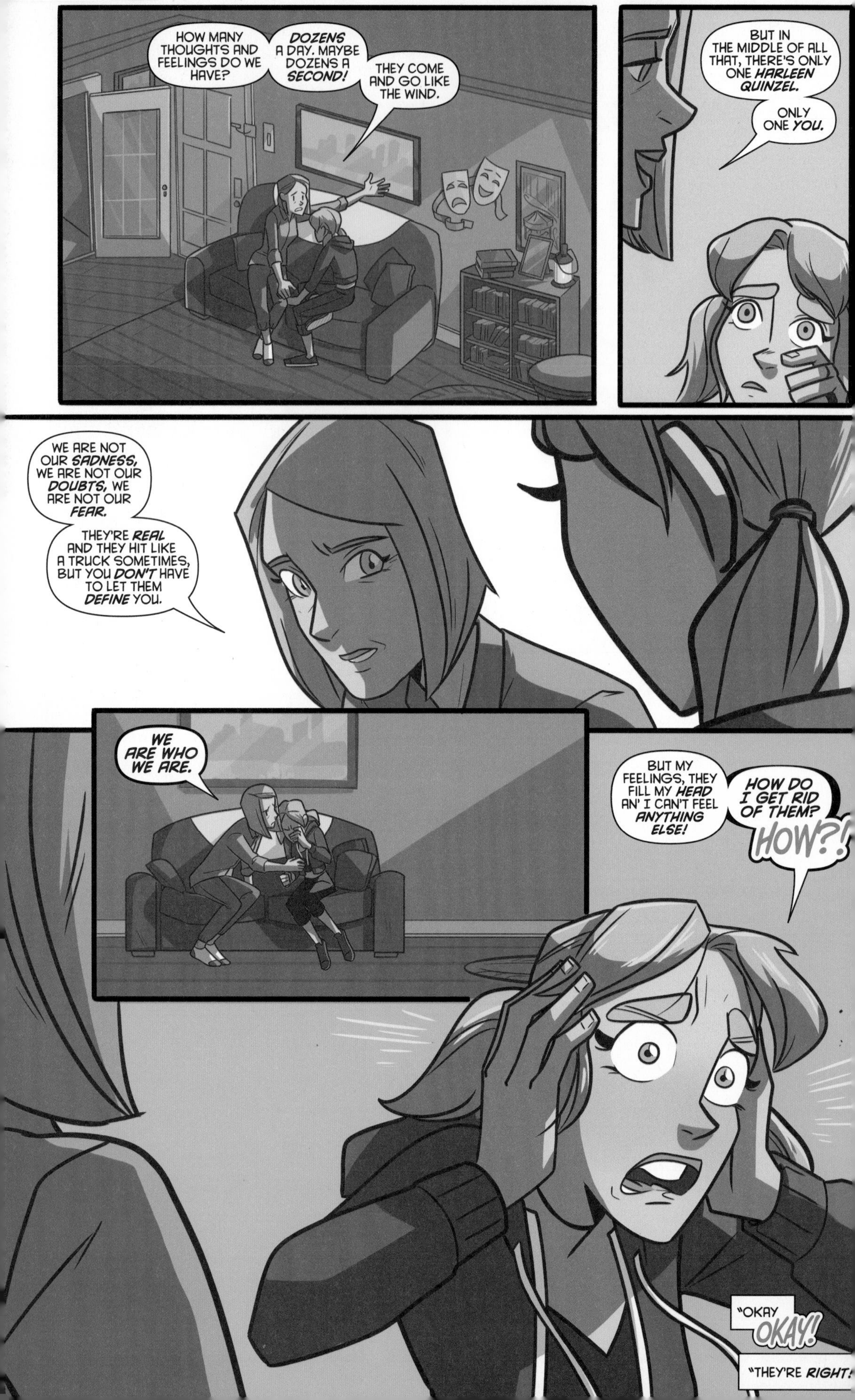
HOW MANY THOUGHTS AND FEELINGS DO WE HAVE?
DOZENS A DAY. MAYBE DOZENS A SECOND!
THEY COME AND GO LIKE THE WIND.
BUT IN THE MIDDLE OF ALL THAT, THERE'S ONLY ONE HARLEEN QUINZEL.
ONLY ONE YOU.
WE ARE NOT OUR SADNESS, WE ARE NOT OUR DOUBTS, WE ARE NOT OUR FEAR.
THEY'RE REAL AND THEY HIT LIKE A TRUCK SOMETIMES, BUT YOU DON'T HAVE TO LET THEM DEFINE YOU.
WE ARE WHO WE ARE.
BUT MY FEELINGS, THEY FILL MY HEAD AN' I CAN'T FEEL ANYTHING ELSE!
HOW DO I GET RID OF THEM?
HOW?!
"OKAY
OKAY!
"THEY'RE RIGHT.

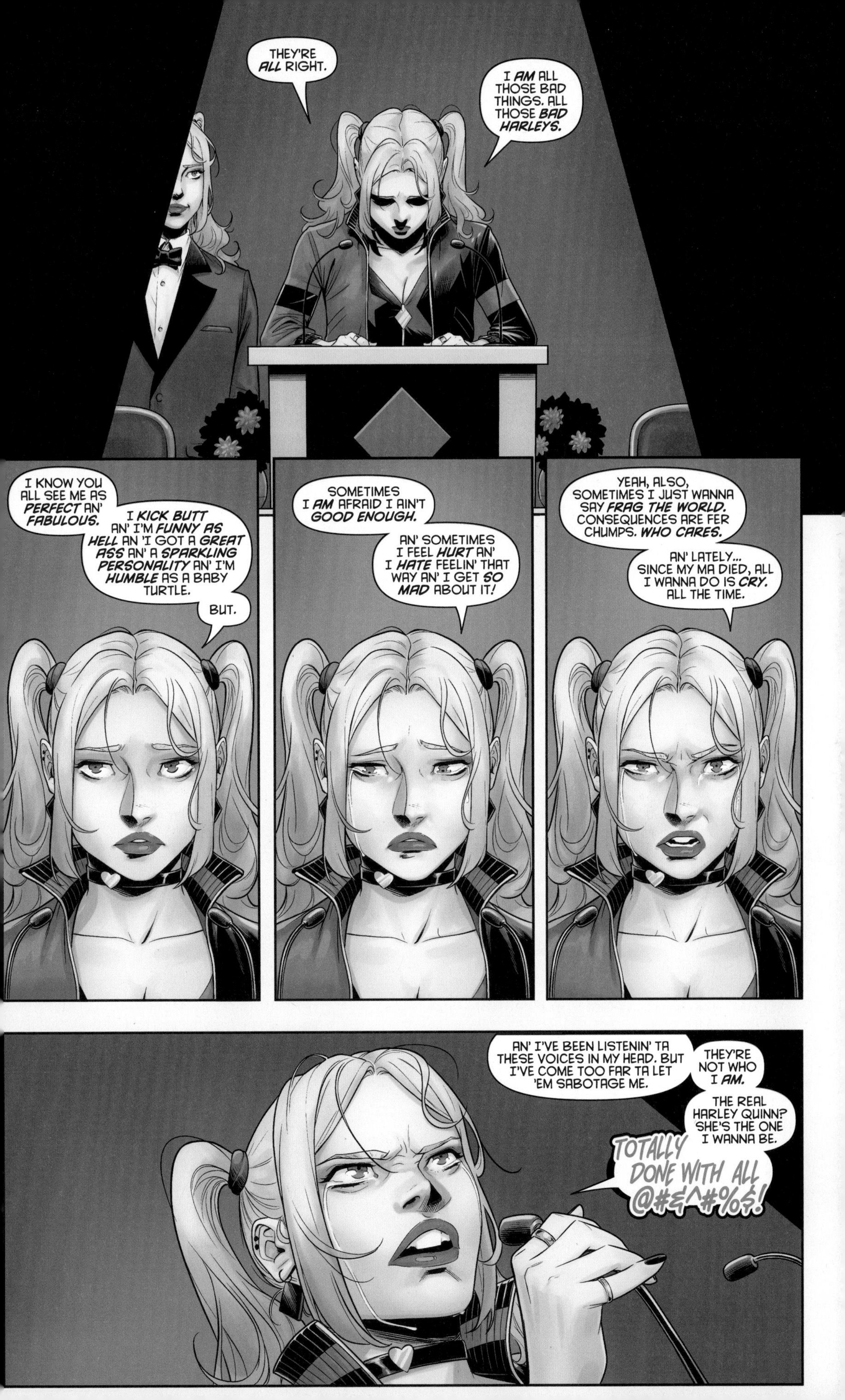

THEY'RE ALL RIGHT.
I AM ALL THOSE BAD THINGS. ALL THOSE BAD HARLEYS.
I KNOW YOU ALL SEE ME AS PERFECT AN' FABULOUS.
I KICK BUTT AN' I'M FUNNY AS HELL AN 'I GOT A GREAT ASS AN' A SPARKLING PERSONALITY AN' I'M HUMBLE AS A BABY TURTLE.
BUT.
SOMETIMES I AM AFRAID I AIN'T GOOD ENOUGH.
AN' SOMETIMES I FEEL HURT AN' I HATE FEELIN' THAT WAY AN' I GET SO MAD ABOUT IT!
YEAH, ALSO, SOMETIMES I JUST WANNA SAY FRAG THE WORLD. CONSEQUENCES ARE FER CHUMPS. WHO CARES.
AN' LATELY... SINCE MY MA DIED, ALL I WANNA DO IS CRY. ALL THE TIME.
AN' I'VE BEEN LISTENIN' TA THESE VOICES IN MY HEAD. BUT I'VE COME TOO FAR TA LET 'EM SABOTAGE ME.
THEY'RE NOT WHO I AM.
THE REAL HARLEY QUINN? SHE'S THE ONE I WANNA BE.
TOTALLY DONE WITH ALL @#&^#%$!

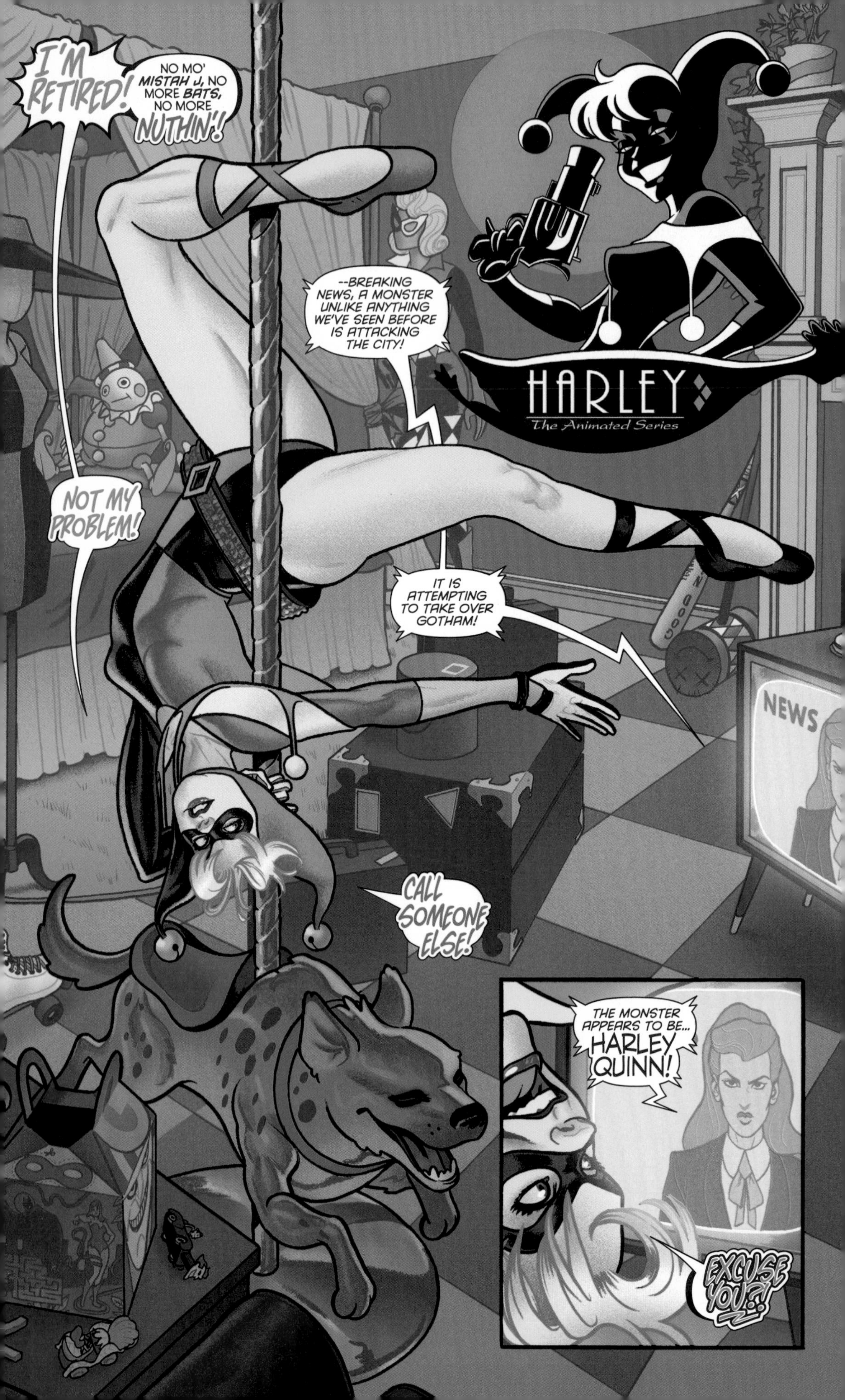

I'M RETIRED!
NO MO' MISTAH J, NO MORE BATS, NO MORE NUTHIN'!
--BREAKING NEWS, A MONSTER UNLIKE ANYTHING WE'VE SEEN BEFORE IS ATTACKING THE CITY!
HARLEY
The Animated Series
NOT MY PROBLEM!
IT IS ATTEMPTING TO TAKE OVER GOTHAM!
CALL SOMEONE ELSE!
NEWS
THE MONSTER APPEARS TO BE... HARLEY QUINN!
EXCUSE YOU?!

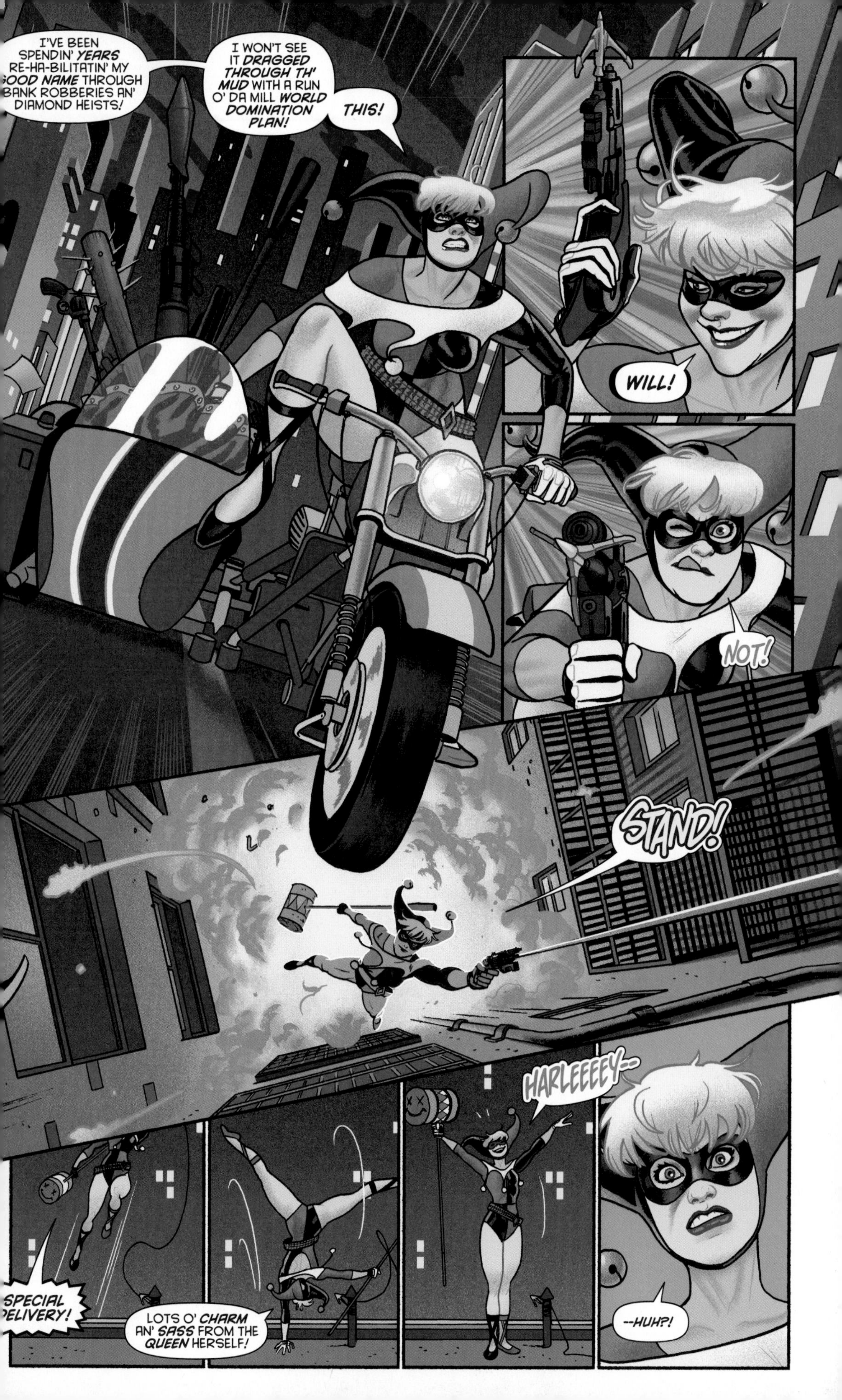
I'VE BEEN SPENDIN' YEARS RE-HA-BILITATIN' MY GOOD NAME THROUGH BANK ROBBERIES AN' DIAMOND HEISTS!
I WON'T SEE IT DRAGGED THROUGH TH' MUD WITH A RUN O' DA MILL WORLD DOMINATION PLAN!
THIS!
WILL!
NOT!
STAND!
SPECIAL DELIVERY!
LOTS O' CHARM AN' SASS FROM THE QUEEN HERSELF!
HARLEEEEY--
--HUH?!

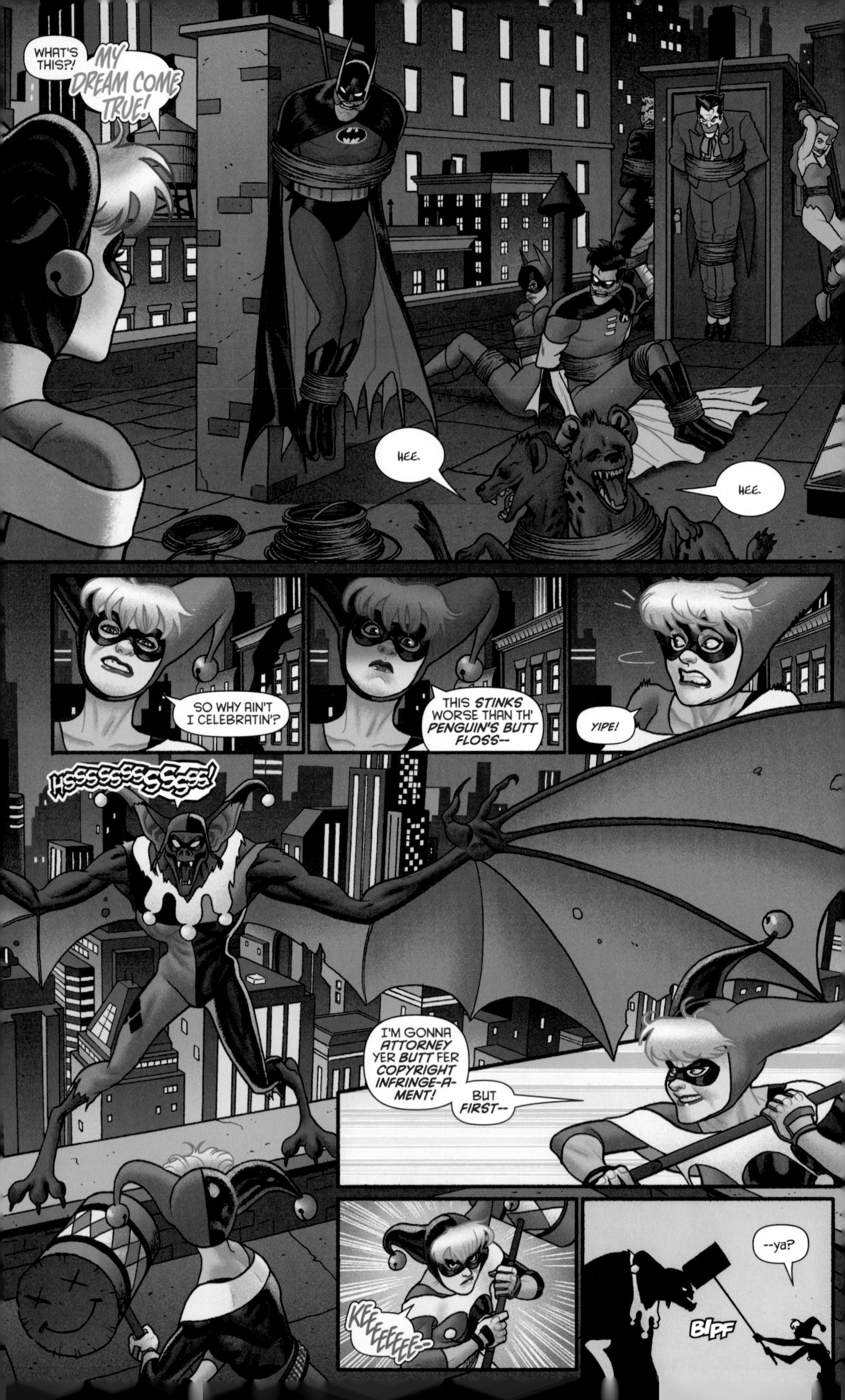
WHAT'S THIS?!
MY DREAM COME TRUE!
HEE.
HEE.
SO WHY AIN'T I CELEBRATIN'?
THIS STINKS WORSE THAN TH' PENGUIN'S BUTT FLOSS--
YIPE!
HSSSSSSSSSSS!
I'M GONNA ATTORNEY YER BUTT FER COPYRIGHT INFRINGE-A-MENT!
BUT FIRST--
KEEEEEEEE--
--ya?
BIPF

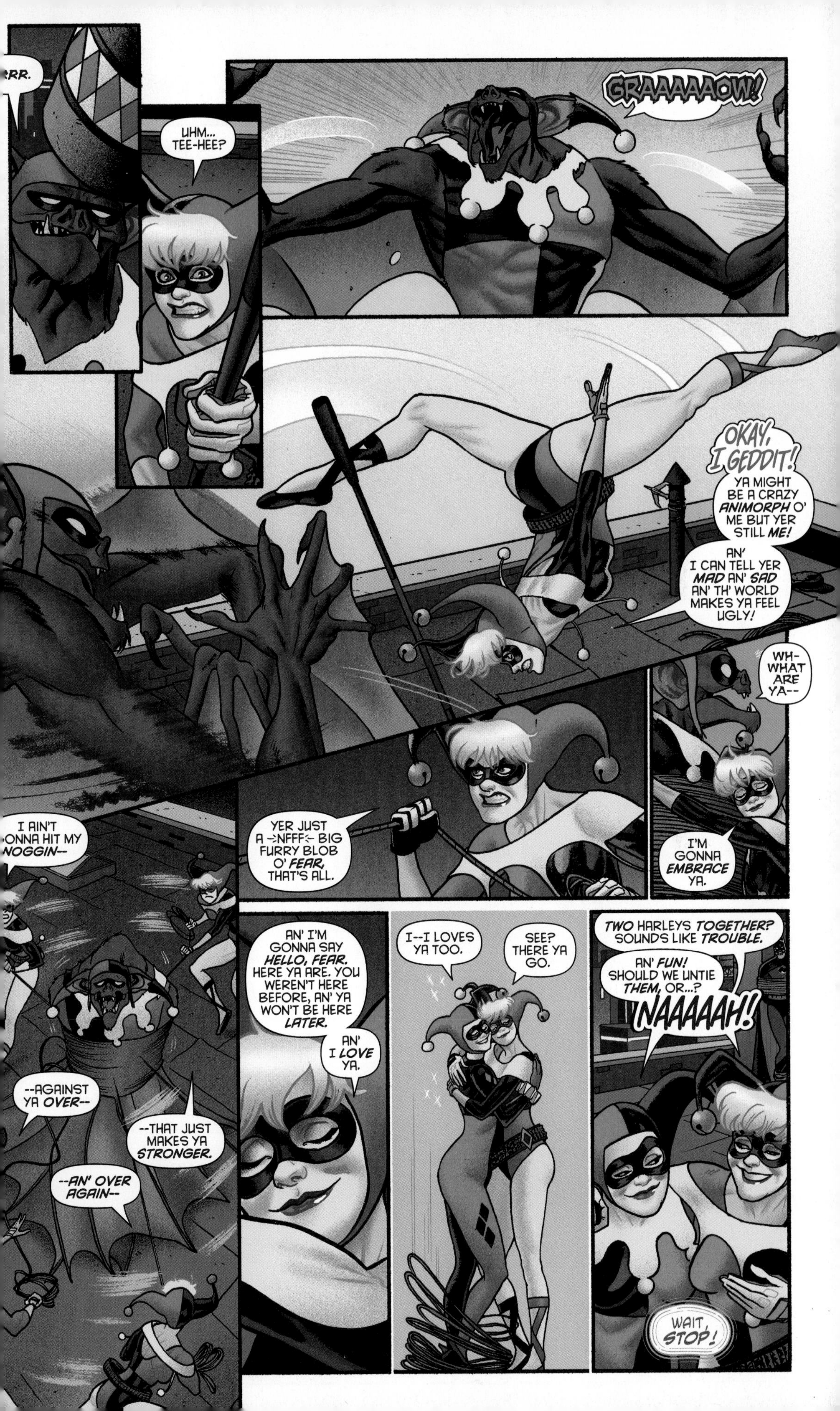

RRR.
UHM... TEE-HEE?
GRAAAAAOW!
OKAY, I GEDDIT!
YA MIGHT BE A CRAZY ANIMORPH O' ME BUT YER STILL ME!
AN' I CAN TELL YER MAD AN' SAD AN' TH' WORLD MAKES YA FEEL UGLY!
YER JUST A -NFFF- BIG FURRY BLOB O' FEAR, THAT'S ALL.
WH-WHAT ARE YA--
I'M GONNA EMBRACE YA.
I AIN'T GONNA HIT MY NOGGIN--
--AGAINST YA OVER--
--AN' OVER AGAIN--
--THAT JUST MAKES YA STRONGER.
AN' I'M GONNA SAY HELLO, FEAR. HERE YA ARE. YOU WEREN'T HERE BEFORE, AN' YA WON'T BE HERE LATER.
AN' I LOVE YA.
I--I LOVES YA TOO.
SEE? THERE YA GO.
TWO HARLEYS TOGETHER? SOUNDS LIKE TROUBLE.
AN' FUN! SHOULD WE UNTIE THEM, OR...?
NAAAAAH!
WAIT, STOP!

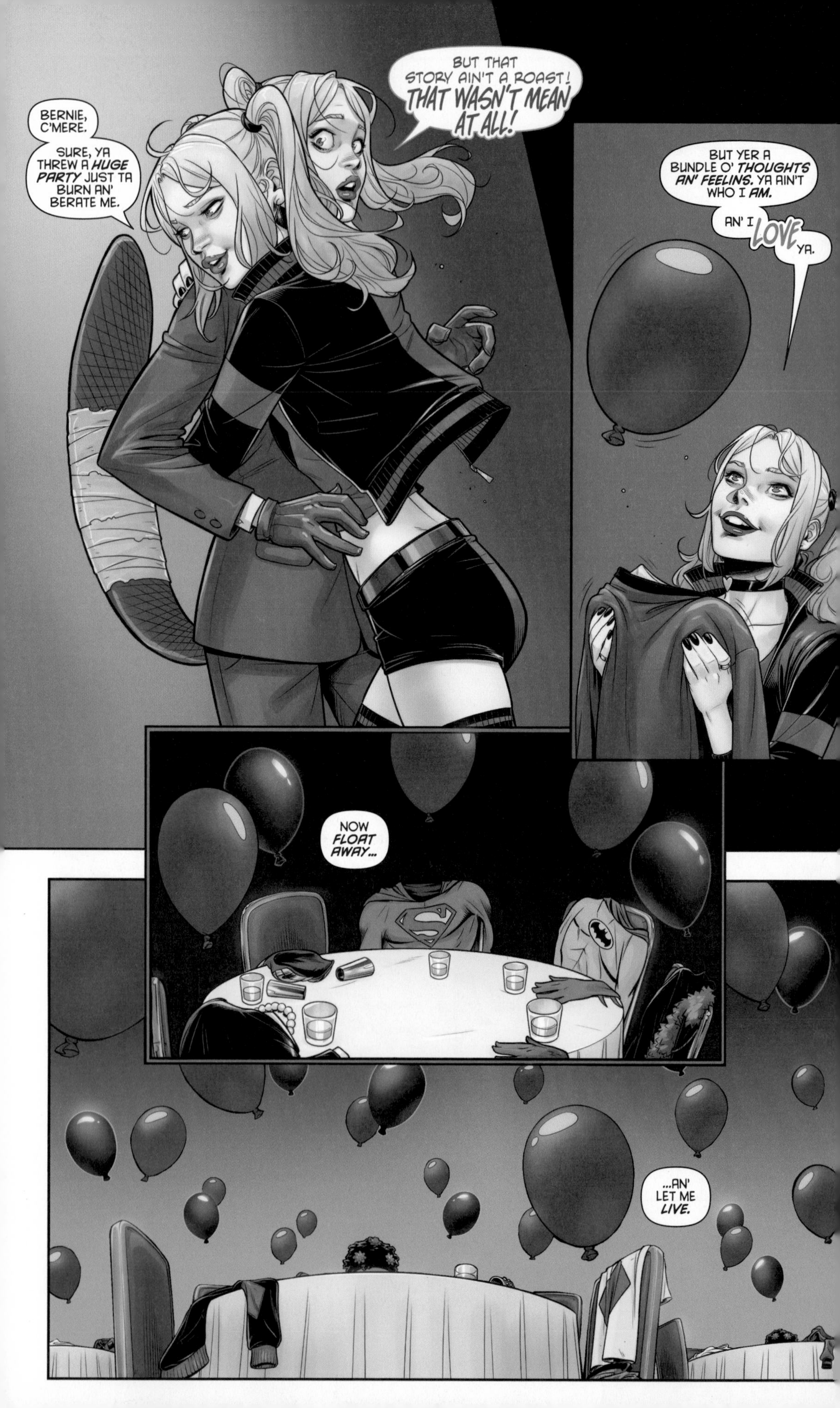

BUT THAT STORY AIN'T A ROAST! THAT WASN'T MEAN AT ALL!
BERNIE, C'MERE.
SURE, YA THREW A HUGE PARTY JUST TA BURN AN' BERATE ME.
BUT YER A BUNDLE O' THOUGHTS AN' FEELINS. YA AIN'T WHO I AM.
AN' I LOVE YA.
NOW FLOAT AWAY...
...AN' LET ME LIVE.

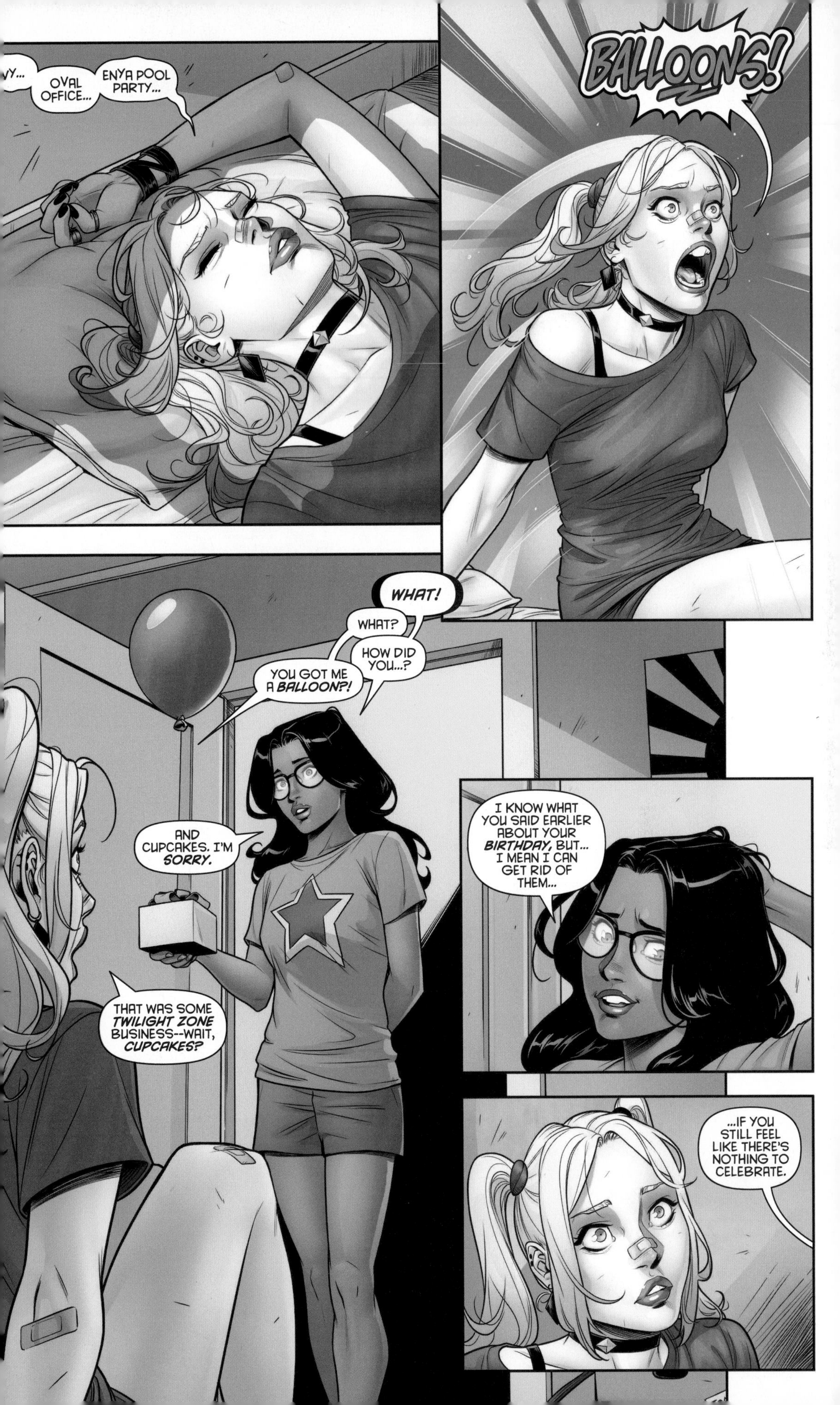
...WY...
OVAL OFFICE...
ENYA POOL PARTY...
BALLOONS!
WHAT!
WHAT?
HOW DID YOU...?
YOU GOT ME A *BALLOON?!*
AND CUPCAKES. I'M *SORRY.*
THAT WAS SOME *TWILIGHT ZONE* BUSINESS--WAIT, *CUPCAKES?*
I KNOW WHAT YOU SAID EARLIER ABOUT YOUR *BIRTHDAY,* BUT... I MEAN I CAN GET RID OF THEM...
...IF YOU STILL FEEL LIKE THERE'S NOTHING TO CELEBRATE.

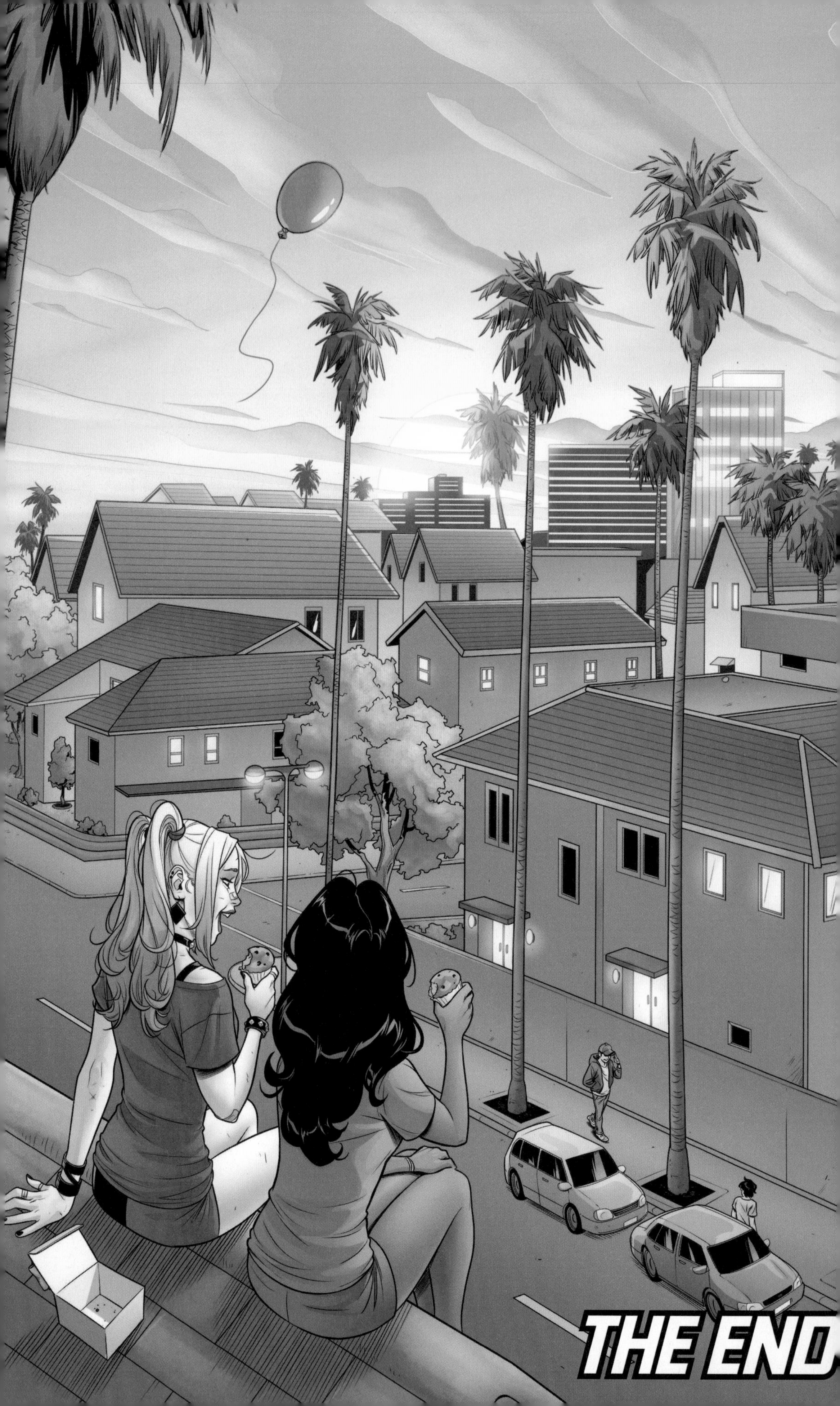
THE END

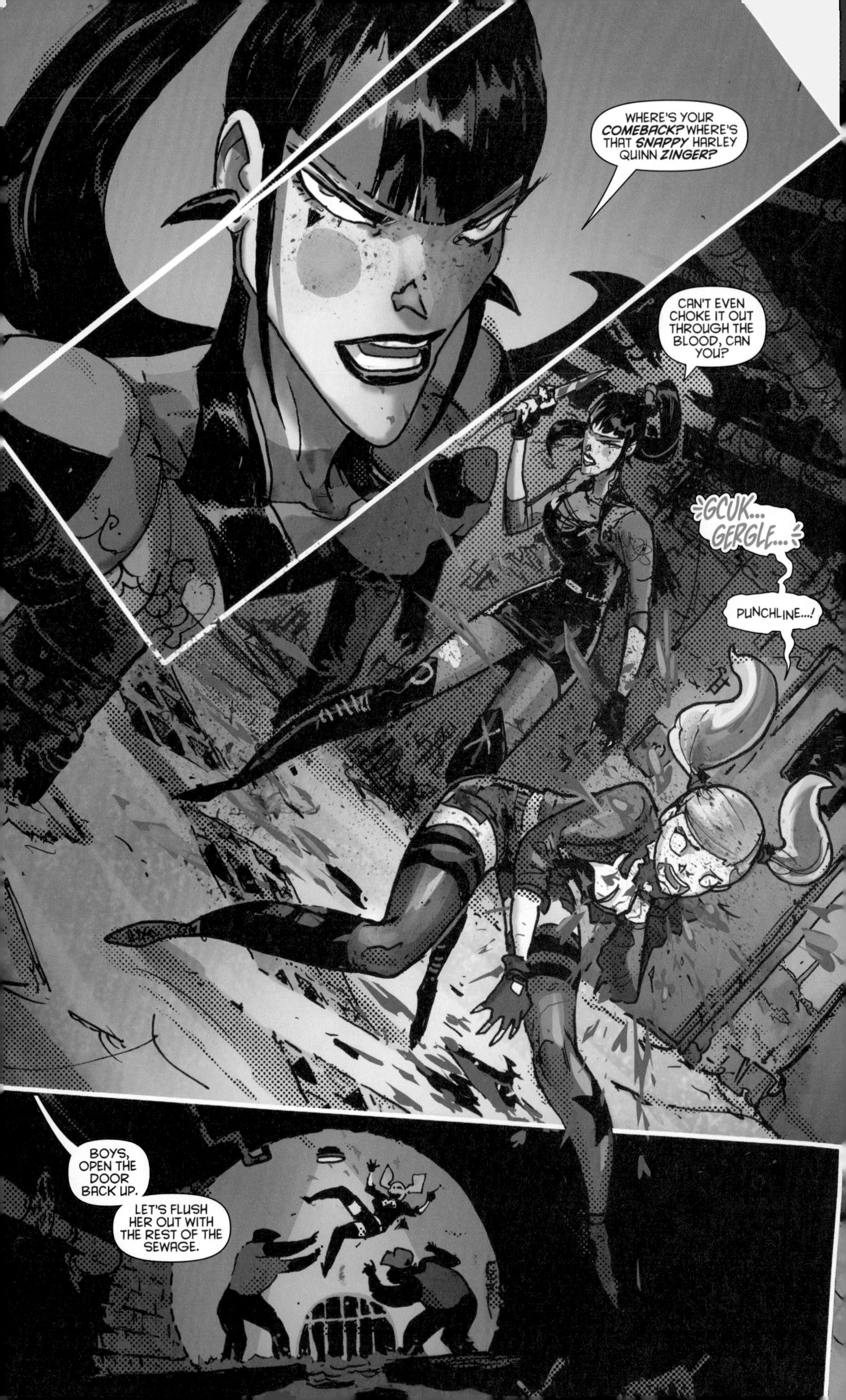
WHERE'S YOUR COMEBACK? WHERE'S THAT SNAPPY HARLEY QUINN ZINGER?
CAN'T EVEN CHOKE IT OUT THROUGH THE BLOOD, CAN YOU?
GCUK... GERGLE...
PUNCHLINE...!
BOYS, OPEN THE DOOR BACK UP.
LET'S FLUSH HER OUT WITH THE REST OF THE SEWAGE.

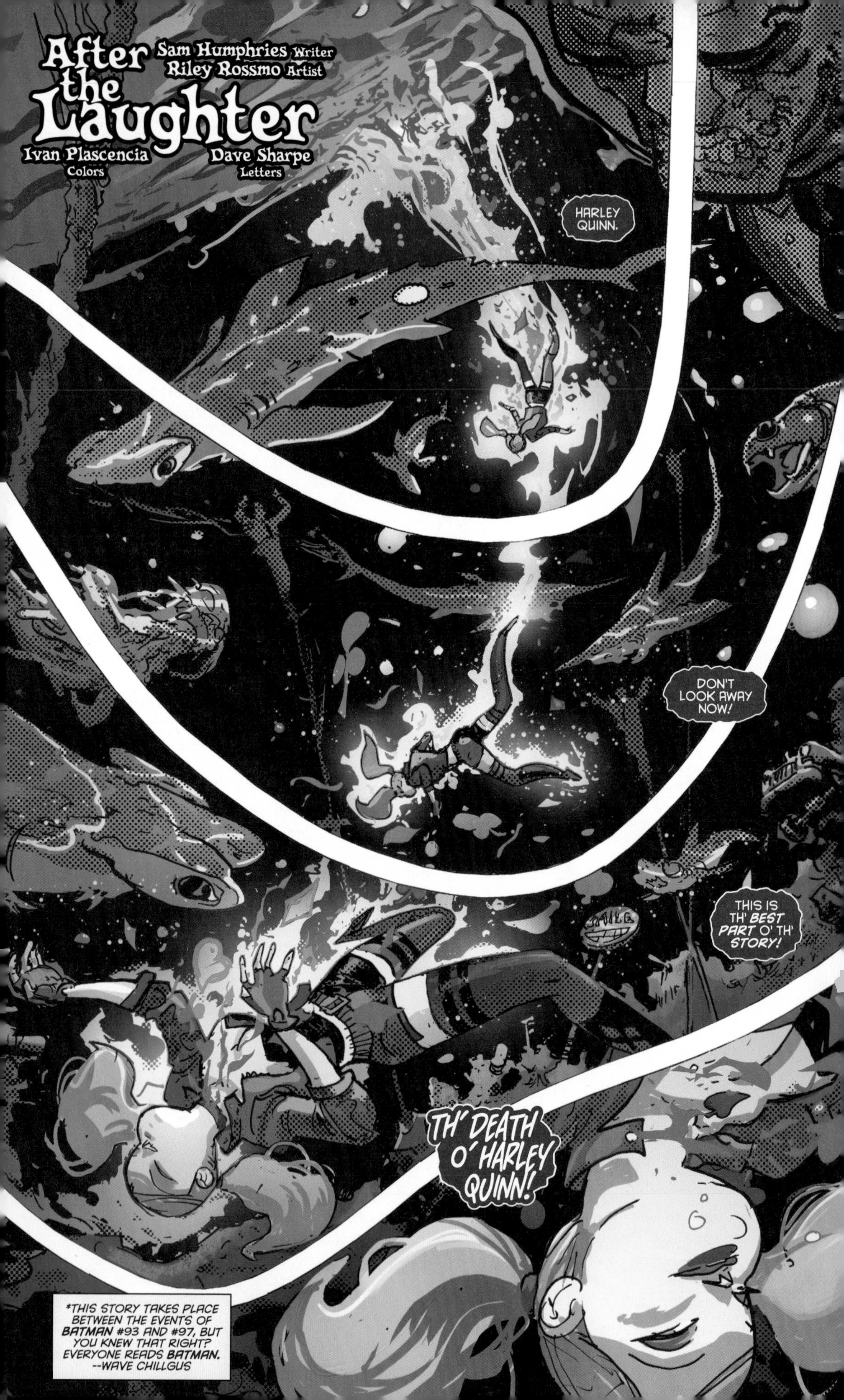
After the Laughter
Sam Humphries Writer
Riley Rossmo Artist
Ivan Plascencia Colors
Dave Sharpe Letters
HARLEY QUINN.
DON'T LOOK AWAY NOW!
THIS IS TH' BEST PART O' TH' STORY!
TH' DEATH O' HARLEY QUINN!
*THIS STORY TAKES PLACE BETWEEN THE EVENTS OF BATMAN #93 AND #97, BUT YOU KNEW THAT RIGHT? EVERYONE READS BATMAN. --WAVE CHILLGUS

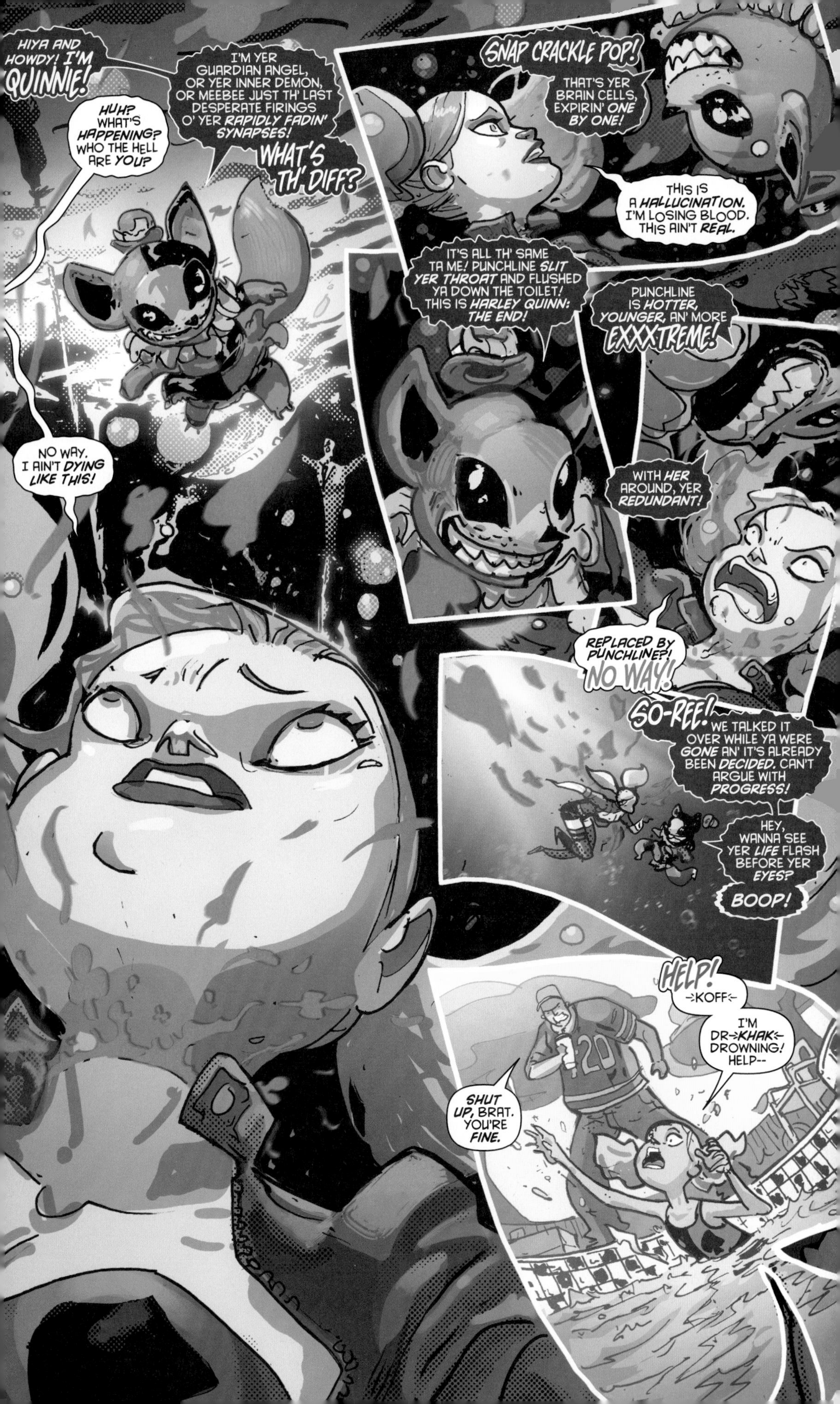
HIYA AND HOWDY! I'M QUINNIE!
I'M YER GUARDIAN ANGEL, OR YER INNER DEMON, OR MEEBEE JUST TH' LAST DESPERATE FIRINGS O' YER RAPIDLY FADIN' SYNAPSES!
HUH? WHAT'S HAPPENING? WHO THE HELL ARE YOU?
WHAT'S TH' DIFF?
SNAP CRACKLE POP!
THAT'S YER BRAIN CELLS, EXPIRIN' ONE BY ONE!
THIS IS A HALLUCINATION. I'M LOSING BLOOD. THIS AIN'T REAL.
IT'S ALL TH' SAME TA ME! PUNCHLINE SLIT YER THROAT AND FLUSHED YA DOWN THE TOILET! THIS IS HARLEY QUINN: THE END!
PUNCHLINE IS HOTTER, YOUNGER, AN' MORE EXXXTREME!
WITH HER AROUND, YER REDUNDANT!
NO WAY. I AIN'T DYING LIKE THIS!
REPLACED BY PUNCHLINE?! NO WAY!
SO-REE! WE TALKED IT OVER WHILE YA WERE GONE AN' IT'S ALREADY BEEN DECIDED. CAN'T ARGUE WITH PROGRESS!
HEY, WANNA SEE YER LIFE FLASH BEFORE YER EYES?
BOOP!
HELP!
-KOFF-
I'M DR-KHAK-DROWNING! HELP--
SHUT UP, BRAT. YOU'RE FINE.

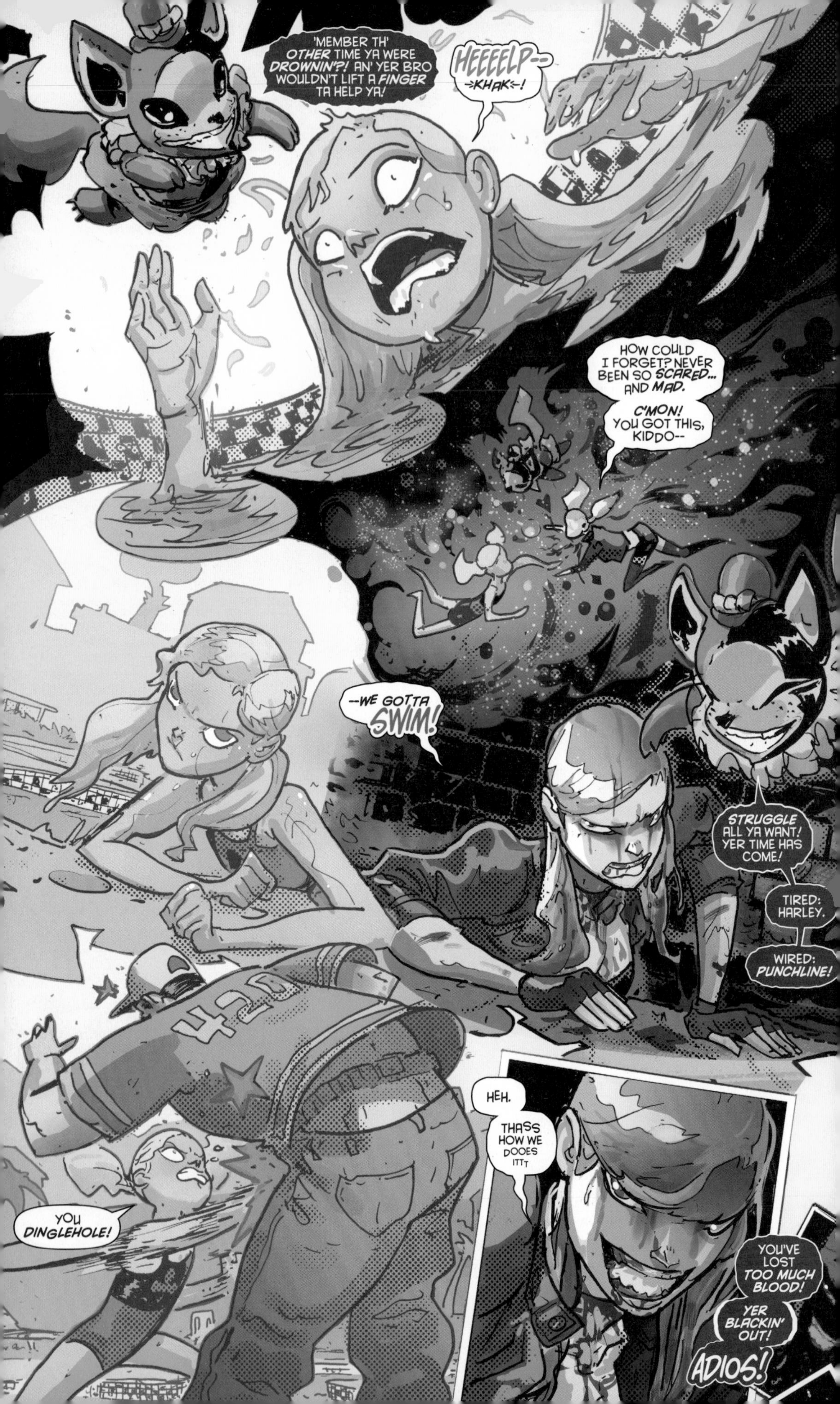

'MEMBER TH' OTHER TIME YA WERE DROWNIN'?! AN' YER BRO WOULDN'T LIFT A FINGER TA HELP YA!
HEEEELP--
-KHAK-!
HOW COULD I FORGET? NEVER BEEN SO SCARED... AND MAD.
C'MON! YOU GOT THIS, KIDDO--
--WE GOTTA SWIM!
STRUGGLE ALL YA WANT! YER TIME HAS COME!
TIRED: HARLEY.
WIRED: PUNCHLINE!
HEH.
THASS HOW WE DOOES ITTT
YOU DINGLEHOLE!
YOU'VE LOST TOO MUCH BLOOD!
YER BLACKIN' OUT!
ADIOS!

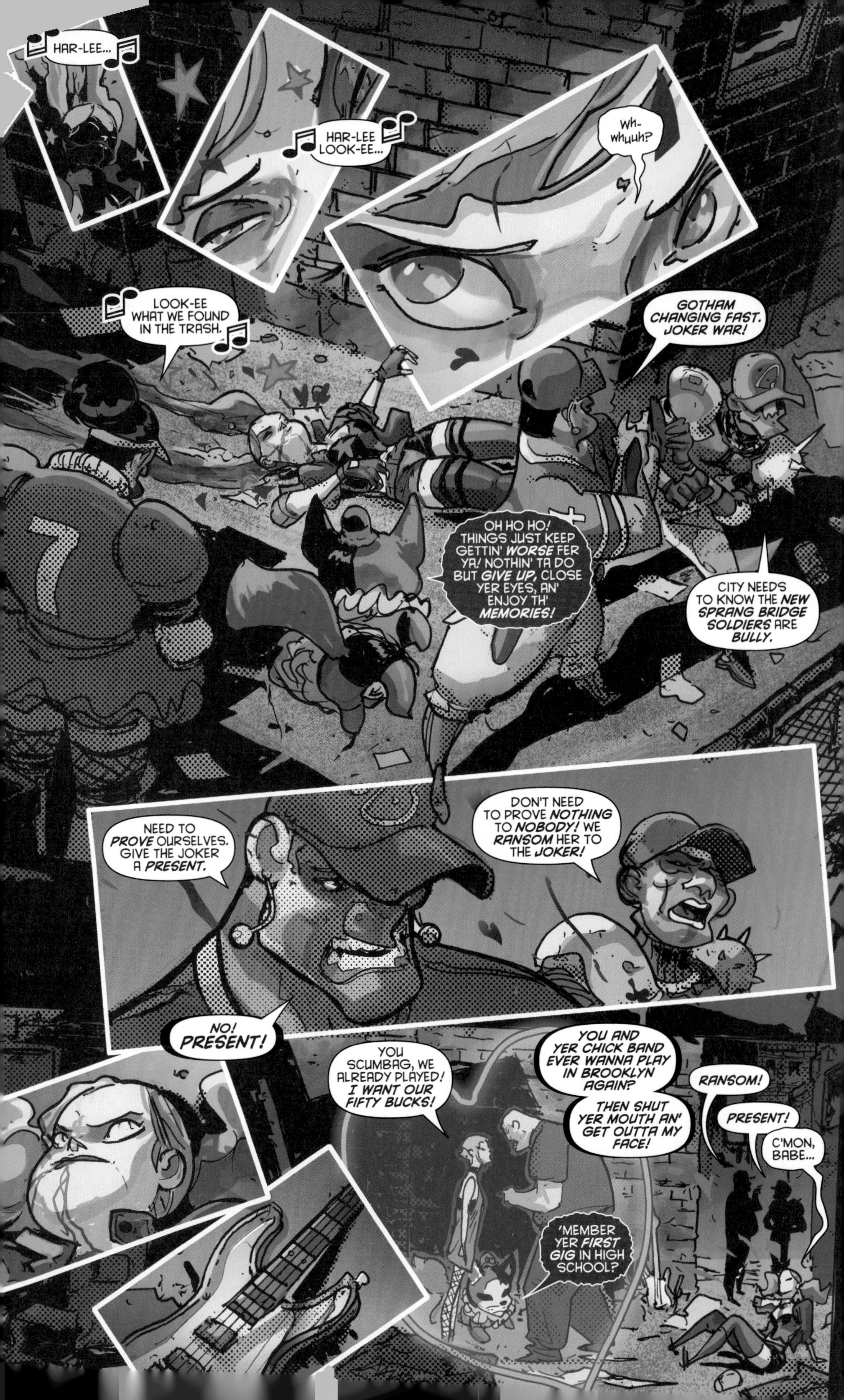
HAR-LEE...
HAR-LEE LOOK-EE...
WH-WHUUH?
LOOK-EE WHAT WE FOUND IN THE TRASH.
GOTHAM CHANGING FAST. JOKER WAR!
OH HO HO! THINGS JUST KEEP GETTIN' WORSE FER YA! NOTHIN' TA DO BUT GIVE UP, CLOSE YER EYES, AN' ENJOY TH' MEMORIES!
CITY NEEDS TO KNOW THE NEW SPRANG BRIDGE SOLDIERS ARE BULLY.
NEED TO PROVE OURSELVES. GIVE THE JOKER A PRESENT.
DON'T NEED TO PROVE NOTHING TO NOBODY! WE RANSOM HER TO THE JOKER!
NO! PRESENT!
YOU SCUMBAG, WE ALREADY PLAYED! I WANT OUR FIFTY BUCKS!
YOU AND YER CHICK BAND EVER WANNA PLAY IN BROOKLYN AGAIN?
THEN SHUT YER MOUTH AN' GET OUTTA MY FACE!
RANSOM!
PRESENT!
C'MON, BABE...
'MEMBER YER FIRST GIG IN HIGH SCHOOL?

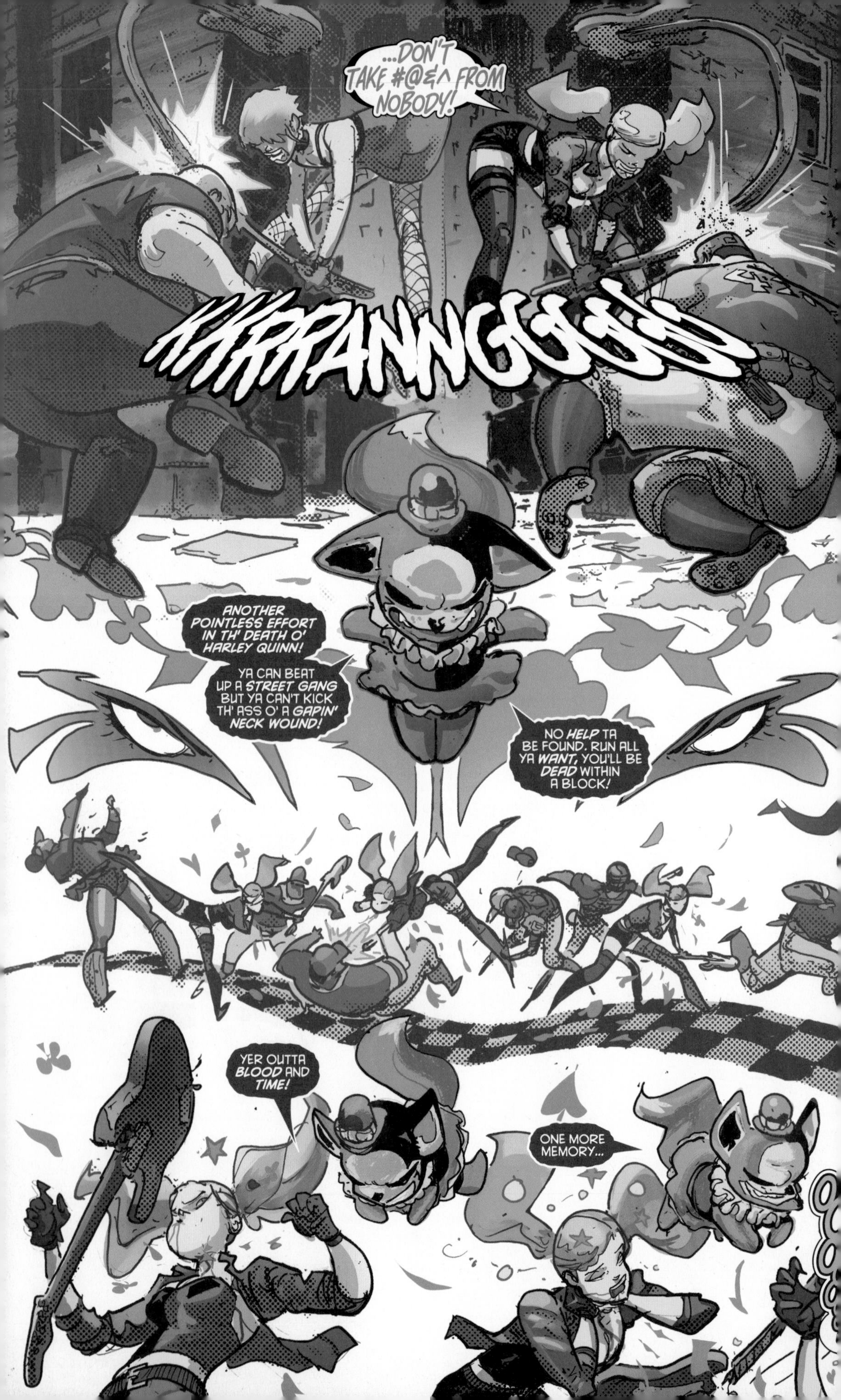
...DON'T TAKE #@&^ FROM NOBODY!
KKRRANNGGGG
ANOTHER POINTLESS EFFORT IN TH' DEATH O' HARLEY QUINN!
YA CAN BEAT UP A STREET GANG BUT YA CAN'T KICK TH' ASS O' A GAPIN' NECK WOUND!
NO HELP TA BE FOUND. RUN ALL YA WANT, YOU'LL BE DEAD WITHIN A BLOCK!
YER OUTTA BLOOD AND TIME!
ONE MORE MEMORY...

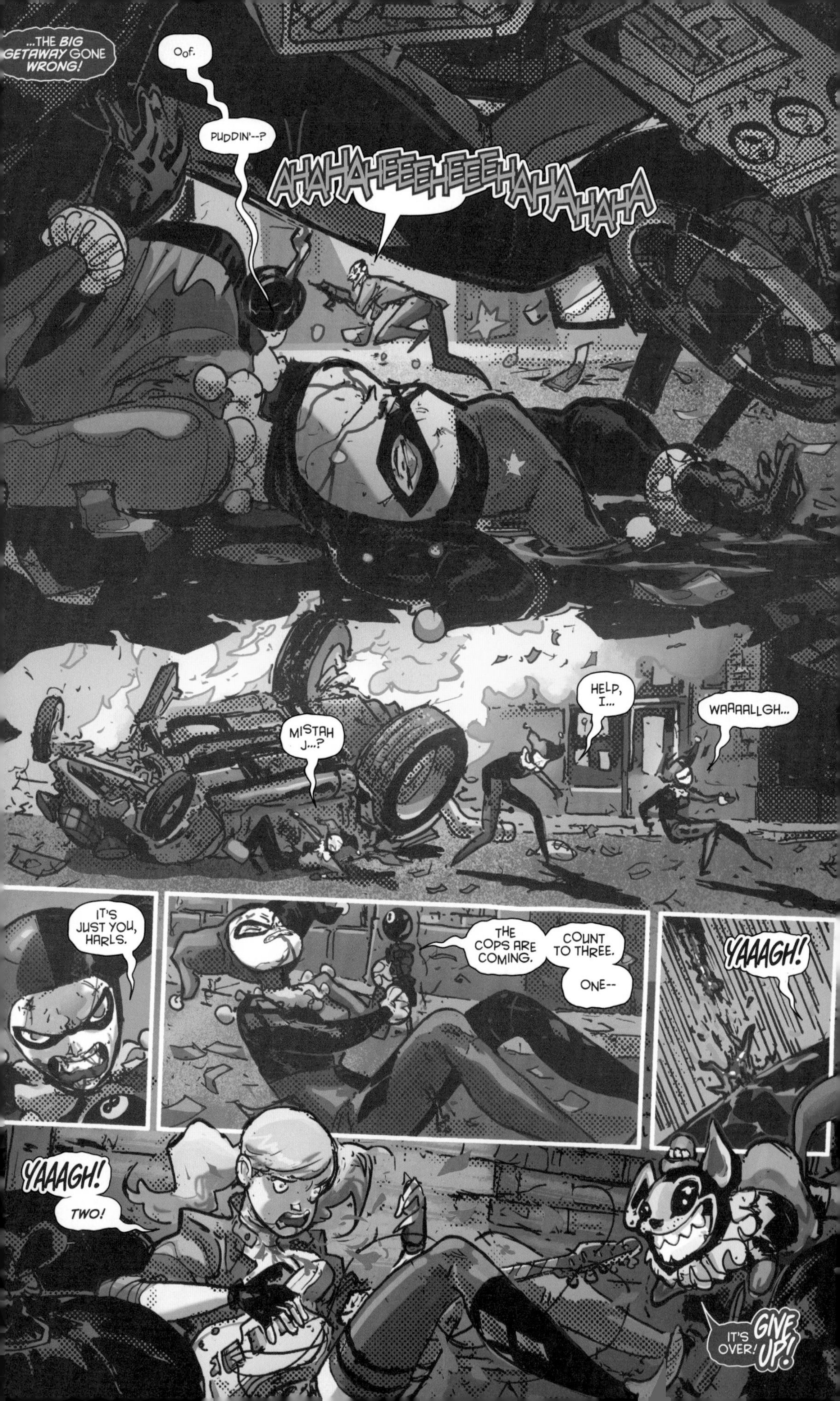

...THE BIG GETAWAY GONE WRONG!
Oof.
PUDDIN'--?
AHAHAHEEEEHEEEEHAHAHAHAHA
MISTAH J...?
HELP, I...
WAAAALLGH...
IT'S JUST YOU, HARLS.
THE COPS ARE COMING.
COUNT TO THREE.
ONE--
YAAAGH!
YAAAGH!
TWO!
IT'S OVER! GIVE UP!

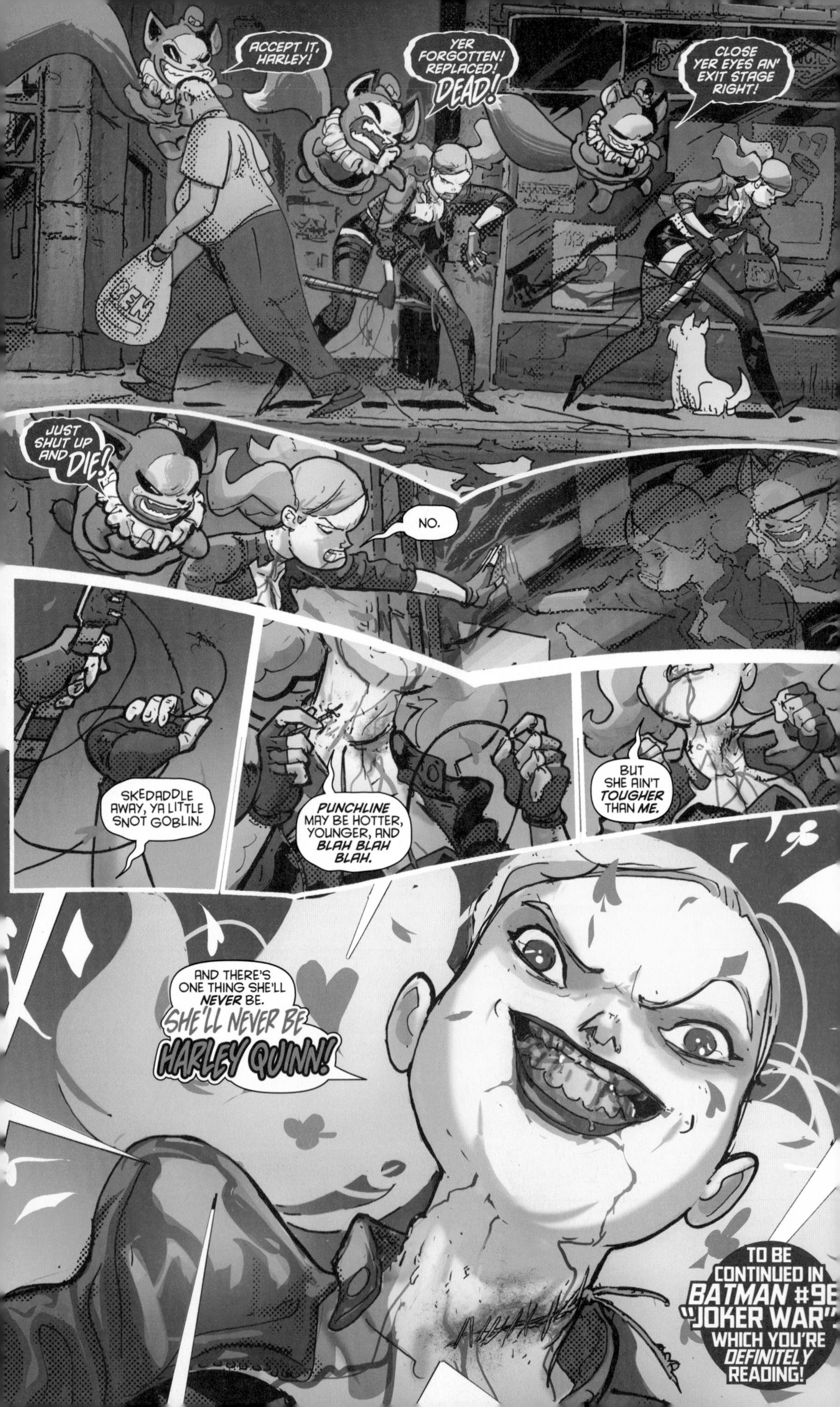

ACCEPT IT, HARLEY!
YER FORGOTTEN! REPLACED! DEAD!
CLOSE YER EYES AN' EXIT STAGE RIGHT!
JUST SHUT UP AND DIE!!
NO.
SKEDADDLE AWAY, YA LITTLE SNOT GOBLIN.
PUNCHLINE MAY BE HOTTER, YOUNGER, AND BLAH BLAH BLAH.
BUT SHE AIN'T TOUGHER THAN ME.
AND THERE'S ONE THING SHE'LL NEVER BE.
SHE'LL NEVER BE HARLEY QUINN!
TO BE CONTINUED IN BATMAN #98 "JOKER WAR" WHICH YOU'RE DEFINITELY READING!

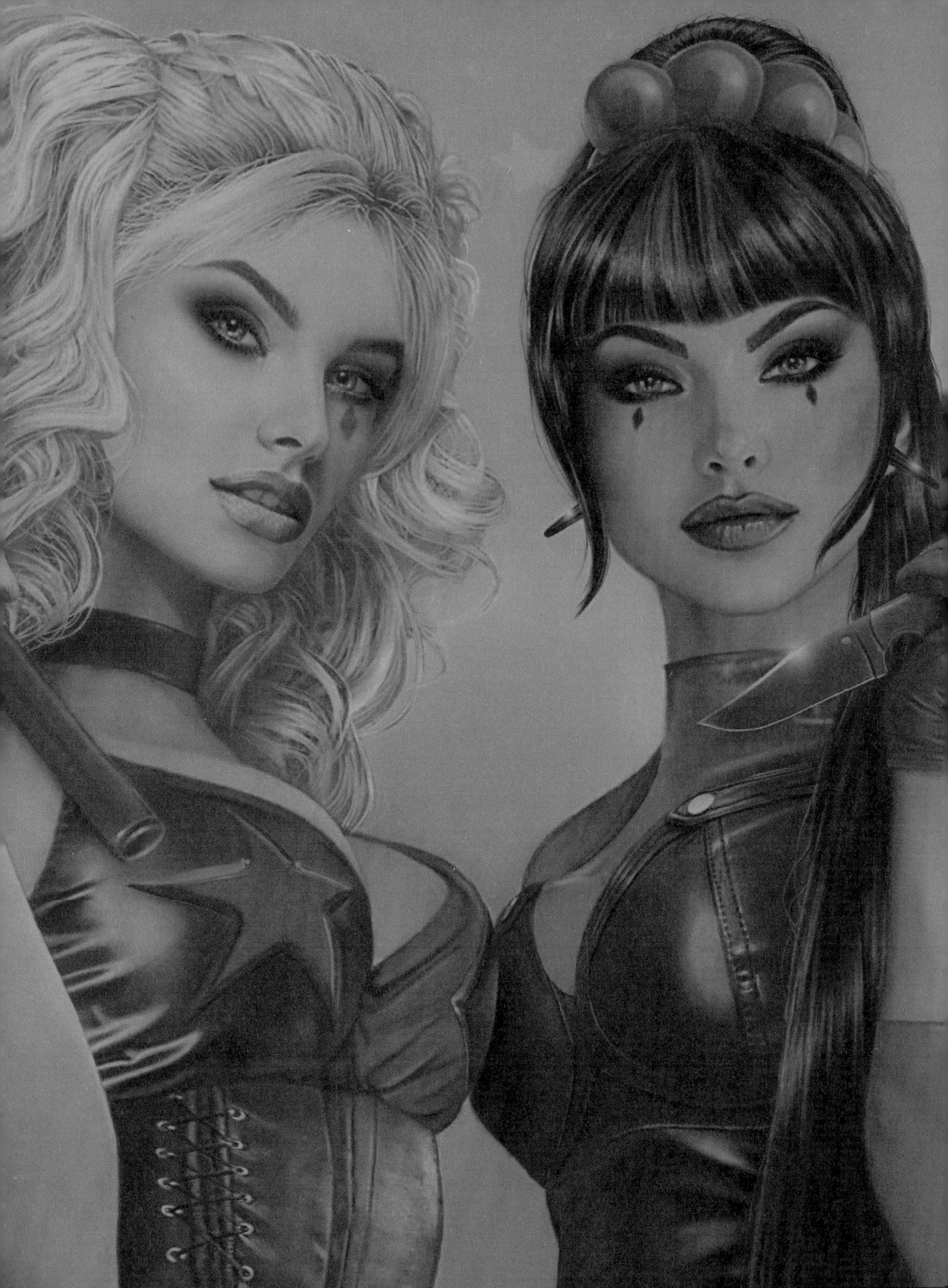

HARLEY QUINN #75
VARIANT COVERS

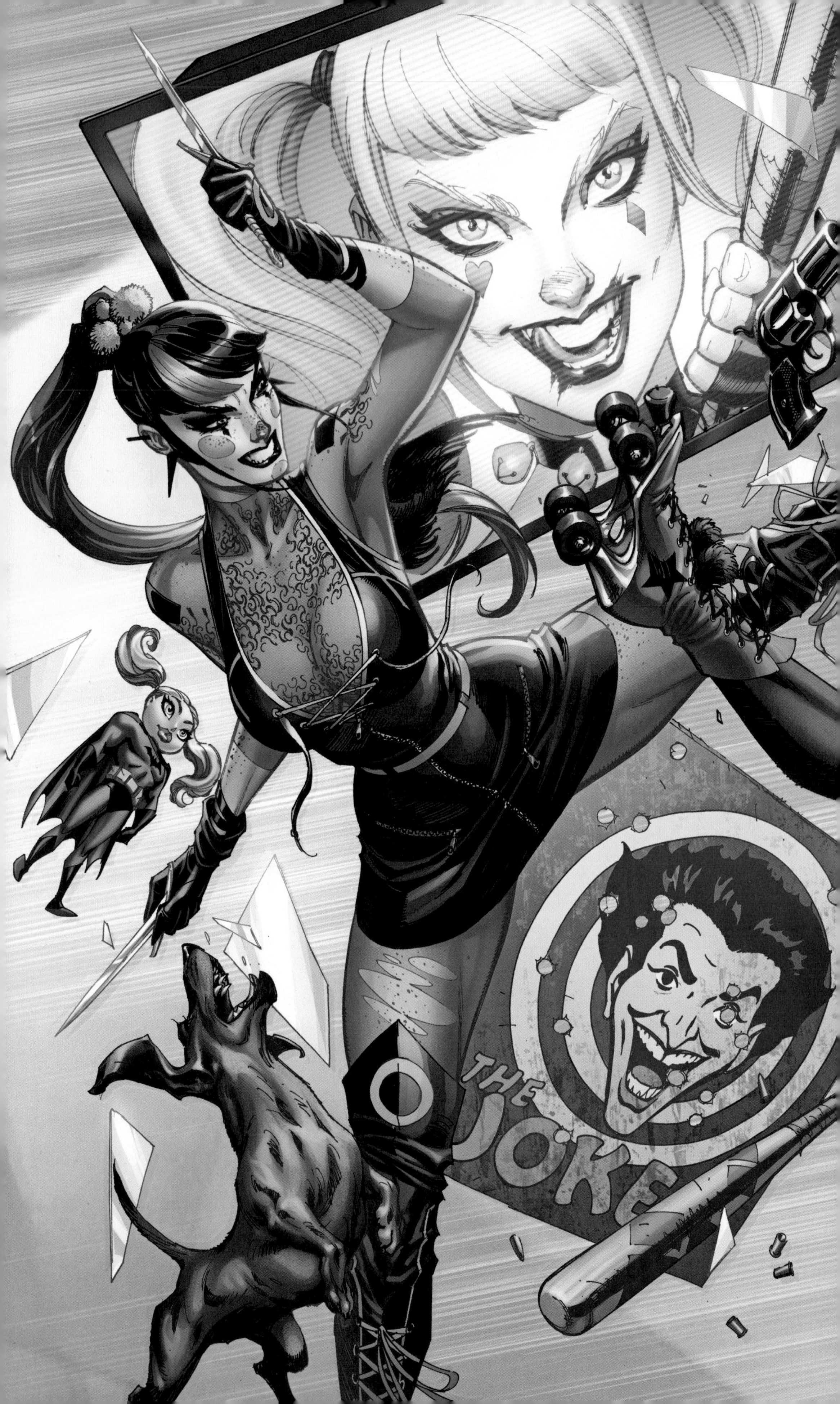
THE

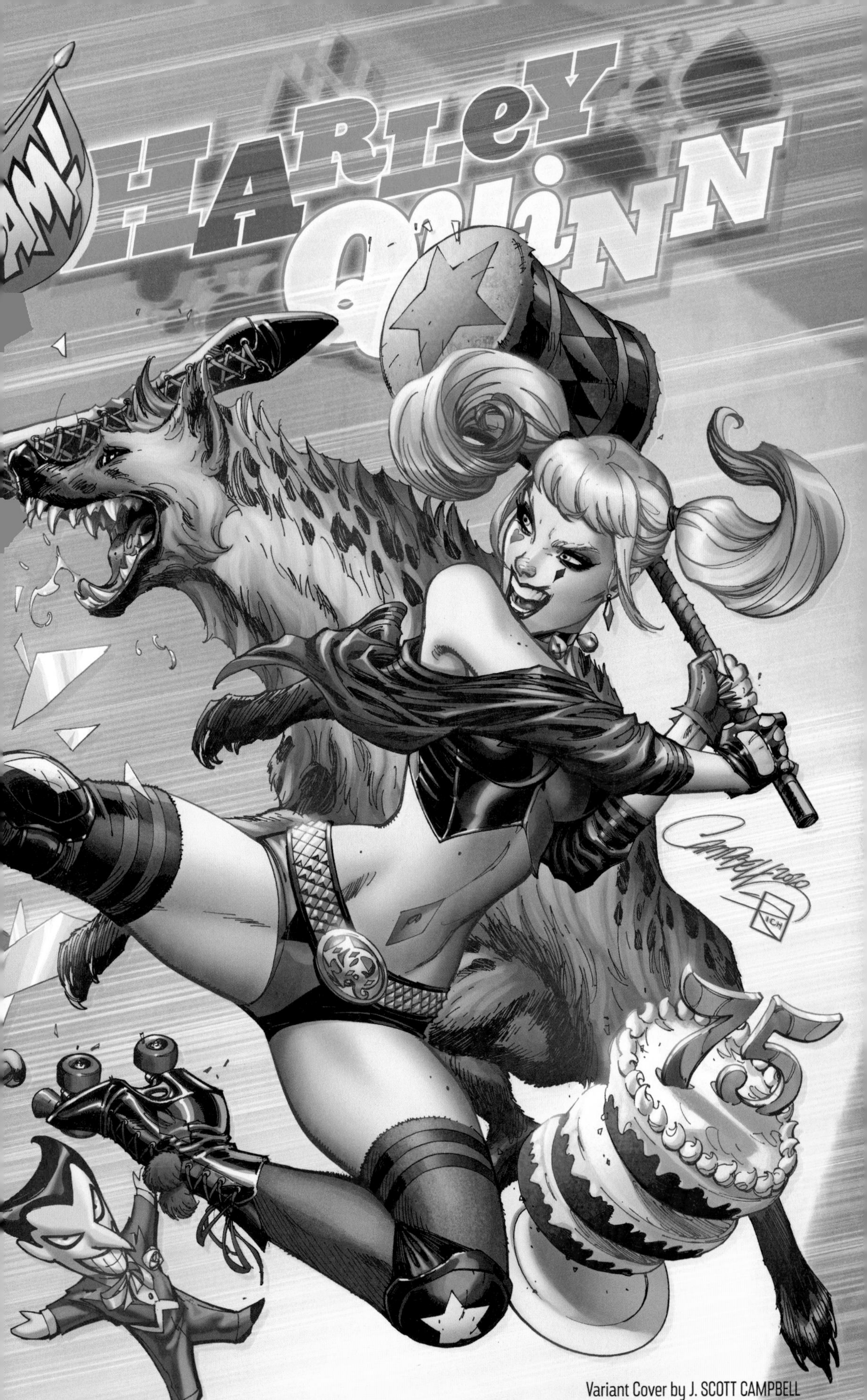
HARLEY QUINN
75

Variant Cover by J. SCOTT CAMPBELL

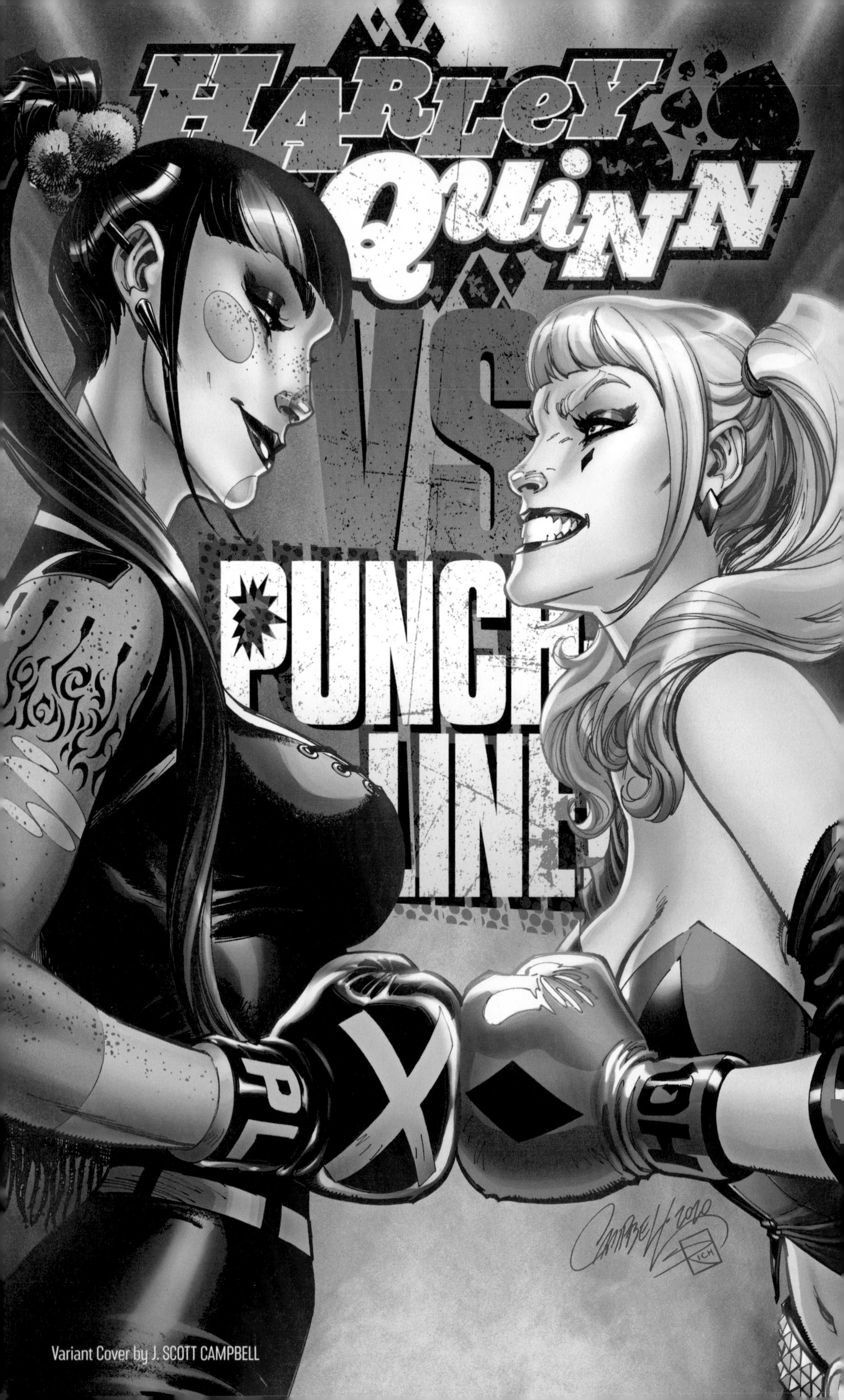
HARLEY QUINN
VS
PUNCHLINE
PL
HQ
Variant Cover by J. SCOTT CAMPBELL

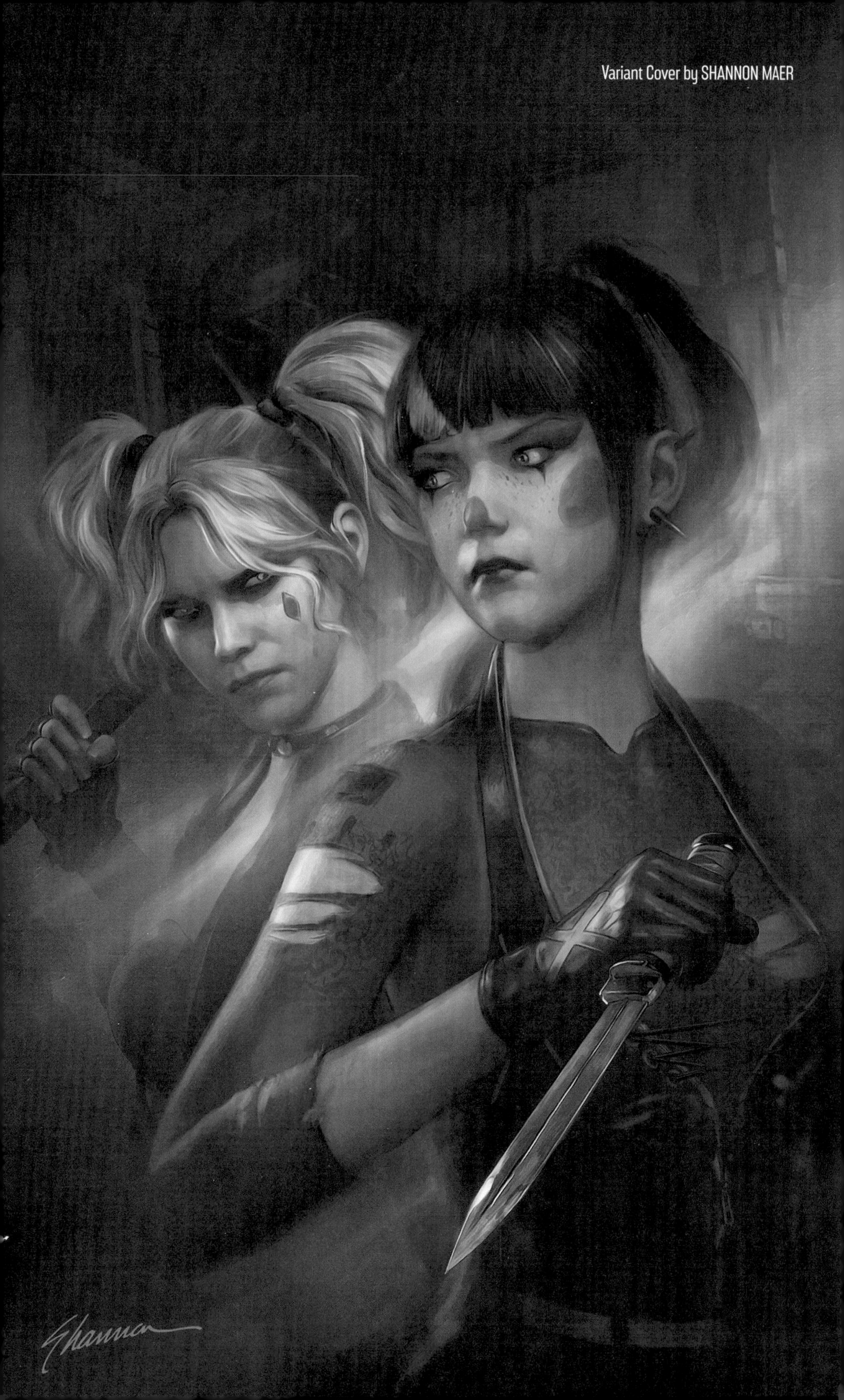

Variant Cover by SHANNON MAER

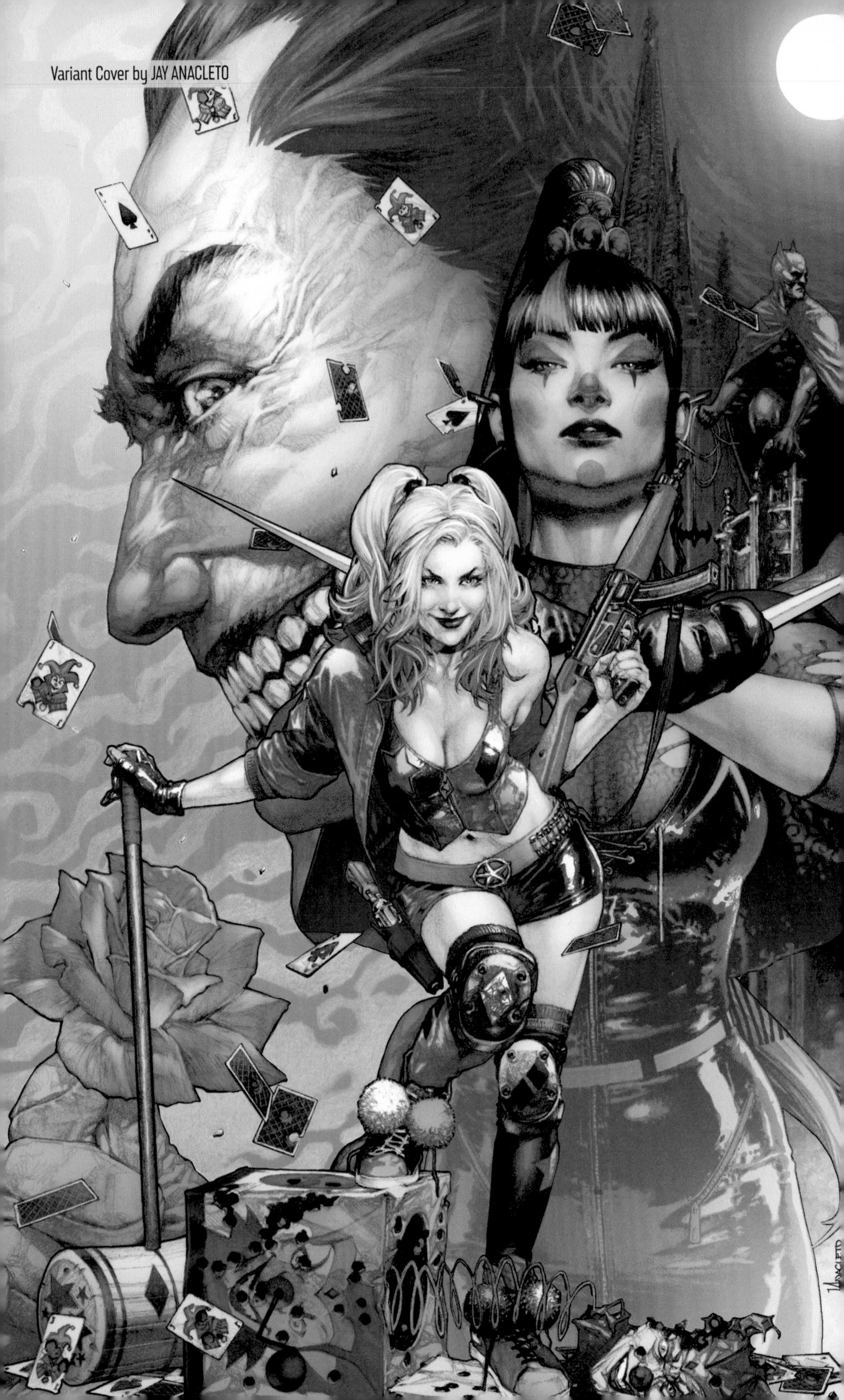

Variant Cover by JAY ANACLETO

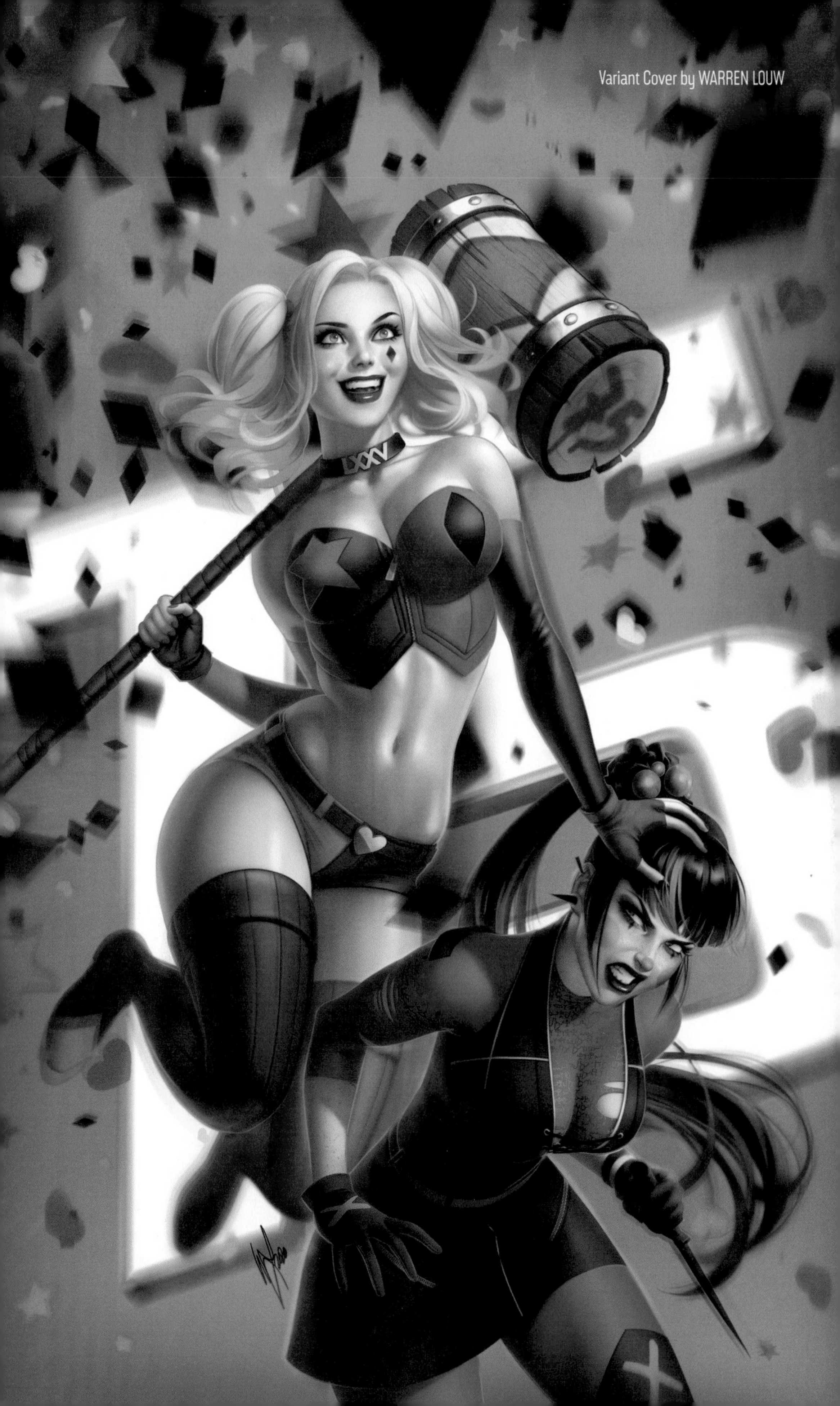
LXXV

Variant Cover by WARREN LOUW

Variant Cover by KAEL NGU

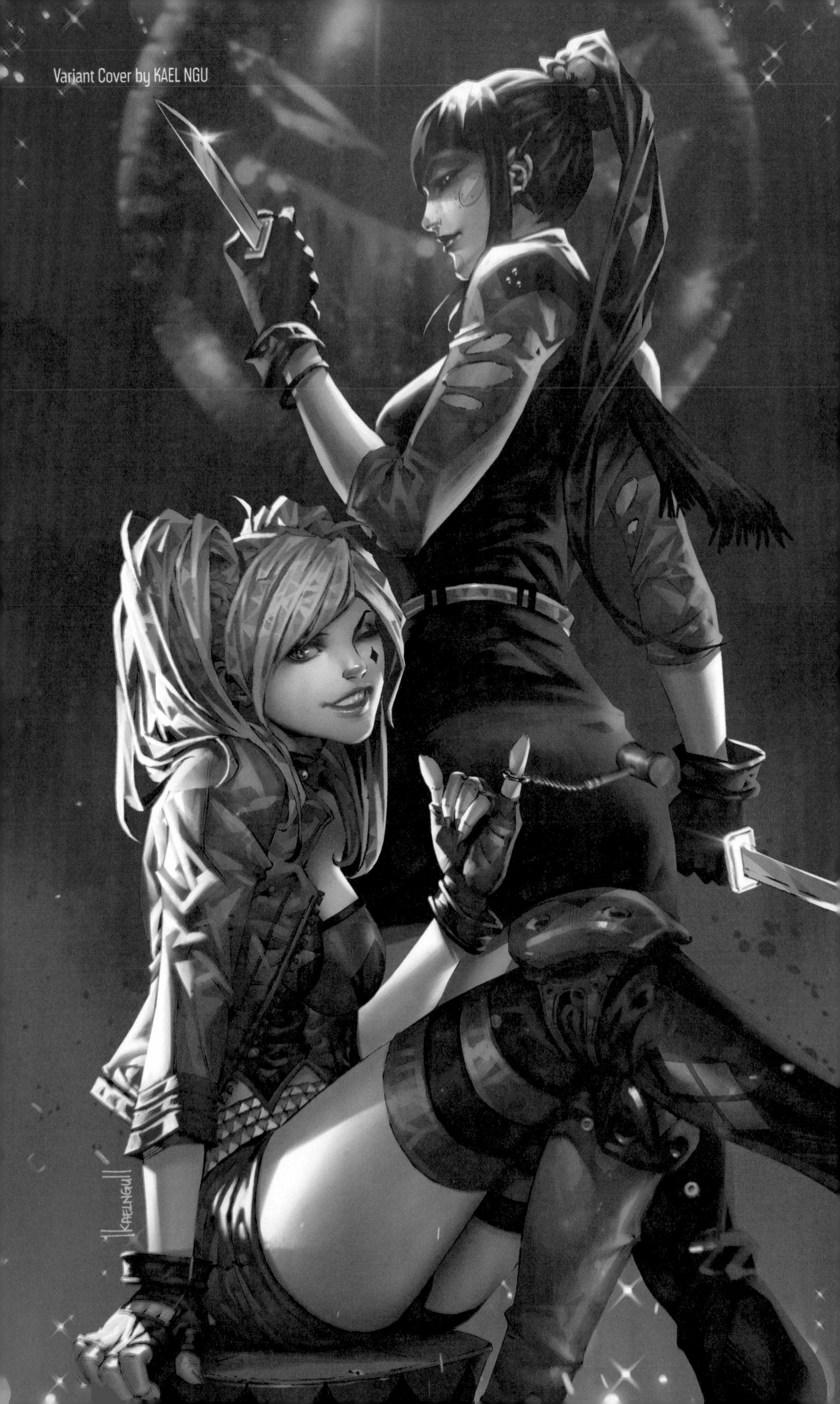
KAELNGU

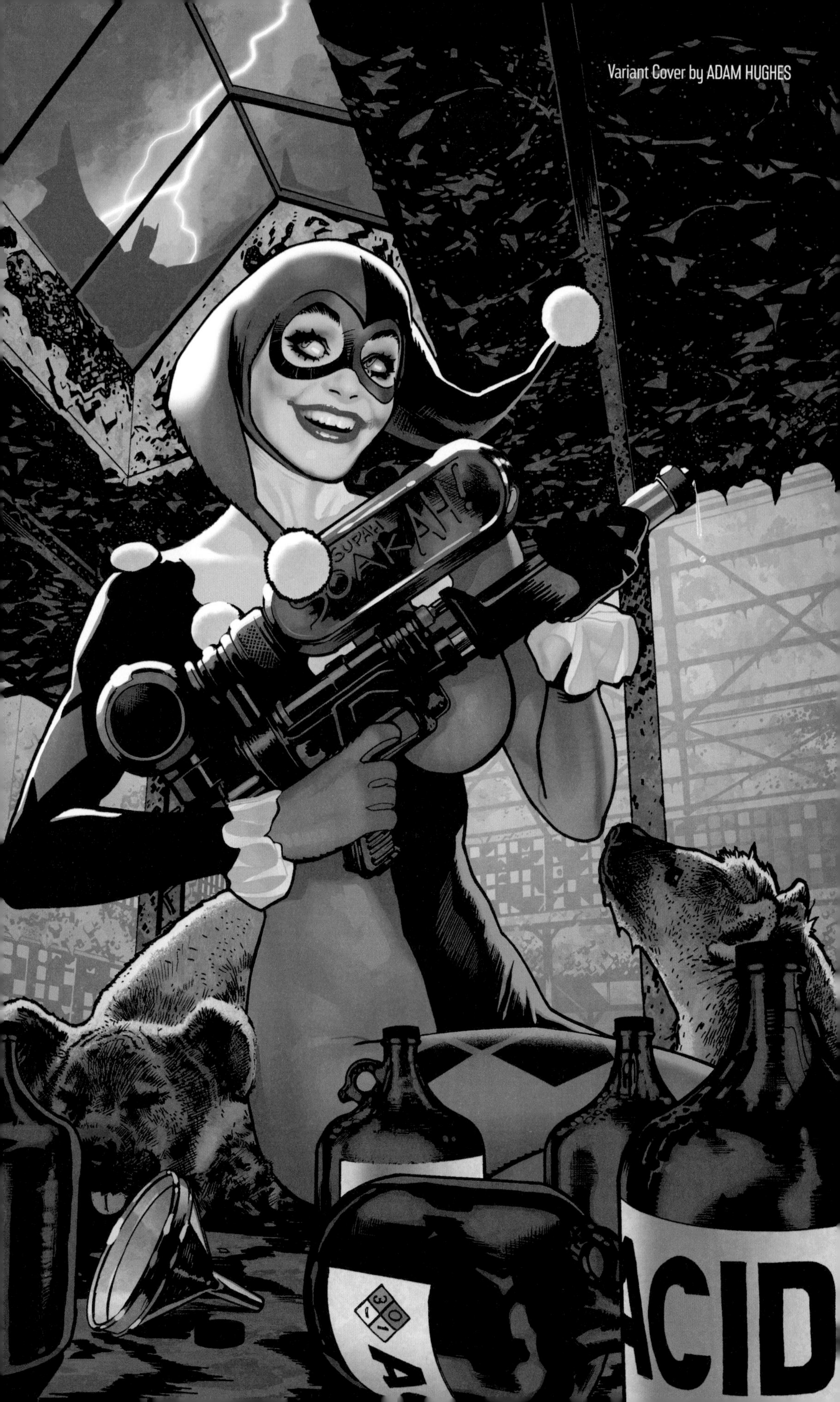
ACID
Variant Cover by ADAM HUGHES

Variant Cover by IAN MacDONALD

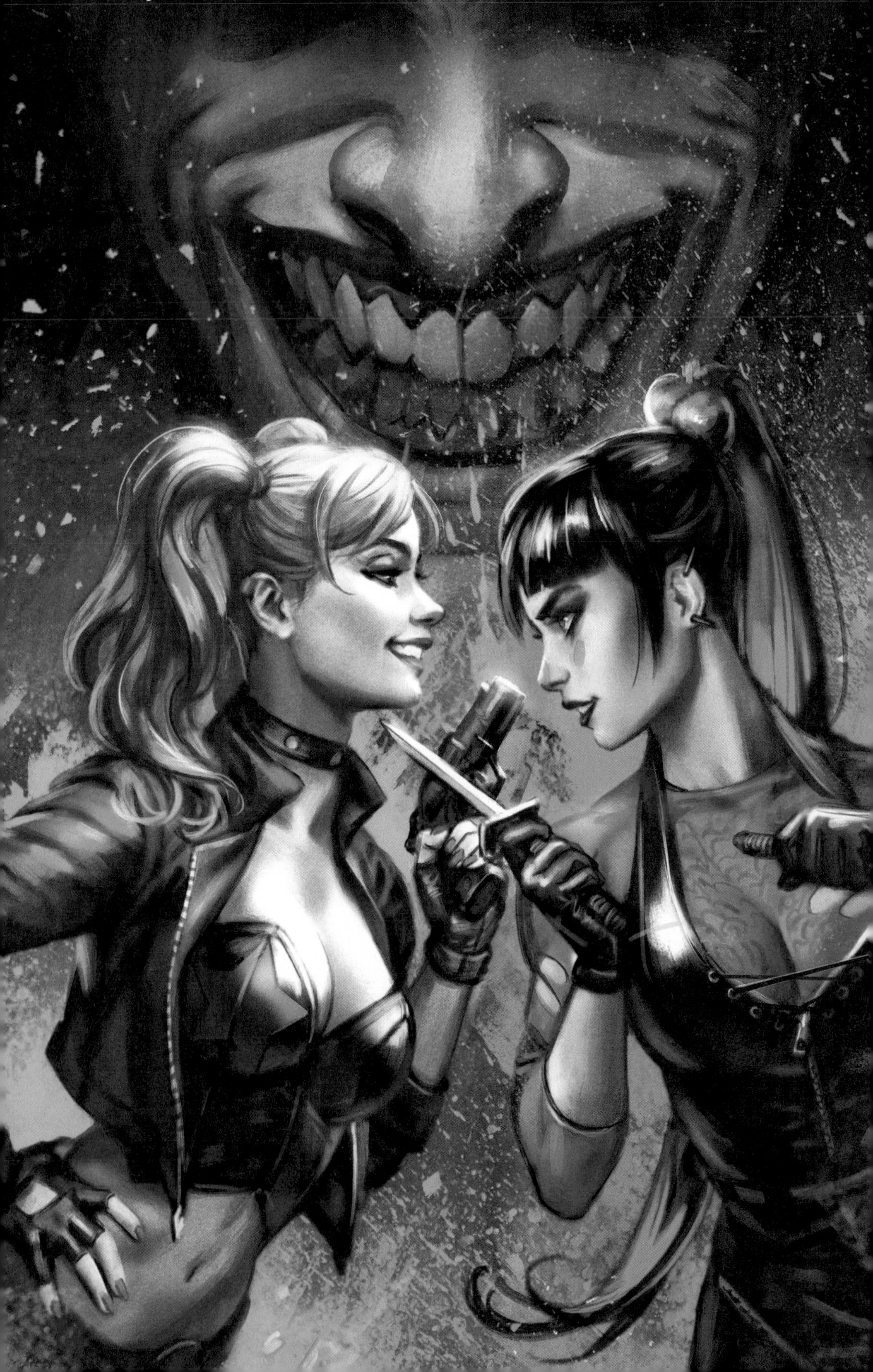

Variant Cover by NATALI SANDERS

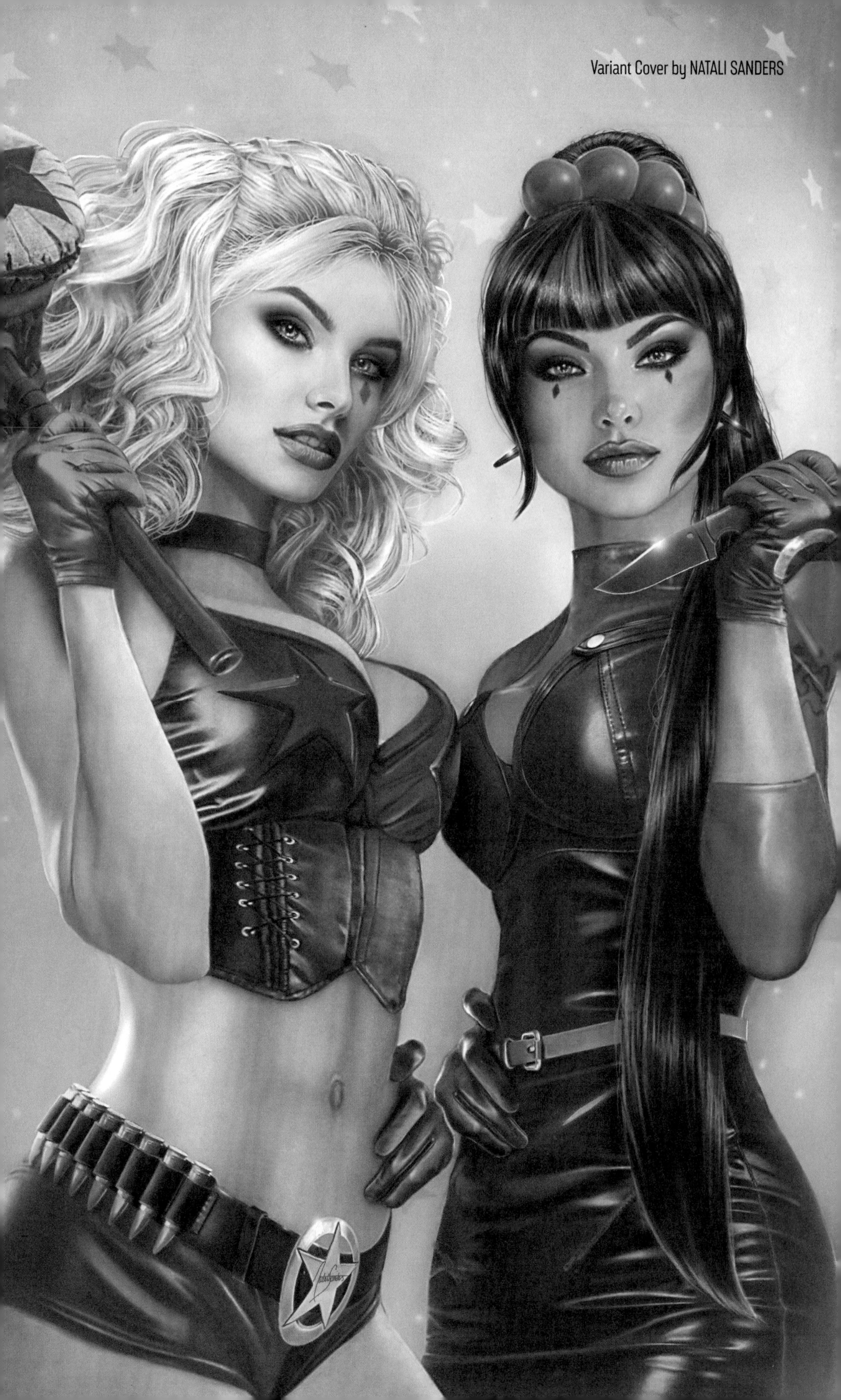

Variant Cover by ANT LUCIA

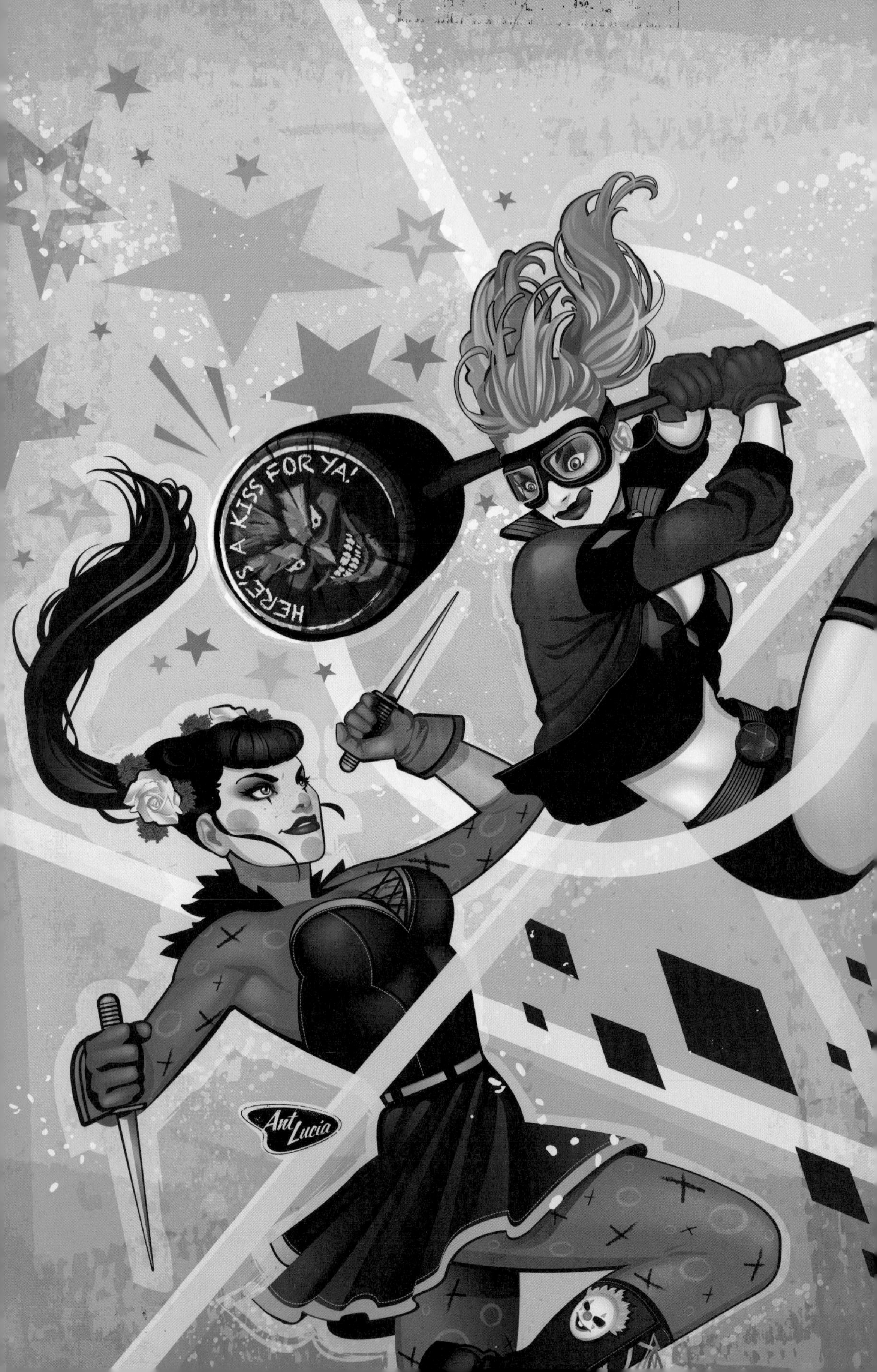
HERE'S A KISS FOR YA!
Ant Lucia